A Tragic Fate

Law and Ethics in the Battle Over Nazi-Looted Art

A Tragic Fate

NICHOLAS M. O'DONNELL

Cover design by Elmarie Jara/ABA Design

Printed in the United States of America.

21 20 19 18 17 5 4 3 2 1

ISBN: 978-1-63425-733-6
e-ISBN: 978-1-63425-734-3

Library of Congress Cataloging-in-Publication Data
Names: O'Donnell, Nicholas M., author.
Title: A tragic fate : law and ethics in the battle over Nazi-looted art / Nicholas M. O'Donnell.
Description: Chicago : American Bar Association, 2017. | Includes bibliographical references and index.
Identifiers: LCCN 2017015050 (print) | LCCN 2017015164 (ebook) | ISBN 9781634257343 (e-book) | ISBN 9781634257336 (hardcover : alk. paper)
Subjects: LCSH: Art thefts. | Art thefts—Europe—History—20th century. | Restitution—Europe—History—20th century. | Cultural property—Repatriation—Europe. | World War, 1939-1945—Claims. | National socialism and art. | World War, 1939-1945—Confiscations and contributions—Europe. | World War, 1939-1945—Destruction and pillage—Europe. | Jewish property—Europe—History—20th century.
Classification: LCC K5219 (ebook) | LCC K5219 .O36 2017 (print) | DDC 940.53/18144—dc23
LC record available at https://lccn.loc.gov/2017015050

FOR AMY

Contents

Introduction

R*ue Saint-Honoré, après-midi, effet de pluie* (*Rue Saint Honoré, Afternoon, Rain Effect*) was painted by Camille Pissarro in 1892. It shows the new Paris of Georges-Eugène Haussmann's design, with a sharp angular perspective rushing to the top left. The soft focus and muted colors mirror the subject: the wide boulevards on a rainy day. Carriages and pedestrians tread the cobblestones amidst leafless trees. It is a depiction of an ordinary day that would normally merit no commemoration. In this way, Pissarro's technique also reflects the history of the painting since World War II. On the surface, the dispute is similar to many others, but digging deeper one finds a multilayered puzzle that embodies the competing narratives often at play in restitution cases: persecution, obfuscation, the murky environment of the art market after the war, and the basic tension between legal systems and who should bear the burden of resolving the competing claims.

The painting once belonged to Fritz and Lilly Cassirer, members of a family that achieved monetary success in electrical component manufacturing and later in the collection and sale of art. The Cassirers were second-generation Jews, integrated members of the Germany of which they were citizens and supporters. They assembled a collection including numerous great works of Western art.

However, the Pissarro is no longer in their collection. Lilly Cassirer was targeted by a Nazi opportunist, and she sold the painting for a fraction of its value before escaping her home country. After a series of sales and donations, the painting hangs today in the Thyssen-Bornemisza Museum in Madrid, a state-run institution that exhibits a world-class collection. One wonders why the painting is in Madrid and not with the Cassirer heirs. One also wonders why the question of who ought to have the artwork only came to a head in the 1990s.

Lilly Cassirer's painting met the same tragic fate as so much of the art that was stolen or purchased under duress during the Nazi occupation. The painting's murky history echoes its former owners' fate and the quiet beauty of the room where it once hung. Its current possessor, the Thyssen-Bornemisza Museum, is a complicated figure in its own right and like many others that will be discussed below, it is a public museum whose mission is dedicated to the display of and access to great art. Unfortunately, the museum's lofty mission only exists in a vacuum because the painting is in a foreign country that had no hand in the repression of the Cassirers and theft of Lilly's property. The case underscores the central paradox posed by disputes in the last twenty years: It is a painting that no one disputes was stolen by the Nazis, yet it has not been, and may never be, returned to the family who owned it.

Litigation is a last resort when there is no agreement to be made. Even to consider how to array the parties and issues in litigation about Nazi-looted art is a dizzying prospect. There are items of movable personal property around the world with heirs in Europe and the United States. The countries of continental Europe and the United States take very different approaches to the varying legal issues from the procedures of dispute resolutions to the substantive laws of property. There is no easy way to reconcile the different perspectives that these myriad jurisdictions offer, and rather than unifying the dispute resolution process, what has instead emerged is a fitful lurching from one victory or defeat to the next.

How did we arrive here? The victorious Allies, the United States in particular, committed massive amounts of energy to the restitution of stolen art after the war ended. The government announced legal principles in the sight of the great tragedy that had just unfolded governing the occupation in the first instance to try to dictate who should bear the burden of proof and who held some sort of presumptive right to restitution of the thousands and thousands of dislocated objects. While those principles—some of which turned into laws, some of which guided judicial interpretations—cast a long shadow into the future, actual private party disputes were relatively rare for the better part of fifty years. After the war, the world was putting itself back together but was becoming entrenched in the new Cold War. It was not until the collapse of the Soviet Union and the breathing room created by that development in world affairs which afforded the various countries a look backwards with fresh eyes and slowly began a comprehensive effort to assess how stolen art ought to be restituted or not.

This book will address comprehensively those cases that have ended in litigation in U.S. courts. While the impact of dispute resolutions in other countries is of critical importance and relevance, this is not a treatise on those foreign processes. Litigation in the United States is based on neutral principles that are not necessarily related to the Holocaust, but the process does reveal a great deal about the policies that the United States has wrestled with for more than seventy years, policies that are interesting to compare with those of other affected countries. To try to recover personal property requires bringing common-law claims such as conversion (the unauthorized control over another's property), replevin (a legal action to compel the return of property in one's possession, often in tandem with a conversion claim), or arguments about bailment (the conditions under which one holds property for another). However, these torts usually have statutes of limitations of three years or so. Sometimes there are conditions under which those deadlines can be delayed and sometimes not.

That is the easiest part. The question of jurisdiction is thornier by far. What court has the power even to hear these disputes? Can a U.S. federal or state court compel a foreign defendant, or even a foreign nation, to defend itself in a U.S. court? Who gets to decide? Are there diplomatic issues to consider?

The nations of the world gathered in the late 1990s to try to answer many of these questions. They enunciated a set of principles that were to apply to the question of Nazi-looted art. These principles are forward-looking, normative rules. Yet again, without the teeth of some enforcement mechanisms, the extent of their effect continues to be debated today. The commitment that those countries have shown toward making real progress in achieving those principles has been inconsistent, and frustration has mounted in the decades since. The inconsistent application of the principles has left many heirs to conclude that that they often have no choice but to go to court to seek legal remedies to recover family property.

Likewise, domestically, museum associations wrestle with how to create ethical rules for their members, yet the resulting lack of legal enforcement of the guidelines or principles causes those same association members to remain silent in the face of claims of irrefutably stolen art. Thus, while it is a truism that every case of looted art and quest for restitution is different, this generalization too often serves as an excuse for deflecting the hard questions and common themes that these cases raise because it requires each claimant to re-prove what should not be in question, to begin anew when so much is already known. The story of legal disputes within the United States regarding Nazi-looted art is also a pendulum. In any given period, the momentum is likely to have swung dramatically opposite to what occurred just a few years before. So, although as the 1990s ended there was little reason to see litigation as a major component of the issues, Maria Altmann's case against Austria, which occurred between 2000 and the Supreme Court's decision in 2004, threw open the courthouse doors. Then, as defendants honed their arguments, claimants' futures in U.S. courts looked dim. Later still, courts took an increasingly nuanced view of the role they had in this international issue and expanded their jurisdictional holdings in particular in recent years. Back and forth, it continues to go today.

However, make no mistake. The very possibility of litigation is in large part the reason that the conversation continues. Obsequious claims of commitments to fair and just solutions are worth just about that and no more. While the fear of litigation is not always salutary, one can be well sure that if the possibility were off the table entirely, the prospect of restitution would also wither before our eyes. In the end, there is no simple, unifying principle to these debates. When approached by the heirs of victims, many current possessors look for the right answer. Some are indifferent. Some see a more complicated story in which their own interests and public service are more important than what happened eighty years ago. Disputes not yet known or filed will be guided by the stories and cases that have already happened. The tactics of and choices made by the parties to such disputes many times reveal the heartbreaking struggles that began in the past and continue to affect the descendants of the original owners today. These are those stories.

PART ONE

Art and Culture in Occupied Europe

Chapter 1

From There to Here: Legislated Plunder in the Third Reich and the Allied Response

The programmatic overhaul of German society by the Nazis took many different forms. And, while many do not associate art with the most prominent aspects of the Third Reich, this is a mistake, not merely because of the oft-repeated observation that Hitler was a failed painter. It is because at the highest level the Nazis saw the creation, treatment, and possession of art as part of their core worldview. A short overview of some related Nazi initiatives is instructive in understanding the disputes that later arose regarding possession and ownership.

As is well known, the Nazis were keenly attuned to symbolism, particularly about expression that either typified—or conflicted with—their worldview. Accordingly, among the first coordinated events after they took power in January 1933 were attacks on authors, culminating in the infamous book burnings. It is no coincidence that the new structures for economic order of cultural institutions fell under Joseph Goebbels's new ministry, the *Reichsministerium für Volksaufklärung und Propaganda* (Reich Ministry for Public Enlightenment and Propaganda RVP). This agency assumed control over what were acceptable and unacceptable forms of creative art. Although German art created between the world wars had become among the most sought after, that quickly changed. In addition, the business of art fell under the *Reichskammer der bildenden Künste* (RBK), the Reich's Chamber for the Visual Arts, itself a subsidiary of the Reich Culture Chamber (*Reichskulturkammer*), each subsidiary under the RVP in the Nazi hierarchy. In 1933, Goebbels issued a report on art, the *Kunstbericht*, laying out his manifesto for the place of visual arts in the new order. This document left no doubt as to the new regime's priorities and intentions. The *Kunstbericht* set forth, among other topics (quotes from the original, author's translation), that any art considered "cosmopolitan" or "Bolshevist" was to be removed from German museums immediately. Museum directors who (in the Nazis' view) "wasted" public money by supporting "un-German" art were to be fired immediately. Artists who did not conform to the regime's taste were to be ignored and not even mentioned. Over and above those works in museums, any publicly displayed sculpture that conflicted with official taste was to be taken down immediately. None of this could have come as a surprise. The renowned dealer Alfred Flechtheim, for example, was the target of anti-Semitic propaganda even before the Nazis' ascension to power in the infamous *So oder so* poster (This? Or this?) that juxtaposed Flechtheim's face and exaggerated Semitic features over a hammer and sickle, contrasted with the swastika.

The other side of the coin was the overall alienation of German Jews from all aspects of society, not just by means of violence and rhetoric, but also through escalating legal and regulatory restrictions on daily and economic life. The RBK was created as of November 1, 1933. It was designed to insinuate itself into all artistic professions, and as a result, Jewish members were barred from the professions overseen by the RBK. The first large-scale restriction, however, came just weeks after the Nazi government was seated. The *Gesetz zur Wiederherstellung des Berufsbeamtentums* (the Law for the Restoration of the Civil Service) took effect on April 7, 1933. The Restoration Law created a nationally administered civil service from which employees could be dismissed, most particularly for political transgressions or ethnic heritage. The law allowed the quick purging from German academia and museums a generation of prestigious art historians and scholars simply for being Jewish. One prominent casualty of the law was Alfred Einstein, then a professor at the Royal Prussian Academy of Sciences. This was the last such Nazi law to have any exceptions (in deference to the still-living President Paul von Hindenburg) for World War I veterans of the front and selected others. In July 1933, naturalized German Jews were stripped of their citizenship. Jewish shops and professionals were subjected to repeated official boycotts, and their complaints for assistance were ignored when locals took matters into their own hands. The infamous Nuremberg Laws of 1935 were actually two laws: the Law for the Protection of German Blood and German Honor and the Reich Citizenship Law. The latter codified what had been true *de facto* since the inception of the regime, that only those who could prove their authentic German heritage were thereafter citizens.

During this period, the regime's expression of its own cultural worldview culminated in the Degenerate Art Exhibition of 1937. This show spotlighted the avant garde art that the Nazis despised, arrayed among captions and wall text mocking the supposed depravity, Bolshevism, and Jewishness of the art and artists. These jibes were leveled regardless of the actual biographical details of the artist whose works were included; while Otto Dix and Max Beckmann were explicit in their criticisms of the warmongering politics of the Nazis, Emil Nolde had actually supported the nascent party but was nonetheless cast in with the supposed offenders.

In any event, authentic German movements like Bauhaus architecture and the painters of *Die Brücke* and *Der Blaue Reiter* movements also found themselves in the crosshairs. While Hitler presided with favor over the opening of the Great German Art Exhibition (*Grosse Deutsche Kunstaustellung*) on July 18, 1937, the Degenerate Art Exhibition premiered a day later, vastly outdrawing the show of approved Aryan art. The contrast was not just the curatorial frameworks within which the two shows were presented, however: Pursuant to the degenerate art legislation, disapproved works were taken out of German museums and sold on the international market, most notoriously at the Galerie Fischer in Lucerne in 1939. Art dealers Hildebrand Gurlitt, Karl Buchholz, Ferdinand Möller, and Bernhard Böhmer were given a license—and a monopoly—to trade in this new form of contraband. These men were eventually given favored access to vulnerable or seized collections in France after the German occupation there.

Even before the chaos and violence of Kristallnacht, the Nazi government stopped waiting for economic pressure and desperation to do the job. Instead, legislated registration of property came in, making it easier to locate and seize desirable objects. So, in quick succession, the April 26, 1938, Ordinance for the Registration of Jewish Property (the Registration Ordinance); the November 20, 1938, Ordinance for the Attachment of the Property of the People's and State's Enemies; and the December 3, 1938, Ordinance for the Employment of Jewish Property were all passed. The Registration Ordinance, and the inventories that were printed for use, quite literally gave German and Austrian officials a list of where to look and whom to coerce. They did so repeatedly. Austria's Jews lost their country and all of their rights inside of barely a month in the spring of 1938.

Thus, by the time Germany began invading other countries, it had perfected its system of marginalization, registration, and opportunism. This was carried out swiftly in the newly occupied countries, particularly in France and the Netherlands, by the Einsatzstab Reichsleiter Rosenberg (ERR): the special Nazi unit organized under and named after Nazi ideologue Alfred Rosenberg, author of *The Myth of the Twentieth Century* (*Der Mythos des 20. Jahrhunderts*), a notoriously racist screed written in the late 1920s. Similar actions followed in Italy and Hungary after the German army invaded their erstwhile allies in 1943 and 1944, respectively. In all these places, starting in Germany and then throughout Europe, a bizarre consistency emerged with respect to cloaking sales made under duress in supposed legitimacy by "paying" for works, when of course the offeror needed only hint—or not—what the consequence might be for a spurned bargain. In addition, this all took place against the backdrop of the planned Führermuseum in Linz (Austria). An entire industry, headed first by Hans Posse of the renowned Dresden Gemäldegalerie, was devoted to identifying and seizing, by whatever means available or necessary, those objects that would create an unparalleled repository of European culture in the city nearest the small town where Hitler was born.

On the other side of the conflict, the Allies were planning for their hoped-for eventual victory. On January 5, 1943—after the German advance in the Soviet Union had been halted, but before the reversal at Stalingrad—the government of the United Kingdom issued the Inter-Allied Declaration against Acts of Dispossession Committed in Territories under Enemy Occupation and Control. Better known since as the London Declaration, sixteen other nations joined the United Kingdom in stating the same principles: Belgium, Canada, China, the Czechoslovak Republic, the French National Committee, Greece, India, Luxembourg, the Netherlands, New Zealand, Norway, Poland, the Soviet Union, the Union of South Africa, the United States of America, Australia, the United Kingdom of Great Britain and Northern Ireland, and Yugoslavia. It assesses the state of affairs with frank candor, with the benefit of having witnessed years of occupation both of the descent into madness in Germany, and then in the occupied countries:

> The systematic spoliation of occupied or controlled territory has followed immediately upon each fresh aggression. This has taken every sort of form, from open looting to the most cunningly camouflaged financial penetration, and it has extended to every sort of property—from works of art to stocks of commodities, from bullion and banknotes to stocks and shares in business and financial undertakings. But the object is always the same—to seize everything of value that can be put to the aggressors' profits and then to bring the whole economy of the subjugated countries under control so that they must slave to enrich and strengthen their oppressors.

The London Declaration took aim not only at the lawless plunder that had spread from the Atlantic to the Urals, but also at the pseudo-transactional seizures guised as purchases. Again, with refreshing directness (emphasis added):

> Accordingly, the Governments making this Declaration and the French National Committee reserve all their rights to declare invalid any transfers of, or dealings with, property, rights and

> interests of any description whatsoever which are, or have been, situated in the territories which have come under the occupation or control, direct or indirect of the Governments with which they are at war, or which belong, or have belonged to persons (including juridical persons) resident in such territories. *This warning applies whether such transfers or dealings have taken the form of open looting or plunder, or of transactions apparently legal in form, even when they purport to be voluntarily effected.*

The message is unambiguous: When the day of reckoning came, it would be no excuse to point to supposed intermediary good-faith purchasers—who were anything but—and bogus sale prices.

The tide did eventually turn, of course, and a massive chore awaited the Allies with respect to stolen art (to say nothing of the larger obliteration of Europe, physically and otherwise). Both the United States and the United Kingdom adopted with respect to their zones of occupation a series of military government laws to put order in place. These laws dealt with all manner of civic and political life, but Military Government Law No. 59 (MGL No. 59) was entitled "Restitution of Identifiable Property." The preamble takes an important position, at odds with the traditional civil law of many of European countries impacted by its enactment (and by the underlying looting):

> Property shall be restored to its former owner or to his successor in interest in accordance with the provision of this Law even though the interests of other persons who had no knowledge of the wrongful taking must be subordinated. Provisions of law for the protection of purchasers in good faith, which would defeat restitution, shall be disregarded except where this Law provides otherwise.

MGL No. 59. Property is defined as confiscated in MGL No. 59 if it was (1) not conveyed in good faith, under duress, or otherwise an unlawful taking; (2) seized by government act or in abuse of a government act; or (3) seized as a result of measures taken by the Nazis. Conformity to the prevailing ideology at the time is explicitly disallowed as an excuse. Article 3 of MGL No. 59 sets forth a critical policy decision that reverberates to this day. It reads:

> **Presumption of Confiscation**
>
> It shall be presumed in favor of any claimant that the following transactions entered into between 30 January 1933 and 8 May 1945 constitute acts of confiscation within the meaning Article 2:
>
> Any transfer or relinquishment of property made during a period of persecution by any person who was directly exposed to persecutory measures on any of the grounds set forth in Article 1;
>
> Any transfer or relinquishment of property made by a person who belonged to a class of persons which on any of the grounds set forth in Article 1 was to be eliminated in its entirety from the cultural and economic life of Germany by measures taken by the State or the [Nazi Party].

The article goes on to say that the presumption may be rebutted only by showing that the transferor was paid a fair purchase price but not if the transferor was then denied the right of free disposal—as was usually the case in Germany with regard to the use of blocked accounts and confiscatory "flight taxes," the sadistic fees that the Nazi government charged Jews for the privilege of leaving Germany.

MGL No. 59 is expansive in its treatment of rights to be vindicated. Dissolved entities' rights can be enforced either by a judicially appointed representative or by individual members of the organization:

> If a partnership, company, or corporation organized under the Commercial Law was dissolved or forced to dissolve under any of the reasons set forth in Article 1, the claim for restitution may be asserted by any associate (partner, member or shareholder). The claim for restitution shall be deemed to have been filed on behalf of all associates who have the same cause of action.

Lastly, to a remarkable extent, the United States in particular took the lead with the establishment and administration of its Monuments, Fine Arts, and Archives Section (MFAA) program, known to history now as the Monuments Men. Actually begun before the war was over, the MFAA was charged with the Sisyphean task of dealing with the vast repositories that were discovered under German control. The MFAA established collecting points at Wiesbaden and Munich and began the meticulous process of examining the objects one by one, interrogating the art historians and museum professionals who had run the cultural institutions of Nazi Germany (including Gurlitt, who it was later revealed had convinced the MFAA into believing his vague story that his entire collection had been burned in Dresden when in fact it was nearby and quite intact). The MFAA and the United States made a choice as to the objects they restituted: Works would be returned to their countries of origin for those governments to restitute to their owners. The MFAA and the United States did not undertake to find individual owners. Remarkably, litigants then, and decades later, argued that this policy decision meant that individual claimants have no right to restitution, but the contemporary MGL Law No. 59 says otherwise. This nuance will play an important role in many of the cases discussed herein.

* * *

MGL 59 and its parallels in the physical restitution procedures coordinated by the victorious Allies left an unanswered question. Namely, would the principles of that legal framework extend beyond the cleanup of the Führermuseum project and other Nazi art depots? Or would the idea of restoring looted art to its source be a finite project that would quickly fade with the memory of the war as the world moved on to the new and looming standoff along the Iron Curtain and as part of the Cold War? The answer turned out to be a little bit of both, and very much a glass half full/half empty situation depending on one's perspective. On the one hand, an important precedent would be set that still casts a shadow on those who try to argue that restitution is not the business of U.S. courts. On the other hand, what one might have expected to be an opening of the floodgates never materialized, and the principles of what presumptions and rules ought to apply to either looted or coerced-for-sale art would go literally decades without being explored again.

It should be noted, however, that 1946 and 1947 were dominated by what was one of the most significant judicial developments in modern history, certainly of Western democracies (and the Soviet Union): the Nuremberg trials. Innumerable volumes have been written about the conduct and importance of those trials, in which the chief surviving Nazi officials and German generals were tried for offenses ranging from waging aggressive and unnecessary war to crimes against humanity. The depravity of their conduct was laid out methodically in a proceeding in which they were nonetheless given a rigorous defense. Excuses such as having followed orders were held insufficient.

For present purposes, the Nuremberg trials were and remain significant because they contrast with many principles of deference to foreign state activity as a judicial prospect. Nazi Germany was a recognized sovereign state, given no deference or immunity on that traditional basis. In addition, the trials made findings about specific Nazi conduct that still resonate with the reconstruction of the legacy of looted art throughout Europe. In particular, the results leave no illusions about the swiftness and severity of Nazi repression from the moment they seized power in 1933—something that has become a creeping form of revisionism in more recent years:

> On the 1st April 1933, a boycott of Jewish enterprises was approved by the Nazi Reich Cabinet, and during the following years a series of anti-Semitic laws were passed, restricting the activities of Jews in the Civil Service, in the legal profession, in journalism and in the armed forces. In September 1935, the so-called Nuremberg Laws were passed, the most important effect of which was to deprive Jews of German citizenship. In this way the influence of Jewish elements on the affairs of Germany was extinguished, and one more potential source of opposition to Nazi policy was rendered powerless.

In re Goering et al., 6 F.R.D. 69, 82 (1946). In conjunction with this formal recognition of the impact of the Nazi regime, matters soon came to a head regarding the ability of U.S. courts to review issues of Nazi looting. It is notable how clearly this question of the availability of judicial review was answered by the generation, and indeed by the very people, without whom Nazi plunder would have taken root in Europe permanently.

Arnold Bernstein was the sole shareholder of a company that bore his name, which was the owner of a ship, the *Gandia*. In January 1937, Bernstein was arrested by Nazi officials and imprisoned in Hamburg. After a period of threats and violence against him and his various interests during two and a half years of imprisonment, under duress, Bernstein signed away the shares of the company to a Marius Boeger. More specifically, an affidavit submitted by Bernstein and cited in the opinion stated:

> On January 25, 1937 I was arrested by the Nazi Gestapo, and from that day until the latter part of July 1939 I was continually in the custody of and imprisoned by the Nazis . . . [pursuant to] certain German foreign exchange laws, and from time to time I was told and led to believe by Nazi officials, by my then attorneys in Hamburg and by others that unless I surrendered my shipping interests to a 'trustee' designated by the Nazis, I would be kept imprisoned indefinitely, my remaining property would be confiscated and my life and the lives of my immediate family would be imperiled.

As shocking as it is that one would actually have to make such an averment, Bernstein noted that he was a Jew, and that the Nazis were carrying on

> a deliberate and openly avowed program of eliminating so-called non-Aryans from German social and economic life. I believed that I and my family were in real danger unless I acceded to Nazi demands, and I signed documents purporting to assign and transfer my ownership and control of the Arnold Bernstein Line to a Nazi designee, one Marius Boeger, while still in prison.

Bernstein v. Van Heyghen Freres Societe Anonyme, 163 F.2d 246, 247 (2d Cir. 1947). Even after signing away his life's assets, he was still not released until he was ransomed from custody in July 1939 and he was allowed to leave Germany. The affidavit concluded by alleging that he had later learned that the ship, which was an asset of the company owned by

Bernstein, had been acquired by the defendant "from the Nazi 'trustee' in June, 1939." *Id.* The District Court quashed Bernstein's writ of attachment, which in the days before the Federal Rules of Civil Procedure was his effort to obtain recovery of his property. Bernstein appealed.

In a now-notorious opinion, the famous Learned Hand issued a decision on appeal. First, Hand held that although an attachment did not require an (in Hand's words) "unassailable case" to proceed:

> The plaintiff's allegations as to the defendant's notice of the duress which compelled him to sign the transfer, are exceedingly fragile, and would not survive challenge under a number of New York decisions.

Id. at 248. That is to say that one of the most respected judges in the history of the United States proclaimed, in 1947 as Europe still smoldered, that three years of imprisonment and torture was a "fragile" basis (again Hand's words) to claim that a sale had been made under duress. The question of the proper view of that transaction under MGL No. 59 was never reached (although conceded). However, because Hand concluded that the Act of State doctrine barred the case from being litigated at all:

> [E]ven though we assume that a German court would have held the transfer unlawful at the time it was made, that would be irrelevant. We have repeatedly declared, for over a period of at least thirty years, that a court of the forum will not undertake to pass upon the validity under the municipal law of another state of the acts of officials of that state, purporting to act as such.

The Act of State doctrine holds that even when a court has jurisdiction, it should decline to hear a case when it would involve the sovereign act against one of the relevant government's own citizens (the chief reason that claims for property crimes by the Soviet Union have not been heard in U.S. courts). Indeed:

> [I]f in 1937 it had been the law of the Third Reich that any private person might seize a Jew and by threats of imprisonment or by

> torture force him to transfer his property, by hypothesis no court of New York would recognize such a transfer as affecting the victim's title, and, if the spoliator came to New York with the property in his possession, the victim could reclaim it. We will moreover assume for argument that anyone who knew how the spoliator had acquired the property would be in like case. The case at bar is indeed a variant of this, because the property of which the plaintiff has been despoiled, never came to New York; nor has the spoliator or his transferee. . . .

Hand was unwilling to consider whether the military occupation or the Allies' victory and Nuremberg prosecution permitted court intervention. The Second Circuit remanded the case, presumably for dismissal.

On remand, the District Court reiterated the holding of the Second Circuit, as it was bound to do. Bernstein sought leave to amend his complaint, which the District Court rejected. *Bernstein v. N. V. Nederlandsche-Amerikaansche Stoomvaart-Maatschappij*, 76 F. Supp. 335 (S.D.N.Y. 1948). This was affirmed on a second appeal to the Second Circuit. 173 F.2d 71 (1949).

An interesting thing then happened, however. On April 27, 1949, the State Department issued Press Release No. 296 entitled *Jurisdiction of United States Courts Re Suits for Identifiable Property Involved in Nazi Forced Transfers.* It stated, *inter alia*:

> As a matter of general interest, the Department publishes herewith a copy of a letter of April 13, 1949 from Jack B. Tate, Acting Legal Advisor, Department of State, to the Attorneys for the plaintiff in Civil Action No. 31-555 in the United States District Court for the Southern District of New York.
>
> The letter repeats this Government's opposition to forcible acts of dispossession of a discriminatory and confiscatory nature practiced by the Germans on the countries or peoples subject to their controls; states that it is this Government's policy to undo the forced transfers and restitute identifiable property to the victims of Nazi persecution wrongfully deprived of such property; and sets forth

> that the policy of the Executive, with respect to claims asserted in the United States for restitution of such property, is to relieve American courts from any restraint upon the exercise of their jurisdiction to pass upon the validity of the acts of Nazi officials.

This was not merely an advisory expression. The Act of State doctrine, after all, is rooted in the idea that diplomatic respect and comity encourages respect for the acts and judgments of foreign sovereigns. But, the rejection of that respect by the United States' chief diplomatic arm specifically regarding Nazi Germany is something that had to affect the manner in which Act of State analysis was done. The letter referenced in the press release, known since that time as the Tate Letter, states:

> This Government has consistently opposed the forcible acts of dispossession of a discriminatory and confiscatory nature practiced by the Germans on the countries or peoples subject to their controls . . . The policy of the Executive, with respect to claims asserted in the United States for the restitution of identifiable property (or compensation in lieu thereof) lost through force, coercion, or duress as a result of Nazi persecution in Germany, is to relieve American courts from any restraint upon the exercise of their jurisdiction to pass upon the validity of the acts of Nazi officials.

In a stunning reversal, the Second Circuit allowed the case to proceed based on the press release and the Tate Letter. 210 F.2d 375 (2d Cir. 1954). Although not a case about looted art, the *Bernstein* case did deal squarely with what would become the heart of so many later restitution cases: the murky intersection between escalating persecution and coercive property transfers. Read in isolation, one might reasonably have expected *Bernstein* to presage a new era of litigation about the validity of those property transfers.

Yet incredibly it was not until more than a decade later that these questions would be raised again in court in a case that was little noticed for many years thereafter. Erna Menzel and her husband were Belgian Jews who fled Brussels in March 1941. The Menzels left in their apartment a painting by Marc Chagall, *Le Paysan a L'echelle (The Peasant and the Ladder). Menzel v. List*, 267 N.Y.S. 2d 804, 806 (N.Y. 1966). Soon after they left, the painting was seized by the ERR (*Einsatzstab Reichsleiter Rosenberg*). *Id.* at 301-02.

Seizure by the ERR is one of the few questions on which there is agreement—now—that a good-faith acquisition thereafter is essentially an impossibility if the work bears the ERR stamp. In 1965, the popular state of understanding about the ERR's activities was much less widespread than it is now. In 1962, Menzel apparently discovered the whereabouts of the painting and demanded that the current possessor, Albert List, return it to her. He refused, citing what he argued was a good-faith purchase. Menzel sued for the return of the painting, and List counterclaimed that the claim was time-barred, and that he had purchased the Chagall in good faith from Klaus Perls in 1955 at the latter's gallery on Madison Avenue. Perls testified that he had purchased the work in July 1955 from the Galerie Art Moderne in Paris. Perls also made an argument that the Court of Appeals summarized in a passage that seems hard to believe today:

> He further stated that title was not warranted in writing or orally to third-party defendants; that Galerie Art Moderne is one of the leading, most representative, reputable galleries in Paris, as is Perls Galleries in New York; and amongst such galleries the offer of sale of any painting is in and of itself, in the custom of the trade as between galleries, warranty of title. Art galleries of such standing assume, without the necessity of inquiry, that an offer of sale constitutes a representation of authenticity and good title.

Menzel, 267 N.Y.S.2d at 808. Under the modern Uniform Commercial Code, a warranty of title is now implicit in every sale of personal property unless explicitly disclaimed and in some jurisdictions, no such disclaimer is permitted. In any event, Perls was brought in as a third-party defendant, and the case was tried before a jury. No information remains about how, if at all, the statute of limitations questions were argued or decided before the case was tried. The jury found that Menzel was the owner of the painting, that the ERR acquisition after she fled constituted theft, and that the defendants were liable to her for the value of the painting.

The defendants moved to set aside the jury verdict on the grounds that it was time-barred, that Menzel had abandoned her property rather than being deprived of it, that in any event the law of war permitted the occupying country to take the painting, and that the defendants were entitled to defend themselves as good-faith purchasers. The Court rejected all of these arguments in turn, setting an important precedent that today still drives the discussion of property transfers.

First, the action was not time-barred, because Menzel brought it within three years of her 1962 demand for its return. *Menzel* thus articulates in a manner that is still relied upon today that in New York the way statutes of limitations are calculated is very different. Most states apply a discovery rule—the statute will begin to run when the plaintiff knows, or with reasonable diligence could know, where the property is and who has it. By contrast, in New York "the cause of action against a person who lawfully comes by a chattel arises, not upon the stealing or the taking, but upon the defendant's refusal to convey the chattel upon demand." *Id.* at 809, *citing Cohen v. M. Keizer, Inc.*, 246 App. Div. 277, 285 N.Y.S. 488 (1st Dept. 1936). When Menzel learned where the property was is not clear, but it was clear that she filed the action fewer than three years after the applicable demand for its return.

Next, the Court dismissed the idea that the Menzels had abandoned their property. Abandonment is a relinquishment of a known right with no intent to reclaim it. *Menzel*, 267 N.Y.S.2d at 809-10, *citing Franmor Realty Corp. v. LeBoeuf*, 201 Misc. 220, 104 N.Y.S.2d 247 (Sup. Ct. Nassau Co., 1951), *Aff'd*, 279 App. Div. 795, 109 N.Y.S.2d 525 (2d Dept. 1952), *In re Johnson*, 294 F. 258 (5th Cir. 1923); *Matter of Kerns' Guardianship*, 74 Cal. App. 2d 862, 868, 169 P.2d 975 (1946). Citing further a Yugoslavian tribunal, the Court held that "personal property temporarily abandoned at the approach of the enemy, without the relinquishment of the owner's right of ownership, is neither foreclosed nor forfeited." *Collac v. Etat Serbe-croate-slovene* [Yugoslavia], IX Recueil des Decisions des Tribunaux Arbitraux Mixtes, 195 (Tribunal Arbitral Mixte hungaro-serbe-croate-slovene, 15 Mai 1929).

Next, the Court refused to sanction the defendants' argument that the painting constituted a legitimate spoil of war. This is expressly outlawed by the 1907 Hague Convention, 36 U.S. Stat. at L. 2259, Art. 53, at 2308:

> An army of occupation can only take possession of cash, funds, and realizable securities which are strictly the property of the State, depots of arms, means of transport, stores and supplies, and, generally, all movable property belonging to the State which may be used for military operations.

By contrast, pillage is the taking of property not necessary for military operations. Incredibly, Menzel appears to be the first articulation of a point that one would presume and hope would be obvious: that the state-sponsored looting organized by the ERR did not enjoy any immunity from judicial review. As with abandonment, pillage does not extinguish the rights of the owner:

> The principle based upon the Roman Law according to which property seized during a war is put on an equal footing with the property seized in the air, in the sea or in the earth, and which in a similar way becomes the property of the captor—since the right of war constitutes a just cause of acquisition—may be applicable to things liable or apt to be used for the needs of the army and belonging to the other belligerent. But it cannot be applied to private property which, if it has not become the object of requisition or sequestration, must be restored or compensated. The objects involved in the present case are private property which had not been requisitioned or sequestrated as it could not be used for the needs of the army. Their seizure must therefore be considered as having been effected by pillage.

Menzel, 267 N.Y.S.2d at 812. As if there were any doubt as to the principle, the *Menzel* Court noted that:

> [T]he very description of the acts of Einsatzstab Rosenberg, in *United States et al. v. Goering et al.*, infra, is entitled "Pillage of Public and Private Property." 6 F.R.D. at 69, 120.

> And in the first order issued by the 21st Army Group, July, 1944, upon the return of Allied Forces to the French beachhead, where the question arose what German property was booty ("butin de guerre"), under the general principles of the laws of war, it was provided:
>
> "The Germans have acquired no title to private movable property which has been acquired by theft, looting, or pillage." Note to Article by Dr. Smith, supra, 23 Brit. Y.B. Intl. L. at 238–239 (1946).

Id. at 812. The Court next considered the possible application of the Act of State doctrine, about which there would be much litigation decades later. The doctrine has four essential elements: (1) the taking must be by a foreign sovereign government; (2) the taking must be within the territorial limitations of that government; (3) the foreign government must be extant and recognized by this country at the time of suit; and (4) the taking must not be violative of a treaty obligation. *Menzel*, 267 N.Y.S.2d at 813. The easiest factor to analyze in the case of the Menzels is the second, because as Belgians they were not targeted on Belgian soil by the Belgian government, nor could they be targeted as Germans on German soil. Thus, the Act of State doctrine defense would have failed in any era. But, the other analysis, as influential a case as *Menzel* is, is dated and worth reviewing for those who so often cite the case for its general principles.

Perhaps most interestingly, the Court concluded that the painting—which was seized by the ERR, which historians recognize as indistinguishable from the German occupation—"was seized not by a foreign sovereign government but rather by 'The Centre for National Socialist Ideological and Educational Research', an organ of the Nazi Party." *Id.* at 815. It is difficult to read that passage without taking into account the state of historical scholarship at that time. In 1966, there was still a tendency to try to distinguish between what was German and what was Nazi.

The reasons are easy to understand. At the height of the Cold War, only three years after the construction of the Berlin wall, historians coalesced around the idea that the National Socialist Party had been some kind of extraneous entity to German sovereignty. Scholarship frequently distinguished between the conduct of the Wehrmacht and the *Schutzstaffel* (SS) on the Eastern Front, for example, a distinction that historians now accept is without a difference. Yet in reading the Court's opinion in *Menzel*, one sees that supposed but ultimately illusory distinction between the army's actions and the Nazis at work: The notion that the army was occupying France, doing what armies do, but that the ERR was an extra layer of domestic politics that just happened to be there.

In fact, the ERR was as much an integrated part of the sovereign government as it could be, indeed as anything that Hitler supported in his overwhelming effort to impress his *Gleichschaltung* on the rest of Europe and the world. It is also, interestingly, directly at odds with Learned Hand's dismissive treatment of the dynamics of sales under duress in *Bernstein*, which went out of its way to establish the Nazis *bona fides* as sovereign actors in dismissing that case before the Tate Letter set him straight.

As with the first factor, the analysis of the third element of the Act of State doctrine set out above seems astonishing today: "The Third Reich was neither extant nor recognized by the Government of the United States at the time of trial." *Menzel*, 267 N.Y.S.2d at 311-12. Obviously, the Third Reich had ceased to exist long before 1966. But treating the Third Reich as something that sprang from nowhere in 1933 and disappeared in 1945 is simply not true. It was the recognized government of a sovereign nation, and it is difficult to imagine even the most ardent present day apologists for leaving looted property in its current location arguing this characterization of the arc of the Third Reich. As noted in the failure of analysis on the first Act of State factor (the requirement that the taking at issue be by a sovereign power), the painting was not seized by a political party, nor a transitory nation. It was seized by Germany, a nation that existed before 1933 and that still existed in 1966—and whose government was not at war with, and which was recognized by, the United States in March 1941 (when the seizure took place). Lest anyone forget, before Pearl Harbor and Hitler's tactical blunder of declaring war on the United States, there was serious discussion in U.S. domestic politics about whether to align against Germany. To suggest in 1966 that U.S.-German relations did not exist on March 31, 1941, is false by every measure.

Lastly, the *Menzel* Court concluded that since the invasion of Belgium violated The Hague Convention, any resulting seizure or dispossession could not be defended under the Act of State doctrine. Given that the doctrine failed on its own terms, the Court expressly declined to consider whether the *Bernstein* exception could or should be applied. *Id.* at 818.

Ironically, it is *Menzel*'s last point of analysis that has provided its most enduring legacy:

> It is of no moment that Perls Galleries may have been a *bona fide* purchaser of the painting, in good faith and for value and without knowledge of the saga of the Menzels. No less is expected of an art gallery of distinction.
>
> Throughout the course of human history, the perpetration of evil has inevitably resulted in the suffering of the innocent, and those who act in good faith. And the principle has been basic in the law that a thief conveys no title as against the true owner.

Id. at 819. And then, with a flourish:

> In the case at bar, the underlying transaction was the looting, plunder and pillage by the Nazis, which was of the very essence of evil.

Id. at 820. *Menzel* went up and back on appeal, but the Appellate Division's initial alteration of the foregoing result was reversed, leaving the holding intact. 298 N.Y.S.2d 979. One might well have expected, with this unequivocal statement of policy, that the floodgates would open—just as one would have expected after the 1954 *Bernstein* decision, and, once again, that that expectation was not to be. Indeed, it was not for another twenty years that the issue received prominent attention, and then only in a short-lived precedent that seemed to set back the cause of reclaiming stolen art.

In 1987, the Second Circuit decided *DeWeerth v. Baldinger*, 836 F.2d 103, 106 (2d Cir. 1987). *DeWeerth* cited *Menzel* for the proposition that even though there is a demand and refusal component to conversion claims, there is also a component of diligence. Specifically, the Second Circuit held that an owner of stolen property may not unreasonably delay making the requisite demand. The Court, interpreting New York law, held that the owner has "a duty of reasonable diligence in attempting to locate stolen property, in addition to the . . . duty to make a demand for return within a reasonable time after the current possessor is identified." *Id.* at 108 (footnote omitted).

That development was short-lived. The Second Circuit, like all federal courts, may interpret the laws of the 50 states, but the final word as to those laws belongs to the courts of those states. *DeWeerth* was thus an effort to synthesize New York law, rightly looking to *Menzel* for guidance. But, the New York courts soon made clear that the Second Circuit had not struck the right balance.

Solomon R. Guggenheim Foundation v. Lubell was not a case about Nazi-looted art. However, it bears review because its effect on later restitution litigation, particularly in New York, has been profound. The Guggenheim Museum had a Chagall work, done in gouache that was known alternately as *Menageries* or *Le Marchand de Bestiaux* (*The Cattle Dealer*, 1912), go missing from its collection sometime in the late 1960s. The Guggenheim believed that it had been stolen by a mailroom employee. In 1967, Rachel Lubell and her husband bought the work, unaware of its history, from the Robert Elkon Gallery on Madison Avenue. The parties disagreed about when the Guggenheim discovered that the work was missing. After an investigation and concluding that it was indeed gone, the Guggenheim board voted to deaccession the work in 1974. The Lubells exhibited the painting on two occasions, once in 1967 and again in 1981, both times at the gallery where they had purchased it. In 1985, bearing a transparency of the work, a private dealer approached Sotheby's for an estimate. By coincidence, the Sotheby's employee who viewed the transparency had worked at the Guggenheim and recognized it as the missing work. Mrs. Lubell notified the Guggenheim and on January 9, 1986, the Guggenheim demanded that Mrs. Lubell return the work or compensate the museum for it. Mrs. Lubell refused, and the museum sued her in September 1986.

Mrs. Lubell answered and asserted the statute of limitations and laches as defenses, among others. Laches is a defensive concept related to but distinct from the statute of limitations. Whereas a statute of limitations is just a statute that prescribes a time after which a claim may not be brought, laches is an equitable defense to be asserted and proved by the defending party. It holds that even when a claim is timely within the statute of limitations, a defendant may still prevail where he or she can show that the plaintiff delayed unreasonably in the claim such that the defendant was prejudiced.

Imagine a case in which Party A steals a work of art from Party B. The statute of limitations would generally provide that Party B will have three years to bring the claim from the time he or she learns that Party A took it or has it. Assume further that within the statute of limitations (possibly two years later), Party B learns that Party A intends to sell it to Party C or at auction. The statute of limitations will not be affected by that transaction. In terms of the timeliness, Party B can sue Party A to restrain the sale beforehand, or Party B for damages and Party C for the return of the artwork afterwards. In turn, Party C can sue Party A for selling a stolen work. That is not the only question, however. Party C can invoke laches and say that whereas Party B may have a claim for damages (money) against Party A for the obvious reason that Party A is a thief, that it would be unfair to punish Party C, a good-faith purchaser, for a transaction that Party B knew was impending. Such a defense is, necessarily, very fact specific.

Citing *DeWeerth*, Mrs. Lubell eventually moved for summary judgment arguing that the Guggenheim had forfeited its right to recover as untimely because it had done nothing in 20 years to find the painting (that period of time being a matter of debate). The trial court allowed the motion, relying on *DeWeerth*. While acknowledging the vitality of the demand and refusal rule, the trial court held that "in order to avoid prejudice to a good-faith purchaser, demand cannot be unreasonably delayed and that a property owner has an obligation to use reasonable efforts to locate its missing property to ensure that demand is not so delayed." *Solomon R. Guggenheim Foundation v. Lubell*, 567 N.Y.S.2d 623, 625-26 (N.Y. 1991). The Appellate Division held that it was more properly a matter of laches than the application of the statute of limitations and that Lubell had to establish that she had been prejudiced by the delay she cited. The Appellate Division certified the question to the Court of Appeals for approval.

The Court of Appeals first summarized the existing law:

> New York case law has long protected the right of the owner whose property has been stolen to recover that property, even if it is in the possession of a good-faith purchaser for value (*see Saltus & Saltus v. Everett,* 20 Wend. 267, 282). There is a three-year Statute

> of Limitations for recovery of a chattel (CPLR 214[3]). The rule in this State is that a cause of action for replevin against the good-faith purchaser of a stolen chattel accrues when the true owner makes demand for return of the chattel and the person in possession of the chattel refuses to return it (*see, e.g., Goodwin v. Wertheimer,* 99 N.Y. 149, 153, 1 N.E. 404; *Cohen v. Keizer, Inc.,* 246 App. Div. 277, 285 N.Y.S. 488). Until demand is made and refused, possession of the stolen property by the good-faith purchaser for value is not considered wrongful (*see, e.g., Gillet v. Roberts,* 57 N.Y. 28, 30–31; *Menzel v. List,* 49 Misc. 2d 300, 304–305, 267 N.Y.S.2d 804, *mod. as to damages* 28 A.D.2d 516, 279 N.Y.S.2d 608, *rev'd as to modification* 24 N.Y.2d 91, 298 N.Y.S.2d 979, 246 N.E.2d 742).

Id. at 626. Then, the Court of Appeals noted, the statute of limitations begins from the time of the theft—even if the owner was not aware of the theft. *Id.*

Reviewing the case at hand, the Court of Appeals overruled *DeWeerth*'s interpretation of the statute of limitations. First, it affirmed the importance of the demand and refusal rule, which *DeWeerth* would have abrogated significantly if not completely. It noted that New York had explicitly considered and rejected the idea of the discovery rule:

> In 1986, both houses of the New York State Legislature passed Assembly Bill 11462-A (Senate Bill 3274-B), which would have modified the demand and refusal rule and instituted a discovery rule in actions for recovery of art objects brought against certain not-for-profit institutions. This bill provided that the three-year Statute of Limitations would run from the time these institutions gave notice, in a manner specified by the statute, that they were in possession of a particular object. Governor Cuomo vetoed the measure, however, on advice of the United States Department of State, the United States Department of Justice and the United States Information Agency.

Id. at 627. The true owner was still under obligation to look for her painting or face a laches defense, but that should be a procedural issue to resolve, not a substantive component of the cause of action in the first instance. As a matter of policy, the Court of Appeals was concerned about how difficult it would be to specify what constitutes reasonable diligence. It noted that reasonable minds differed, for example, about whether and how to publicize the fact of a theft, and whether publicity would deter or encourage such thefts. Thus:

> [I]t would be particularly inappropriate for this Court to spell out arbitrary rules of conduct that all true owners of stolen art work would have to follow to the letter if they wanted to preserve their right to pursue a cause of action in replevin. All owners of stolen property should not be expected to behave in the same way and should not be held to a common standard.

Id. at 628. Furthermore, the Court of Appeals was eager to distinguish New York as a sophisticated jurisdiction for art disputes and its "worldwide reputation as a preeminent cultural center." The Court of Appeals thus concluded that the Appellate Division was right, *DeWeerth* was wrong, and that the case should return to the trial court to explore as a matter of fact the extent of the Guggenheim's diligence and/or the Lubells' prejudice, if any. A day after the trial began in December 1993, the dispute settled on confidential terms. Although the Iron Curtain had fallen just four years earlier, it was not yet obvious that a new era had begun.

PART TWO

The New Era

Chapter 2

The Washington Conference and Its Ethical Parallels

In 1992, the year after *Lubell*, Lynn Nicholas published her seminal book, *The Rape of Europa*, followed soon after by Hector Feliciano's *The Lost Museum* and the scholarship of Jonathan Petropoulos. Suddenly the past seemed alive again with the fantastical details of looted art schemes and conspiracies to strip the continent of its greatest treasures for Hitler's amusement. As this wave built, 1998 was a signal year regarding the issues of restitution. In addition to the intense focus early in the year on the *Portrait of Wally* and *Dead City III* seizure case, the year provided two important efforts for establishing updated guiding principles to address the issue of potentially looted art. Although the Washington Conference is rightly the best known, America's museum industry associations also took important steps to give some shape to resolving questions that many institutions had not thought about in decades and were ill-equipped to handle.

Late in 1998, the U.S. Department of State hosted a remarkable event: the Washington Conference on Holocaust-Era Assets. This was spawned by what writers and scholars now consider the new era of restitution. The reasons are hard to pin down with precision, but certainly a new perspective on the world after the Cold War and the new availability of people and sources previously obscured by the Iron Curtain played a major role.

More than 40 nations sent representatives to discuss issues related to the topic. Judge Abner Mikva chaired the proceedings, which began with an address by U.S. Secretary of State Madeleine K. Albright. Secretary Albright invoked the 1997 London Gold Conference as a model for success. She identified what she described as the imperatives of the conference: (1) the pursuit of justice, even if relative; (2) openness and full access to archives and records; (3) the obligation to seek truth; (4) the urgency created by the passage of time; and (5) what she called a "twin purpose": to "forge a common approach to the issues still surrounding Holocaust assets," and "to advance Holocaust education, remembrance and research." *See* Madeleine Albright, opening remarks to Washington Conference, available at https://fcit.usf.edu/holocaust/resource/assets/heac1.pdf. Secretary Albright closed her remarks with the poignant observation that she had recently learned of her family's Jewish heritage and that her grandparents had perished in the Holocaust. Undersecretary Stuart E. Eizenstat, Elie Wiesel, and Judge Mikva all gave opening remarks as well, underscoring the importance of the issue at hand.

Many of the remarks made at the conference are publicly available and are fascinating in hindsight. Several are particularly notable. As befitting their significant contributions to the field, both Lynn Nicholas and Jonathan Petropoulos gave historical overviews of the looting itself as discussed above. Dr. Ernst Bacher, chairman of the Austrian Committee, addressed the contemporary state of restitution in that country. Valeriy D. Kulishov offered a distinctly Russian take on the historical question:

> By the end of the war the cultural assets confiscated by the Nazis from their victims in the East were literally burning a hole in the pockets of those who had possession of them. They could have become material evidence of their current owners' complicity in Nazi crimes in the East. It is not surprising that these individuals tried to get rid of them at any cost. There is no doubt that these artworks ultimately found their way to the West. The facts uncovered to date confirm this.

See statement to the Plenary Session on Nazi-Confiscated Art Issues by Valeriy D. Kulishov, Chief of the Office of Restitution, Department for the Preservation of Cultural Assets, Ministry of Culture Russia, statement translated from the original Russian by the U.S. Department of State Office of Language Services, Translating Division, available at https://fcit.usf.edu/holocaust/resource/assets/heac4.pdf. Kulishov went on to extoll the virtues of Soviet fulfillment of its obligations in returning stolen property. This conclusion implicitly accuses the Western art market of being somewhat compromised by a looted art problem, but leaving Soviet expropriation of cultural goods unaddressed except as follows:

> In searching for and identifying cultural assets that belonged to the allies and their citizens, the Soviet Military Administration in Germany could proceed only on the basis of restitution claims submitted by the interested countries and backed up by documentation. In the case of state property this was relatively simple. It was much more difficult in the case of property belonging to Holocaust victims. Nevertheless, I can solemnly state that Russian archives do not contain any information or documents which would indicate that the Soviet Military Administration knowingly or intentionally kept property that belonged to Holocaust victims, including cultural assets, when it was aware of the origin of these items.

Id.

Given the retributive plunder of German museums by the Red Army, it is hard to believe that statement. Ronald Lauder made a number of overview statements that still carry weight even today. As he noted, given the scale of the looting, it was inconceivable that nearly every museum in the world would not be affected somehow (not knowingly, he was quick to add). He was particularly critical of France, which he accused of having "stopped trying to find owners after 1959"[1] and of still being in possession of 2,000 works that he said should be returned to families or, where that was not possible, to the Jewish communities of France. (This comment drew a sharp response from the French delegation, as noted below.) He extolled the efforts of Austria (to which he had been U.S. ambassador, and which shortly thereafter would stumble so badly in the *Portrait of Wally* and *Altmann* cases discussed below), but criticized the Netherlands for inadequate progress on work that he said should take no more than six months, and Germany for simply creating a trust for unclaimed works, a trust that subsequently distributed them to German museums. He also lamented the amount of work that had passed through Switzerland, both traceable and untraceable. His assault on France on the one hand and his compliments to Austria on the other was interesting given his obvious personal connection to Austria, which was hardly in the vanguard at the time. (Indeed, as discussed later, it was among the most resistant until later and meaningful progress.) It was the kind of potential conflict of loyalty that would shadow his advocacy again in the future when the Museum of Modern Art (MoMA), of which he was a board member, was faced with claims. Interestingly, Lauder also took the position that the United States "is perhaps the most active country in finding works of art through its Association of Art Museum Directors [the AAMD]."[2]

A. "Rusty" Powell III, director of the National Gallery of Art in Washington, D.C., also spoke early in the conference. He described the work of the Roberts Commission after the war. He said that at the time of the conference, the National Gallery had received only one claim for a work that had been restituted by the Allies after the war.

Dr. Oliver Rathkolb of the Kreisky Archives in Vienna also addressed Austrian restitution in remarks entitled "From 'Legacy of Shame' to New Debates over Nazi Looted Art." He traced the genesis of awareness in many ways to the Waldheim crisis—the public revelation that Kurt Waldheim, former Austrian president and U.N. Secretary General, had been a member of the Nazi Party. In Austria, of course, interest in the *Portrait of Wally* case was greater than elsewhere and heightened in prominence starting in 1997. He addressed the *Beethoven Frieze* case—not in active dispute at the time—as one of "ransom," in the following way:

> The famous Klimt [frieze] in the Lederer collection was, however, not included in the export license, and it took until the 1970s when Chancellor Bruno Kreisky himself started negotiations for the Republic of Austria to buy the Klimt Fries from Lederer. When Erich Lederer had tried to get back the Bellini painting in the 1950s the Austrian Ministry for Education refused, although

> a confidential internal evaluation of the Ministry opposed to the use of the Export Control Law for such deals ("Vorgang immerhin im Ausfuhrverbotsgesetz nicht gedeckt"). The Minister, Heinrich Drimmel, himself decided not to restitute, but at least admitted that the Export Control law should be changed.

Summing up the bureaucratic resistance to restitution, he noted the "first victim" mythology that only began to change during the Waldheim crisis.

Richard Bevins, a historian at the Foreign and Commonwealth Office, spoke about the British experience. The U.K. was unique among European nations to have been both a belligerent with, but never actually occupied or invaded by, the German army. The U.K. did play a significant role in postwar restitution, but from a more detached perspective. The first notable step in this regard, Bevins observed, was the London Declaration.

Another interesting perspective on the reaction and synthesis of the contributions at the conference itself was the delegation statements submitted by the various countries at or shortly after the conference. These are particularly instructive in considering the eventual principles themselves. The approach that each of these countries brought to the issues was, not surprisingly, informed by the respective country's experience during the war; however, even those countries that had generally been more open about the war submitted statements that are laden with subtext.

For obvious reasons, Germany's and Austria's submissions would have been the most interesting—except Germany did not make one. Germany's central role in the Holocaust requires no further elaboration. However, as artist Ruth Bekkerman noted in 2015[1] in dedicating her multimedia work, *The Missing Image* (about the spontaneous humiliation forced on Vienna's Jews after the *Anschluss*),[2] Austria's progression from the popular myth of the "first victim" of National Socialism—which was driven by and allowed the desire to break free of four-party occupation in the 1950s—to a more nuanced confrontation with the nation's history had barely begun in the 1990s.

Austria's submission "Aryanization" (the takeover of Jewish property by non-Jews) is one of the most detailed to have been made public. It discusses the Aryanization of various asset classes, including but not limited to art, and Austria's postwar restitution administration. In preparation for the return of properties taken from the rightful owners by the Nazis, a law regarding the submission of claims was passed as early as 1945. The holders of Aryanized properties were requested under threat of penalty to register those assets and to refrain from any legal transactions regarding the property in question, except ordinary administrative activities. Between 1946 and 1949, seven restitution laws were passed by the Austrian Parliament which provided for restitution in several phases. The immediate victims, as well as their direct descendants and siblings, were eligible for restitution. In addition, four laws dealt with claims for restitution of property, for example to democratic institutions, including Jewish and non-Jewish religious institutions.

Not all Aryanized and registered property was actually claimed, and therefore not everything could be restored. A law regarding the collection of those assets was passed in 1957, and the Collection Points A and B were created. Collection Point A received all unclaimed property of persons who, in 1937, had belonged to the Jewish community; Collection Point B received other claims. After the disbursement of the proceeds to victims of persecution, the collection points were liquidated in 1972. While the legal framework for the resolution of restitution cases (with the exception of leases which were not included) was generally accepted by the Allies and victims' organizations, questions concerning the practical implementation of the laws remain. There is no systematic overview of the files or any historical analysis on that subject. Of the 42,096 claims submitted, approximately one-fifth were granted, one-third were settled by agreement, and one-third were rejected or withdrawn. There exist no reliable data about the monetary value of the restored property.

By January 1949, of the more than 18,500 items that had been seized during the Nazi era or that had been voluntarily given up to air raid shelters, more than 13,000 art objects had been returned to their rightful owners or their legitimate heirs. Restitution of the remaining objects was spread out over the subsequent years. For this purpose, two specific laws pertaining to the settlement of claims regarding art and cultural heritage were passed in 1969 and 1986. The latter law was amended in 1995 to allow for the Mauerbach sale: In 1996, an auction of Nazi-confiscated works of art that could not be restituted to former owners or their heirs was held to benefit Holocaust victims.

Three major laws had been passed in the 1940s and 1950s. Pursuant to the First Restitution Act, Federal Law Gazette No. 156/1946, property was returned under the administration of the country or its states when the law was enacted in 1946. Likewise, the Second Restitution Act, Federal Law Gazette No. 53/1947, concerned confiscated property in Austria's possession because of forfeiture. Specifically, the second law addressed the restitution of property that had been taken from rightful owners and then passed into the hands of private individuals who were themselves subject to forfeiture laws as war criminals pursuant to the Nazi Prohibition Act and the War Criminal Act. In other words, the Second Restitution Act applied where the intermediary was a top Nazi or convicted war criminal. Lastly, the Third Restitution Act, Federal Law Gazette No. 54/1947, regulated the restitution of property that was taken from its owner during the German occupation of Austria by the Nazis.

Not mentioned in the submission is any reference to Austria's postwar export laws. As would soon come to the fore in a number of disputes (the Beethoven Frieze dispute in particular), even works whose title was restituted to survivors and heirs were often subject to an export prohibition. That prohibition presented survivors with a quandary regarding whether to return to the place of their persecution or to sell the works (with the unavoidable negative effect on the price that could be obtained). The silence on the topic of Austria's postwar export laws is notable particularly because within ten years that very discrepancy would be addressed by new legislation in Austria.

Most important for the long term, however, was the description of the Commission for Provenance Research, which would assume prominence in the years that followed. In order to gain comprehensive knowledge of historical facts related to assets looted by the Nazis and of restitution of property after the war, the Austrian government established an independent Commission of Historians, which also included international participation, to study all aspects of Aryanization and the country's restitution efforts regarding victims of the Nazi era after the war. The mandate of the Commission ranged from dispossessed property within the territory of Austria to restitution and/or compensation as well as economic and social efforts by Austria after 1945. The Commission had its inaugural session on November 26, 1998.

Belarus also submitted a statement, which referred to many cultural losses during the Nazi occupation. As documented so well in Timothy Snyder's *Bloodlands*, Belarus was among those countries that suffered incalculably during successive Soviet, Nazi, and then Soviet occupations. The Belarus statement is short on specifics, however, while generally committing to the wisdom of comprehensive negotiations on looted art.

Belgium's statement begins with an overview of the occupation of its territory that began in May of 1940. With regard to cultural plunder, two groups—the Sicherheitspolizei-Sicherheitsdienst (SIPO-SD) and Einsatzstab Reichsleiter Rosenberg (ERR)—took the most prominent roles. Belgium was also subjected to the Möbelaktion that took place in France, the organized plunder of furniture from the Jewish population. Despite major cultural losses, the immediate postwar apparatus was focused on commodities such as trains, coal, ships, steel, etc. A small unit within that organization (the Office de Récupération, or ORE) was dedicated to finding cultural goods that had been taken to Germany and Austria. That unit worked until 1952 and recovered 492 works of art and 2,749 books, including the Van Eyck brothers' *The Mystic Lamb* and *Madonna* by Michelangelo from the Bruges cathedral.

According to the Belgian delegation, that ORE unit then worked in a second phase until 1964 without achieving results and later disbanded in 1967. Its records, regrettably, are lost. As of the date of the Washington Conference, the Belgian delegation counted 3,273 works as still missing, though it cautioned that the looting itself was only barely documented. Not until 1993 did this work in Belgium resume, which the delegation attributed to the end of the Cold War and the newly found access to previously unavailable resources. In 1997, a commission formed to further investigate the loss of cultural property.

Croatia was less than ten years old as a country at the time of the Washington Conference, and like Belarus, had its own complicated history of occupation, collaboration, and Communist-era repression. Even so, however, the Croatian delegation noted its irritation regarding the (lack of) access to previously accessible Yugoslavian archives.

A provisional governmental authority was created in Croatia in 1945 to address property abandoned during the German occupation. According to the Croatian delegation, many cultural objects (which may have been deemed abandoned, although under what standards it is not known) were placed into collection centers. Not surprisingly, the delegation had no specific data to offer on that de facto nationalization. A number of commissions did begin working at the Institution for Conservation of the Republic of Croatia in Zagreb, however, for the "collection and preservation of surviving cultural monuments, antiquities and libraries following the period of the Holocaust."[3] While the delegation statement does describe the loss of cultural objects because of the Holocaust, it quickly shifts course to talk about Croatian losses during the Yugoslavian wars of 1991–95, which were many times worse than the damage suffered during World War II.

Finland's wartime history, its delegation noted, is unique. It first fought against the Soviet Union—an ally of Nazi Germany at the time—while Germany was conquering other parts of Scandinavia. Having prevented a Soviet invasion, it then staved off Nazi incursions from the north. There was, according to the Finnish delegation, no seizure of Jewish-owned artwork in Finland. At the time of the report, two paintings had been discovered that might have been stolen. Any restitutions since that report are unknown.

France, as is now well known, was among the most heavily affected countries by virtue of its Jewish population and the country's centrality to the international art market. The French delegation's statement opens, combatively, by taking issue directly with a statement made earlier in the conference by Lauder, that "the French Government knew the identity of the owners of the 2,000 works of art deposited with the Museums of France at the end of the restitution campaign that permitted the return of more than 45,000 of the 61,000 works of art recovered in Germany."[4] Adolph Steg, Deputy Chairman, Fact Finding Mission on the Looting of Jewish Assets for the Musée Nationaux Récupération (MNR), stated his commission's guiding principles:

> 1) The MNR assets are not integrated in the national patrimony. 2) When seeking a solution (and for us a general rule in all fields) we refer ourselves only to the interest of victims. Clearly we do not protect any institution, or organization or corporation, but only the victims. 3) Finally, our mission will now begin a reflection on the definitive statute of the MNR and we will make proposals on the destination of these works of art.

See Adolph Steg, Opening Statement on Art Works (Washington, December 2, 1998), available at https://fcit.usf.edu/holocaust/resource/assets/heac3.pdf.

Greece's contribution was relatively brief. With regard to Jewish property, the statement noted that archival materials of the Jewish community of Thessaloniki that were forcibly removed to Germany had only recently been discovered in Russia. It notes the following losses, among other financial looting:

> The Library of the Religious Tribunal (Beth-Din), containing approximately 2,500 volumes of rare editions. The Library of the Community Schools' Teachers, with about 600 volumes of reference books, etc. The Library of the Monastirioton Synagogue, that included exclusively books of religious and hieronomic interest. The Library of the Religious Establishment Haimoutcho Kovo located on 8, Menexe st. and of its annex on 74, Queen Olga Avenue, to which the personal libraries of its founder, the Great Rabbi Haim Asher Kovo, and the precious library of Chief Rabbi Asher Kovo had been added. The 250 manuscripts of the Holy Jewish Law (Pentateuque) treasured in the city's Synagogue, many of which had been brought from Spain in 1492.

Hungary's statement is one that has become even more interesting with the passage of time and Hungary's specific involvement in litigation, as discussed later. The statement noted the initial alignment of Hungary with Germany in the war, followed by the German occupation of the country starting in 1944 until the Red Army arrived in 1945. The delegation statement noted the organized looting of property from Hungary's Jewish population began in March 1944 and lasted until April 1944, under the direction of the Government Commission for the Registration and Safeguarding of Art Work. The statement[5] read:

> These treasures were then - with a few exceptions - transported to Germany. There was a so-called Hungarian gold train with two trucks at the end of World War II, full with gold, jewelry, precious stones and a large amount of artifacts looted from Jews, and which were never returned to Hungary. We do not know anything about their fate.

The delegation statement asserted that "[a] significant portion of all cultural property found was returned to Holocaust survivors." The statement noted further that certain objects had been located in Russia, but that "[t]he return of these objects is blocked by the Russian attitude of indifference towards international norms on restitution and also by the uncertain situation of their restitution law." The statement cited comments by Eizenstat in 1996 to the effect that the Hungarian government had, at that point following the fall of Communism, been forward thinking about the issue. Presciently, with regard to the state of objects whose provenance was under review, the delegation statement quoted above further framed the obligation of the Hungarian museums thusly:

> Some of these cultural objects are registered as unclear deposits, some others as part of the basic collection of the museum. In fact, it is one of the museum's most important missions to safeguard its holdings from being sold or alienated until unlawful ownership has not been proved incontestably.

The delegation statement claimed "full commitment" to restitution or compensation of Holocaust victims and pledged that a state commissioner for that purpose would be designated.

The Israeli delegation was in a unique position, as the self-described "central representative of the survivors and their offspring . . . dedicated to achieving justice on their behalf and to the remembrance of the Holocaust."[6] As a result, and in calling for continued work on the topic through the World Jewish Restitution Organization (WJRO) in particular, the delegation statement to the Washington Conference[7] said this:

> People or institutions who knowingly acquired looted property should pay restitution. We appeal to financial institutions such as banks and insurance companies to accept responsibility for their Holocaust era clients. This also applies to those who acquired art works and ritual objects looted from homes and houses of worship. Though these items may have passed through a number of hands, the original owners have an indisputable claim to what is rightfully theirs. We welcome the openness and the cooperation of

> the countries researching the facts regarding property seized during the Holocaust. We note with satisfaction that many countries have established commissions to investigate their own past. We join the initiative to persuade all countries, groups and individuals to allow immediate and unrestricted access to all archival and state archive materials relevant to the period. This applies especially to church records and archives of private concerns, corporations and individuals, as well as documentation not stored in archives. Any entity that withholds information from public access compounds the indifference and crimes of the past.

This is a common sense appeal to do the right thing. The Israeli delegation's basic directive was that if one received something one should not have, one should give it back.

Italy, like Hungary, held an unusual role as both a co-belligerent but also a forcibly occupied country. As in Hungary, the Jewish population suffered throughout but at an increased rate after the German army moved in. Minister Franco Tempesta delivered the Italian delegation statement, which is broken down by subject matter, including education, research, and gold. There is a separate chapter devoted only to gold. Remarkably, given Italy's artistic heritage and interest, there is no specific mention of art at all.

Latvia's statement provided another example of the importance of the starting point perspective. It refers to a historical commission to address "the tragic events in Latvian history from 1939 through 1991."[8] This is an interesting choice, because that period encompasses three distinct eras: (1) the Soviet occupation following the Molotov-Ribbentrop Pact; (2) the German occupation starting shortly after the beginning of Operation Barbarossa in June 1941; and (3) the incorporation of Latvia as a Soviet Republic until the collapse of the U.S.S.R. at the end of 1991. Each era affected Latvia harshly but in very different ways; yet, the commission was organized to address them all as a continuous era of history. The Latvian statement nonetheless spotlights the return of Jewish property as an issue of particular importance. The statement claimed that "to date property rights on most pieces of property have been restituted."[9]

The statement by Luxembourg recounted the demographic situation at the time of Germany's 1940 invasion of the small principality. Of the roughly 3,700 Jews in the country when the invasion began, some 2,000 were German refugees. By September 5, 1940, the Nuremberg Laws were in full effect, and every remaining Jew in the country had to provide to authorities a detailed description of his or her property. After a period of rampant corruption by officials administering the seizure of Jewish property, Gauleiter Gustav Simon announced the creation of the Verwaltung des jüdischen und Emigranten-Vermögens (Administration of Jewish and Emigrants' Property). Private works of art in Luxembourg were seized by the Aussenstelle des Gaupropagandaamtes in Luxembourg (External Affairs of District Propaganda Office). The 1998 statement claimed limited evidence was available as to the fate of those works in the art market. Public museums were less affected, according to the statement.

After the war, laws enacted by the Luxembourg government in exile came into play. First and foremost, the government had enacted a law in 1941 that declared all forced sales null and void. A 1950 law, however, restricted compensation to Luxembourg nationals who had been victimized for what were described by the Luxembourg delegation as "patriotic reasons."[10] This excluded, by its terms, victims of racial or ethnic persecution (principally Jews, of course).

The Macedonian statement referred to the Holocaust as having effectively eliminated Judaism in that country, a history that stretched back to the sixth century. The Macedonian delegation pointed the finger at Bulgarian authorities with respect to the looting of personal property. This related to the manner in which Yugoslavia—of which Macedonia was a part when the war began—was invaded. Bulgaria, allied with Germany, was given administration and occupation of most of the territory until 1945.

As Croatia did, Macedonia lamented the inability (in 1998) to access archives in Sofia, Belgrade, and Salonika. The statement listed a number of laws that affected the seizure of Jewish property and the location of their enactment, in nearly all cases, in Sofia. The statement was silent on efforts to restitute works of art.

Few countries were as affected by the Holocaust more than Poland. The Polish delegation statement described itself as a "shortened copy of texts on most important issues from the above-mentioned"[11] submission made to all delegates at the Washington Conference itself. The statement included a promise to host a conference on restitution of communal property in post-Communist countries.

With regard to all property classes, Poland's delegation statement noted that national archives, once quite comprehensive, were devastated by the wars of the twentieth century (not just WW II). The statement made no mention of the restitution of artwork or any national-level plans to address the restitution of artwork.

The Russian delegation statement stressed the importance of "the humane idea of seeking possibilities to provide aid to victims of the Nazis, regardless of their nationality, who have not previously received such aid in sufficient volumes and require it due to their health conditions and low income."[12] The statement made no mention of Jewish victims at all, let alone in any special proportion. That alone betrays a creeping relativism that has infected a great deal of Holocaust-minimizing discourse: the notion that since the war claimed victims of all nationalities, none deserve any special status. The delegation claimed that Russia would continue searching for confiscated objects, but that "claims for these values could be submitted only within the 18-month period beginning from April 21, 1998."[13] A nonspecific suggestion was offered that the government would consider claims after that date, but with no further detail.

Like the Czech Republic, the Slovak Republic faced two legacies to address in 1998: the Nazi occupation of what Germany called the Protectorate of Bohemia and Moravia as well as communist Czechoslovakia. The Slovak delegation statement made heavy reference to both. Between them, addressing expropriations from the communist era of 1948–1989 had assumed much greater legislative priority by 1998. But in 1993, the adoption of the National Council of the Slovak Republic's Act n.282/1993 of 27 October 1993 on Mitigation of Some Property Injustices Inflicted to Churches and Religious Communities formed the basis for compensation of victims of Nazi persecution. Section 1 of that Act made explicit provision for Jewish property, which, the delegation statement noted, was confiscated as part of the systematic destruction of the historic Jewish community within what is now the Slovak Republic. Somewhat vaguely, the statement [14] claimed that "[i]n the restitution of the property of Jewish congregation, the Ministry of Culture provided consultation services which resulted mostly in fruitful restitutions." Art was not specifically mentioned.

Slovenia, also part of Yugoslavia when the war began, submitted a brief delegation statement. It primarily discussed monetary and gold restitution and made no mention of art or Jewish property specifically.

Spain's statement will be of greater interest in subsequent chapters when discussing litigation involving Spanish museums, but it began by laying out the 1997 establishment of a commission to investigate the role of Spain in economic relations with Germany during the war.[15] That may seem unexceptional in light of other countries' similar commitments, but Spain was arguably the lone country allied with Germany that did not face any real consequences for it at the end of the war, because Spain did not take part in the war. Historical examination of Spain's fascist past, then less than a generation removed, is an extraordinarily fraught topic in Spain.

Spain's delegation statement was devoted primarily to the question of gold. Given the discussion to follow here, its language concerning art—which made no mention of art belonging to Jews—is worth quoting in its entirety (emphasis added):[16]

> Indeed, in what pertains to works of art – and apart from smuggled items, difficult to trace – the cases registered are few in number and of minor importance. It was estimated that only one percent of all the art dealers operating in Europe did business in Spain at the time. Therefore, this issue was barely examined in the course of the negotiations between the Spanish Government and the Allies at the end of the war.
>
> *The only case worth noticing is that of Alois Miedl, Goering's art dealer, who brought to Spain a total of twenty-two paintings,* that were deposited in the Tax Exempt Warehouse in Bilbao (Northern Spain). What happened to these paintings after 1949 is not known. Eight of the twenty-two paintings belonged to the Goudstikker Collection. The origin of the other fourteen is not known to this day.

Sweden emphasized the question of looted art, even without a history of Nazi occupation (a notable contrast with Spain). Already by the time of the Washington Conference, the delegation referenced efforts to interview trade organizations, auction houses, and storage companies active during the Nazi period. The Swedish commission had advertised in newspapers and sent a questionnaire to the Jewish communities in Sweden. Purchases made before the war by national collections were checked for provenance, which revealed some overlap with works taken out of German museums and then sold in the "degenerate art auction." The delegation claimed to have investigated private works with connections to Goering's looting activities. The statement promised a final report by February 1999 (barely two months hence). As later reported by the WJRO, "The Commission's final report 'Sweden and Jewish Assets,' released in 1999, concluded that cultural property looted from Jews might have entered Sweden but more research was needed. As a result, the 'Swedish Committee of Enquiry' was set up and in 2002 was able to present its own final report."[17]

Switzerland presents another unique case. Although the country was neutral during the war but heavily involved in the art trade before, during, and after it, Switzerland had a different sort of legacy with which to wrestle. The Swiss delegation statement was necessarily informed by two issues that were far more problematic than looted art: insurance and gold. Yet, the Swiss submitted what is easily the most detailed and thoughtful series of contributions, equaled only by the United States' submissions in a leadership role (and about art in particular).

The first encounter that Switzerland had with the Nazi-denounced art was the appearance of the so-called degenerate artworks in the late 1930s. The best known of these exchanges, of course, was the infamous Galerie Fischer sale in June of 1939 in Lucerne. At that auction, Fischer sold 126 works that were removed from the German public museums: Works by Braque, van Gogh, Picasso, Klee, Matisse, Kokoschka, and 31 other artists were included in the sale. Of the some 350 attendees, 40 bought two-thirds of the artworks. The works were mainly sold to buyers from Switzerland, Belgium, and the United States.

In addition, Switzerland's status as a neutral country and its culture of banking and custodial work made it a natural repository for artwork, licit and otherwise. As Stephanie Barron wrote[18] in her seminal exhibition catalogue regarding the Degenerate Art Exhibition of 1937 at the Los Angeles County Museum of Art in 1991:

> After Hitler's rise to power, neutral Switzerland became a haven, albeit temporarily, for German artists (and collectors who emigrated

> to keep their collections intact), writers, musicians, actors, theatrical directors, and other refugees. Many settled in Swiss cities, hoping to pursue their careers with relatively little disruption. Some stayed only long enough to make arrangements to emigrate elsewhere in Europe or to Palestine or the United States. Some remained permanently; others returned to Germany after the war.

As the Swiss delegation noted, even though the wartime closing of borders dampened trade, it did not cease entirely. The delegation cited the examples of Theodor Fischer's sales to Emil Bührle of looted artworks, as well as the acquisition by Oskar Reinhart of works that were later bequeathed to the Swiss Confederation.

When the war ended, MFAA personnel visited Switzerland in connection with their work. British Wing Commander and art historian Douglas Cooper compiled a list of seventy-seven works stolen by the Nazis. The Swiss Confederation issued two related directives, one on December 10, 1945, and another on February 22, 1946. According to the Swiss delegation statement, all seventy-seven works on Cooper's list were restituted to their original owner, Paul Rosenberg among them. Interestingly, the conclusion that the delegation drew from all this is that "it [was] safe to assume that despite Switzerland's relatively important role as an art market during the war, the number of stolen art works that might still be located in Switzerland should be limited."[19] However, merely because many works left Europe hardly means that others were not left behind.

The Swiss delegation shifted to talking about the modern era, but it also put the national apparatus on record with the following assertions as of August 1998: "[N]o object in collections belonging to the Swiss Confederation was found which had been acquired through illegal dealings."[20] With regard to efforts then under way, the delegation also noted a study published in December 1998 concerning the development of the Swiss art market between 1930 and 1955.

Turkey opened its delegation statement with a bold (and untrue) assertion: "Turkey is one of the few countries in the world where the Jews have never been persecuted."[21] The statement went to great lengths to portray Turkish diplomats throughout Europe as solicitous of the welfare of Jews in various countries, citing records of the International Committee for the Red Cross (ICRC). The statement's primary focus, however, was refuting claims made by other delegations about the role that Turkey played with respect to Nazi wartime gold sales and the sale of chromium to Germany between 1942 and 1943.

Ukraine also falls into the short list of areas most harshly affected by the war and occupation. Its delegation submission was focused mostly on questions of banking and commodities. Artwork was referenced only in general terms, and in the context of the need for further research, and with the need to remember that forty-five more years of Soviet rule followed, with its attendant privations and deprivations of property.

The United States' submission offers unique insight into the proceedings. Stuart Eizenstat's preface made explicit a key point highlighted above: It is difficult to overstate the importance and influence of Jonathan Petropoulos and Lynn Nicholas in reviving awareness of and interest in the issue of Nazi-looted art. Eizenstat also recognized the remarks given by Kulishov for his insight into the suffering of the Russian people,[3] by Ronald Lauder touting the need for guiding principles and guidelines, by Bacher concerning the recent Austrian legislation, and by Rusty Powell about the new results of the AAMD Task Force on the Spoliation of Art during the Nazi/World War II Era (1933–1945).

In his remarks, entitled "Explanation of the Washington Conference Principles on Nazi-Looted Art," Eizenstat noted the evolution of the intent and language of the Principles in the form in which they existed and had been proposed at the time (they would change):[22]

> Several weeks ago, we prepared a discussion paper laying out eleven general principles, which was used as the basis of extensive consultations and which all of you have today. These principles are not, in themselves, a solution. They are a means by which nations can fashion their own solutions consistent with their own legal systems. The principles try to capture the spirit of this Conference for nations to use in this task.

Eizenstat called attention to an announcement by the Russian Federation of its intended participation in the creation of a database. He then clustered the principles thematically. The first three, he noted, "envision a massive cooperative effort to trace this art."[23] The fourth dealt with gaps and ambiguities of provenance, noting that given the destruction of the war, some leeway in establishing a record must be allowed. Principles five through seven addressed publicity, information, and encouragement toward resolution. Eizenstat praised France's display on the Internet of unclaimed art restituted to France by Allied military authorities. *Fair and just solutions*—buzzwords that later would be used as a sword and a shield—are the focus of principles eight and nine, Eizenstat observed. He made a critical point that was still novel at the time:[24]

> We can begin by recognizing that as a moral matter, we should not apply rules designed for commercial transactions of societies that operate under the rule of law to people whose property and very lives were taken by one of the most profoundly illegal regimes the world has ever known.

Eizenstat commended, rightly, the resolution of the *Landscape with Smokestacks* dispute, discussed in Chapter 5, as an imaginative solution to a dispute. Where victims or heirs have died, Jewish communities should be prioritized for restitution, which is an important point that does not demand the existence of a claimant with legal standing to compel action.

The tenth principle invited the inclusion of members on commissions from outside the government and expert in the fields of art and history, in addition to representatives of communities affected by the Holocaust. The final principle in Eizenstat's formulation urges participating nations to take specific measures to implement the principles.

Like the Claims Conference (The Conference on Jewish Material Claims Against Germany), the WJRO also submitted a statement on par with the participating nations. The WJRO was established in 1992, and its statement described negotiations it had undertaken with eight governments in Europe over the subsequent years "for the restitution of Jewish communal and public properties which were confiscated and/or nationalized by the Nazi occupation regime and by the Communist authorities."[25]

The WJRO described its experience in universally negative terms. In Poland, the WJRO made a specific request for legislation concerning communal and public property that belonged to Polish Jews before the German invasion on September 1, 1939. The WJRO noted a 1997 law but expressed dissatisfaction with its scope, noting a failure to deal with the fact that when the government nationalized Nazi property in 1946, much of that property in fact belonged to Jews. As of the conference, the WJRO said that it had received no response.

According to the WJRO statement, there were fewer than 3,000 Jews in the Czech Republic in 1998, compared to a prewar population of 100,000. The WJRO lauded a more flexible response by the Czech Republic, but noted that only a small portion of the relatively low number of objects claimed by the WJRO had been returned. The WJRO applauded Slovakia as even more forthcoming than the Czech Republic, with some 360 of 800 claimed objects returned as of the statement.

The WJRO's statement concerning Hungary reflected an early success, it seemed at the time. The statement noted that the Hungarian government had signed an agreement with the Jewish community to settle claims for communal real estate worth HUF13,511 billion ($60,000,000) and in return would receive an annual payment of about $3 million for religious, educational and charitable activities. Romania had also agreed to return roughly 20 properties out of approximately 3,000.

The WJRO criticized Ukraine more harshly, noting that its efforts to convince the Ukrainian president and prime minister to return Jewish property had been without success. Croatia, according to the WJRO, had not agreed to anything by that point. Addressing the Baltic nations (Latvia, Lithuania, and Estonia) collectively, the WJRO praised Latvia for a positive outlook toward the restitution issue, and mentioned an agreement to start a foundation to process restitutions. WJRO's statement described Lithuania somewhat less positively. Lithuania had a relatively robust prewar Jewish population of 250,000, which as of 1998 only 5,000 to 7,000 remained. The WJRO noted that its outreach to officials in Vilnius had been ignored.

WJRO praised Norway for a constructive approach. In 1998, stated the WJRO, the Norwegian government proposed a bill to commit some $60 million to Holocaust survivors and the Jewish community.

Although Germany made no general Holocaust-era asset position paper submission, numerous papers were presented on the topic of Nazi-looted art in particular. Prof. Dr. Carla Schulz-Hoffmann, then deputy general director, Bavarian State Paintings Collection, made the following claim in her paper:[26]

> Yesterday Mr. Rusty Powell quoted the necessity for research work including provenance checks in each museum. I would dare saying that this largely has been done in German governmental museums for art works in question till the end of the 19th century including roughly impressionism. 20th century art is surely not as thoroughly covered. In Munich we just finished the catalogue raisonné of the Brücke collection and in a few months, the Klee collection—till now without any new results concerning questionable property. But of course every work of art coming to the collection—regardless if it is an acquisition or a donation—has been and will be checked for any hint to a doubtful provenance.
>
> Everything helpful and useful to trace and return art property confiscated by the Nazis should be done keeping in mind that here a "statute of limitations" never can be a justified question. And with regard to this conference one result for me personally is to strengthen our efforts to clarify museum provenances especially for works which came to the collection after 1937 till today and thus to contribute as far as possible to a restitution of works of art confiscated during the Holocaust-Era to their legal owners and heirs.

This is an unambiguous declaration of accomplishment, of a job mostly completed with only minor work remaining to be done. It was, as will be seen, also quite premature.

Ultimately, of course, the conference adopted the Washington Conference Principles on Nazi-Confiscated Art as follows:

1. In developing a consensus on non-binding principles to assist in resolving issues relating to Nazi-confiscated art, the Conference recognizes that among participating nations there are differing legal systems and that countries act within the context of their own laws.
2. Art that had been confiscated by the Nazis and not subsequently restituted should be identified.

3. Relevant records and archives should be open and accessible to researchers, in accordance with the guidelines of the International Council on Archives.
4. Resources and personnel should be made available to facilitate the identification of all art that had been confiscated by the Nazis and not subsequently restituted.
5. In establishing that a work of art had been confiscated by the Nazis and not subsequently restituted, consideration should be given to unavoidable gaps or ambiguities in the provenance in light of the passage of time and the circumstances of the Holocaust era.
6. Every effort should be made to publicize art that is found to have been confiscated by the Nazis and not subsequently restituted in order to locate its pre-War owners or their heirs.
7. Efforts should be made to establish a central registry of such information.
8. Pre-War owners and their heirs should be encouraged to come forward and make known their claims to art that was confiscated by the Nazis and not subsequently restituted.
9. If the pre-War owners of art that is found to have been confiscated by the Nazis and not subsequently restituted, or their heirs, can be identified, steps should be taken expeditiously to achieve a just and fair solution, recognizing this may vary according to the facts and circumstances surrounding a specific case.
10. If the pre-War owners of art that is found to have been confiscated by the Nazis, or their heirs, cannot be identified, steps should be taken expeditiously to achieve a just and fair solution.
11. Commissions or other bodies established to identify art that was confiscated by the Nazis and to assist in addressing ownership issues should have a balanced membership.
12. Nations are encouraged to develop national processes to implement these principles, particularly as they relate to alternative dispute resolution mechanisms for resolving ownership issues.

* * *

Domestic associations of museums were moving forward on the issue as well. In fact, while the Washington Conference is rightly the more well-known policy development of 1998, it was actually not the first. That distinction belonged to the Association of Art Museum Directors (AAMD). In 1998, the AAMD published what is, even twenty years later, a forward-looking and thorough statement. After convening a Task Force on the Spoliation of Art During the Nazi/World War II Era (1933–1945), the designated panel issued its report on June 4, 1998 (the AAMD report). Ironically, this was the very same year that the AAMD and so many of its members lent their voices not to the Bondi family in their efforts to reclaim the *Portrait of Wally*, but to the idea that the painting should be returned to Austria and not restituted.

A notable aspect of the AAMD report that is easily overlooked, but increasingly important as time goes on, is its title. The AAMD Task Force, and then the AAMD report, took as a given that the Nazi era of spoliation extends to the whole Nazi era, not just some later part of it. As any Jew living in Germany on January 30, 1933, could attest, while the Nazis laboriously and exhaustively entrenched their racial persecution into the laws of Germany, they did not wait for the 1935 Nuremberg Laws to strip Germany's Jews *de facto* of any and all of their rights as citizens, even their right to be considered Germans. Additionally, as noted above, art was at the very forefront of the Nazis' worldview from the start, and thus the targeting of art collectors and art collections was at the top of the Nazis' to-do list upon assuming the authority of a sovereign nation. Both the AAMD and its members deserve credit for recognizing this with elegant simplicity.

The AAMD report reviewed the role of American museums in post-war restitution, noting the prominent place many museum professionals had in the MFAA. It stated as a priority the creation of informational resources, and "a process of reviewing, reporting, and researching the issue of unlawfully confiscated art which respects the dignity of all parties and the complexity of the issue."[27] The AAMD report also began with what now (through no fault of its authors) has become a double-edged sword much like the recitation of the Washington Principles' "fair and just solutions": the idea that "[e]ach claim presents a unique situation which must be thoroughly reviewed on a case-by-case basis."[28] This is actually only half-true, as subsequent chapters will demonstrate. Obviously, each dispute has idiosyncratic aspects that must be sorted out factually. But, the notion that every case is unique has actually been used as a tool to make claimants prove the obvious; a common tactic is to bemoan generally the horrors of Nazi Germany but suggest that maybe, in this case, things were not so bad for the person in Germany in 1934 or 1935. That is not what *unique* means, and the persecution faced by German, Austrian, or Hungarian Jews is not unique simply because those affected were unique human beings.

But what of action? Here, the AAMD report directed its members to three points:

1. As part of the standard research on each work of art in their collections, members of the AAMD, if they have not already done so, should begin immediately to review the provenance of works in their collections to attempt to ascertain whether any were unlawfully confiscated during the Nazi/World War II era and never restituted.
2. Member museums should search their own records thoroughly and, in addition, should take all reasonable steps to contact established archives, databases, art dealers, auction houses, donors, art historians and other scholars and researchers who may be able to provide Nazi/World-War-II-era provenance information.
3. AAMD recognizes that research regarding Nazi/World-War-II-era provenance may take years to complete, may be inconclusive and may require additional funding. The AAMD Art Issues Committee will address the matter of such research and how to facilitate it.[29]

Like all self-governance, these principles are aspirational and depend entirely on the good faith of their adherents. It is difficult to gauge the extent to which members plunged into the task and how thoroughly. But it is beyond question that many museums, large and small, did expend considerable time at least identifying which objects in their collection might be of potential concern, and it changed the landscape about diligence with respect to future acquisitions.

In response to this directive, the author of this book spent the better part of a year at the Sterling and Francine Clark Art Institute examining the provenance files of every object in the collection older than 1945 to determine first where it was created and, if not in America, when it first entered the United States. For any object that came into the collection after 1945, the most critical question was the provenance of the acquisition prior to its arrival in Robert Sterling Clark's possession in New York and then in Williamstown. This was begun with some apprehension, given Clark's particular fondness and skillful eye for French painting, and the general knowledge at the outset that he had bought many of his paintings in France. The remaining set of paintings was relatively low in number, but the task even from there was arduous and time-consuming. Provenance information in 1998 was not standardized nor often even computerized, let alone easily searchable. Previous owners had to be checked by hand against MFAA reports, the Art Loss Register (ALR), and lists of individual collections that had been targeted (most of which, to the extent then known, were in Amsterdam and Paris).

While still relatively new, the utility of the ALR was profound; the service was a pioneer in due diligence for potentially stolen art. It grew out of efforts over the years by the nonprofit International Foundation for Art Research (IFAR), which was founded in 1969. For years, IFAR began publishing a stolen art alert, which began in 1976. Beginning in 1990, IFAR increased the frequency of the alert to ten times per year, which soon outpaced the scope of the organization's personnel resources.

To meet the need, the ALR was founded in 1990 as a for-profit entity. Julian Radcliffe formed a partnership with IFAR and the major auction houses, who had a substantial need for the information services, and which own a minority stake in the company. There is little question that in the first decade of this new phase of awareness of Nazi-era art looting, the ALR was a critical resource. The ALR allowed (and allows) users either to register notice of a claim of a work having been stolen (which goes into the ALR database), or inquire about a specific work under consideration for purchase or sale. The advances that this permitted in real-time diligence cannot be overstated; for Nazi-looted art, the alternative was essentially to review Allied interrogation reports and other primary source documents around the world.

In the Clark's case, it came down to a single painting that was not in America until after the war: a vibrant red flag in the modern era that was unremarkable to most for so many decades. The painting was a small Peter Paul Rubens oil on panel, *Holy Family Under an Apple Tree.* Given Rubens's typically grand scale, and the painting's somewhat unfinished detail, the painting is clearly a sketch, not a final work. A work referred to as Rubens's *Holy Family Under an Apple Tree* had been stolen from a prominent Dutch collection, that of the van Gelder family. The report in which that information was contained did not include any additional details about the size or medium of the looted work, however. This was the dreaded development that had hovered over the project from its inception: a concern that the trail would reach a dead end and the Rubens painting could not be ruled in or out. Thankfully, however, within a year an additional resource about that plundered collection became available, and it was determined that the stolen Rubens was in fact a finished painting, several feet high by several feet wide. The Clark's painting was not the looted work.

The point of this anecdote is to illustrate the value of the AAMD report. It was a call to action. As described above, in researching the Rubens sketch, the Clark heeded that call in earnest, without tipping the scales on the investigation. Others, such as the Museum of Fine Arts Boston, have created either temporary or permanent staff for similar projects which have, as the Internet and museum resources have evolved, identified works about which there were questions.

For its part, the American Association of Museums (the AAM, now named the American Alliance of Museums) also took upon itself to craft a policy on the topic. The AAM had consulted the AAMD, as well as the Presidential Advisory Commission on Holocaust Assets in the United States (PCHA). The resulting "Recommended Procedures for Providing Information to the Public about Objects Transferred in Europe during the Nazi Era" laid out some of the practical and deductive tools that museums such as the Clark had used to distinguish artwork worthy of further investigation. Its overarching directives were that each AAM member:[30]

1) Identify all objects in its collection that were created before 1946 and that it acquired after 1932, that underwent a change

of ownership between 1932 and 1946, and that were or might reasonably be thought to have been in continental Europe between those dates (hereafter, "covered objects"). In the event that a museum is unable to determine whether an object created before 1946 and acquired after 1932 (a) might have been in continental Europe between 1932 and 1946 and/or (b) underwent a change of ownership during that period, it should still be treated as a covered object;

2) Make currently available object and provenance (history of ownership) information about covered objects accessible online; and
3) Give priority to continuing provenance research on those objects as resources allow.

Additionally, the creation and enhancement of searchable tools was recommended. The report suggested a list of twenty categories of provenance information that should be examined. It also launched a Nazi-Era Provenance Internet Portal. The rub lies in the basis for searches:

> Museums should submit to the Alliance a set of descriptive data about covered objects in their collections. This information will constitute the registry. It will be the responsibility of the museum to update this information whenever there are changes, additions, or deletions.

That is to say, in the best of circumstances the information would be extensive, but that was not a foregone conclusion. The AAM committed to developing the portal for three years, but stated its intention to transfer management thereafter "to a more appropriate organization" given "that a project of this technological complexity falls outside the range of the Alliance's customary activities and services."[31] It also announced that an independent commission would be established to guide the development of the portal.

None of this was new ground, but its importance lay, at least theoretically, in the difference in reach. While the AAMD is a smaller group of the most significant museums of art, the AAM includes nearly every museum in America. And, as the twenty-first century began, the creation of a searchable Internet database was essential to staying current with the issue and providing a meaningful tool for researchers; compliance and commitment would not have lasted long had the only means of research remained having interns labor through photocopies of manifests of looted collections.

The AAMD issued more guidance in 2007. After reviewing the changes in perception and progress in the intervening years, it posed these questions to its members:[32]

- Has the museum identified—or is it in the process of identifying—all objects in its collection that underwent a change of ownership between 1933 and 1945, and that were in continental Europe between those dates?
- Has the museum made it a priority to conduct provenance research on those objects, while balancing this commitment of financial and staff resources with its ongoing educational responsibilities to its community?
- Has the museum made public the results of its provenance research, and is it continuing to do so?
- Is the museum sharing its findings with peer institutions to assist them with their research into comparable works, and is the museum contributing information to centralized databases and related art recovery information resources?
- Given the complicated nature of ownership claims, is the museum balancing a swift and compassionate response to claimants with its responsibility as an institution to act with care and prudence in protecting the works it holds in trust for the public?
- Is a prospective ownership claim accompanied by definitive proof, or is further research required to confirm the claim, and is the museum able to assist with that research?
- What are the steps a museum should take in establishing whether a claim is legitimate?
- When new research provides conclusive evidence of prior rightful ownership, is the museum taking responsible action even if no formal claim has been made?

- Before purchasing a work or accepting a gift or a loan with an incomplete ownership history, has the museum undertaken additional research to determine its Nazi-era provenance status?
- Is the museum updating its provenance research to the best of its ability as new information becomes available?

The update also addressed the question of accountability:[33]

> Museum directors are responsible to their trustees, staff, donors and community for ensuring that museums fulfill their public service mission and reinforce the leadership position of museums as cultural and educational resources.

However, there was one notable omission from the foregoing list of accountable parties: the AAMD itself. And, while that may seem a heavy burden for a voluntary association of independent museums, accountability for adherence to its principles is something about which the AAMD has had no hesitation whatsoever. Most relevantly, the AAMD has set the tone of the national conversation about the topic of deaccessioning: the process by which a museum sells or otherwise conveys a work of art in its collection. Put simply, the AAMD takes the position that a museum may only sell a work of art if the proceeds are used to purchase other art, not for operating or overhead expenses. It has publicly shamed and sanctioned members that disobey the principle and has even sanctioned a nonmember (the Delaware Art Museum) for violating the precept. The AAMD in effect directed its members to shun the Delaware Museum of Art and not participate in exhibitions with it, thereby punishing a museum for violating a set of rules set by an organization of which it was not a member.

Yet, in all the years since the AAMD Task Force was convened in 1997, it has never publicly criticized, let alone sanctioned, a single museum, with respect to its principles, on the subject of provenance and ownership. Is it because they have all complied fully? That seems unlikely. Closer to the truth is that the guidelines, while useful when taken up in the spirit they were intended, are not absolute. Normative rules shape behavior but also create or at least suggest a consequence for noncompliance. These rules have no consequence in the application. As museums have become increasingly aggressive in their assertions of time-based defenses or in their assertions of the right to retain indisputably Nazi-looted art, the AAMD has been silent, either by way of support or condemnation. And here is where the tricky aspect of uniqueness comes into play. If the rule is a categorical prohibition never as with the deaccessioning guidelines, then it is easy to say when that rule has been broken. If the rule is somehow to be "fair and just," but to allow every aspect of every case to start from square one, then who is to say? In the end, this is why the early hope created by these publications has gone largely unfulfilled. If every case is special, then no case is special.

These policies created important awareness and even priorities, but as foreign sovereigns and private defendants have since pointed out, often smugly, they did not provide a direct mechanism for those seeking the return of art that had once belonged to them or their families. Thus, as with most disputes, it is easy to bemoan the inefficiency and expense of litigation, these well-meaning developments really left those claimants (or indeed those who believed they were rightly in possession of disputed works) with no other choice.

Chapter 3

Portrait of Wally and the Politics of Seizure

Quite possibly nothing has focused popular attention more on the question of looted art and the dilemmas it creates than a story that began to break late in 1997. Lea Bondi was a Viennese art dealer. She owned and operated the Würthle und Söhne (Würthle and Sons) Gallery. Like the Bloch-Bauers and the Altmanns, she straddled the delicate balance of Jewish assimilation and the prejudices of the late Austrian Empire. After the Anschluss, a Nazi functionary, Friedrich Welz, Aryanized her gallery and then visited her again to indicate that he wanted another painting that was hanging in her home: *Portrait of Wally*, by Egon Schiele, to which she acquiesced.

Bondi managed to emigrate from Vienna to London, where she opened another gallery. Bondi went to the restitution court in Austria after the war to seek restitution of the Galerie Würthle und Söhne (Würthle and Sons). She was successful, insofar as the Austrian court recognized that the gallery had been wrongfully taken and title to the business was returned to her, but she was actually ordered to pay Welz for his supposed improvements to the gallery. *Portrait of Wally* was not among the subjects of her restitution claim. Bondi apparently discussed the painting with Welz after the war as well. He told her it had been confiscated as part of the collection of Heinrich Rieger, another persecuted and ultimately murdered Viennese Jew, and sold to the Austrian National Gallery.

Welz, for his part, was remarkably candid in his interrogation with the U.S. Army, which was in the process of assembling recovered art for return to national governments. *Wally* was among the property seized by the U.S. Army. Welz had works from many sources, including Bondi and Rieger. Rieger's son and his attorneys, for their part, wrote to the authorities and requested that Welz be prevented from reacquiring art he had obtained from Rieger, including Schiele's *Liebespaar* (*Lovers*), *Kardinal and Nonne* (*Cardinal and Nun*) and *Bildnis seiner Frau* (*Portrait of His Wife*). That last work, was a drawing that had been taken from Rieger. *Wally* is an oil painting on wood. No curator—or even a layperson—would mistake the two works for each other. The reverse of the painting said "Wally aus Krumau."[34] The museum inventory noted explicitly that the painting was of Wally Neuzil, even though the fiction that it was the Rieger drawing (which was not of Wally Neuzil) was put forward as a defense to its retention.

Dr. Christian Broda (Rieger's attorney) also wrote to Dr. Otto von Demus, director of the Austrian Federal Office for the Care of Monuments (Bundesdenkmalamt [BDA]). The list he included of Rieger works cited *Bildnis seiner Frau* (*Portrait of His Wife*) but not *Portrait of Wally*.

The Reparations, Deliveries, and Restitution Division (RDR) of the U.S. Forces advised in November 1947 that it had several paintings that the Rieger heirs were looking for, including *Portrait of His Wife*. On December 4, 1947, it released to the BDA fourteen works of art that were in Welz's possession. The works were described as "[p]aintings purchased during the war by Frederic Wels, Salzburg, from the confiscated collection of Dr. Heinrich Rieger (deceased), former Jew of Vienna, and recovered from his collection in Salzburg." *United States v. Portrait of Wally*, 663 F. Supp. 2d 232, 240 (S.D.N.Y. 2009).

Portrait of Wally was also among the paintings the RDR delivered to the BDA. *Id.* at 240. This was where the plot thickened. Whether by mistake or otherwise, the BDA returned to the Riegers not the *Portrait of His Wife* drawing, but *Portrait of Wally*, a painting. The Riegers then had to contend with Austria's export laws and negotiated the sale of a number of their pieces to the Österreichische Galerie Belvedere, a national institution. The Belvedere's director, Dr. Karl Garzarolli, sent a letter the next day cataloguing the items inspected by his team as part of the negotiation. Item number three is *Frauenbildnis* (*Portrait of a Woman*). To the left of this typewritten list is a handwritten note stating "Vally Neuzil aus Wien" (Wally Neuzil from Vienna). A later list from the Belvedere's files from 1950 does not include *Portrait of a Woman* but instead lists "E. Schiele, Vally aus Krumau" (Wally from Krumau). *Id.*

In early December 1950, Garzarolli sought permission from the Austrian Federal Ministry of Education for the Belvedere's purchase of the artworks he had inspected. He was given permission to purchase, eleven pictures, *Umarmung* (*Embrace*), *Kardinal and Nonne* (*Cardinal and Nun*), and *Frauenbildnis* (*Portrait of a Woman*), which it later became clear was *Portrait of Wally. Id.*

Dr. Rudolph Leopold was an important collector and expert on Schiele. Leopold's own catalogue raisonné made clear that the Riegers only had two Schiele paintings: *Embrace* and *Cardinal and Nun*. *Id.* at 241. Leopold went to Bondi's gallery in London in 1953. After they had struck a deal about some other drawings, she asked where *Portrait of Wally* was. According to Leopold's later deposition testimony, he candidly replied that it was in the Belvedere. She asked him for help in retrieving it, but Leopold said that it would not be possible, because if he went to the gallery and asked, they would simply "throw him out."[35]

Yet the following year, Leopold indeed went to the Belvedere to inquire about *Wally*, and far from being thrown out, he left with *Portrait of Wally* for his own collection. In June 1954, Dr. Leopold discussed with Garzarolli the possibility of Leopold's acquisition of *Cardinal and Nun* and *Wally* from the Belvedere in exchange for other paintings. Leopold relied by reference on the 1930 catalogue raisonné by Otto Kallir, which had clearly identified Bondi as the owner. On July 12, 1954, in a meeting attended by Garzarolli, the Exchange Commission of the Belvedere approved the trade, referring to it as *Vally aus Krumau*. Leopold acquired *Wally* on September 1, 1954, but did not tell Bondi, which was more than a year after Bondi had told him she could not find the painting and had asked him for his help. As a journalist at Austria's largest daily paper *Der Standard* later pondered in a documentary interview,[4] the museum may well have worried that it would have to give the painting back and exchanged it more or less to launder the title to it. Bondi asked for help from other quarters to shame Leopold into doing the right thing but declined to file suit in Austria because, as she said in correspondence, "[i]t is probably very hard to have lawsuits in Vienna against a medical doctor residing in Vienna because the judges always take the side of the resident of Vienna, and if the lawsuit is lost, I have lost my picture forever." *Portrait of Wally*, 663 F. Supp. 2d at 245.

In October 1966, Lea Bondi (now married, and adding the surname Jaray) wrote to Otto Kallir, now in New York, asking him to help her recover another Schiele painting. She set out the history and her frustrations with what she felt were a stacked deck in Vienna, where the painting was being exhibited. She wrote:[36]

> [A] few days before we left Vienna, Welz came to me to discuss something regarding Würthle. He saw [*Portrait of Wally*] hanging on my wall and demanded that I give it to him. I explained that the painting was my private property and had nothing to do with Würthle. But he would not stop pressuring me in the most unpleasant manner, until finally my husband (who was there) said "Give it to him already. We may want to leave as soon as tomorrow, don't make difficulties. You know what he can do." So that is how [Portrait of Wally] came into the possession of Welz.

In 1966, Kallir published an updated catalogue raisonné, which stated the provenance as:

Emil Toepfer, Vienna
  Richard Lanyi, Vienna
  Lea Bondi, Vienna
  Dr. Rudolph Leopold, Vienna

In 1972, Leopold wrote his own book, *Egon Schiele, Gemälde, Aquarelle, Zeichnungen* (*Egon Schiele: Paintings, Watercolours, Drawings*). It made no mention of the alleged Rieger provenance of *Wally*. In 1994, Leopold transferred his art collection, including *Wally*, to the foundation that bears his name. In 2001, the Austrian state built the museum where the collection now resides. As part of the transaction, he was named a director for life.

The exhibition "Egon Schiele: The Leopold Collection" opened at the Museum of Modern Art in 1997, featuring *Portrait of Wally* and another Schiele, *Dead City III* (which had belonged to persecuted Jewish actor Fritz Grünbaum), among others. On Christmas Eve 1997, Judith Dobrzynski wrote an article reviewing the show in the *New York Times*, "THE ZEALOUS COLLECTOR—A special report; A Singular Passion For Amassing Art, One Way or Another." Dobrzynski's article noted the history of Bondi's gallery and detailed Leopold's history as a collector, including his skill at taking advantage of art that was subject to Austria's infamous export ban.

The Bondis wrote to the Museum of Modern Art (MoMA), which merely advised that the museum was contractually obligated to return the painting. On January 7, 1998, the Manhattan district attorney (DA) served a grand jury subpoena to secure possession of the painting as allegedly stolen property.

Leopold responded caustically, "They're looking for a way to tighten the laws, and on the other hand there is greed. Now, Schiele fetches very high prices, far more than at that time. And when it is being said by [the Bondis] that this is only about justice and not money, one can only laugh bitterly."[37] Betraying his mindset when the controversy caused some to label him a collector of stolen art, Leopold later argued: "If a mushroom collector buys a poisonous mushroom, he doesn't become a poisonous mushroom collector."[38]

MoMA and other museums opposed the subpoena publicly. Glenn Lowry, MoMA's director, argued that the seizure "deals a heavy blow to the international exchange of art." Lowry said, "[T]he District Attorney's action has the potential of seriously affecting the future of art loans in this country. Unless we can assure the lenders that American museums will return borrowed works of art, lenders, fearing seizure, will simply not lend."[39] Years later, a former Metropolitan Museum of Art official, Ashton Hawkins, told a documentarian, "It's not a moral matter. It's a money matter. The moral issues get shady pretty fast, especially when there's a chance to get money out of it."[40]

While all this was going on, MoMA complained about National Public Radio's (NPR) coverage, arguing that the radio broadcast should have mentioned MoMA's denial of having taken a position on the case. Yet this was pure farce: Lowry had testified on the record that Bondi was not an heir with title to the painting. MoMA's objection was entirely disingenuous. Nonetheless, NPR issued a retraction, which was particularly galling given that MoMA declined a request to comment, and fired the reporter (whose report was completely accurate).[41] Morley Safer of *60 Minutes* called NPR's reaction "appalling" and that the network "should be ashamed of itself."[42] For their part, the AAM and AAMD filed amicus briefs urging that the paintings be released to the Leopold Museum.

MoMA moved to quash the grand jury subpoena pursuant to N.Y. C.P.L. 190.50 (7). N.Y. Arts and Cultural Affairs Law § 12.03, which prohibits seizure of any art lent to a cultural institution by a nonresident exhibitor. MoMA had argued that the statute was absolute and had no exception, while the DA argued that it applied only to attachments in civil proceedings. The law reads:

> No process of attachment, execution, sequestration, replevin, distress or any kind of seizure shall be served or levied upon any work of fine art while the same is enroute to or from, or while on exhibition or deposited by a nonresident exhibitor at any exhibition held under the auspices or supervision of any museum, college, university or other nonprofit art gallery, institution or organization within any city or county of this state for any cultural, educational, charitable or other purpose not conducted for profit to the exhibitor, nor shall such work of fine art be subject to attachment, seizure, levy or sale, for any cause whatever in the hands of the authorities of such exhibition or otherwise.

The N.Y. Supreme Court weighed principles of statutory interpretation and the legislative history of the law to decide the question. It concluded that the law was intended to provide "the broadest possible protection for out-of-State art work on loan to New York cultural institutions." *In re Grand Jury Subpoena Duces Tecum Served on the Museum of Modern Art*, 177 Misc. 2d at 991–92. In addition to the conclusion that the DA was seeking "to complicate an otherwise simple statute," (*Id.*) the court also noted that the grand jury was in no way impeded in its investigation. It simply could not retain the paintings.

The DA also argued that the New York law was preempted by the Immunity from Seizure Act (IFSA), 22 U.S.C. § 2459. IFSA provides:

> (a) Whenever any work of art or other object of cultural significance is imported into the United States from any foreign country, pursuant to an agreement entered into between the foreign owner or custodian thereof and the United States or one or more cultural or educational institutions within the United States providing for the temporary exhibition or display thereof within the United States at any cultural exhibition, assembly, activity, or festival administered, operated, or sponsored, without profit, by any such cultural or educational institution, no court of the United States, any State, the District of Columbia, or any territory or possession of the United States may issue or enforce any judicial process, or enter any judgment, decree, or order, for the purpose or having the effect of depriving such institution, or any carrier engaged in transporting such work or object within the United States, of custody or control of such object if before the importation of such object the President or his designee has determined that such object is of cultural significance and that the temporary exhibition or display thereof within the United States is in the national interest, and a notice of that effect has been published in the Federal Register.

A painting that is immune from seizure cannot be seized by the government, or to satisfy a judgment in a civil lawsuit. By all accounts, and for all its bluster about the consequences that would ensue if seizure were allowed, MoMA had made a catastrophic error from the perspective in regard to what it was trying to accomplish: It borrowed the foreign paintings without getting IFSA immunity first. Had it done so, the New York subpoena would still have failed, but so would the federal seizure (if the U.S. Attorney had even tried, which it likely would not have had IFSA immunity been in place). This minute detail caused the entire affair to unfold over the better part of thirteen years. MoMA later argued that it had not applied for IFSA immunity because it never did, having done so in only four out of eighty-nine instances of loans in the three years prior.

On May 13, 1998, the Supreme Court (New York's trial-level court) ruled that the DA lacked the authority to seize the painting. *In re Grand Jury Subpoena Duces Tecum Served on the Museum of Modern Art*, 177 Misc. 2d 985 (N.Y. Sup. Ct. May 13, 1998). As the N.Y. Supreme Court opinion put it:

> According to the Museum, New York cultural institutions often eliminate this time-consuming process, relying instead on what they believed to be the automatic protection from any kind of seizure afforded by the New York law.

In re Grand Jury Subpoena Duces Tecum Served on the Museum of Modern Art, 177 Misc. 2d at 988. The court concluded that IFSA did not preempt the New York Arts and Cultural Affairs Law because "[n]othing within the IFSA or its supporting regulation suggests that Congress considered the mechanism it created necessarily to provide the exclusive means for the protection of foreign art." *Id.* at 999.

Regarding the question of interference in foreign affairs, an argument that would be raised repeatedly by foreign sovereign actors trying to retain Nazi-looted art, the DA argued that the New York Arts and Cultural Affairs Law intruded on areas entrusted to the federal executive branch. The court disagreed:

> The sole purpose of the Federal statute is to provide protection to art work. The law does not limit art from entering the country even if approval under the statute is not obtained.

Id. at 1001.

The DA appealed, and the Appellate Division reversed. *People v. Museum of Modern Art In re (Grand Jury Subpoena Duces Tecum)*, 253 A.D.2d 211 (1st Dep't 1999). Citing a New York Court of Appeals decision, the Appellate Division noted that:

> [A] subpoena *duces tecum*, such as the one in question, "does not authorize the seizure, impoundment or other disruption in

> possession of records or property. . . . Its function is to cause the physical evidence to which it is directed to be brought before the court. It is not intended to deprive its custodian of control which is compatible with its production. So '[o]bedience to the subpoena will be complete when the books called for are presented to the grand jury in an actual session, and are taken away again . . . as soon as the particular session adjourns.'"

Id. at 214, *citing Matter of Heisler v. Hynes,* 42 NY2d 250, 252 (1977). It rejected MoMA's and its amicus museums' concern about interrupting the flow of art: "[I]t is not contended, nor could it be, that the public interest is served by permitting the free flow of stolen art into and out of the State." *Id.* at 216. The Appellate Division concluded:

> There is no question that, pursuant to section 12.03 of the Arts and Cultural Affairs Law, the alleged heirs, whose complaint prompted the District Attorney's action, may not attach or otherwise seize the subject paintings as a prelude to a civil action seeking to establish ownership, their return, or payment in lieu thereof. However, that does not prevent the District Attorney, the official charged with the duty, from investigating alleged crimes.

Id. at 218.

Now it was MoMA's turn to appeal, seeking leave in the first instance for further appellate review before the Court of Appeals (such petitions to hear the case are granted only at the discretion of the state's highest court). There, the pendulum swung again, and the subpoena was quashed. *People v. Museum of Modern Art In re (Grand Jury Subpoena Duces Tecum),* 93 N.Y.2d 729 (1999). The Court of Appeals agreed with the N.Y. Supreme Court's earlier reasoning that the statute was intentionally as broad as possible. *Id.* at 736–37. "Seizure," in its ordinary sense, does not distinguish between the reason, only the outcome. *Id.* at 738.

The U.S. Attorney's Office in the Southern District was watching the grand jury subpoena proceedings unfold too, and it was ready. It had filed a Complaint for civil forfeiture on September 22, 1999. On the day that the Court of Appeals ruled (which standing alone would have allowed the paintings to be released and returned to Austria), the U.S. Marshal issued a seizure warrant for *Portrait of Wally* but not *Dead City III*. The Complaint was for civil forfeiture under customs laws that provide that goods must be forfeited if they were brought into the United States illegally, or if they are to be removed from the United States illegally. 19 U.S.C. § 1595a(c); 22 U.S.C. § 401(a). The United States contended in its petition that *Portrait of Wally* was stolen and that, therefore, it was imported and would be exported in violation of the National Stolen Property Act, 18 U.S.C. § 2314 (1994).

The Leopold Museum moved to dismiss the forfeiture action, advancing a number of arguments. First, it argued that when the RDR seized the paintings from Welz, they ceased to be considered stolen. The court then had to decide what law to apply to determine whether *Wally* was, in fact, stolen when it entered the United States. To answer that, the court reviewed prior cases involving the importation of pre-Colombian artifacts from Mexico. *United States v. McClain*, 545 F.2d 988 (5th Cir. 1977) and *United States v. McClain*, 593 F.2d 658, 664 (5th Cir. 1979), which concerned violating § 2314 by bringing Mexican antiquities into the United States. Ultimately:

> Under both the *McClain* cases and *Long Cove*, federal law controls the question of whether an item is stolen, and local law—Mexican law in *McClain*, and New York law in *Long Cove*—controls the analytically prior issues of (a) whether any person or entity has a property interest in the item such that it can be stolen, and (b) whether the receiver of the item has a property interest it. These issues are wholly distinct from the question of the conditions under which a once-stolen item ceases to be stolen. The answer to the latter question is determined by federal law and not local law. . . .

United States v. Portrait of Wally, 105 F. Supp. 2d 288, 292 (S.D.N.Y. 2000). The Court then reviewed federal law and concluded:

> In this case, the U.S. Forces were charged with recovering stolen items and acting on behalf of the items' true owners. Accordingly, when they recovered the painting they did so as agents of Lea Bondi Jaray—even though they did not know her name, or that

> the painting was hers. . . . This recovery purged the painting of the taint that it had. Although the painting may not have been placed in the correct hands when the Rieger heirs received it, in the eyes of the law it was no longer stolen.

Id. at 294. Accordingly, the court dismissed the forfeiture action.

At this point, the government moved the court either to reconsider its ruling or to grant leave to amend its Complaint for forfeiture. The court denied the former but allowed the latter, over the Leopold Foundation's strenuous objection. *United States v. Portrait of Wally*, 99 Civ. 9940 (MBM), 2000 U.S. Dist. LEXIS 18713, at *4 (S.D.N.Y. Dec. 28, 2000). After yet another amendment to the initial Complaint, MoMA and the Leopold Foundation again moved to dismiss. The court denied the motion. *United States v. Portrait of Wally*, 99 Civ. 9940 (MBM), 2002 U.S. Dist. LEXIS 6445 (S.D.N.Y. April 12, 2002). The threshold issue this time was whether MoMA had standing to contest the proceedings at all, since it did not own or claim to own the painting. The question was whether as a bailee, it had a possessory interest. The court concluded that while the law was confusing, it allowed MoMA to make its argument either for itself or on behalf of the Leopold Foundation. *Id.* at *14–15. Further, "MoMA has demonstrated lawful possession pursuant to its contract with the Leopold. The seizure has interfered with MoMA's rights and obligations under the contract, and the Leopold has threatened MoMA with liability for any damage it suffers." *Id.* at *15.

Next, the Leopold Foundation argued that the Austrian Treaty of 1955 barred the forfeiture action because the treaty vested solely in Austria the responsibility for disposing of property improperly seized by the Nazis. The court summarily rejected this argument:

> As the government argues, had the Republic of Austria taken control of Wally as unclaimed property within the meaning of the Treaty, it would have breached the Treaty to allow the painting to remain with the state-owned Belvedere or to give it to Dr. Leopold. Under Austrian law pursuant to the Treaty, all such property was to be transferred to Assembly Centers, whose contents have since been liquidated for the benefit of the victims of the Nazis.

> Whether or not U.S. courts would review such a breach need not be decided, however, because it makes no logical sense to apply this provision to Wally, which was not and could not have been taken under Austria's control as "unclaimed" property, but rather was mistakenly transferred to the Belvedere as part of the sale of the Rieger collection before the Treaty was enacted.

Id. at *24–25.

The District Court then turned to a question made interesting by the period between the end of the war and the full independence of Austria from the occupying powers in 1955: the Act of State doctrine. As noted above in considering the *Bernstein* case, the Act of State doctrine addresses those circumstances when a claim concerns the act of a sovereign state against one of its own citizens, a circumstance that courts will typically decline to adjudicate. The Leopold Foundation contended that the doctrine put the transfers from the Belvedere to Leopold beyond U.S. judicial review. The court, however, disagreed:

> Contrary to the conceptualization by the Leopold and MoMA, Wally was never legally transferred to the Rieger heirs pursuant to an official Austrian government determination of ownership. Rather, the BDA erroneously attributed it to the Rieger collection and mistakenly shipped it to the Belvedere with the Rieger collection. Although the court might be reluctant to second-guess the public acts of a sovereign, this does not seem to have been such an act. The court is notably not being asked to review a decision by a Restitution Commission regarding the restitution of Wally.

Id. at *28. Similarly, the court rejected the comity argument because U.S. interests were at least as great in determining whether there had been a National Stolen Property Act (NSPA) violation. *Id.* at *33–34.

Returning to the same recovery doctrine question—the idea that the painting had ceased to be stolen when it was recovered by the RDR—the court concluded that the new Complaint defeated the argument. The government had retracted the allegation that the United States armed forces were holding stolen works of art with an eye toward their eventual restitution. Now, the new Complaint alleged that pursuant to Military Decree No. 3, the Allies seized property of suspected war criminals, regardless of how it was acquired. As a result, the theory of the case was no longer that the government was the agent of victims like Bondi (which, if true, would have terminated the status as stolen property). Under the new view, the owner or her agents had never recovered the painting, and it had never ceased to be stolen. *Id.* at *46.

Importantly, the District Court in Manhattan also rejected the idea that the Belvedere, or Austria, or Leopold, had acquired title by prescription. That doctrine requires, in the first instance, that the acquirer have taken the property in good faith, which the Complaint squarely alleged to the contrary: (1) the BDA had been put on notice of *Wally*'s mistaken inclusion in the Rieger collection; (2) the director of the Belvedere listed *Wally* merely as *Portrait of a Woman* on his typed inventory, even though he knew it was Wally Neuzil; and (3) the Belvedere failed to investigate *Wally*'s provenance. Further, Bondi's letter to Kallir describing her request for assistance to Leopold made that presumption impossible to sustain. *Id.* at *57. Leopold definitely knew that Bondi believed the painting was hers, and the Complaint certainly alleged and implied so sufficiently. *Id.* at *83–84.

Lastly, the District Court had to determine whether Austrian law provided that Bondi's claim was barred by a statute of limitations such that the Leopold Foundation was safe from claims, and therefore had imported property that did indeed belong to it. Leopold asserted laches as a defense, too, suggesting that Bondi and her heirs had been lax in enforcing their rights. These defenses were tolled from the beginning to accrue until the painting was imported, however. *Id.* at *69.

The case was now more than three years old, and the District Court had not really begun to probe the facts. With the motions to dismiss resolved, the parties set to the exchange of discovery, though even that was a challenge. Very few restitution cases have proceeded deep into discovery with foreign parties, and the conflict between U.S. discovery methods and the complete hostility to this process in Europe can pose a challenge. U.S. discovery takes the view that the parties must preserve, unearth, and exchange every conceivably relevant piece of information. The concept is that if a case gets to trial, there are no surprises. All parties know what information is available and craft their arguments accordingly. The downside of this approach is the intrusion and expense that it imposes on the parties, which can range from significant to exorbitant.

By contrast, European law (and Austrian law in particular) takes a narrower view, namely, that the parties should essentially present their best cases and make their arguments. This has a considerable practical advantage in terms of speed and expense but of course allows for the possibility that a party could fail to disclose a harmful document without the other party knowing it existed. Along with this hostility to foreign discovery is the distaste for depositions. Leopold's deposition, as is often the case with a witness unfamiliar with the process, is revealed as a combative affair, with Leopold repeatedly answering the U.S. Attorney's questions contemptuously, with a sneer of derision.

After years of discovery, all the parties moved for summary judgment. In other words, each party argued that the facts material to the legal standards set forth in the motions to dismiss (that had assumed the allegations of the Complaint) were undisputed such that no trial was necessary to sort them out. The District Court denied the summary judgment motions, concluding that a triable issue existed regarding whether or not Leopold (subjectively) knew at the time the painting entered the country in 1997 that the painting had been stolen in 1939. *Portrait of Wally*, 663 F. Supp. 2d at 246. The legal arguments addressed largely the same issues. The Leopold Foundation did advance a new take on the Act of State doctrine, namely, that an Austrian Federal Finance Ministry's May 10, 1950, approval of the BDA's restitution of Schiele artworks to the Rieger heirs required deference pursuant to the Act of State doctrine because the BDA was making a decision as a sovereign act. The District Court disagreed, finding that approval did not constitute a "formal or purposeful act of the Austrian judiciary, executive, or legislature with respect to [*Wally*] rising to a level that would implicate international comity." *Id.* at 249.

Concerning the merits of the customs claims, the court made a number of findings. First, Welz stole *Portrait of Wally*. This point is beyond serious debate, but the Leopold Foundation had continued to press it: "[N]o reasonable juror could find the Museum has introduced a preponderance of the evidence indicating otherwise." *Id.* at 253. There was a considerable issue to be resolved about the evidentiary sufficiency of much of the documentary record. Although historians might reasonably agree on the authenticity of primary source documents, that does not necessarily make them admissible under the Federal Rules of Evidence. Written documents, if introduced to prove the proposition stated therein (*e.g.*, "Leopold stole my painting"), are hearsay. There are, however, numerous hearsay exceptions, and the court was satisfied that the correspondence with Kallir met the authentication requirements of Fed. R. Evid. 901(b)(8), and having been found authentic, met the hearsay exception of Fed. R. Evid. 803(16) for ancient documents.

The decision goes over the same history in meticulous detail, reaching the important point:

> The Government has thus far shown probable cause to believe that *Wally* was stolen and remained so until it arrived in this country, whereas the Museum has not met its burden of showing otherwise. However, this is not alone sufficient to render the Painting subject to forfeiture under the pre-[Class Action Fairness Reform Act] NSPA. The Government must also show that the Museum imported *Wally* into the United States *knowing* it was either stolen or converted. To this end, the Government contends that Dr. Leopold either knew *Wally* was stolen or himself converted it and that his knowledge should be attributed to the Museum under agency principles. I conclude that the trier of fact must determine whether Dr. Leopold knew the Painting was either stolen or converted. Should the jury find that he did, his knowledge will be imputed to the Museum.

Portrait of Wally, 663 F. Supp. 2d at 269.

Therefore, that question was what was set for trial; a date was scheduled for July 2010, more than twelve years after the first *New York Times* article had opened the case to scrutiny. There was little doubt that the trial could be avoided given the lengths to which that the museum had gone to retain ownership and the persistence that the Bondi heirs had shown in pursuing their family's property.

However, Leopold died just weeks before the scheduled trial. While the negotiations that followed his death are not matters of public record, there is simply no question that with the death of Leopold, the potential for a resolution became a real possibility. The same long shadow cast by Leopold that Bondi had described remained true in the twenty-first century. Leopold was a giant figure of Viennese art and culture, and the museum is one of the most popular in the country. His intransigence was something that was difficult to overcome. Put more bluntly, Leopold was a man who was willing to take advantage of Lea Bondi's circumstances to scoop up *Portrait of Wally* for himself; thus, he was not the kind of person to yield to moral pressure.

Leopold knew the painting was stolen. He had always known it. With his arrogance and pride out of the way, a real negotiation was possible. On July 20, 2010, the U.S. Attorney announced a settlement. The Leopold Foundation agreed to pay the Bondi heirs $19 million, and under the agreement, would be allowed to retain and return the painting to Vienna. It hangs on the wall of the Leopold Foundation today.

The settlement frames well the often diametrically opposed perspectives characteristic of restitution battles. On the one hand, Leopold's decades of deceit and manipulation were exposed, and the heirs were compensated, albeit belatedly, for the theft of their family property (obviously the settlement does not itself concede liability as a matter of adjudication). On the other hand, the painting will hang on the wall indefinitely in a museum dedicated to the glory of the man who snatched it up. In the end, however, it is impossible to overstate the significance of the case in drawing attention to the issue in the nation at large. When the case began, only two restitution litigations had been filed since 1990: those over *Landscape with Smokestacks* and *Femme en Blanc*, discussed further below. Over the years during which the case was making news, the views regarding stolen art as worthy of adjudication shifted, and thus the restitution landscape bears *Wally*'s influence even today.

*　　*　　*

Customs played a key role in two other cases, one that was resolved quickly, and another that was contested much more aggressively. In 1922, Pablo Picasso painted *Femme en Blanc* (*Woman in White*). Carlotta Landsberg, a German Jewish woman, bought the painting in 1926 or 1927. Carlotta and her husband, Robert, lived in Berlin through the time of the Nazi takeover of power. Robert died in 1932. At some point thereafter, as she was preparing to flee Germany, Carlotta transferred the painting to Justin Thannhauser in France. After the invasion of France in 1940, Thannhauser's own possessions were looted by the Nazis. Thannhauser described the 1940 theft in a June 12, 1958, letter to Carlotta:

> Dear Mrs. Landsberg,
>
> As I remember very clearly, and as I therefore can confirm to you in writing, in 1938 or 1939 you sent your painting by Picasso, of a woman, from the so-called classical period of the artist, to me in my house in Paris, 35 Mirosmenil. At this time, as we were forced to leave our home in Paris in 1939, your Picasso hung in the middle of a narrow wall. Upon the occupation of Paris in 1940, when we were no longer in Paris and the house was closed, the entire contents of the four-story building—and with it your painting—were stolen. This was confirmed to us by the property manager after the end of the war. Further we heard from the porter of the house on the occasion of a later visit certain facts, revealing that during the four day long violent German national socialist plundering everything was taken out of the four-story house during the night and placed in trucks.
>
> Your painting is pictured in Christian Zervos' large Picasso work, Volume 4, No. 389, Page 160 with the title "Femme en blanc" 1922, oil painting, 65:54 cm. As you know, I have often tried to find a trace of this oil painting, as well as all of the other property that disappeared at the same time, but until now without success.
>
> In conclusion may I especially state that I have set forth the foregoing to the best of my knowledge and conscience.

As it turns out, the Picasso was collected and/or identified by the Allied Command. The provenance from there is a blank until 1975, when Maurice Covo (a French art dealer) asked Stephen Hahn (a gallerist in New York) whether Hahn would be interested in buying it. Covo represented that he might be able to acquire it. Hahn traveled to Paris and purchased the Picasso, with Covo making no mention of its Nazi connection (according to Hahn). That same year, Hahn sold the painting to Marilyn Alsdorf of Chicago.

In 2001, Alsdorf delivered the painting to David Tunkl Fine Art in Los Angeles, for an exhibition that ran from September 20, 2001, through October 28, 2001. Tunkl then returned the painting to Alsdorf in Chicago. In 2002, Tunkl suggested to Alsdorf that he might be able to sell the Picasso for her. At Tunkl's suggestion, the painting was sent from Chicago to Geneva, Switzerland, for inspection by the art advisor Didier Imbert, for an unknown European collector. Imbert contacted the ALR.

After Imbert made inquiry of the ALR, Sarah Jackson, the ALR's historic claims director, informed him that the painting had been stolen by the Nazis. Imbert then wrote to Adam Cirker in New York to alert him to the ALR's report. On April 25, 2002, the ALR formally notified both Imbert and Tunkl that the Nazis confiscated the painting from a Jewish owner during World War II. Imbert then notified Alsdorf. In the meantime, Jackson had located Thomas Bennigson in Berkeley, California; Bennigson was Carlotta Landsberg's grandson and sole heir.

On June 7, 2002, Jackson got in touch with Alsdorf's attorney, Stephen Bernard. She stressed that the Nazis had stolen the Picasso, and that the ALR had extensive records. In the summer of 2002, these documents were shared with Alsdorf's and Bennigson's attorneys, as well as with Tunkl. By this point, the painting had returned to Los Angeles from Geneva, but on December 13, 2002, Alsdorf gave instructions to have it shipped to Chicago. It went back on December 20, 2002.

Bennigson filed suit in California Superior Court on December 19, 2002. Alsdorf was served with the Summons and Complaint on December 27, 2002, after the painting had returned to Illinois. Alsdorf then moved to dismiss for lack of personal jurisdiction. The concept of personal jurisdiction was summarized by the California Court of Appeals, Second Division:

> Personal jurisdiction is either general or specific. If the defendant's forum-related contacts are extensive and wide-ranging, or substantial, continuous and systematic, the defendant may be subject to the court's "general" jurisdiction. . . . In those circumstances, the specific claims at issue need not be connected with the defendant's

> business relationship to the forum. Instead, the defendant is subject to the California court's jurisdiction for all causes of action raised against it. . . .
>
> "Specific" personal jurisdiction, on the other hand, exists if the defendant's forum-related activities are not so pervasive as to justify an exercise of general jurisdiction.

Bennigson v. Alsdorf, B168200, 2004 Cal. App. Unpub. LEXIS 3681, at *11 (Cal. Court App. 2nd Div. April 15, 2004) (citations omitted). Alsdorf argued that she did not have the minimum contacts with the state to satisfy either California's long-arm statute, Code Civ. Proc., § 410.10, or the Due Process Clause. Any challenge to personal jurisdiction is evaluated under a two-step analysis. First, does the state authorize the contact in question to confer jurisdiction, and second, is hauling that person into the court in question consistent with the constitutional requirements of due process?

Bennigson argued, not surprisingly, that Alsdorf met the contact requirement with the statute because she had brought the painting there. Moreover, she purposefully tried to evade jurisdiction by shipping the painting out of state before she was served with process, just as an emergency temporary restraining order (TRO) was being sought by Bennigson's attorney. On June 16, 2003, the motion to quash the summons was allowed, and the case was dismissed. *Bennigson*, 2004 Cal. App. Unpub. LEXIS 3681, at *8. Bennigson appealed.

The intermediate appellate court affirmed the dismissal in 2004. Only specific jurisdiction was at issue, based on Alsdorf's shipment of the Picasso to Los Angeles. The appellate court concluded:

> The record reflects Alsdorf did not purposefully avail herself of forum benefits with respect to the matter at issue, nor is there any evidence this particular controversy arose out of any of Alsdorf's extremely limited contacts with California.

Id. at *13. This is manifestly wrong. Alsdorf sent the painting to California as part of a potential sale. Any sale necessarily implicates title to the work. The fact that a title investigation would follow is not only reasonably foreseeable, it is presumptively expected. Nevertheless, the court did not agree:

> Alsdorf's extremely minimal contact with California, all of which appears largely to have been at Tunkl's direction, is simply too passive, isolated and attenuated to constitute deliberate action directed at this state.

Id. At *14. This was because, in the trial court's view, the substance of the claim arose because of Nazi theft, not Alsdorf's shipment into California. Even if Alsdorf's actions met the statutory basis for specific jurisdiction, the appellate court concluded that it would offend the "traditional notions of 'fair play and substantial justice'" enunciated by the Supreme Court. *Id.* at *19, *citing Burger King Corp. v. Rudzewicz,* 471 U.S. 462, 477–478 (1985):

> There can be no dispute this litigation bears no relationship to Alsdorf's activities in California, or that an alternative forum is not available. The lawsuit seeks only to establish *Bennigson*'s ownership of a painting he claims was stolen in Europe. Undoubtedly other courts, including those in Alsdorf's home state, are available to *Bennigson* to assert his claim.

Id. at 21.

The California Supreme Court accepted review of this decision on July 28, 2004, but never issued a decision because of the resolution that eventually followed, detailed further below.

Meanwhile, Alsdorf was seizing the initiative on her own. On September 10, 2004, Alsdorf filed a federal quiet title action against Bennigson in Chicago, pursuant to 28 U.S.C. § 1655. She sought a mirror-image declaration that she was indeed the owner of the painting, free and clear of any claims by Bennigson. Bennigson moved to stay the Illinois action as preceded by the California case, under what is known as the *Colorado River* abstention doctrine:

> Pursuant to the Colorado River doctrine, federal district courts may abstain from the exercise of their jurisdiction in deference to

concurrent proceedings in a state court, only in "exceptional circumstances." *See Colorado River Water Conservation Dist. v. United States*, 424 U.S. 800, 813, (1976).

Alsdorf v. Bennigson, No. 04 C 5953, 2004 U.S. Dist. LEXIS 24696, at *13 (N.D. Ill. Dec. 2, 2004). *Colorado River* abstention involves its own two-step analysis. First, the court must determine whether the proceedings are "parallel." *Id.* at 17. Second, the court must look to a number of factors to balance the relative interest, which include (but do not exhaustively require) the following:

> (1) whether the state has assumed jurisdiction over the property; (2) the inconvenience of the federal forum; (3) the desirability of avoiding piecemeal litigation; (4) the order in which jurisdiction was obtained by the concurrent forums; (5) the presence or absence of concurrent jurisdiction; (6) the source of governing law, state or federal; (7) the adequacy of the state court action to protect the federal plaintiff's rights; (8) the relative progress of state and federal proceedings; (9) the availability of removal; and (10) the vexatious or contrived nature of the federal claim.

Id., citing Caminiti and Iatarola, Limited v. Behnke Warehousing, Inc., 962 F.2d 698, 701 (7th Cir. 1992).

As to the first part of the analysis, although Tunkl was a party in California but not Illinois, both cases involved resolving ownership of the Picasso. *Bennigson*, 2004 Cal. App. Unpub. LEXIS 3681, at *20. That left the more amorphous remaining factors. The U.S. District Court held that with the California appeal still pending, the question of assumption of jurisdiction was unresolved. The court was unconcerned about the inconvenience to Alsdorf of litigating in California, but was circumspect of the risk of piecemeal litigation if the California case survived. The court did not determine which law applied, but did determine that the California proceedings were further advanced. *Id.* at 31–32. The court did not consider Alsdorf's case vexatious; she had a live dispute over title to the painting. *Id.* at 32. Based on all this, the District Court entered a temporary stay, to be revisited based on progress in the California case.

Incidentally, according to an affidavit filed by Jackson in the Illinois federal case, the evidence that the painting had been stolen from Thannhauser, but that he was not the owner, "was found in May 2002 in a letter in the Wiedergutmachungsamt (Restitution Office), in Berlin Germany, in a letter from Dr. Otto Weise, dated February 22, 1965, in which he asked that the Painting be struck out of Thannhauser's compensation claim, as it belonged to Carlota Landsberg." *Alsdorf*, 2004 U.S. Dist. LEXIS 24696, at *6, n.4.

It was at this point that something remarkable happened: The U.S. government got involved. On October 6, 2004, the United States filed an action for civil forfeiture pursuant to 18 U.S.C. §§ 981(a)(1)(C), 2314, and 2315 in California federal court, alleging that Alsdorf transported property in interstate commerce that she knew was stolen when she transported it in interstate commerce. On January 3, 2005, the government and Alsdorf entered into a stipulated Order, allowing her to retain physical possession of the painting during the pendency of the proceeding.

Alsdorf moved to dismiss for lack of subject matter jurisdiction or alternatively to transfer the case to the District Court for the Northern District of Illinois where her case was pending. Bennigson also cross-claimed in the Los Angeles federal court on similar grounds to those asserted in his first lawsuit, cross-claims that Alsdorf also moved to dismiss for lack of personal jurisdiction.

The District Court in Los Angeles denied both motions. *United States v. One Oil Painting Entitled "Femme En Blanc" by Pablo Picasso*, 362 F. Supp. 2d 1175 (C.D. Cal. 2005). The subject matter jurisdiction argument was premised on the doctrine of prior exclusive jurisdiction, which prohibits "a court from 'assuming *in rem* jurisdiction over a *res* that is already under the *in rem* jurisdiction of another court.'" *Id.* at 1180, *citing Penn Gen. Casualty Co. v. Pennsylvania*, 294 U.S. 189, 195 (1935). Alsdorf thus argued that because she filed the Illinois action before the civil forfeiture action, the Illinois court obtained jurisdiction first, to the exclusion the Los Angeles court. *Femme en Blanc*, 362 F. Supp. 2d at 1181. The mere filing of the Complaint is not enough; however, the court held:

> In order for the Illinois court to have obtained prior exclusive jurisdiction, the painting must have been in the custody or control of

> that court. Such a conclusion is consistent with the general and long-standing rules regarding *in rem* jurisdiction. Actions under § 1655 are no different from any other *in rem* proceedings. Therefore, Alsdorf has failed to establish that the Illinois court obtained jurisdiction to the exclusion of this Court.

Id. at 1184.

The District Court in Los Angeles also denied Alsdorf's 28 U.S.C. § 1404 transfer request, as well as the first-filed rule because the latter applies only to the same parties and issues. The Illinois suit concerned title to the painting (ownership), whereas the forfeiture action concerned the allegation that Alsdorf had knowingly transported in interstate commerce stolen property. As to the transfer request, the District Court found both venues adequate, but California better. Alsdorf was the only witness in Illinois, whereas most were in California. *Id.* at 1185–86. Summing up, the court concluded:

> Because the painting was transported from this district to Illinois, and this transportation in interstate commerce is the basis for the forfeiture action, at least one of the acts or omissions giving rise to the action occurred in this district. Furthermore, the fact that the painting is currently in Illinois is irrelevant. It is within the Court's power to bring the painting before the Court. The painting remains in Illinois because the parties so stipulated, with the understanding that Alsdorf's possession of the painting would not serve as the basis for a challenge of jurisdiction.

The last task was the personal jurisdiction motion on Bennigson's cross claims, which were similar to the previously litigated and still-pending California state court case. However, now the difference was that Alsdorf had appeared as a claimant in the civil forfeiture action. That made it reasonable, in the Los Angeles District Court's view, to subject her to its jurisdiction. In fairness to Alsdorf, it seems a bit circular to say that. She had successfully defended the idea (so far) that she had not availed herself of California. Once the government started the forfeiture action—which Alsdorf duly challenged—she had no choice but to appear or otherwise lose the painting that she claimed to own. In any event, the case survived.

It was at this stage that the prospect of multi-front litigation had the effect that it so often does: creating the pressure to reach an accommodation. On August 10, 2005, the *Chicago Tribune* reported that Alsdorf had agreed to pay Bennigson $6.5 million to resolve the claim—and keep the painting. "I think she has very personal reasons for doing it,"[43] Alsdorf's attorney, Richard Chapman told the *Tribune*. Bennigson's attorney at Burris & Schoenberg LLP spoke more pointedly: "It was clear that Mrs. Alsdorf had no [legal] defense, that this painting had been stolen during the Nazi era."[44]

Surprisingly, *Alsdorf* and *Wally* are rare examples of the impact of customs and forfeiture laws. The most recent such case never really came to be a contested matter. Girolamo Romano's *Christ Carrying the Cross Dragged by a Rogue*, from 1538, was owned by a French Jew, Giuseppe Gentili, before the collaborationist Vichy government in France seized the painting and sold it at auction in 1941. In 2011, the Mary Brogan Museum of Art in Tallahassee borrowed the work from Pinacoteca di Brera in Milan for a temporary exhibition. The painting did not receive immunity from seizure, and the United States filed a civil forfeiture action under the same statute at issue in *Wally:* 19 U.S.C. § 1595a, justifying seizure of property that is known to be stolen when imported into the United States. Happily, however, the Italian museum was amenable to restitution, and the heirs were found. The painting was handed over to them in February 2012. *U.S. v. Painting Known as Cristo Portacroce Trascinato da un Manigoldo*, Docket No. 14, 4:11-cv-00571-RH-WCS (N.D. Fla. Jan. 31, 2012).

Chapter 4

A New Door Opens: Maria Altmann and the Portrait of Adele Bloch-Bauer

As a general proposition in Anglo-American law, a sovereign cannot be sued without its consent. That principle can extend to a nation, such as the United States or Hungary; to a subdivision, such as Massachusetts or Bavaria; or further still to a municipality. Domestically, the United States and the fifty individual states all have a framework of statutes pursuant to which they permit lawsuits, mostly for tort liability and for other causes of action in which the state defendant is more like a commercial or private actor than a sovereign. As such, the Federal Tort Claims Act, 28 U.S.C. §§ 2671–2680 (FTCA), and analogous state laws abrogate state immunity under certain circumstances.

What about foreign sovereigns, however? While the FTCA dates to 1946, it was not until thirty years later that the U.S. Congress passed a law concerning the ability to bring actions against other countries. The Foreign Sovereign Immunities Act (FSIA), 28 U.S.C. § 1605 *et seq.*, was that law.

The FSIA addresses both the circumstances of immunity and the remedies available. It is not a substantive law; rather, it is a means to get into court. It also functions in many instances like a long-arm statute (a law that provides the circumstances under which an out-of-state defendant may be subject to the state's jurisdiction); once a defendant is held to have satisfied an exception to sovereignty, it must content itself with defending the lawsuit, and a personal jurisdiction defense that might apply to a private litigant is not available.

The FSIA has many exceptions to sovereignty, which refer to circumstances in which a defendant appears to behave less like a sovereign and more like a commercial actor. For example, there are exceptions for enforcement of a lien in admiralty (28 U.S.C. § 1605(b)), to enforce an agreement or arbitration or personal injury or death (28 U.S.C. § 1605(a)(5)), or to foreclose a preferred mortgage (28 U.S.C. § 1605(d)). None of these would seem to raise the prospect of entangling a foreign sovereign in possession of fine art that someone alleges was stolen by the Nazis. The provisions that have come to be so important are found in the law's first paragraph. It reads:

> (a) A foreign state shall not be immune from the jurisdiction of courts of the United States or of the States in any case—
>
> (1) in which the foreign state has waived its immunity either explicitly or by implication, notwithstanding any withdrawal of the waiver which the foreign state may purport to effect except in accordance with the terms of the waiver;
>
> (2) in which the action is based upon a commercial activity carried on in the United States by the foreign state; or upon an act performed in the United States in connection with a commercial activity of the foreign state elsewhere; or upon an act outside the territory of the United States in connection with a commercial activity of the foreign state elsewhere and that act causes a direct effect in the United States;
>
> (3) in which rights in property taken in violation of international law are in issue and that property or any property exchanged for such property is present in the United States in connection with a commercial activity carried on in the United States by the foreign state; or that property or any property exchanged for such property

is owned or operated by an agency or instrumentality of the foreign state and that agency or instrumentality is engaged in a commercial activity in the United States.

28 U.S.C. § 1605.

Maria Altmann's story spans the late Austrian empire and the years between World War I and World War II. Maria Victoria Bloch was born in Vienna in 1916. She was a member of the successful Austrian Jewish Bloch family and the daughter of Gustav Bloch and Marie Therese Bauer. Her uncle, Ferdinand Bloch-Bauer, was a sugar magnate and patron of the arts. In particular, Ferdinand commissioned numerous works by Gustav Klimt, including two of his wife Adele Bloch-Bauer (Maria's aunt). The paintings are now known as *Adele Bloch-Bauer I* and *Adele Bloch-Bauer II.* Adele was an archetypal turn-of-the-century figure in Vienna in a way that reflects the allure and complexity of that era.

Austria at the dawn of the 20th Century

In 1900, Austria stood at the tail end of the Habsburg dynasty that had spanned hundreds of years of dominance over the Holy Roman Empire and its remnants. The Habsburgs cemented their traditional leadership of the Holy Roman Empire as the kings of Bohemia, one of the fixed set of prince electors of the Holy Roman Empire (Kurfürsten), hereditary houses that then elected the emperor pursuant to the Golden Bull of 1356. The Habsburgs withstood the carnage of the Thirty Years' War, diminished but in control. Seeing this weakness, the Ottomans soon advanced to the gates of Vienna. After withstanding the Siege of Vienna in 1683 with the last-minute help of Jan Sobieski, the king of Poland-Lithuania, and the leadership of Eugene of Savoy, the Austrian coalition drove the occupying Ottomans back through Hungary and the Balkans. The Austrians absorbed into their sphere of influence the areas that the retreating Turks left behind after hundreds of years of administration. When Frederick II of Prussia and the monarchs of Europe refused to recognize the Pragmatic Sanction under which Maria Theresa in 1740 would be recognized as empress, she was left to defend the War of Austrian Succession. She steered the war to a successful stalemate, losing only minor Silesian territory, but in so doing cemented her reputation as a formidable monarch. When

Poland was subjected to successive partitions starting in 1772, Austria acquired the newly named territory of Galicia, which comprises large parts of southeastern Poland and Ukraine.

Thus, even when the Holy Roman Empire fell apart before the advance of Napoleon, leaving the Austrian empire for the first time, it was still a major European land power that encompassed more cultures and ethnicities than any other. Even after the greater autonomy of the Hungarian compromise, or Ausgleich, in 1867, Austria looked inward to augment its cultural importance. The historic urban renewal of the Ringstrasse (the Ring Road) in Vienna commenced to ease the sting of losses in the Austro-Prussian War. The Ring stands on the outer edge of the *glacis* that encircled the medieval wall, the very territory where Ottoman soldiers had dug towards the besieged city in 1683. The wall was torn down and in its place the magnificent boulevard was constructed, surrounded by the grand palatial buildings of Théophile Hansen, architecturally echoing the functions of the structures: neoclassical for the parliament, medieval gothic for the city hall, or *Rathaus*, baroque for the Naturhistorisches (Natural History) and Kunsthistorisches (Art History) Museums, and so on. On the outer edges of the Ring, the new grand buildings, known as *Palais*, were constructed by successful Viennese, many of them Jewish. In sum, it was without question the cultural capital of central Europe, if not the continent.

Yet there were other undercurrents developing in Vienna at the turn of the century. At the same time as Austrian lawyer Theodor Herzl was writing *Der Judenstaat* and planting the seeds of Zionism, Karl Lüger was elected mayor of the city on a frank, transparent platform seething with anti-Semitism. In a manner far more overt than anything happening in Germany at the time—where Otto von Bismarck's firm hand steered the unification of the German states into the German Empire—Vienna and Austria began the new century with a fascinating and complicated mix of cosmopolitanism and nativism, avant garde ideas, and regressive populist *völkisch* culture that would ascend to power in the 1930s. Perhaps even more so than in Germany, the tragedy of the Vienna Jewish community—where, it cannot be forgotten, Hitler made a go at the Academy of Fine Arts only to be turned away as he seethed at the modernity of Vienna—has its roots a generation earlier.

This was the world that Adele and Ferdinand Bloch-Bauer inhabited and embodied. As Viennese Jews, they themselves stood astride the collisions and conflicts of that community: the successful business people of the Ringstrasse Palais (the "Zionstrasse," or "Zion Street," as detailed brilliantly in Edmund de Waal's tale of the losses of the Ephrussi family, *The Hare with the Amber Eyes*) and the *shtetl* Jews from the empire's eastern reaches. Adele had a passionate relationship with Klimt himself, and the family's fortunes came through the disaster of World War I more or less intact. After the boundaries were set by by the victors, instead of an empire spanning the scenic far reaches of Eastern Europe, Austria was a republic, a landlocked state that few thought would survive independently.

Adele died in 1925 of meningitis. In her will, she expressed a desire that Ferdinand bequeath the paintings that she left to him to the Austrian national collections. This was hardly surprising; Adele considered herself as much Austrian as Jewish, a recurrent theme among many of the persecuted Jews of Germany and Austria. Ferdinand did make such a gift of one painting, *Schloss am Attersee II,* in 1936.

Maria Bloch was married in 1937 to Victor Altmann. However, the Nazi takeover that swept through Austria in March 1938 swept away everything before it. While it does not appear that the Altmanns were immediately subjected to the horrific *Reibpartie* in which Viennese Jews were forced to scrub the sidewalks with toothbrushes on their hands and knees in front of leering crowds, their prominence did not take long to attract the attention of the nascent Nazi authorities. Maria's husband, Victor, was repeatedly arrested and mistreated.

On April 28, 1938, Ferdinand Bloch-Bauer was accused of and charged with a variety of trumped-up offenses and fined RM 700,000 (Reichsmark). On May 14, 1938, a judicial seizure order deprived Bloch-Bauer of the legal authority to dispose of his own property. Local attorney Erich Führer was appointed administrator of the Bloch-Bauer estate.

Führer was an enthusiastic Nazi, a Party member since 1932 and a reserve officer and *Obersturmführer* (the rough equivalent of a First Lieutenant but specific to the Nazi paramilitary groups) in the SS Standorte 89. Führer began to liquidate Bloch-Bauer's assets in January 1939, and strong-armed Altmann out of her property as well. *Adele Bloch-Bauer I* and *Apple Tree I* were traded in 1941 to the Austrian Gallery for *Schloss Kammer am Attersee III. Adele Bloch-Bauer II* was sold in March 1943 to the Austrian Gallery. *Houses in Unterach am Attersee* was kept by Dr. Führer for his personal collection.

Ferdinand escaped to Switzerland, where he survived the war before passing away in 1946. In 1947, a Swiss court recognized Altmann as heir to 25 percent of Ferdinand's estate. She then retained an Austrian lawyer, who pursued several of the paintings at issue from the Austrian National Gallery, as it was known at the time. The gallery argued that it owned the paintings by virtue of a bequest by Adele in 1926. Amazingly, as the District Court later held (emphasis added):

> In March 1948, Dr. [Karl] Garzarolli of the Austrian Gallery learned of the contents and probate proceedings of Adele's will. Specifically, Garzarolli learned that Adele had expressed the wish that Ferdinand donate the paintings to the Gallery, but that Adele had not herself bequeathed the paintings to the Gallery. Garzarolli acknowledged as much in a March 8, 1948, letter to his predecessor wherein Garzarolli expressed his concern at his predecessor's failure to obtain a declaration of gift in favor of the state from Ferdinand. . . . *Dr. Garzarolli did not reveal to the heirs or their lawyers the files from Adele's probate proceedings that he had in his possession;* rather he prepared to sue the heirs for the remaining paintings.

Altmann v. Republic of Austria, 142 F. Supp. 2d 1187, 1194 (C.D. Cal. 2000). Karl Garzarolli, of course, is the same director who was in involved in the underhanded postwar acquisition of *Portrait of Wally*.

A negotiation ensued concerning the paintings that had belonged to Ferdinand (including *Houses in Unterach am Attersee*) that had been recovered by Altmann's brother—who was a member of the Allied Armed Forces—specifically Austria's assertion of its now infamous export ban on ostensibly restituted works. In 1946, Austria had enacted its law declaring that all transactions that were motivated by discriminatory Nazi ideology were to be deemed null and void but which still required payment of some compensation to the current possessors. In addition, the law prohibited the export of artworks that were deemed to be significant Austrian cultural heritage. As is now well known, the Austrian government routinely used the law as leverage to force Jews who were trying to get their recovered property out of a country to which they had no interest in returning "to trade artworks for export permits on other works." *Id.* at 1193–94. Dr. Garzarolli, unbeknownst to the Bloch-Bauer heirs, expressed in writing a plan to deliberately delay the export licenses they sought in order to encourage putative donations of some of the paintings.

Interestingly, the District Court seemed not to be aware of the intervening provenance of another Bloch-Bauer work, Klimt's *Portrait of Amalie Zuckerkandl*, before the art dealer Vita Künstler gave the work to the nation of Austria in 1988. The work appears on the very same property inventory (*Verzeichnis*) of Ferdinand Bloch-Bauer at issue in the federal court litigation. During the Nazi era, Künstler bought *Portrait of Amalie Zuckerkandl* for RM 1,600 from the Müller-Hoffmann family. The unknown provenance at the time of the litigation was how *Portrait of Amalie Zuckerkandl* went from Bloch-Bauer's collection to Künstler's. The Müller-Hoffmann family later produced evidence that Ferdinand Bloch-Bauer had either given it to Hermine Müller-Hoffmann, who also happened to be Amalie Zuckerkandl's daughter, or requested that Erich Führer do so. As the Austrian restitution panel (*Kunsrückgabebeirat*, or *Beirat* for short) would later and controversially find, "[t]he most plausible possibility is that the painting may have been given by Dr. Führer to Ms. Müller-Hofmann at the inducement of Ferdinand Bloch-Bauer without exchange or consideration, with whom Führer was in regular contact."[46] The respective families apparently agreed that Müller-Hoffmann had sold it to Künstler for RM 1,600. The painting remains today in the possession of the Belvedere in Vienna.

In the midst of the furor surrounding the seizure of *Portrait of Wally* and *Dead City III*, an Austrian journalist, Hubertus Czernin, took note of the Altmann story and the story of *Adele*. Czernin published a series of stories exposing the Austrian government's use of the export licenses after the war to obtain donations of artwork to the national collections. Czernin unearthed the smoking gun: Contrary to the museum's assertions that the paintings had been donated pursuant to Adele's will, *Adele Bloch-Bauer I* had been conveyed to the museum by Erich Führer himself.

On the heels of this development, Altmann brought a claim to the *Beirat.* The panel recommended that the paintings not be returned, notwithstanding Austria's then-recent and much improved restitution law. This result was itself controversial. Austria refused to arbitrate the dispute and indicated that Altmann's only recourse was to go to court. This, too, was a formidable obstacle, however, because she would have been required to post a bond in proportion to the value of the property at stake, paintings worth more than $150 million by any measure.

Altmann instead brought her claim to the U.S. District Court for the Central District of California, in Los Angeles, where she lived. She filed suit in 2000, invoking the FSIA's jurisdiction over the Republic of Austria. She sought a declaration of ownership concerning six paintings *Adele Bloch-Bauer I, Adele Bloch-Bauer II, Beechwood, Apple Tree I, Houses in Unterach am Attersee,* and *Amalie Zuckerkandl.*

The first obstacle that the Los Angeles court wrestled with was the applicability of the FSIA. The statute, if you recall, was not passed until 1976. The Tate Letter featured centrally in this analysis. The Tate Letter, as the court pointed out, takes what is known as the "restrictive view" of sovereign immunity. "Under the restrictive principle of sovereign immunity, the immunity of a foreign sovereign is recognized with regard to a sovereign's public acts (*jure imperii*), but is not recognized with respect to a sovereign's private acts (*jure gestionis*)." *Altmann v. Republic of Austria,* 142 F. Supp. 2d at 1199. At the time *Altmann* was filed, Austria argued that it was unsettled whether the policy embodied in the Tate Letter could be applied to events that preceded the letter (Austria not surprisingly arguing that it should not). The question had not even come up until 1986, in the Eleventh Circuit, which ruled that pre-1952 events were not covered by the FSIA's restrictive view. *Jackson v. People's Republic of China,* 794 F.2d 1490 (11th Cir. 1986), cert. denied, 480 U.S. 917, 107 S. Ct. 1371, 94 L. Ed. 2d 687 (1987). The District Court for the District of Columbia followed *Jackson*'s reasoning to hold that the FSIA did not apply to a claim under a 1922 agreement between that plaintiff and Mexico. *Slade v. United States of Mexico,* 617 F. Supp. 351, 356 (D.D.C. 1985). However, a case that was not even about the FSIA, let alone looted art, changed the conversation.

In *Landgraf v. USI Film Products, Inc.*, the Supreme Court found that to determine whether a law should be applied retroactively, a court must first consider whether Congress expressly stated the statute's temporal reach. *Landgraf v. USI Film Products,* 511 U.S. 244, 114 S. Ct. 1483, 229 (1994). Following *Landgraf,* the D.C. Circuit implied that pre-Tate Letter events were indeed covered by the FSIA. *Princz v. Federal Republic of Germany,* 26 F.3d 1166 (D.C. Cir. 1994). *Princz* thus concluded that the FSIA is to be applied to all cases decided after the enactment of the FSIA, whether or not the plaintiff's cause of action had accrued when the law was passed. *Altmann,* 142 F. Supp. 2d at 1201. Based on this history, the District Court concluded that the FSIA was applicable to events before the Tate Letter.

Altmann was not in the clear yet, however. She still had to persuade the court that her claims fit within the "expropriation exception" of § 1605(a)(3). The court adopted the standard that so long as she had alleged claims that were "substantial and non-frivolous, there would be a sufficient basis for the exercise of the court's jurisdiction." *Id.* at 1202. A taking requires three elements to be valid under international law; thus, in their absence, it violates international law: "First, the taking must serve a public purpose; second, aliens must not be discriminated against or singled out for regulation by the state; and third, payment of just compensation must be made." *Id., citing Siderman de Blake v. Republic of Argentina,* 965 F.2d 699 (9th Cir. 1992). Altmann's claims qualified under this standard, in a holding that still resonates today. The Aryanization of Altmann's property was "clearly" such a violation. *Altmann,* 142 F. Supp. 2d at 1203. "The taking was not for public purpose; instead, some of the art was distributed to the collections of Hitler, G[ö]ring, and Dr. Führer." *Id.* Further, in a point that Germany still resists in litigation today:

> [T]he Nazis' aryanization of art collections was part of a larger scheme of the genocide of Europe's Jewish population.

Id. Not only that, the court found that the coercion in 1948 was also such a taking in violation of international law.

In addition, the court would have none of Austria's argument that Altmann should first have exhausted her remedies in Austria: "[T]his exhaustion requirement is excused when the domestic remedies are a sham, are inadequate, or would be unreasonably prolonged." *Id.* at

1203, *citing* Restatement (Third) of Foreign Relations Law, § 713, cmt. f (1986).

Having found that the allegations set forth a taking in violation of international law, Altmann still had to persuade the court that the claims were addressed to an agency or instrumentality of the state that was engaged in commercial activity. The former was not terribly complicated: The republic itself claimed ownership. With respect to commercial activity, critically the court made clear that the property did not have to have been used in the United States (although *Adele I* had been lent to an exhibition in America at least once and the Belvedere published books in the United States). The court rejected Austria's argument that "the property be present in the United States" because that language comes from § 1605(a)(1) (another exception to sovereign immunity not at issue in *Altmann*), not the expropriation exception. That construction means the physical presence requirement cannot be read into the latter, because it was considered and expressed in the former.

Next, the question of personal jurisdiction was raised, namely, whether it would satisfy constitutional due process for Austria to be required to defend itself. Here, the court found, the law suffices as a long-arm statute and a determination by Congress that meeting the statute is sufficient due process. That assumes that a foreign sovereign is a "person" entitled to due process, which was an unsettled question at the time. The *Altmann* District Court found the District Court for the District of Columbia's reasoning decisive on the question, and that they are not a "person" to which a due process analysis even applies. *Id.* at 1207, *citing Flatow v. Islamic Republic of Iran*, 999 F. Supp. 1, 19 (D.D.C. 1998).

The Austrian defendants also made a number of arguments concerning the addition of indispensable parties under Fed. R. Civ. P. 19, arguing that complete relief could not be afforded without other people not then part of the lawsuit. Even though the plaintiffs candidly claimed less than a 100% interest in the paintings, the court rejected these arguments as well. Acknowledging the existence of the Müller-Hoffmann claim to *Amalie Zuckerkandl*, the court concluded that those who believed they had an interest could join if they wished.

Finally, the court rejected Austria's argument that *forum non conveniens* compelled dismissal. Under the doctrine of *forum non conveniens*, a district court "may decline to exercise its jurisdiction, even though the court has jurisdiction and venue, when it appears that the convenience of the parties and the court and the interests of justice indicate that the action should be tried in another forum." *Piper Aircraft Co. v. Reyno*, 454 U.S. 235, 250, 102 S. Ct. 252, 70 L. Ed. 2d 419 (1981). That doctrine requires as a threshold the existence of an adequate alternative forum, without which there is nothing further to discuss. The *Altmann* court concluded that Austria did not provide an adequate forum. Both the likely assertion of the statute of limitations in Austria, and the extortionate filing fee, made Austria an inadequate forum.

The decision was a decisive shift, and one that few observers and commentators had given Altmann a chance to achieve. It was purely a jurisdictional decision, of course, but it held for the first time that a foreign sovereign in possession of art that was the subject of a claim of Nazi looting and duress would have to defend itself in a U.S. federal court. Austria appealed. While ordinarily an unsuccessful movant to dismiss must await a final judgment to appeal (*i.e.*, to lose the case), the FSIA allows such intermediate or interlocutory appeals. Austria fared no better in the U.S. Court of Appeals for the Ninth Circuit, however: "[I]f true, the facts alleged by Altmann establish a taking in violation of international law that confers jurisdiction upon our federal courts, and thus *Altmann* has presented a substantial and nonfrivolous claim." *Altmann v. Republic of Aus.*, 317 F.3d 954, 958 (9th Cir. 2002). In addition, "[b]ecause Appellants profit from the Klimt paintings in the United States, by authoring, promoting, and distributing books and other publications exploiting these very paintings, these actions are sufficient to constitute 'commercial activity' for the purpose of satisfying the FSIA, as well as the predicates for personal jurisdiction." *Id.* at 959.

First considering the extent to which the FSIA could be applied to claims that predated the Tate Letter, the Ninth Circuit focused on *Landgraf* and the extension of that logic in *Princz*. It also surveyed the considerable case law that had considered whether 1952 was the date on which the restrictive approach to sovereign immunity should begin. For example:

> Although the issuance of the 1952 Tate Letter has been recognized as the moment when "the American position changed

> and the 'restrictive theory of sovereign immunity' was adopted," for purposes of determining whether Austria could have settled expectations of immunity in a United States court, we note the observation of Judge Re, Chief Judge Emeritus of the Court of International Trade, that it was announced in 1948 that the State Department was reconsidering the policy. Edward D. Re, *Human Rights, Domestic Courts, and Effective Remedies*, 67 St. John's L. Rev. 581, 583–84 (1993).

Id. at 964. In the end, the Ninth Circuit looked to what it termed the Austrian government's legitimate expectation

> to receive immunity from the executive branch of the United States for its complicity in and perpetuation of the discriminatory expropriation of the Klimt paintings. Mindful that such seizures explicitly violated both Austria's and Germany's obligations under the Hague Convention (IV) on the Laws and Customs of War on Land, Oct. 18, 1907, 1 Bevans 631, 1907 U.S.T. LEXIS 29 (entered into force Jan. 26, 1910),[3] and that Austria's Second Republic officially repudiated all Nazi transactions in 1946, we hold that Austria could not expect such immunity.

Id. at 965. Dismissing Austria's protestations of comity, the Ninth Circuit held that "we are certain that the Austrians could not have had any expectation, much less a settled expectation, that the State Department would have recommended immunity as a matter of 'grace and comity' for the wrongful appropriation of Jewish property." *Id.* Both the Tate Letter and the 1949 State Department press release underscore that the cessation of armed conflict did not suddenly ally the Axis power with the United States. Thus, the application of the FSIA to Altmann's case infringed on no rights held at the time the act was issued (1976). Importantly, the Ninth Circuit distinguished *Jackson* and *Slade*, as well as *Carl Marks & Co. v. Union of Soviet Socialist Republics*, 841 F.2d 26 (2d Cir. 1988), because those cases involved contracts and the settled expectations at the time of the contract. *Altmann* was distinguishable because of Austria and/or Germany's expectations *at the time of the looting* were distinct from

Austria's expectations at either the time of the FSIA enactment or the time of suit.

Turning to the elements of the expropriation exception, the Ninth Circuit was forceful in its holding that the requirements had been met. "There is no question but that rights in property are in issue. The Austrian Republic and Gallery insist on Adele's will as the basis for their legal ownership of the Klimt paintings." *Id.* at 968. Because the Austrian museum had not paid Altmann or her family, there was no argument to be had about just compensation either.

Lastly, the Ninth Circuit agreed with the District Court's holding on commercial activity. "Authoring, editing, and publishing in the United States both a book entitled *Klimt's Women,* as well as an English-language guidebook, containing photographs of the looted paintings" was sufficient. *Id.* at 969. The touchstone of the commercial activity analysis under § 1605(a)(3) is not whether the Belvedere is a commercial, rather than sovereign, enterprise in Vienna; rather, it is whether the foregoing constitutes commercial activity by the instrumentality within the United States. To ask that question was to answer it in the affirmative. Indeed, the principal museum guidebook at the Belvedere featured *Adele Bloch-Bauer I* on its cover.

At this point Austria faced a choice: accept the Ninth Circuit holding and proceed to litigate the case, or seek review from the U.S. Supreme Court. While appeals from District Court judgments are the right of any litigant, and the FSIA gave Austria interlocutory review rights, appeals to the Supreme Court are entirely discretionary under writs of certiorari. The applicant must petition the Supreme Court to take the case and convince at least four justices that a split among Courts of Appeal or other important factors merits review by the highest court in the land. Austria did so, and the Supreme Court agreed to hear the case.

Even at this point, with two important and carefully reasoned holdings under their belt, Altmann and her legal team faced daunting odds and widespread skepticism regarding their chances. It must be said, however, no small amount of snobbery occurred in the legal community at the idea that they could prevail at the high court, a place of familiar faces and seasoned Supreme Court advocates. They were, as always, undeterred, and, in the end, they were victorious.

In 2004, the Supreme Court held that Altmann's interpretation of the FSIA to cover the events at issue was correct. The Supreme Court carefully circumscribed its ruling, however, and did not reach the deeper analysis of whether the Ninth Circuit's holding that Altmann's Complaint met the FSIA was correct. The high court's interest was in addressing the retroactivity question. First, it clarified that its own recent *Landgraf* decision was not controlling. *Landgraf* had set a test that:

> [I]f a federal law enacted after the events in suit does not expressly prescribe its own proper reach but does operate retroactively—*i.e.,* would impair rights a party possessed when he acted, increase his liability for past conduct, or impose new duties with respect to transactions already completed-it does not govern absent clear congressional intent favoring that result.

Altmann v. Republic of Austria, 541 U.S. 677, 678 (2004). The Court held that that test, however, did not answer the question posed by Altmann.

Instead, the Supreme Court reviewed a long history of sovereign immunity jurisprudence dating all the way back to Justice Marshall, citing *Schooner Exchange v. McFaddon,* 7 Cranch 116, 3 L.Ed. 287 (1812). As the high court noted, until 1952 it was the policy of the executive branch to request immunity for all "friendly" sovereigns. *Altmann*, 541 U.S. at 689. Interestingly, and in partial answer to the implicit question posed much later, "the change in State Department policy wrought by the 'Tate Letter' had little, if any, impact on federal courts' approach to immunity analyses: 'As in the past, initial responsibility for deciding questions of sovereign immunity fell primarily upon the Executive acting through the State Department,' and courts continued to 'abid[e] by' that Department's 'suggestions of immunity.' *Id.* at 690, *citing Verlinden B.V. v. Central Bank of Nigeria,* 461 U.S. 480, 486, 103 S.Ct. 1962, 76 L.Ed.2d 81 (1983).

Ultimately the challenge that the Supreme Court wrestled with actually had nothing to do with Altmann, Austria, or the Nazis:

> Under *Landgraf,* therefore, it is appropriate to ask whether the Act affects substantive rights (and thus would be impermissibly retroactive if applied to preenactment conduct) or addresses only matters

> of procedure (and thus may be applied to all pending cases regardless of when the underlying conduct occurred). But, the FSIA defies such categorization. To begin with, none of the three examples of retroactivity mentioned in the above quotation fits the FSIA's clarification of the law of sovereign immunity. Prior to 1976 foreign states had a justifiable expectation that, as a matter of comity, United States courts would grant them immunity for their public acts (provided the State Department did not recommend otherwise), but they had no "right" to such immunity. Moreover, the FSIA merely opens United States courts to plaintiffs with pre-existing claims against foreign states; the Act neither "increase[s those states'] liability for past conduct" nor "impose[s] new duties with respect to transactions already completed." 511 U.S., at 280, 114 S.Ct. 1483. Thus, the Act does not at first appear to "operate retroactively" within the meaning of the *Landgraf* default rule.

Id. at 694–95. Instead, "we think it more appropriate, absent contraindications, to defer to the most recent such decision—namely, the FSIA—than to presume that decision *inapplicable* merely because it postdates the conduct in question." *Id.* at 697 (emphasis in original).

That is the whole of the Supreme Court's holding. It did not consider, and therefore did not reach even in *dicta*, the application of the expropriation exception to Altmann's allegations. Nor did it take a position on the possible applicability—or inapplicability—of the Act of State doctrine. *Id.* at 700. Most notably, however, while noting the relevance of the State Department's views on *future* cases after the FSIA, the statute itself removed the centrality of that view. Put another way, the Tate Letter changed everything because, at the time, there was no FSIA, and the views of the executive branch of the federal government were paramount. The FSIA invested the judiciary with that determination, subject to weighing whatever persuasive argument the State Department could offer. However, the courts were not bound by those views, and as history will show, did not feel obligated to bow to them.

Chapter 5

Landscape with Smokestacks and Early Trends

With regard to claims for allegedly looted art, the bulk of early litigation concerned cases between private parties within the United States: heir against museum, museum against heir, and private person versus private person. Among the most difficult issues these many cases grappled with was the passage of time. As a historical matter, the topic of wartime looting was new and fresh; as a legal matter, it ran against neutral dictates of property law that did not fit neatly into the larger questions posed by the Washington Conference and the AAMD. The results have been frustrating from many angles.

One of the first disputes to end up in court concerned a Degas monotype, *Landscape with Smokestacks* (*Paysage avec Fumée des Cheminées*) (1890–93), which belonged at one time to the descendants of Bernhard Gutmann. Gutmann was the founder of the Dresdner Bank, a particular irony given the prominent role that the Dresdner Bank would later play in laundering plundered acquisitions from German Jews in the 1930s.[5] His grandson, Friedrich Bernhard Gutmann, went to London in 1912 to head the bank's London branch. He married Louise von Landau, and they had a son, named Bernard (dropping the German *h* for the more British spelling).

As World War I began, Louise and young Bernard were deported from England as enemy aliens. Friedrich was interned at a prison camp on the Isle of Man. When the war ended, he wished to go to back to Germany, but the family persuaded him to head to the Netherlands to oversee bank operations there. By the 1920s, in addition to acting as trustee for his father Eugen's art collection, Friedrich had begun to amass a notable collection of his own. He purchased *Apple Tree in Bloom* by Pierre-Auguste Renoir in 1928, and the Degas monotype from Paul Cassirer (see below) in 1932.

The 1930s treated Friedrich as grimly as one might expect. His banking ventures failed, and his diversified wealth and possessions were liquidated to provide him with the means to carry on. In April 1939, Friedrich sent the Degas *Smokestacks*, the Renoir, and other works of art to the Paul Graupe auction house in Paris. When the war began in 1939, Friedrich did not react or move, even expressing that he was not concerned. But, when the Netherlands were invaded and occupied in 1940, things turned worse quickly. It made no difference that Friedrich and his wife had converted to Christianity in England decades before; their ethnic heritage was all that mattered to the Germans. Friedrich was replaced with an administrator to run his business and the company Aryanized. While he remained in limbo, he managed to write a few letters to his daughter Lili, then living in Italy. He noted that he had sent some paintings to Graupe at Place Vendôme. Friedrich tried to leave Holland for Italy, and Lili received permission from the Italian government for her parents to live with her. She eventually got word that they had left the Netherlands, but they never arrived.

As it turned out, an SS officer had come to Friedrich and Louise's home and announced that he had their visas. They were taken to The Hague and put on a train bound for Berlin, where they were told they would change trains because there were no direct connections. They did change trains in Berlin, but their train went to Theresienstadt, not Italy. Once there, Friedrich was tortured for information about the location of the remainder of the art collection. Unsatisfied with the information he provided, the Nazis killed him on the spot. Louise was deported to Auschwitz shortly thereafter and murdered there. Lili survived, and she and Bernard (who further Anglicized his name to Goodman) filed claims with the Dutch government.

Like the majority of instances and families, the trail went cold with the exigencies of the war. Not until the mid-1990s did the Gutmann/Goodman family locate the Degas and make a claim. In 1987, in a private sale, Daniel Searle had acquired it from Emil Wolf, a collector in New York. The provenance that Searle's investigation had unearthed was as follows:

> Atelier Degas (Vente IV, July 2-4, 1919, no. 45, illustrated); Nunes et Fiquet, Paris;
> Collection of SS (Vente Galerie Georges Petit, Paris, June 9, 1932, no. 5);
> Lutjens Collection, Holland;
> Hans Wedland, Paris;
> Emile Wolf, New York (since 1951)

In December 1995, the heirs' attorney sent a letter to Searle. The letter laid out the claim to the family's superior title and demanded the work's return. An initial exchange between the parties' counsels focused on whether the work in Searle's possession was indeed the same as the Degas sent by Gutmann to Graupe. A letter in the hands of a Swiss art dealer, Walter Feilchenfeldt (whose father had been presented at the Cassirer auction in 1932), settled the question. The Lutjens on the Searle provenance had been Gutmann's agent. With that resolved, such as it was, it was clear that there was a dispute about who should get to keep the painting.

The parties could not reach an agreement, and the Goodmans sued Searle in New York, where he had acquired the work, with Lili and her nephews Nick and Simon (Bernard's sons) as plaintiffs. Well before *Portrait of Wally*, the case was big news because it was the first litigation in the new era of awareness (and since the publication of *The Rape of Europa* and *The Lost Museum*). In addition to print coverage from the *New York Times* and the *Los Angeles Times*, National Public Radio and *60 Minutes* covered the story.

Searle's first tactical move was to argue for the transfer of the case to the Northern District of Illinois, where he lived. Searle briefed a motion to dismiss, asserting a lack of personal jurisdiction over him in New York, improper venue, or, in the alternative, asking that the case be transferred to Chicago for administrative efficiency. While the argument for specific jurisdiction was reasonably strong (Searle had come to New York, investigated the title, and bought the painting there), the judge expressed a clear view at oral argument that the case did not belong in New York. As is often the case, without ruling, the court suggested strongly that the parties might not like the result; therefore the parties all agreed to the transfer.

Once in Chicago, the legal battle focused on several issues. First, which party ought to bear the burden of proof to establish title to *Smokestacks*? Searle had moved for summary judgment, arguing that there were no material facts in dispute about the sequence that would establish ownership. Lynn Nicholas was consulted as an expert to cast doubt on the idea that no trial was necessary. In addition, Searle argued that the family had delayed unreasonably in seeking to recover the painting, relying on the logic of *DeWeerth,* which was difficult, given the precedent of the *Lubell* case. In addition, Searle asserted that the postwar transfer of possession in Switzerland had passed title in good faith, and even if not, that it triggered the running of the statute of limitations such that the claim could no longer be brought.

Ultimately, the court denied the motion as marred by too many disputed facts and ordered the parties to prepare for trial. At this point, the parties reached a creative solution. They would agree that they each owned half the work. Searle would donate his half to the Art Institute of Chicago, and the Art Institute would purchase the Goodmans' half. The upshot would be that the work would end up at the museum, and the family would be compensated. It seemed a promising start to the new age; even though it had taken litigation to get there, the whole dispute had lasted barely two years and had ended with an agreement recognizing the difficult truth of the work's history.

Landscape with Smokestacks did not turn out to be the harbinger of negotiated resolutions, however. Instead, the era of pitched battles was about to begin.

Chapter 6

The Max Stern Estate

In 1913, a man named Julius Stern opened an art gallery in Düsseldorf. The Galerie Julius Stern, as it was named, specialized in Dutch and Flemish Old Masters, as well as German paintings. When Julius Stern died in 1934, he left the gallery to his son, Dr. Max Stern. By that time, of course, the official persecution of Jews was well under way. Beginning in 1935, Dr. Stern began receiving letters from the *Reichskammer der bildenden Künste* (the RBK). As discussed before, the RBK had broad supervisory authority over the arts industry. The RBK began demanding that Dr. Stern, as a Jew, liquidate the gallery and its inventory. Finally, the demands coalesced into a single and unambiguous directive. On August 29, 1935 (before the enactment of the Nuremberg Laws), the RBK forbade Dr. Stern from operating a gallery because he was a Jew and ordered him to close the gallery and liquidate its contents. Dr. Stern attempted to appeal this instruction but without success. On September 13, 1937, the RBK sent him a final order to comply immediately. He was given barely two months—until December 15, 1937—to comply.

In keeping with this instruction, Dr. Stern consigned the bulk of the gallery's inventory to the Kunsthaus Lempertz, an auction house in Cologne. Among the works in the November 13, 1937, sale entitled Die Bestände der Galerie Stern–Düsseldorf (the inventory of the Stern Gallery, Düsseldorf) was a painting by Francis Xavier Winterhalter known as *Mädchen aus den Sabiner Bergen* (*Girl from the Sabine Mountains*). After the sale, Dr. Stern fled Germany for Paris on December 23, 1937—the same day he was sent a letter from the RBK demanding proof of compliance with the liquidation order.

Dr. Stern eventually made his way to England where, unfortunately, he was interned as an enemy alien (a German) for a time after the outbreak of war. After being released, he emigrated to Canada, where he was again briefly interned. Eventually, he became a prominent Canadian art collector and the director of the Dominion Art Gallery in Montréal. When he died in 1987, he bequeathed his collection to the Dr. and Mrs. Max Stern Foundation.

Dr. Karl Wilharm acquired the Winterhalter painting at the Lempertz sale. According to the Stern estate's court filings, Wilharm was a physician who at some point was a high-ranking member of the Sturmabteilung (SA) and who joined the Nazi Party in 1932.[6] Wilharm was interned after the war by the Allies as a Category 1 offender. He later married a Baroness von Morsey Pickard, whose daughter by another marriage, Maria-Louise Bissonnette, eventually obtained the painting from either or both of them by putative inheritance.

Little of the foregoing history in the aftermath of the Lempertz sale was known to the Stern family until representatives of the estate learned in 2005 that the Winterhalter painting had been consigned for sale to a company called Estates Unlimited, an auction house in Rhode Island. Upon learning of the painting's whereabouts and intended sale, the estate sought help from the Holocaust Claims Processing Office (HCPO) in New York. The HCPO was created in 1997 as a division of the New York State Department of Financial Services. The HCPO describes itself on its website thusly:[7]

> [H]as advocated on behalf of Holocaust victims and their heirs, seeking the just and orderly return of assets to their original owners. In fulfilling this mission, the HCPO has facilitated the restitution of over $157 million in bank accounts, insurance policies, and other material losses and the resolution of cases involving more than 56 works of art.
>
> The HCPO works as a bridge between claimants and the various international compensation organizations and/or the current

holder(s) of the asset be it a bank account, insurance policy or artwork. Claimants pay no fee for the HCPO's services, nor does the HCPO take a percentage of the value of the assets recovered. Our goal is to advocate for claimants by helping to alleviate any cost and bureaucratic hardships they might encounter in trying to pursue claims on their own.

We provide institutional assistance to individuals seeking to recover:

1. Assets deposited in banks.
2. Monies that insurance companies failed to pay policy beneficiaries.
3. Artwork that was lost, stolen, or sold under duress between 1933 and 1945.

See http://www.dfs.ny.gov/consumer/holocaust/hcpoindex.htm. On behalf of the Stern estate, the HCPO sent a demand to Estates Unlimited on February 8, 2005, though still unaware of the painting's actual location. Bissonnette refused to relinquish the painting.

After a year or so of attempted negotiations, the Stern estate learned that the painting had been moved to Germany. On May 8, 2006, Robert Vineberg, as trustee of the Max Stern estate, brought suit against Bissonnette in her home state of Rhode Island, asserting a variety of common law claims for conversion, replevin, and fraudulent concealment (on the theory that the Wilharm and Bissonnette possessors had intentionally concealed the painting because they knew or should have known that it had been wrongfully obtained).

Bissonnette answered the Complaint and generally denied the Stern estate's theory of ownership. She asserted no Counterclaim for ownership, interestingly, but among her defenses claimed that Stern's prior litigation in Germany had settled the question of the extent of his losses as a result of persecution and that the estate was not permitted to relitigate that question.

After about a year, the Stern estate moved for summary judgment, arguing that no facts that bore on the legal questions of ownership were in dispute. In sum, the estate argued that the facts of persecution could not be disputed: (1) The Lempertz sale could not have conveyed title to any subsequent owners because no one could have purchased a painting at that auction believing in good faith that the owner intended to sell of his own free will; and (2) In any event, Wilharm and Bissonnette knew, subjectively, that the painting had been sold under duress.

As in any litigation, however, there was an intervening procedural development that undoubtedly influenced what would follow substantively. In this case, it was a major one. After an unsuccessful motion to dismiss by Bissonnette arguing that the claims did not amount to a legally recognizable injury even assuming the facts as alleged in the Complaint to be true, the Stern estate sought a preliminary injunction to require Bissonnette to confirm that the painting would be secured in its present location. In making this request, the Stern estate revealed that after the HCPO made a demand for the painting's return, Bissonnette had sent the painting to Germany. As unconventional as that would be in a case about ownership of that very painting, the application for a preliminary injunction divulged that Bissonnette had[47]

> sent the Painting to Düsseldorf, Germany – not Cologne – through the U.S. Postal Service, declaring its value to be the outrageously low figure of $50.00 for U.S. Customs purposes. (U.S. Postal Service, Customs Declaration and Dispatch Note, dated Sept. 15, 2005 (Kline Prelim. Inj. Decl. Ex. 2).) In contrast, Defendant informed this Court that the Painting's value was about $80,000.

Bissonnette promptly opposed the request for preliminary injunction. She argued that there was no real dispute over the painting's location, which the initial Complaint had alleged was already overseas, and that the disagreement was really over discovery logistics: where the painting would be viewed. Most notably, the opposition stated Bissonnette's lawyer's intention to seek to withdraw from the case. This is a most unusual thing to file; ordinarily, a lawyer may not withdraw from a case with a motion pending. In any event, her lawyer indeed moved to withdraw just four days later—with the preliminary injunction request still pending. Shortly thereafter, the U.S. District Court for Rhode Island allowed the motion for preliminary injunction, ordered Bissonnette to permit inspection of the painting, and restrained her from moving the painting from its current location in the United States without the court's permission.

This was an extremely shrewd tactic by the Stern estate's attorneys. The painting was the subject of the lawsuit already, and had Bissonnette sold it during the pendency of the case, it would not have affected her potential liability. It would obviously prevent her from physically returning the painting, but the subsequent possessor would not have been able to acquire good title in any event. Moreover, even if the painting were out of reach but the estate were deemed to be the owner, then Bissonnette would be liable to the estate for its value. However, the larger point is that the disagreement over the painting's location and accessibility caught Bissonnette unprepared. The disarray that was presented to the court was, in one sense, an impression that could not be undone, particularly about the misstatement of value, which compromised her credibility, likely for good.

The Stern estate quickly seized the initiative and moved for summary judgment. First, the estate argued that there were no facts relevant to the determination of ownership that were in dispute. The dictates of the RBK left no doubt, it argued, that the conveyance in the Lempertz auction was coercive, submitting historical and legal affidavits attesting to that conclusion. As a result, no subsequent possessor—whether it was Wilharm or Bissonnette—could have obtained good title. Lastly, the Stern estate argued that the claims were timely either under German law or under the forum statute of limitations, because, even assuming Bissonnette's good faith acquisition from her stepfather (a presumption to which she is entitled in considering a motion for summary judgment), the nature of her possession only changed in 2005 when the Stern estate unconditionally demanded the return of the painting and Bissonnette refused. Having brought suit well within three years of that demand and refusal, the estate argued, the claim was timely and ripe for adjudication.

Similarly, the estate argued that Bissonnette could demonstrate none of the prejudice required to assert laches, because Stern had diligently sought the painting but could not have known where it was. Even if he had, laches will only lie if the possessor is harmed by some acquiescence; so, even if Stern knew that Bissonnette had it, the dispute came to a head immediately upon her efforts to sell it. By contrasting example, laches is more viable when the personal property is in a known location and the rightful owner does nothing when the work is transferred. There were no disputes of fact to make out such a theory, the estate argued.

Bissonnette argued in response that the laches defense was indeed a dispute of fact that was premature for resolution at summary judgment, in large part based on the argument that the Stern estate was not sufficiently diligent in searching for its property. She identified the prejudice she believed to have suffered from what she characterized as the Stern estate's supposed inaction as becoming "embroiled in a protracted litigation in federal court and having her family's name disparaged in the process"[48] and she would otherwise have sold the painting. This assertion is nonsensical; if the painting were stolen, no one could be disparaged by being revealed to be in possession of such stolen property (particularly if the family were actually involved in the illicit acquisition). Being involved in litigation is not a recognizable burden if there is a genuine dispute about the ownership. This too fails to persuade. It effectively argues that she was prejudiced in her inability to sell stolen property. Happily, for the Stern estate the law does not recognize that as a real burden.

The court allowed the Stern estate's motion. In the absence of a coherent opposition, there were no facts to adjudicate about the Lempertz auction and the effectiveness of any transfer of title by Dr. Stern. Bissonnette made no arguments at all to suggest there were any disputes of fact about the initial transfer. That allowed the court to make an important holding about sales in the 1930s. First and foremost, the court cited the rarity of Holocaust restitution claims—only ten were filed between 1945 and 1995—but without holding it against the Stern estate. *See* Benjamin E. Pollack, 43 Hous. L. Rev. at 208. That implicit acknowledgment that a new era had arrived remains an important holding.

As to the substantive questions, the court found that the undisputed facts compelled the conclusion that Dr. Stern was still the owner of the Winterhalter when he died (and thus his estate would now be the owner). As to the sale, the court held that the Lempertz auction sales "are properly classified as looting or stealing." *Vineberg v. Bissonnette*, 529 F. Supp. 2d 300, 307 (D.R.I 2007). The court found that Bissonnette had acquired a stolen painting through no fault of her own, but that Wilharm could not have and did not acquire title before her.

The court disagreed sharply with Bissonnette's argument that both Dr. Stern and the estate had not been diligent. The decision lists the numerous attempts, beginning right after the war, which Dr. Stern and the estate made to find the painting over the intervening decades. Nor did the court have any patience for the idea that Bissonnette had been prejudiced. The court expressly rejected the notion that the mere fact of having to litigate a property claim is prejudice within the meaning of a laches defense. The idea that her inability to sell the painting because of the Stern estate's claim failed to persuade the court also.

> The only prejudice alleged by [Defendant] is [her] inability to sell [the property] due to the pending lawsuit. This allegation simply does not rise to the level of material prejudice [in order to invoke the defense of laches]. *Junkins v. Spinnaker Bay Condominium Assoc.*, No. OT-01-007, 2002 WL 337780, at *12 (Ohio Ct. App. March 1, 2002).

Id. at 311. The court entered judgment for the Stern estate, confirming its ownership and ordering Bissonnette to turn over the painting.

Bissonnette appealed to the First Circuit Court of Appeals. The appellate court affirmed the judgment of the trial court. *Vineberg v. Bissonnette*, 548 F.3d 50 (1st Cir. 2008). The First Circuit repeated the factual history of Dr. Stern's persecution, since it was not contested by Bissonnette in the trial court. The decision focuses largely on Bissonnette's laches defense under Rhode Island law. The First Circuit observed uncontroversially that laches is an affirmative defense; to rely on it at summary judgment, Bissonnette would have had to identify facts in dispute that, taken in the light most favorable to her, could have supported the defense at trial. *Id.* at 56–57. The appeals court found two deficiencies in the assertion of laches. First, the Court of Appeals held that the Stern estate and Dr. Stern had diligently pursued the painting before filing suit. Second, the Court of Appeals rejected Bissonnette's assertion of prejudice emphatically:

> Typically, the kind of prejudice that will support a laches defense arises out of a loss of evidence, the unavailability of important witnesses, the conveyance of the property in dispute for fair market value to a bona fide purchaser, or the expenditure of resources in reliance upon the status quo ante.

Id. at 58–59. Summing up in view of that standard, the First Circuit pointed out that Bissonnette had not specified any kind of evidence or testimony that would have created a factual dispute required to make that showing. In words that might have provided a guidepost for future courts, the opinion stated:

> A de facto confiscation of a work of art that arose out of a notorious exercise of man's inhumanity to man now ends with the righting of that wrong through the mundane application of common law principles. The mills of justice grind slowly, but they grind exceedingly fine.

Id. at 58–59.

PART THREE

Out of Time?

Chapter 7

Bakalar and the Defense of Laches

The facts underlying claims for Nazi-looted art are decades old. While historians and heirs renewed their interest in the stories of looted art in the 1990s in particular, that alone did not answer the question of whether the age of the claims would be something for which the U.S. legal system could (or should) make an exception to its typical rules about the deadlines for filing claims. Statutes of limitations vary by state, but claims for property are subject to approximately three-year limitations. The occasions when those deadlines can be extended (or delayed from beginning) have been the subject of many of the cases to be litigated in the United States. The question is, even when the deadlines have not expired, are there, or should there be, other mechanisms to draw some limits around such claims in the interests of fairness to the current possessors? For the most part, claimants have generally struggled to avoid these limitations.

One of the first cases to address limitations periods on allegations of looted art is also one of the few ever to go to trial, and it occurred twice. In 2012, the U.S. Court of Appeals for the Second Circuit affirmed the judgment in favor of plaintiff David Bakalar concerning ownership of the drawing *Seated Woman with Bent Left Leg* (*Torso*) by Egon Schiele, ending a long battle. It was a notable decision because it affirmed the U.S. District Court for the Southern District of New York's ruling on the merits of whether the drawing was stolen by the Nazis from the Austrian-Jewish collector Fritz Grünbaum. The finding was that it was not stolen. Such a ruling on the merits of the allegation of theft is a rarity among wartime restitution cases. Ironically, even though the court ruled that that the current owner could not prove good title, the current owner still prevailed by arguing successfully that the plaintiff's inaction had prejudiced him.

Fritz Grünbaum owned the 1917 work prior to the start of World War II. In 1938, Franz Kieslinger, a Nazi art appraiser, inventoried Grünbaum's collection pursuant to the then-recent property declaration law and forms. The District Court never determined, however, whether the drawing at issue was still a part of Grünbaum's collection at the time of the inventory (it did not appear to be). In 1938, Grünbaum was arrested and imprisoned at Dachau. There, he signed a power of attorney in favor of his wife, Elisabeth. Fritz died in Dachau in 1941, and Elisabeth was later interned and died in another concentration camp. The court found that the drawing was eventually sold to the Galerie Gutekunst in 1956 by Mathilde Lukacs, which later that same year sold it to the Galerie St. Etienne.

Bakalar was the current possessor of the Schiele drawing, having purchased it in 1963 from the Galerie St. Etienne in New York. According to Bakalar, Otto Kallir—whose name is at the intersection of more than one case in this area—advised Bakalar that the drawing had come from Galerie Gutekunst and Klipstein in Switzerland. After the purchase from Galerie St. Etienne, the drawing stayed in his possession, which was revealed in the 1990 catalogue raisonné by Jane Kallir, Otto's granddaughter and successor director of Galerie St. Etienne.

In August 2004, Bakalar consigned the drawing to Sotheby's to be sold at auction. The prior ownership by Fritz Grünbaum caused Sotheby's to contact Bertha Salomon-Herzl. According to Bakalar's later Complaint, Salomon-Herzl said she had no claim to the work, and the auction went forward. The drawing was sold on to an unnamed buyer for $675,000 on February 8, 2005.

After the auction, Gabriel Lansky, a Viennese lawyer, wrote to Sotheby's and claimed that Leon Fischer and Miloš Vávra were the drawing's true owners. Miloš Vávra is the nephew of Fritz Grünbaum's niece (Fritz's sister Elise Zozuli's daughter). Zozuli lived in Czechoslovakia after the war, and, according to the court, made various efforts to obtain the return of Grünbaum property. Leon Fischer is a relation of Elisabeth Grünbaum, Fritz's wife. Elisabeth was survived by four siblings, one of whom (Max Herzl) survived the war but died in 1946. Leon Fischer is his grandson, daughter of Rene Herzl.

Lansky's letter to Sotheby's included a number of documents, including documents asserted to show that Vávra and Fischer were heirs of Grünbaum, and a document that the Complaint attached (the *Verzeichnis über das Vermögen von Juden* [Inventory of the Property of Jews]), which was the notorious list that Jews were required to submit of their assets pursuant to the April 1938 law. Lansky thus disputed that title had ever validly passed to Lukacs or later to Bakalar. The Verzeichnis, whose authenticity Bakalar did not contest in his Complaint, makes no reference to the drawing.

Sotheby's eventually responded that it had reviewed the claim and stood by its original conclusion that Bakalar had marketable title to sell. Out of an abundance of caution, however, Sotheby's notified the successful bidder of the claim, and the bidder rescinded the sale.

In view of this, Bakalar seized the initiative and filed suit against Fischer and Vávra, notwithstanding that he (Bakalar) still had the painting. He asserted three claims: (1) a declaratory judgment that he had acquired good title in 1963; (2) slander of title disparaging his ownership; and (3) interference with contractual relations with regard to Bakalar's inability to sell the drawing because of the threatened litigation. In particular, Bakalar argued that laches applied to bar any claim of title by Vávra and Fischer. In layman's terms, laches is the equivalent of sitting on your hands and failing to enforce your rights in a way that prejudices your opponent.

Not surprisingly, Vávra and Fischer told a different story in their Answer and Counterclaims, and attached many of the documents referenced. The first is the *Verzeichnis* itself, a printed form. Grünbaum identifies himself as an actor and author in his own handwriting. The person completing the form is required to identify any life insurance that he or she has. Fritz and

Elizabeth signed the form, dated August 7, 1938. The April 27, 1938, date referenced in the Complaint is in fact the prospective date of the printed form itself.

The Kieslinger appraisal was also attached to the Counterclaims. It identifies five works by Schiele, but even acknowledging that the list consists of Kieslinger's descriptions, not necessarily the actual titles, none seem to be the drawing. They are (1) a "self-portrait," oil on canvas; (2) a portrait of a woman, oil on canvas; (3) "City on a River"; (4) "Small Landscape with Trees"; and (5) "Ships at Harbor." It is depressingly clinical and methodical. The Counterclaims argued that either items 37 and 37a, a reference to color drawings, or other mentions of Schiele sketches and etchings were meant to refer to the drawing at issue.

Particularly disturbing is the power of attorney that Fritz signed, which was filed as an exhibit to the Counterclaims. It begins by identifying Grünbaum as: "Franz Friedrich (known as Fritz) Grünbaum, Actor in the 4th District, Vienna, Wienzeile 29," and then, as though it were an unremarkable detail of his whereabouts, "*currently Dachau*." It goes on to name Elizabeth as his attorney in fact with the power to effect any and all property transactions. Curiously, despite the notation of his presence in Dachau, it is notarized in Vienna. It is dated July 16, 1938.

Elizabeth later put works into storage with a shipping company (Schenker), after which she was deported to a Nazi camp and murdered on October 5, 1942. Vávra and Fischer argued that the Grünbaum property was stolen by Schenker employees and sold in Switzerland after the war.

The defendants and/or counterclaimants asserted pointedly from all this that the drawing, along with Grünbaum's art collection, had been expropriated. Critically, Vávra and Fischer disputed Bakalar's allegations that the chain of title had passed in good faith; rather, they alleged that the Kallirs and other intervening owners knew that the drawing was stolen.

Various correspondences in the 1950s referred to the "Brussels sister," taken to be Mathilde Lukacs—Elisabeth's last surviving sibling—after which Zozuli made reference to the matter being settled. Later letters from Galerie Kornfeld in Bern—remember that name—claimed that Lukacs had approached the Swiss gallery with the works, but not until the 1990s did Galerie Kornfeld realize that they had once belonged to Grünbaum.

The case was eventually tried in 2008. On a critical point, the court found that Swiss law, not New York law, applied to the question of title in Bakalar's chain of title. Bakalar's attorney put the question thusly in his letter[49] to the District Court on May 6, 2008:

> New York's choice of law rules, grounded in comity, direct the Court to the law of the place where the allegedly stolen Drawing was sold or transferred to a third party. New York recognizes that foreign jurisdiction, unlike New York, may recognize good faith acquisitions of even stolen property, thereby clearing title for future transactions that take place in New York.[49]

Under New York's choice of law rules, "choice of law dictates that questions relating to the validity of a transfer of personal property are governed by the law of the state where the property is located at the time of the transfer." *Kunstsammlungen zu Weimar v. Elicofon*, 536 F. Supp. 829, 845-46 (E.D.N.Y.). Bakalar's experts in Swiss law presented evidence that Swiss law presumes good faith by the purchaser and places the burden on the former owner to disprove good faith. Thus, he argued, Kornfeld acquired good title to the painting when he acquired it from Lukacs; this was the transfer in question under the choice of law analysis, not the allegation of the confiscatory taking from Grünbaum. Put another way, assuming that the drawing was stolen from Grünbaum, Kornfeld acquired good title that he was then free to pass on to others, eventually Bakalar.

The court agreed on May 30, 2008. *Bakalar v. Vávra*, 2008 WL 4067335, No. 05 Civ. 3037 (WHP) (Sep. 3, 2008). In addition, the court accepted Bakalar's argument that the concern over endorsing the title of a Nazi-looted work offended New York's public policy. "Even where a plaintiff has claimed the application of foreign law according to choice of law principles would impede the return of art that had been stolen by the Nazis, New York's public interest in protecting original owners has not been considered more important than applying law." *See also Warin v. Wildenstein & Co., Inc.*, 2001 WL 1117493, 2001 N.Y. Slip Op. 40127

(N.Y. Sup. Ct. Sep. 4, 2001). The court found that Swiss law applied to the defense of laches.

Under this ruling, the parties tried the case to the court in the summer of 2008. The court found[50] that Bakalar had good title to the drawing:

> Under Swiss due diligence standards, a purchaser of an object has no general duty to inquire about a seller's authority to sell the object, or to inquire about the object's origins, unless suspicious circumstances exist... (1) the seller offers to sell the object well below its market value, (2) the seller has a notoriously bad reputation, (3) the seller tries to sell the object unusually quickly, (4) there are marks on the object indicating the likelihood of another owner, or (5) the seller makes unusual demands for cash.

The relationship between Kornfeld and Lukacs, the court found, did not fail any of these indicia of stolen property. Lukacs's explanation that the works came from an Austrian family—where she herself was from—struck the court as plausible and not suspicious. From there, the result[51] was that:

> [b]ecause Kornfeld purchased the painting in good faith, he acquired good title to it and had the authority to pass that title to Galerie St. Etienne. Thus, when Bakalar acquired the painting in good faith for value in 1963, title to the Drawing validly passed to him and he gained ownership to it with all accompanying property rights.

Because the court found that Bakalar's title was good, it did not reach the question of laches, because it did not have to.

The defendants appealed. The U.S. Court of Appeals for the Second Circuit vacated the judgment and remanded the case for a new trial. Writing for a unanimous panel, the Honorable Edward R. Korman held that:

> The problem with the traditional situs rule, upon which Judge Mishler relied in part and upon which the district judge here relied exclusively, is that it no longer accurately reflects the current choice

> of law rule in New York regarding personal property.... The interest analysis, which generally applies in all choice-of-law contexts, *see Istim*, 78 N.Y.2d at 347, 575 N.Y.S.2d 796, 581 N.E.2d 1042, begins with an examination of the contacts each jurisdiction has with the event giving rise to the cause of action. *See Karaha Bodas*, 313 F.3d at 85. "Once these contacts are discovered and analyzed they will indicate (1) that there exists no true conflict of laws...as in most choice of law cases, or (2) that a true conflict exists, i.e., both jurisdictions have an interest in the application of their law." *In re Crichton's Estate*, 20 N.Y.2d at 135 n. 8, 281 N.Y.S.2d 811, 228 N.E.2d 799. "In property disputes, if a conflict is identified, New York choice of law rules require the application of an 'interests analysis,' in which 'the law of the jurisdiction having the greatest interest in the litigation [is] applied and...the facts or contacts which obtain significance in defining State interests are those which relate to the purpose of the particular law in conflict.'"

Bakalar v. Vávra, 618 F.3d 136, 143-44 (2010). Under this analysis, the Second Circuit concluded that New York's interests were stronger:

> Judge Mishler's analysis of the compelling New York interest to "preserve the integrity of transactions and prevent the state from becoming a marketplace for stolen goods," which preceded the clear articulation of this interest by the Court of Appeals in Lubell, is relevant here. However the Drawing came into the possession of the Swiss art gallery, New York has a compelling interest in the application of its law.

Id. at 144. The court viewed the question prospectively: "The application of New York law may cause New York purchasers of artwork to take greater care in assuring themselves of the legitimate provenance of their purchase." *Id.* at 145. Judge Korman took the occasion to write a separate concurrence—reciting cases from *Menzel* to *Vineberg v. Bissonnette*, 548 F.3d 50 (1st Cir. 2008)—regarding the presumption of coerciveness under similar circumstances: "the power of attorney Grünbaum signed in the fourth month of his confinement in Dachau does not appear to be any more voluntary a relinquishment of his legal interest in the Drawing than the acts discussed in *Vineberg* and *Menzel*." *Id.* at 150.

On the remand, Vávra and Fischer asked to reopen expert discovery, but the District Court denied the request. Bakalar renewed his motion for declaratory judgment on the existing record, and the court accepted further briefing but did not hold a second trial.

In its August 17, 2011, decision, the District Court found that the most reasonable inference from the fact that the drawing was in Grünbaum's possession before his arrest in 1938, and later with Lukacs in 1956, was that the drawing remained in the family's possession the entire time. The alternative (the drawing was looted but returned to his sister-in-law) seemed implausible. The mere fact that the collection was inventoried was almost certainly a prelude to stealing it; however, there was no evidence that the confiscation ever took place. In sum, the court found that the drawing was not looted by the Nazis. *Bakalar v. Vávra*, 819 F. Supp. 2d 293, 299-300 (S.D.N.Y. 2011). The opinion also addressed Judge Korman's observations about the power of attorney, sidestepping the question of the validity of that authority to conclude that there was no evidence that the drawing had ever been transferred pursuant to it. *Id.* at 300-01.

Next, the court addressed the argument that even if not stolen, Lukacs did not hold good title. Bakalar responded to that argument by suggesting that the most logical explanation was that Lukacs obtained the work as a gift. The defendants (relying on a passing observation from the Court of Appeals during the first appeal) suggested that no one could have made a gift of the painting because the power of attorney that Grünbaum signed in Dachau was made under duress and therefore void (and, therefore, any disposition thereafter by anyone other than Grünbaum was ineffective). The District Court rejected this argument, pointing out that earlier cases cited for that proposition were ones in which the collector had "sold" the painting to the Nazis, a forced sale that was later voided. The District Court did hold, though, that however plausible the notion that Lukacs had received the drawing as a gift, there was no evidence at all of how she got it or a sufficient legal argument that she would have come to it as an heir under Austrian law. As the party bearing the burden of proof, Bakalar failed, in the court's view, to prove that Lukacs ever acquired good title to the drawing.

Yet, Bakalar won the case on the defense of laches. The District Court went through the history of the Vávra and the Fischer families' awareness of the drawing and their failure to seek to claim it. The lack of any documented efforts to find or claim the work while it changed hands ultimately prejudiced Bakalar enough, the District Court held, so that his defense carried the day and he won the trial. Since this was not a preliminary determination but a trial, the court was charged with actually addressing and ruling on the competing facts. That is significant because it requires more deferential review by the Second Circuit, and without evidence of clear error by the District Court (as opposed to a re-weighing of the evidence), the Second Circuit had little difficulty in upholding the result.

Vávra and Fischer appealed again, but the Second Circuit affirmed this time. In a far more cursory opinion, the Second Circuit dismissed the challenge as a matter of fact to the conclusion that the drawing was not stolen and rejected the defendants' arguments that they should have been entitled to more discovery.

This is one of the very few restitution claims that has made it to trial—twice—yet the claimant came away empty-handed again. Although there was a ruling on the merits about whether the work was stolen, the outcome actually makes sense. As the court noted, it is hard to imagine a scenario where the drawing could have been looted but still end up back in the same family that was part of the persecuted minority. In addition, despite the objections that are often raised to laches as a defense, perhaps the simplest explanation really is correct: The family never sought to get the drawing back because it was sold by the person who had the right to do so (Lukacs).

Chapter 8

California Legislative Amendments and the Legacy of Jacques Goudstikker

In the midst of the cases on the East Coast, two private ownership disputes related to California began that have had consequences on claims both foreign and domestic. The first involved the fate of the renowned collection of Jacques Goudstikker, probably the most successful interwar art dealer in the Netherlands. Goudstikker was born in 1897 and named after his grandfather Jacob Goudstikker. Jacob founded the J. Goudstikker Gallery plc in 1845, which focused on decorative arts and furniture. Jacques's father, Eduard, took over the business just before the turn of the century and branched out into Dutch and Flemish Masters of the seventeenth century. Jacques studied art history and became a specialist in Old Masters. Not only did he establish expertise in the art of the Low Countries, but as a dealer, he also bought Italian, German, and French works of the fifteenth and sixteenth centuries. With some later irony given the *Cassirer* case discussed further on, he acted as a personal advisor to Baron Hans Heinrich Thyssen-Bornemisza, among others. As the 1920s came to a close, Goudstikker demonstrated the depth of his formidable skill and scholarship by sponsoring an exhibition of modern Dutch painters, including Vincent van Gogh, Kees van Dongen, and Piet Mondrian, at a time when they were far from the household names that they are today (even van Gogh). Indeed, Goudstikker's endorsement enjoys responsibility in some part for those painters' roles in the pantheon today. By the early 1930s, he was established, successful, and famous, and his ethnicity as a Jew was of little consequence in his civic and economic life.

In 1937, he met Desirée von Halban-Kurz (Desi) at a party he hosted at his castle. She was an opera singer at the Vienna State Opera and the daughter of Selma Kurz, once the object of Gustav Mahler's romantic attention. Jacques courted her and urged her to come to the Netherlands instead of the increasingly unsettled Austria. They married later that year.

Goudstikker observed the ominous developments in Europe and had the foresight to apply for American visas. He booked passage for himself and sent about twenty paintings ahead on the *Simon Bolivar,* which struck a German mine and sunk with 100 fatalities and the last trace of those paintings. The Goudstikkers had still not left when the Wehrmacht invaded on May 10, 1940. On May 14, Goudstikker gathered his staff to his office. He also told his wife to pack. He hastily drove to Amsterdam, where he met with employees Jan Dik Sr. and Jr. He instructed the Diks to take care of the collection and left some 1,400 works of art with them for safekeeping.

Jacques and Desi were able to get aboard the *SS Bodegraven,* one of the last ships to leave the occupied Netherlands. The ship docked in Dover, England, but no one was permitted to disembark. As with the infamous *St. Louis,* the ship began a tragic odyssey from there, heading first to South America. Jacques Goudstikker never made it there, however. On May 16, less than a week after making the agonizing decision to leave his home country, he went out to the deck in the evening to smoke a cigarette. When he did not return, Desi sounded the alarm and a search ensued. His body was found at the bottom of a deck hatch; he had fallen down in the darkness and broken his neck. A sailor was injured looking for him, and the ship docked in Falmouth, England, to allow the sailor to go to the hospital. Desi was able to arrange for Jacques's burial there, but she and their son Eduard were not allowed to stay. The ship then headed for Liverpool, and they were allowed to get out. After obtaining a visa with the assistance of friends, they traveled to the United States via Canada.

Just a few weeks after all this, Goudstikker's gallery had been taken over by none other than Hermann Goering and Alois Miedl. Miedl was a Munich-born banker who had lived in the Netherlands for some time. Goering and Miedl hatched a plot that underscores the complexities of the inter-Party rivalries among even high-level Nazis. Had they simply liquidated the Goudstikker gallery business, the collection would have come under the jurisdiction of Arthur Seyss-Inquart, the Reichskommissar für die besetzten niederländischen Gebiete (Reich Commissioner for the occupied Dutch territories), over whom Goering had no direct control, even as *Reichsmarschall*. Instead, Goering used Miedl as an agent for the business, even after Goudstikker had fled. Miedl paid Max Model to make an introduction to Jan Dik. In a paradigmatic example of the Nazis' and Goering's desires to cloak their thefts in legitimacy, Miedl actually held a series of ostensible board meetings that also included Goudstikker's mother, who was now in mortal danger as a Jew. Before the end of the month, Miedl's attorney was promoted to president of the gallery. Amazingly, Desi was able to keep apprised of this and even sent a telegram objecting in the strongest possible terms to this takeover. Dik and Miedl's attorney (the titular president) spread rumors that the gallery was on the brink of insolvency, for which they were paid some 210,000 guilders (from Goudstikker's bank account no less).

With control of the still-extant Dutch company in hand, Goering and Miedl purchased the gallery outright for 2,550,000 guilders. Goering took possession of Goudstikker's art inventory for the fictional share of 2,000,000 guilders, and Miedl took the real estate for the supposed consideration of 550,000 guilders. This was the masterstroke Goering had been waiting for. He had 780 works of art crated and sent to Germany, particularly Dutch Baroque paintings. Some 300 of the most valuable soon ended up in his estate, Karinhall, in particular works by Frans Hals, Salomon van Ruysdael, Pieter de Hooch, and Rembrandt.

In the United States, Jacques's son Eduard Goudstikker married a woman named Marei von Saher-Langenbein, who became Jacques's sole heir when both Marei's mother-in-law and husband died. Earlier, in 1946, Desi had returned to the Netherlands to seek compensation for her lost property. She had the now-famous book in which Jacques had recorded the most significant works in his collection; he documented 1,241 works in 165 small, typed pages. In a horrid irony, Goudstikker plc was now in the hands of the Dutch state as an enemy enterprise, because Goering and Miedl were the record owners. Goering was in jail awaiting the Nuremberg trials. It was revealed at Goering's trial that the painting *Christ with the Adulteress* attributed to Vermeer was actually a forgery by Han van Meegeren—a revelation at the Nuremberg trials that was the only testimony to prompt a reaction from Goering despite the litany of his other murderous deeds. Miedl had fled to Fascist Spain, where he lived the rest of his life in relative comfort, supported in considerable part by the art he had stolen from Jews in the Netherlands.

Desi filed suit in the Netherlands against the Dutch government and litigated for several years. In 1952, she reached a settlement, under which she received the supposed purchase price paid during the Goering and Miedl's 1940 confiscation. She repurchased her own real estate with this money, as well as the gallery stock, which still included 165 pictures. Desi had remarried in 1950, and she and her son Eduard took Desi's new husband's surname: Von Saher. Not until 1997 did the Netherlands acknowledge its role in this compounded injustice, but when Marei von Saher formally filed a claim to the same effect, she was rebuffed and told that her family had relinquished its claims in 1952. Against all odds, however, the government set up a new restitution-related commission following the Washington Conference.

While all of this was going on, a pair of important paintings from the Goudstikker gallery were already in the United States: *Adam* and *Eve* by Lucas Cranach the Elder. Goudstikker had purchased the works at auction in Berlin in 1931. After the war, the paintings (and others in Goering's possession) were sent first to the Allied Collecting Point and then to the government of the Netherlands, following standard Allied procedure. The Cranachs were restituted not to Desi Goudstikker/Von Saher but to George Stroganoff. As it turned out, Stroganoff claimed that the paintings had been taken from him by the Soviet Union. It is rarely remembered today, but in an effort to raise foreign currency that the Soviet command economy could not provide, the Soviet Union conducted several high-profile fire sales of expropriated bourgeois art at Berlin galleries just before the Nazis' rise to power. This tactic, of course, was later repeated during the 1937 Degenerate Art Action run by the Nazis, when modern works were taken out of German museums and sold. Stroganoff eventually sold the Cranachs in 1971 to the Norton Simon Art Foundation, and they went from there to the well-known museum of the same name. They remain there today.

In the meantime, in 2002, the California legislature had taken up the issue of Holocaust restitution and amended its statute of limitations. Cal. Code Civ. Prod. § 354.3 read in relevant part:

> (b) Notwithstanding any other provision of law, any owner, or heir or beneficiary of an owner, of Holocaust-era artwork, may bring an action to recover Holocaust-era artwork from any entity described in paragraph (1) of subdivision (a). Subject to Section 410.10, that action may be brought in a superior court of this state, which court shall have jurisdiction over that action until its completion or resolution. Section 361 does not apply to this section.
>
> (c) Any action brought under this section shall not be dismissed for failure to comply with the applicable statute of limitation, if the action is commenced on or before December 31, 2010.

With this in mind, von Saher sued the Norton Simon Museum, unburdened by any statute of limitations. There were no jurisdictional questions to resolve; the case was a state law claim brought in the district where the Norton Simon is located. Nonetheless, the museum moved to dismiss, arguing that the amendment of § 354.3 (above) was unconstitutional as an impermissible intrusion into the foreign affairs of the United States and thus barred by preemption. The District Court agreed and dismissed the case. *Von Saher v. Norton Simon Museum of Art,*

Case No. CV 07-2866-JFW (JTLx), 2007 U.S. Dist. LEXIS 95757, at * 7–8 (C.D. Cal. Oct. 19, 2007).

The initial opinion was brief and adopted the Norton Simon's view of preemption as applied to the law, particularly given another similar abolition of the statute of limitations as it related to slave labor (§ 354.6) held unconstitutional in *Deutsch v. Turner Corp.*, 324 F.3d 692 (9th Cir. 2003):

> As with Section 354.6, by enacting Section 354.3, "California seeks to redress wrongs committed in the course of the Second World War"—a legislative act which "intrudes on the federal government's exclusive power to make and resolve war, including the procedure for resolving war claims." *Id.* at 712. There can be no doubt that, as Judge Reinhardt stated in *Deutsch*, the Holocaust was "the most atrocious act ever perpetrated by a civilized (or uncivilized) people" and "represents the worst historic manifestation of the perpetual human condition known as anti-Semitism." There are no words which can adequately describe the atrocities suffered by the victims of the Holocaust, and the harms suffered continue to have an effect on the victims and their descendants. For that reason, the Court shares the Ninth Circuit's reluctance in finding unconstitutional a statute which attempts to provide at least some measure of redress to those victims and their families. However, the Court is not only compelled to apply the foreign affairs doctrine, it is bound by the interpretation of that doctrine as set forth by the Ninth Circuit in *Deutsch.*

Von Saher, 2007 U.S. Dist. LEXIS 95757, at * 8–9. With § 354.3 struck down, the question was whether von Saher had brought her claim in time. Because von Saher inherited her claims in 1996, and the museum had had the works since 1971, the court concluded that the claims were time-barred and dismissed the case. *Id.* at 10.

Von Saher appealed to the U.S. Court of Appeals for the Ninth Circuit. As the Ninth Circuit noted, the Supreme Court has consistently voided state laws when they conflict with federal action such as a treaty, federal statute, or explicit executive branch policy. *Von Saher v. Norton Simon Museum of Art,* 578 F.3d 1016, 1020 (9th Cir. 2009), *citing Am. Ins. Assoc.*

v. Garamendi, 539 U.S. 396, 413–14 (2003) (invalidating California's attempt to regulate insurance claims for Holocaust victims by requiring any insurer doing business in California to disclose information about all policies sold in Europe between 1920 and 1945).

The Ninth Circuit first considered the argument that § 354.3 was actually in conflict with some federal law or policy. The court concluded that there was no such conflict. Since the London Declaration on war, the U.S. policy favored facilitating restitution. Similarly, the State Department noted the sham transactions through which the Nazis seized many of the artworks, and that it might "be impossible to locate the original owners or their heirs and the governments involved will have to decide what should be done with the property or proceeds therefrom." U.S. Dep't of State, Memorandum from Interdivisional Comm. on Rep., Rest., & Prop. Rights, Sub-comm. 6, Recommendations on Restitution, Apr. 10, 1944, 1, NACP, RG 59, Lot 62D-4, Box 49, State/Notter. The Ninth Circuit took note of the substantial restitutions that the United States oversaw to artworks' countries of origin before 1948, under the policy that it would be best to let those countries handle further restitution in "whatever way they see fit." *Von Saher,* 578 F.3d at 1024. That termination of national-level restitution policy meant that individual restitutions, or any law that furthered them, no longer conflicted. Thus, there was no conflict preemption. *Id.* at 1025.

That left the question of foreign affairs field preemption. While von Saher was correct, the court held, that statutes of limitations are quintessentially state concerns that are not international in nature, this one was different. *Id.* at 1026. That was because:

> § 354.3 cannot be fairly categorized as a garden variety property regulation. Section 354.3 does not apply to all claims of stolen art, or even all claims of art looted in war. The statute addresses only the claims of Holocaust victims and their heirs.

Id. Expressing sympathy with California's concerted efforts to aid Holocaust survivors (including in the law at issue in *Garamendi*), the Ninth Circuit still concluded that it could not allow the law to stand.

Rejecting the idea that the law was a neutral regulation of the art trade, the Ninth Circuit observed that:

> The scope of the statute as enacted belies California's purported interest in protecting its residents and regulating its art trade. The amended version of § 354.3 suggests that California's real purpose was to create a friendly forum for litigating Holocaust restitution claims, open to anyone in the world to sue a museum or gallery located within or without the state.

Id. The upshot of this statement was that the statute was effectively, if not explicitly, expressing dissatisfaction with the lack of progress on a generally applicable federal forum. But the decision to create, facilitate, or not to create such a forum at the federal level encroached on international commitments made by the United States (*i.e.*, the Washington Principles), and thus into the foreign affairs domain. Here, the court was at its most uncomfortable with the potential reach of the law:

> Claims brought under this statute, including the instant claim, would require California courts to review acts of restitution made by foreign governments. For example, in this case, the parties contest the provenance of the Cranachs. In order to determine whether the Museum has good title to the Cranachs, a California court would necessarily have to review the restitution decisions made by the Dutch government and courts. This example illustrates that § 354.3 claims cannot be separated from the Nazi transgressions from which they arise.

Id. at 1028. From there it was a short step to find preemption because "the Constitution divides the war power between the Executive, who is the Commander-in-Chief of the Armed Forces, and the Congress, who has the power to declare war. U.S. Const. art. II, § 2; Id. at art. I, § 8…'[m]atters related to war are for the federal government alone to address,' and state statutes which infringe on this power will be preempted. *Deutsch*, 324 F.3d at 712."

Having affirmed the constitutional invalidity of the statute, the Ninth Circuit turned to whether von Saher's claims were time-barred, as the

District Court had held. It disagreed that the Complaint was sufficient to answer the question. Instead, it remanded the case back to the District Court to find whether von Saher had exercised reasonable diligence in discovering her claims, and whether the statute of limitations had expired by that point.

After a petition for rehearing was denied—*Von Saher v. Norton Simon Museum of Art at Pasadena*, 592 F.3d 954 (2010)—von Saher petitioned the Supreme Court for certiorari review, the discretionary procedure by which the high court decides whether to hear a case. The Supreme Court denied the petition without comment, as it usually does. *Von Saher v. Norton Simon Museum of Art*, 131 S. Ct. 3055, (2011). But an ancillary filing was notable. After the Supreme Court solicited the views of the United States, the Solicitor General actually filed a brief[52] urging the high court not to hear the case and arguing that not only did § 354.3 conflict with the foreign affairs powers of the United States, but so did the very notion of individual litigation:

> The court of appeals erred in dismissing the external restitution policy as irrelevant to this case because it "ended" on September 15, 1948 – the deadline set by the United States for filing restitution claims. The United States established a deadline to ensure prompt submission of claims and achieve finality in the wartime restitution process. The United States has a continuing interest in that finality when appropriate actions have been taken by a foreign government concerning the internal restitution of art that was externally restituted to it by the United States following World War II.

Back in the U.S. District Court in Los Angeles, on remand following the certiorari denial, the landscape had changed yet again. In direct response to the Ninth Circuit's 2009 decision in *Von Saher*, California tried to remedy the constitutional infirmity in its statute of limitations. New Cal. Code. Civ. Prod. § 338(c) now read:

> the bill retroactively amended § 338 and (1) extended the statute of limitations for specific recovery of a work of fine art from three to six years if the action is brought against a museum, gallery,

> auctioneer or dealer; and (2) clarified that such claims do not accrue until "actual discovery" rather than "constructive discovery" of both the identity and whereabouts of the work and information supporting a claim of ownership.

Von Saher v. Norton Simon Museum of Art at Pasadena, 862 F. Supp. 2d 1044, 1048 (C.D. Cal. 2012). This should fare no better, the Norton Simon had argued, because it conflicted with express federal policy and should again be found to be preempted. *Id.* at 1049. The District Court felt it permissible to go against the Ninth Circuit's earlier holding that amended statutes of limitations did not conflict with U.S. policy because external restitution had ended in 1948. The District Court relied on the views in the Solicitor General's Supreme Court brief, noted above, including that "the Solicitor General concluded that contemporary United States policy 'does not support relitigation of all art claims in U.S. courts,' but rather 'supports the fair and just resolution of claims involving Nazi-confiscated art, while also respecting the bona fide internal restitution proceedings of foreign governments.'" *Id.* at 1052. The District Court concluded that the new statute could not survive, either, as it impermissibly conflicted with foreign policy:

> In this case, the United States made a decision and chose its favored remedy for the restitution of Nazi-looted art, *i.e.*, a country of origin's bona fide restitution proceedings. This external restitution policy has not changed since it was first adopted by the United States after World War II. However, Plaintiff's action seeks to trump and interfere with United States foreign policy, by relying on an entirely different remedy for the restitution of Nazi-looted art, i.e. the laws of the State of California. Although the United States and California both share a goal of returning Nazi-looted art to its rightful owners, "[t]he fact of a common end hardly neutralizes conflicting means."

Id. at 1052–53. Regrettably, this finding ignored the claims on their face had never purported to relitigate a foreign nation's restitution decision. Von Saher did *not* ask the District Court to second-guess the Dutch restitution panel but rather to reach a decision about the current state of the painting's title. Nonetheless, the District Court dismissed the claims as untimely on the face of the Complaint, which is interesting given the Ninth Circuit's admonition about making a record on von Saher's reasonable diligence in discovering the basis for her claims.

Von Saher appealed and the parties briefed the questions with essentially the same arguments that they had put before the District Court. The Ninth Circuit held its hearing on August 22, 2012, before a panel comprised of judges Harry Pregerson, Dorothy Wright Nelson, and Kim McLane Wardlaw. Von Saher's attorney argued[53] that the issue on remand should have been a simple, factual one: Namely, even without the benefit of the more recent statute of limitations abolishment, were von Saher's claims timely? Von Saher's attorney pointed out that the Solicitor General's Supreme Court brief was limited to the question of preemption of the statute of limitations. That leaves, he argued, common law claims for the recovery of art. More to the point, he argued for von Saher that the District Court's findings about the Dutch proceedings were premature findings of fact when the court should have deferred to the allegations of the Complaint. In response to a question from the bench about how it could write an opinion without criticizing the Dutch government's process, he argued that the Dutch government had already deemed the dispute private.

The Norton Simon's attorney opened that von Saher's case was a direct attack on foreign policy as expressed in the Solicitor General's brief. Judge Pregerson initiated a ten-minute, back-and-forth discussion about what evidence the Norton Simon had of the U.S. policy. The Norton Simon's lawyer was prepared, quoting the brief where it said, "[w]hen a foreign nation, like the Netherlands here, has conducted a bona fide investigation." His fundamental point was that once the United States has spoken on policy, whether it was correct is not for federal courts to decide.

Pregerson was clearly unconvinced and veered into some slightly odd questioning, invoking his personal experience in WWII (which should have had no bearing on the outcome), criticizing (incorrectly) the attorney's pronunciation of *Goering* and chastising him for not knowing the 1940s sale price. The lawyer was ready, however, and noted that the

United States had long stated that it does not want to untangle questions of title in, for example, cases of inadequate compensation (i.e., coerced sales) as opposed to outright appropriation. The bottom line was that once the executive branch has stated its satisfaction with another country's claims process, the federal courts cannot step in and second-guess a specific adjudication.

Before issuing a decision in *Von Saher*, however, the Ninth Circuit had upheld the revised § 338(c). *See Cassirer v. Thyssen-Bornemisza Collection Found*, 737 F.3d 613 (2013). Reviewing the standards of field preemption, the Court of Appeals held in *Cassirer* that the revised statute did not create an independent remedy for wartime injuries of the sort that would intrude on the federal government's authority in that area, nor was it functionally equivalent to the § 354.3 that was struck down in *Von Saher I*. First, the court noted that the extension of limitations for artworks was unrelated to wartime claims on its face. It applies equally to artworks taken under far more mundane circumstances. Indeed, the law is silent on matters of foreign affairs. Critically (see more below), the court rejected the idea that allowing the claim to proceed was necessarily an adjudication of the fairness of what Lilly Cassirer had been paid by Germany, citing the important then-recent decision concerning the Hans Sachs painting collection. In that case, the high German commercial court (Bundesgerichtshof) restituted a collection to the heirs of Hans Sachs from the Deutches Historisches Museum, notwithstanding the compensation paid to Sachs after the war. Had the newer California statute provided a method to attack those German payments collaterally, it might well have intruded on the foreign affairs function, but this law did not do so, stated the court. Second, the *Cassirer* court gave short shrift to the argument that the six-year statute of limitations was functionally equivalent to the one already struck down. The latter addressed Holocaust claims specifically, while the former was silent, as noted above.

It was hardly a surprise, then, when the Ninth Circuit followed suit several months later and restored von Saher's claims, subject to the caveat that they might be vulnerable to the Act of State doctrine with respect to Desi Goudstikker's treatment in the 1950s by the Dutch restitution proceedings. *Von Saher v. Norton Simon Museum of Art at Pasadena*, 754 F.3d 712, 714 (9th Cir. 2014). The Ninth Circuit's inquiry in its 2014 opinion was focused on whether individual claims (such as von Saher's) conflict with the foreign policy of the United States, as the Solicitor General had suggested. The Ninth Circuit held that the views of the executive branch, while important, were not the final word. Importantly, the Ninth Circuit undertook to state what the policy was, rather than what it was not:

> In sum, U.S. policy on the restitution of Nazi-looted art includes the following tenets: (1) a commitment to respect the finality of "appropriate actions" taken by foreign nations to facilitate the internal restitution of plundered art; (2) a pledge to identify Nazi-looted art that has not been restituted and to publicize those artworks in order to facilitate the identification of prewar owners and their heirs; (3) the encouragement of prewar owners and their heirs to come forward and claim art that has not been restituted; (4) concerted efforts to achieve expeditious, just and fair outcomes when heirs claim ownership to looted art; (5) the encouragement of everyone, including public and private institutions, to follow the Washington Principles; and (6) a recommendation that every effort be made to remedy the consequences of forced sales.

Id. at 721. With that in mind, "Von Saher's claims do not conflict with any federal policy because the Cranachs were never subject to postwar internal restitution proceedings in the Netherlands, as noted in the complaint, the district court's order and the opinion of the Court of Appeals of The Hague." *Id.* Notably, Desi had brought a claim in the Netherlands for some, but not all, of Jacques Goudstikker's artwork. Because the claim had not encompassed the Cranachs, there was no decision about restitution concerning Desi to review or risk second-guessing the act of a foreign sovereign, which deference to the foreign affairs power of the executive forbids. By the time that von Saher returned to the Netherlands with a request for *all* Goudstikker paintings, the Cranachs were no longer in the Dutch government's possession, and thus were not part of the claim. That is to say, nothing about the U.S. litigation was a revisiting of the denial of von Saher's claim after the newer restitution law.

Importantly, the Court of Appeals held affirmatively that von Saher's claims were *consistent* with U.S. policy and not merely not in conflict with them:

> Von Saher is just the sort of heir that the Washington Principles and Terezin Declaration encouraged to come forward to make claims, again, because the Cranachs were never subject to internal restitution proceedings. Moreover, allowing her lawsuit to proceed would encourage the Museum, a private entity, to follow the Washington Principles, as the Terezin Declaration urged. Perhaps most importantly, this litigation may provide Von Saher an opportunity to achieve a just and fair outcome to rectify the consequences of the forced transaction with Goering during the war, even if such a result is no longer capable of being expeditiously obtained.

Id. at 723. Further, there were factual discrepancies that made the Solicitor General's brief less persuasive, particularly its sweeping statement that the paintings "have already been the subject of both external and internal restitution proceedings."

The Court of Appeals sent the case back down to the lower court, but with a new sword of Damocles hanging over von Saher's case: the possible applicability of the Act of State doctrine, pending further factual development. *Id.* at 726-27. This was because of the return of Stroganoff-Scherbatoff to prominence in the case. He, after all, had been the victim of Soviet expropriation, a taking of the sort that ordinarily cannot be reviewed by virtue of the Act of State doctrine.[9]

The Supreme Court again denied certiorari review. *Norton Simon Museum of Art v. Von Saher*, 135 S. Ct. 1158 (2015). Von Saher survived another motion to dismiss in April 2015, with the court holding that the case had been filed within California's often-revised statute of limitations. The District Court held that it was. Although the case was filed more than six years after von Saher's discovery of the location of the Cranachs, at some point in the interim the parties apparently signed a tolling agreement, which suspends the expiration of any statutes of limitations while the agreement is in effect. These are typically entered into when parties are trying to negotiate a resolution, and they believe such a resolution might be possible. Avoiding litigation in the short term can often make negotiations more productive.

Lastly, the court dismissed the idea that forcing the museum to defend itself was unfair:

> Finally, the Court finds that there is nothing unfair about affording Plaintiff an opportunity to pursue the merits of her claims against Norton Simon. As the California Legislature recognized by enacting AB 2765, museums are sophisticated entities that are well-equipped to trace the provenance of the fine art that they purchase. After carefully weighing the equities, the Legislature determined that the importance of allowing victims of stolen art an opportunity to pursue their claims supersedes the hardship faced by museums and other sophisticated entities in defending against potentially stale ones. Plaintiff, whose family suffered terrible atrocities at the hands of the Nazis, will now have an opportunity to pursue the merits of her claims, and Norton Simon will have an opportunity to pursue any and all defenses to those claims.

See Von Saher v. Norton Simon Museum of Art At Pasadena, et al., Case No. 2:07-cv-02866-JFW-SS, Order Denying Defendants' Motion to Dismiss Pursuant to Fed. R. Civ. P. 12(b)(6) for Failure to State a Claim Upon Which Relief Can Be Granted, filed 3/2/2015, Docket No. 112, at p. 11. A trial date was scheduled for September 20, 2016.

With the case seemingly headed for trial, the parties filed comprehensive cross-motions for summary judgment. Both parties' submissions were exquisitely written and argued, and each side's argument reflects well the starkly different perspectives that claimants and possessors take on so many of these issues. The District Court's award of judgment to the Norton Simon on August 15, 2016, was, in the end, a stunning misapprehension of restitution history. It remains to be seen how broadly it will damage further claims if left undisturbed.

Von Saher filed her motion first. With regard to the facts, many had been presented to the court before, and the summation of the record was reviewed in many respects. However, the critical outlier in von Saher's brief was the treatment of Stroganoff. Now, Stroganoff was cast as an equal villain in the story, a bad-faith opportunist who knew that the painting was not among those confiscated by the Soviets. Rather than a question of mistaken identity, the plaintiff's brief lays out a very different story. The record showed the Dutch court's initial disbelief that Stroganoff had any claim at all. The 1966 transaction was not a restitution, von Saher argued, but a commercial sale to dispense with a nuisance claimant for compensation. Thus, she pointed out, the 1966 sale would not answer any questions about the state of von Saher's title to the paintings. In other words, the 1966 sale would not resolve whether the painting was Stroganoff's to sell to the Norton Simon.

Instead, von Saher reiterated, the Dutch government was holding the Cranachs in trust or at least in custody for the Goudstikker firm. She pointed out that Dutch Royal Decree A6 from 1940 (in exile) voided automatically any transactions with Germans (such as Miedl or Goering). That was modified by the Dutch postwar restitution commission described in more detail in Chapter 20, the Commissie Rechtsverkeer in Oorlogstijd (CORVO), which used its power in 1947 to:

> Sanction all acts and agreements, performed or entered into in violation of [Decree A6]. Insofar as these acts or agreements related to matters, which were found in enemy territory, after such territory was liberated or occupied by the allied forces, [that] since then have returned to or will have been returned to the Netherlands.

See Von Saher -v- Norton Simon Museum of Art At Pasadena, et al., Case No. 2:07-cv-02866-JFW-SS, Order Granting Defendants' Motion for Summary Judgment, filed 6/13/2016, Docket No. 186, at p. 3.

The critical question became whether that decision applied to the Goering's thefts, and if so, whether the Goudstikker firm had to do anything further to protect its rights, as opposed to having the Miedl sale automatically invalidated. A later Royal Decree 100 set up a procedure to challenge CORVO's decision. The District Court in Los Angeles concluded that the Goudstikker firm had not followed the procedure. In the absence of a Royal Decree 100 restitution claim, the District Court found a claimant was left to seek (financial) reparations under Royal Decree 133.

Critically, the court agreed with the Norton Simon's arguments that Royal Decree 133 made such property recovered from the enemy and covered by CORVO's 1947 opinion property of the Dutch state.

Von Saher's central argument was also her shrewdest: That rather than fear the obstacles to claims that this book has laid out (such as the Act of State doctrine), those principles actually compelled victory for her. The argument is as follows: Because Stroganoff was not a successful restitution claimant but rather a purchaser, the 1966 proceedings and transaction had no sovereign character and thus were an entirely commercial event. As such, she argued, the Norton Simon could not deflect inquiry into the state of title as of 1966, the way that the Metropolitan Museum of Art and Yale University could against Pierre Konowaloff. Put another way, because von Saher made a compelling, factual presentation that Stroganoff had never owned the paintings, that the Soviets had not taken the paintings from him, and that the Netherlands sold the works to him in commerce, the Act of State doctrine should not shield to the sale.

Conversely, von Saher argued, the Washington Conference's Restitutions Committee's decision in 2006 to return all Goudstikker work "purchased" by Miedl was a sovereign act that the Norton Simon was bound to accept and that U.S. courts were powerless to reconsider. This two-step argument brilliantly turns on its head the setback that has bedeviled so many claimants. In other words, von Saher argued that the Netherlands has spoken as to the question of postwar title, and spoken in her favor such that no one could argue otherwise in U.S. court.

The District Court did not agree. Instead, it concurred with the Norton Simon's argument that when the Goudstikker firm failed to file a Decree 100 claim before 1951, the Cranachs became the property of the Dutch state. At that point, the court held, the Netherlands had title to do what it wanted. The court also took the Norton Simon's view of the scope of the settlement between Desi and the Netherlands, which hardly seemed undisputed, and which in any event with proper historical context now looks much more like the pressures faced by Lea Bondi or the Lederer family after the war. It is largely disingenuous to say (as the Norton Simon did) that simply because the Dutch were occupied but the Austrians were complicit, the Dutch settlement merits no scrutiny at all.

In a further critical holding, the District Court stated that:

> Military Law 59, which was enacted for U.S.-occupied Germany, provided that if a former owner failed to file a restitution claim before the deadline, that former owner "lost his right to restitution" and was "Forever barred from making any claim for restitution of that such property."

Id. at p. 15.

This is a catastrophic conclusion for restitution claims—and it is also incorrect. The court's holding was based on an Advisory Opinion by the Court of Restitution Appeals from 1950, Advisory Opinion No. 1, 1 Court of Restitution Appeals Reports 489, 492 (Aug. 4, 1950). However, that case concerned the deadlines within MGL No. 59 for successor organizations. That scenario, within the regulations of the MGL itself, applied only

> [i]f a juridical person or unincorporated association was dissolved or forced to dissolve for any of the reasons set forth in Article 1 [e.g., racial persecution], the claim for restitution which would have appertained to such juridical person and unincorporated association had it not been dissolved, may be enforced by a successor organization to be appointed by the Military Government.

MGL No. 59, Article 8(1). However, that has no application to the Goudstikker firm because it was not dissolved but was taken over. It continued to exist through the war and after. Thus, the deadline imposed on successor organizations, even if it applied, would not apply to von Saher.

Additional skirmishes did not reach a decision, but they are notable in the context of the themes of this book. First, again seeking to turn defeat into victory, von Saher argued that the adverse possession and/or prescriptive ownership in *Cassirer* (to be discussed further) at the very least confirmed that in California, there is no law of adverse possession of personal property; no matter how long one has a piece of tangible property, that fact alone will never convert ownership. Von Saher also raised the stakes by arguing for the application of a California criminal statute that punishes those who knowingly possess stolen property.

Laches was argued strenuously by both sides, and in so doing, the Norton Simon made a particularly appalling argument. It is common practice, indeed necessary, when the principle of laches is in play, to argue that one's opponent cannot claim the equitable defense because of some defect. Yet, in countering von Saher's motion, at the very end of its brief, the Norton Simon buries the ad hominem argument that because von Saher's father may have been a member of the Nazi party, she has no claim to the paintings. How does that matter? She holds the claim of Jacques Goudstikker, chased out of his own country to die while fleeing the Nazis. The parentage of the future spouse of one of his descendants could not possibly matter less. In addition, for good measure, the Norton Simon cast a shadow over Goudstikker by suggesting that he must have believed the works to have been stolen art from the Soviet Union.

What meaning do the AAMD guidelines possibly have left in the face of tactics such as this? The Norton Simon's brief conceded without quarrel that the Cranachs were sold under duress by Goudstikker to the very worst of the Nazis' international art thieves. Somehow, rather than agree to return it or reach a compromise, can disparaging the plaintiff's father (and Goudstikker) be considered a "fair and just solution" as the Washington Principles urge? Hardly. Did it give credence to the mandate to "balanc[e] a swift and compassionate response" that those same Washington Principles exhort? No. So now, *Von Saher* has headed to the Ninth Circuit for the third time, and the case will pass into its second decade.

That is not all, either. In possession of a work that all sides agree was looted by the Nazis, the Norton Simon filed a motion for what is known as the taxation of costs. In the American legal system, unless a specific rule or statute says otherwise, all sides to the litigation pay their own attorneys' fees. This has the effect of both permitting the filing of meritorious cases that might otherwise fear the penalty of paying the opponents' legal fees on the one hand (a positive), and failing to deter frivolous cases because the risk of bringing such a case in the first place is lower. For better or worse, that is the American system regarding legal fees, which is contrasted with the approach generally used in the United Kingdom and Europe. An exception to this rule, however, is the taxation of costs. Distinct from the hourly fees billed by attorneys, costs typically refer to out-of-pocket charges for things such as deposition transcripts or photocopies. Different courts have different rules, and among the things that vary in terms of whether they are allowable are things such as legal research fees, expert witness hourly fees, or travel expenses. In any event, the taxation of costs is almost universally regarded as intended to cover only an incidental cost of defending oneself.

After the District Court ruled in favor of the Norton Simon, the museum filed such a motion on August 29, 2016, seeking $94,821.06 in costs (of which the clerk allowed $84,834.62, which von Saher has challenged). This is a retributory tactic. Consider the museum's litigation tactics. It besmirched von Saher's name based on her father's activity when she was a small child. It filed a motion earlier in the case in which the museum attempted to have von Saher's attorneys sanctioned for speaking to a trustee of the Norton Simon Foundation (who contacted the attorneys and strenuously insisted he was not represented by the museum's attorneys) in supposed violation of the ethical rules against speaking with a represented party. Against all this it is difficult to imagine how anyone could characterize the museum's defense as consistent with the AAMD guidelines. The AAMD presumably disagrees, as it has never commented publicly on the litigation in a period when it has vocally sanctioned and criticized members (and nonmembers) concerning other AAMD guidelines. This is particularly disappointing because of how revolutionary the AAMD guidelines were when promulgated, apparently now replaced by an ends-justify-the-means result. Museums and nonprofits are statutory entities, beneficiaries of tax law, primarily. They have no mandate or excuse to possess once-stolen property, nor any excuse to claim the public good to keep it. A museum can either find possessing stolen art to be acceptable, or not.

* * *

The second case involving California's attempted statute of limitations reform was brought by the heirs of Margarethe Mauthner, a German Jew. Mauthner owned *Vue de L'Asile et de la Chapelle de Saint-Rémy*, a painting by Vincent van Gogh. Van Gogh painted it in 1889 while at the Saint-Paul-de-Mausole asylum. The painting shows either the Church of Labbeville near the town of Auvers-sur-Oise or a monastery within the asylum. Van Gogh committed suicide within a year of completing the painting. The painting went to his brother Theo, along with the bulk of Vincent's oeuvres that had gone unsold during his lifetime. The works later went to Theo's widow, Johanna, when Theo died six months later. Paul Cassirer, the noted art dealer, bought *L'Asile et de la Chapelle de Saint-Rémy* in 1906 or 1907. Cassirer was an early proponent of van Gogh at a time when the artist's name was hardly the byword for expensive paintings as he is today. Cassirer sold the painting to Mauthner shortly thereafter, around 1914. She owned it for decades thereafter.

The actress Elizabeth Taylor purchased the painting in 1963 at a Sotheby's auction. The Sotheby's provenance apparently included a mistake. First, it listed Paul Cassirer as the owner after 1928, but he had died in 1926. In addition, the Sotheby's catalogue referred in turn to two catalogues raisonnés, each of which identified Mauthner in the chain of title, contrary to the Sotheby's listing. One catalog published in 1928 (*L'oeuvre de Vincent Van Gogh. Catalogue Raisonné*), shows Margarethe Mauthner as the owner of the painting at that time. Another catalog by J. B. de la Faille, published in 1939, also identifies Mauthner as the owner, clearly contradicting the notion that Cassirer owned it in 1939 or any time after.

Mauthner fled Germany in 1939, leaving her possessions behind. The fate of the van Gogh in that period is unknown. A 1970 catalogue raisonné from the Netherlands identifies Alfred Wolf as the next owner. The 1963 Sotheby's catalogue provenance identifies three owners prior to Wolf. It asserted that the ownership of the painting went from Mauthner to Paul Cassirer, to Marcel Goldschmidt, and then to Alfred Wolf.

The Orkins were Mauthner's heirs and took notice of the issue of looted art along with many others at the end of the twentieth century. They retained a law firm and wrote to Taylor in 2003 demanding that she return the painting. Some negotiation ensued, but Taylor refused and eventually sued the Orkins for a declaration quieting title. The Orkins asserted state law claims for conversion, specific recovery, and a constructive trust but this was also a novel claim by arguing that the Holocaust Victims Redress Act (HVRA) of 1998 (the passage of which piqued their interest in the topic), gave them a cause of action to recover the van Gogh.

Taylor moved to dismiss, arguing that the claims were time-barred. California's 2002 statute discussed above was actually not the first amendment to its statute of limitations. In 1983, the law was amended to incorporate a discovery rule that governed accrual of claims before that for recovery of any article of historical, interpretive, scientific, or artistic significance after the claimant learned of the object's whereabouts. Before that amendment, the statute of limitations was silent on the availability of a discovery rule. The District Court observed that § 354.3, which was still on the books, applied only to suits against museums or galleries, not individuals. *Adler v. Taylor,* Case No. CV 04-8472-RGK, 2005 U.S. Dist. LEXIS 5862, at *11 (C.D. Cal. Feb. 2, 2005). As such, it did the Orkins no good against Taylor. As to whether the discovery rule applied, the District Court noted a conflict among appellate courts had not resolved. *Naftzger v. American Numismatic Society*, 42 Cal. App. 4th 421, 49 Cal. Rptr. 2d 784 (1996); *cf Society of California Pioneers v. Baker*, 43 Cal. App. 4th 774, 783, 50 Cal. Rptr. 2d 865 (1996). On balance, the District Court concluded that the *Naftzger* court failed to address California precedent that rejected the application of a discovery rule and that the Orkins could not claim it. *Adler,* 2005 U.S. Dist. LEXIS 5862, at *12. Even if the Orkins could claim it, the District Court held they could not meet its requirements:

> Plaintiffs' own Complaint establishes several key facts: (1) the world knew of Mauthner's prior ownership of the painting for years; (2) Mauthner was aware that the painting was lost or stolen; and (3) Taylor's purchase and ownership of the painting was common knowledge and easily discoverable. The facts establish that Plaintiffs, "by exercise of reasonable diligence," should have discovered Taylor's ownership in 1963.

Id. at 13.

The District Court also considered and rejected the Orkins' argument that the HVRA gave them a cause of action. Using the well-known *Cort* factors to determine whether Congress intended to create a private right of action in a statute, the court concluded that it had not. *Id.* at 14-15, *citing Cort v. Ash*, 422 U.S. 66, 78, (1975). They require determination of (1) whether the plaintiff is a member of a class that the statute especially intended to benefit, (2) whether the legislature explicitly or implicitly intended to create a private cause of action, (3) whether the general purpose of the statutory scheme would be served by creation of a private right of action, and (4) whether the cause of action is traditionally relegated to state law such that implication of a federal remedy would be inappropriate. Unless there is affirmative evidence of that intent, no right of action will exist. The court thus held:

> Here, under any Supreme Court methodology, the Congressional Record does not indicate an intent to create a private cause of action. Rather, it indicates a Congressional intent to encourage governments to aid in the restitution of property through currently existing laws. Plaintiffs completely fail to address the fourth *Cort* factor. This factor makes it clear that courts should not create a new federal law where a state law already exists.

Adler, 2005 U.S. Dist. LEXIS 5862, at *16.

The Orkins appealed, and the Ninth Circuit affirmed. *Orkin v. Taylor*, 487 F.3d 734 (9th Cir. 2007). The Ninth Circuit also noted the split in authority over whether the discovery rule applied to pre-1983 events, specifically a 1939 theft or a 1963 conversion. But even where discovery rules applied, they contain an element of constructive notice under California law. *See Jolly v. Eli Lilly & Co.*, 44 Cal.3d 1103, 1109, 245 Cal. Rptr. 658, 751 P.2d 923 (1988). With that in mind:

> From the face of the Orkins' complaint, it is apparent that Taylor's acquisition of the painting was certainly discoverable at least by 1990, when she held it out for sale in an international auction, and most probably as early as 1963, when she acquired the painting in a highly publicized international auction. In fact, the complaint alleges—and demonstrates by attachment—that Taylor bought the painting at a publicized auction in 1963, that Taylor was listed as the owner of the painting in a publicly available 1970 *Catalogue Raisonné*, and that Taylor publicly offered the painting for sale in 1990.

Taylor, 487 F.3d at 741–42.

The District Court also affirmed the dismissal of the HVRA claims on the same basis as the District Court had. The Orkins relied on a "Sense of the Congress" resolution that had stated:

> It is the sense of the Congress that consistent with the 1907 Hague Convention, all governments should undertake good faith efforts to facilitate the return of private and public property, such as works of art, to the rightful owners in cases where assets were confiscated from the claimant during the period of Nazi rule and there is reasonable proof that the claimant is the rightful owner.

HVRA, § 202, 112 Stat. at 17–18.

But, senses of the Congress are insufficient, the Ninth Circuit held. *Taylor*, 487 F.3d at 739. The court also reviewed the legislative history and noted that the most ardent supporter of the HVRA, Jim Leach (R-IA), thought that existing law was adequate and no new cause of action was necessary. The Ninth Circuit held that the HVRA failed the first *Cort* factor because Holocaust victims were not a required beneficiary class; the statute's focus is on governmental remedies, not private ones. There is no explicit conferral of a benefit on Holocaust victims; there is rather a preference that the victims benefit from existing law. The overarching purpose of the statute, the *Taylor* court held, was not private litigation, but research and declassification of records. *Id.* at 740. This fails the third *Cort* factor. Lastly, "there can be no doubt—as this case amply demonstrates—that state law provides causes of action for restitution of stolen artworks." *Id.* By implying a federal claim where none was explicitly stated would reach too far into that area.

Chapter 9

The Museum of Fine Arts Boston, Oskar Reichel, and Provenance Research

Oskar Reichel was a Jewish doctor and art collector in Vienna. Before the *Anschluss*, Reichel and his wife Malvine lived with their son Raimund at Chimanistrasse 11 in Vienna's leafy 19th District. They also had two other sons, Hans and Max. At some point, the Reichels opened an art gallery at Seilergasse 1 in the city center, right off the famous Graben street at the heart of the old city. Vienna had a large and integrated Jewish community, Reichel among them. In 1914, he acquired a 1913 painting by Oskar Kokoschka known by various titles, including *Two Nudes (Lovers)*, *Skizze (Doppelakt)* (*Sketch, Two Nudes*); *Liebspaar* (*Two Lovers*); and *Tanzpaar* (*Dancing Couple*).

By 1917, Reichel had amassed within his collection at least eight paintings by Kokoschka. Over the succeeding years, he sold some of them but retained the 1913 painting. In May 1924, Reichel lent the painting to a man named Otto Nierenstein, owner of the Neue Galerie. That month,

Reichel and Nierenstein corresponded about whether the painting might be for sale. Reichel indicated that it might be. The topic recurred many times over the next several years.

In or around 1933, Nierenstein changed his surname to Kallir. In June of that year, Reichel again lent him the 1913 painting. In 1937, Reichel was approached about loaning his Kokoschka paintings to the Museum für Kunst und Industrie (Museum of Art and Industry), known today as the Museum für Angewandte Kunst (Museum of Applied Art, or MAK). On April 22, 1937, Siegfried Troll of the museum wrote to Reichel at his home to confirm receipt of five works. Later correspondence confirms the receipt and insurance of the 1913 painting. The exhibition proceeded in May and June, and the painting is identified in the catalogue with Reichel as the owner and lender.

The annexation of Austria by Germany, or *Anschluss*, in March 1938 was an immediate catastrophe for Vienna's Jews. With shocking swiftness, mobs began turning Jews out of their homes. The Ringstrasse, redeveloped around the old medieval wall of the city under Emperor Franz Joseph in the nineteenth century, is bounded both by monumental civic buildings, as well as palaces that were both residences and social centers. These buildings, like the Altmann residence on Elisabethstrasse, still define the visual character of the grand boulevard with which Vienna is now identified. As it happened, a large number of the beautiful homes were owned by Vienna's Jews, who were targeted immediately.

On the second to last page of Reichel's mandatory property inventory (Verzeichnis), with several other items, notation appears in one place *Tanzpaar* (*Dancing Couple*) and in another *Liebespaar in Landschaft* (Lovers in a Landscape), an oil painting on canvas by "O. Kokoschka." The list of paintings, attested by art dealer Amatus Caurairy, is dated June 25, 1938.

These inventories, as Jonathan Petropoulos has written, were hardly incidental or perfunctory. Instead, they were literally a road map for enterprising Nazis and looters[54]:

> [T]he Nazi Authorities instituted the Property Declaration requirement to monitor and control the property of Jews in Germany and Austria, with the ultimate goal of curtailing their economic

> influence. Property Declarations in fact were a prelude to the formal Nazi confiscation and seizure of all Jewish-owned property in Austria and Germany. Nazi legal decrees required Jews to report any sales of property items identified on the Property Declaration to an official Nazi authority and later to deposit the proceeds of such sales in to blocked accounts denominated in the name of the Jewish payee.

The compulsion to file these property declarations was accompanied by the creation of a centralized bureaucracy to enforce them. The *Vermögensverkehrsstelle* (property registration office) was empowered to seize and document Jewish property.

Jews in Austria suffered on Kristallnacht just as those in Germany did. In addition to the brutal violence across the newly enlarged Germany, a series of dispossessing decrees followed. On November 12, 1938, the *Verordnung zur Ausschaltung der Juden aus dem deutschen Wirtschaftsleben* (Order Regarding the Elimination of Jews from the German Economy) was enacted. This decree explicitly did just that by forbidding any trade or commercial activity by Jews. The Reich Economic Ministry soon adopted the tone described by Professor Petropoulos's summary of the immediate availability of Jewish property but for limited exceptions (including, for the moment, a non-Jewish spouse).

Sometime on or after February 1, 1939, Reichel transferred five paintings to the Galerie St. Etienne in New York, Kallir's new enterprise in the United States. On that date (February 1), Kallir wrote from New York to Reichel in Vienna to confirm the authorization for a shipping company to retrieve the works. An inventory reflecting the acquisition remains in the possession of the Galerie St. Etienne.

Kallir exhibited the 1913 Kokoschka in the United States over the course of the next several years. After the war, the painting was exhibited as part of a show entitled "Forbidden Art in the Third Reich: Paintings by German Artists Whose Work Was Banned from Museums and Forbidden to Exhibit," sponsored by the Nierendorf Gallery in New York and shown there as well as the Institute of Contemporary Art in Boston and the Worcester Art Museum. According to papers later filed by the Museum of Fine Arts, the painting was by then owned by the Nierendorf Gallery, but curiously, those papers do not explain how or when the ownership was conveyed from Kallir and St. Etienne. Nierendorf records indicate that the painting was sold from the show to E. Silbermann of the Silbermann Galleries in New York.

The painting was loaned to, among other places, the Museum of Modern Art in New York. Kallir wrote to James Plaut at MoMA on April 12, 1948,[55] and references the paintings as in private hands at that point, with a reference to "Mrs. John Blodgett, of Grand Rapids, Michigan."[56] Over the intervening decades, the painting was loaned to a number of exhibitions, attributed to the ownership of Sarah Reed Blodgett, of Portland, Oregon. That same Sarah Reed Blodgett (Pratt) bequeathed the painting to the Museum of Fine Arts, Boston, in 1973, where it has been ever since. Since then, it has appeared in catalogues raisonnée and exhibition catalogues identifying the MFA as its owner.[57]

Reichel's fate was far less salutary. Malvine Reichel, the titleholder to their Döbling home, sold it in 1939 to a couple she knew, Alfred and Herta Karrer. The Karrers' ethnicity is unknown, but presumably, they were not Jewish. Malvine, who miraculously survived the war, later relinquished any claim to the home. By contrast, the Reichels sought restitution concerning their share in a building owned by Oskar at Börsegasse 12, which was adjudicated by the Restitution Commission in Vienna in 1953. Raimund, now living in Argentina, submitted two applications to the Fund for Assistance to Political Persecutees.[58] This petition concerned both the livelihood that he and Hans had lost as Jews, as well as "[a] large art collection [owned by my father that] was forcibly sold: 47 pictures by the painter Anton Romako, which are today to be found in Austrian museums and private collections."[59] In 1953, however, the *Verzeichnis* were deemed classified by the Austrian government and unavailable to the public. Hans's application was formally denied over a notarization issue that could not be resolved.

According to Reichel's heir Claudia Seger-Thomschitz in her Counterclaim:[60]

> By the time Reichel died in Vienna in 1943, the Nazis had seized all of his material possessions, and had either murdered, incarcerated, or forced other Reichel family members to emigrate. The National Socialists murdered son Max in 1940, the year after the transfer of

> the painting to Kallir. Dr. Reichel's wife, Malvine, was deported on January 15, 1943 to the Theresienstadt concentration camp in Prague, where she remained until the end of the war. She lived the rest of her life in Illinois.

Hans and Raimund were thus Oskar's sole surviving descendants. When Hans died, he left Raimund as his residual heir, and when Raimund passed away, he designated Claudia Seger-Thomschitz of Vienna (where he had returned) as his universal successor and heir.

According to Seger-Thomschitz, she first learned of the confiscated artworks when contacted by a Viennese museum in 2003 about the museum's intention to return four Romako works to her as Dr. Reichel's heir. After first retaining Austrian counsel to investigate, Seger-Thomschitz retained an American lawyer, who made a written demand on the MFA for the 1913 painting's return on March 12, 2007. After some discussion, the MFA and Seger-Thomschitz agreed to a tolling agreement while the museum investigated further.

A tolling agreement is simply another way of describing an agreement to freeze the status quo with respect to the statute of limitations. Put another way, if a claim is timely, a tolling agreement allows the plaintiff to hold off on filing a case after what would otherwise be the deadline so long as the agreement is still in effect. Thus, if a claim subject to a three-year state of limitations is addressed in a tolling agreement the day before the deadline, the claimant could file the claim a day or a month after what would ordinarily be the deadline unless the tolling agreement has been terminated. By contrast, a tolling agreement does not provide a claimant with any rights she does not already have. So (as eventually happened), if Seger-Thomschitz's claims were eventually deemed to have expired before March 2007, the tolling agreement could not revive them unless the agreement waives the limitations period regarding that party rather than suspending it (which it likely would not). Tolling agreements often make good practical sense for everyone, especially a defendant who is certain that he or she is right. Such agreements provide breathing space for a discussion and explanation, if there is one to be made, and avoid immediately entering the contentiousness and expense of full-blown litigation.

The MFA's response has become a kind of Rorschach test for perspective about looted art restitution. Certain components are undisputed. The MFA engaged Victoria Reed, an art historian on its staff, to research the claim. Dr. Reed described her investigation in a lengthy affidavit that was eventually filed in court. Interestingly, there was not a sharp dispute between Seger-Thomschitz and the MFA (resulting from Dr. Reed's investigation) about the provenance of the painting. Indeed, much of Dr. Reed's exhaustive affidavit is addressed to the history and public availability of its whereabouts after the war.

After reviewing the history, the MFA came to a few salient conclusions. First, it maintained that the 1939 sale was entirely voluntary and not the subject of compulsion. The MFA made much of Reichel's relationship with Kallir and the failure to include the 1913 painting explicitly in any of the various efforts at restitution after the war. Reed's affidavit, interestingly, includes what might be regarded as the thesis statement of the MFA's position only at the very end. It cites a November 10, 1982, letter from Raimund Reichel Marie-Agnes von Puttkamer, a Viennese art historian. Raimund's letter states (in the MFA's translation):[61]

> In the house on Chimanistrasse 11, my father put all the paintings he had by O.K. in the 'Kokoschka room' on the second floor. . . . Further: [I]n 1938 my father transferred the entire collection of O.K. paintings to the art dealer Dr. Kalier [*sic*], so that he could sell them in the U.S.A.

The clear implication of this, the MFA argued, was that Dr. Reichel had involved Kallir voluntarily for the purpose of selling the paintings for Reichel's benefit and without any duress.

Seger-Thomschitz took an entirely different tack from a factual perspective. She noted the secrecy of the *Verzeichnis* until at least 1993, arguing that the very contents of Reichel's declaration were unknowable between the *Anschluss* and decades later (and critically, after the 1982 letter). There is another aspect of the 1982 letter that was never adjudicated because of the approach that the court eventually took, as will be seen. Review again the MFA's translation of the letter. The original document is attached to Dr. Reed's affidavit, and not surprisingly, it is in German. The ostensible purpose of the letter is to discuss not the 1913 painting at issue, but rather a portrait of Ernst Koessler and whether it was by Kokoschka or Max Oppenheimer, referred to as "MOPP."[62] It reads with regard to the Kallir transaction (author's translation):[63]

> Further: [I]n 1938 my father gave collected OK pictures to the art dealer Kallier [sic], with which to sell them in the USA. "Ernst Koessler" was not among them. This picture remained in Vienna, as with other pictures by MOPP, Schiele, Gütersloh, Romako, and so on. Which route these pictures took, unfortunately I do not know.

This is a critical document. Raimund's statement certainly implies familiarity with the contents of his parents' house, as well as at the very least the fact of the transfer to Kallir. In addition, he makes a point of saying when he does not know the fate of the paintings under discussion. One reading of that statement is to conclude that Raimund did have information about the others. If he did, it would undercut Seger-Thomschitz's position that he (and then she) could not have known about the Kokoschka paintings until the contents of the property declarations were brought to their attention.

On the other hand, the statement about Kallir and the United States has its own ambiguity. If Reichel gave the paintings to Kallir to sell them in the United States, is the likeliest meaning that Reichel sold the paintings to Kallir and that the eventual decision to sell them in the United States was Kallir's decision alone after taking title to them, or that Reichel entrusted the works to Kallir for eventual sale in the United States, or that Reichel consigned the works to Kallir? If it were the first scenario, then certainly no successive holders would have a title problem; they would be Reichel's proper successors just as much as Kallir's. If it were the last scenario (consignment), it might not make a notable difference either. A consignee has legal authority to sell a consigned object, and a subsequent good-faith purchaser for value from a seller in the ordinary course could claim title. They would, in that case, not be taking title from a thief. The consignor—who gave the property to someone with the legal power to sell it—has a remedy against the consignee (Kallir), not the subsequent owner. But, what of the middle scenario? It would certainly be fact-intensive—if there were more facts. In any event, none of this can be examined further, because Raimund died and cannot be asked what he meant.

The MFA satisfied itself that the painting was not stolen from Reichel. Seger-Thomschitz disagreed and did not waiver in her claim for it, however. At this point, the MFA took a controversial step and sued Seger-Thomschitz to "quiet title." This procedural maneuver, which is not unusual as a general matter, asks a court to answer the same question but posed by a different actor (and is a routine event in real estate title questions in particular). Rather than the person without the property asking the court to compel the possessor to give it back, a quiet title declaratory judgment action seeks a statement from the court that the current possessor is, in fact, the owner, superior to any other claimants. Although not odd procedurally, the optics were jarring to many, whereas others praised the MFA's thoroughness. According to the *Boston Globe:*

> Ori Soltes, cofounder of the Holocaust Art Restitution Project in Washington, D.C., said he was impressed by the museum's research. "It strikes me the MFA's case has a lot of merit," Soltes said.

"MFA sues to bolster claim to disputed 1913 painting," *Boston Globe*, January 24, 2008. On the other side, Rabbi Howard Berman wrote to the *Globe* and said:

> THERE MAY well be legal merit to both sides of the argument regarding the ownership of the disputed Kokoschka painting by the Museum of Fine Arts ("MFA sues to bolster claim to disputed 1913 painting," City & Region, Jan. 24). However, it is appalling that deputy director Katherine Getchell would equate the horrors already facing the Jews of Austria by 1939 with the "duress" of financial pressures during the Depression, or the current mortgage problems in America.
>
> The violent persecution of the Jews of Germany and Austria was well underway by the time the Reichel family sold the painting. There can be no question that the elderly couple faced enormous fear and desperation as their sons fled the country and one was interred in a concentration camp. Getchell's insensitivity to these

realities is very disturbing, and diminishes the MFA's moral stature in this complex controversy.

"Rabbi: MFA Director Insensitive," *Boston Globe*, January 26, 2008.

Regardless of the public reaction, the battle was underway. Seger-Thomschitz answered the Complaint and filed a Counterclaim of her own for return of the painting. She articulated the foregoing history, and argued that any uncertainty should be resolved against the MFA and not her. Notably, she cited the presumption that any transfer in Nazi Germany (as Austria, literally speaking, was in 1939) involving a Jew is presumptively invalid. This unassailable notion has many roots in both common sense and legal action by the Allies. In particular, Seger-Thomschitz articulated the importance of MGL No. 59, whose stated purpose was "to effect to the largest extent possible the speedy restitution of identifiable property... to persons who were wrongfully deprived of such property within the time period from January 30, 1933 to May 8, 1945 for reasons of race, religion, nationality, ideology or political opposition to National Socialism." 12 Fed. Reg. 7983§ 3.75(a)(1). As discussed, the touchstone of this presumption is that it could be rebutted only where it could be shown that the seller was paid a fair price and had free disposal of the proceeds. Making explicit common-law concepts of the priority of the true owner over subsequent holders, even those innocent and in good faith, it states that "property shall be restored to its former owner or to his successor in interest... even though the interests of persons who had no knowledge of the wrongful taking must be subordinated. *Provisions of law for the protection of purchasers in good faith, which would defeat restitution, shall be disregarded except where Law No. 59 provides otherwise.*" See MGL No. 59. (Emphasis added.)

The MFA moved for summary judgment. Summary judgment, distilled to its essence, asks the court to conclude that no factual resolution is necessary. If all the facts that are material to the causes of action are undisputed, then the legal consequence of those facts can, and indeed should, be determined by a judge, not a jury. By contrast, if something essential to the claim is in dispute, then a trial is necessary for either a jury, or a judge as fact finder, to resolve conflicting versions of events, credibility, and similar competing facts.

The legal thrust of the motion was purely procedural. Whatever the circumstances in 1938, the MFA argued, Seger-Thomschitz's claim was too late to bring in a Massachusetts court. To advance this argument, the MFA first had to convince the court to apply a particular law. Federal courts have various avenues to assert jurisdiction, as we have seen. Among them is so-called diversity jurisdiction, which refers to conflicts between parties from different locations under the right circumstances. Thus, the MFA's case was brought in diversity pursuant to 28 U.S.C. § 1332 as a dispute in excess of $75,000 between citizens of different states (in this case, Massachusetts and Austria). In such a case in federal court, however, there is no federal cause of action or federal law to apply. The question then becomes which law to apply. A federal court in diversity looks first to the choice of law rules of the forum (which is distinct from, and does not presuppose the eventual application of, the substantive law of the forum). *Klaxon Co. v. Stentor Elec. Mfg. Co.*, 313 U.S. 487 (1941).

The MFA argued that Massachusetts law should apply to the dispute over a painting in Massachusetts against a Massachusetts nonprofit entity. Like many states, Massachusetts looks to the Restatement (Second) of the Conflict of Laws, § 142. In that view, the forum court will apply its own substantive statute of limitations if it bars the claim. *New England Tel. & Tel. Co. v. Goudreau Constr. Co.*, 647 N.E.2d 42,45-46 (Mass. 1995). If it does not bar the claim, then the forum state will apply its law to permit the claim unless the defendant establishes that the claim serves no substantial interest in the forum and the claim would be barred by a state with a more significant interest. *Fedder v. McClennen*, 959 F. Supp. 28, 35 (D. Mass. 1996).

With that in mind, the MFA argued that the various tort claims brought by Seger-Thomschitz (replevin, conversion) were barred by Massachusetts's three-year statute of limitations. Generally, that limitation period will run from the time of the injury. That would have ended the timeliness of any claim in 1942.

Massachusetts, like most states (critically excluding New York's demand and refusal rule as described further herein) also use the discovery rule for torts, however. That is to say:

> The limitations period begins to run 'when a plaintiff discovers, or at an earlier date when she should reasonably have discovered, that

> she has been harmed or may have been harmed by the defendant's conduct.'... The limitations period is tolled until 'events occur or facts surface which would cause a reasonably prudent person to become aware that she or he has been harmed. A person is considered to be on 'inquiry notice' when the event first occurs that would prompt a reasonable person to inquiry into a possible injury.

Epstein v. C.R. Bard, Inc., 460 F.3d 183, 187 (1st Cir. 2006). This is the fundamental basis of the Museum of Fine Art's motion. It avoids arguing or undertaking to prove whether the 1939 sale was, in fact, legitimate. Instead, it argues that the circumstances of the transaction, and the subsequent history and location of the painting, were sufficiently knowable that a reasonably prudent person would have discovered it at some point in the time between the transfer by Kallir in Vienna and more than three years before the case was filed.

Although the MFA's motion was not directed toward proving that Reichel freely sold the painting, those same facts were squarely targeted to arguing that the Reichels—Oskar and then Raimund—knew who had sold the painting thereafter (Kallir) and that the painting's whereabouts were reasonably ascertainable in the intervening period. Indeed, Raimund's correspondence as referenced in Dr. Reed's report is referenced heavily for just that purpose. Not only, argued the motion, did the 1982 letter refer to the rooms filled with Kokoschka paintings that were sold in the United States (with no apparent complaint), but the motion identifies another letter from 1985[64] in which the specific painting is mentioned. By the terms of that letter, Raimund later spoke with Kallir in New York, who claimed to have "lost his shirt."[65] Lastly, although the MFA contested the idea that the 1939 conveyance was under duress, it suggested that the belief would have compelled only a reasonable owner to inquire immediately, if he thought he had been robbed.

Lastly, even accepting for the sake of argument that Raimund might never have had sufficient facts to discover the basis for his claim, the MFA noted that more than three years had elapsed since Seger-Thomschitz's U.S. counsel had made a demand for the return of the painting. The point is that even if the statute of limitations were tolled, ignored, or otherwise set aside from the 1939 conveyance to the modern era, Seger-Thomschitz knew enough by no later than 2003 that she had an argument as to the painting's ownership.

Seger-Thomschitz countered with a different theory. Although the MFA's claim was brought in diversity, Seger-Thomschitz argued that her claims actually implicate federal, not state law. In that event, there would be no choice of law analysis; rather, federal law would apply. Seger-Thomschitz went on to articulate that her claims were supported by the allegation that MFA's acquisition and retention of the paintings were in violation of its implicit promises under the Internal Revenue Code, specifically § 501(c)(3) that confers charitable status. These breaches of the museum's obligations, in Seger-Thomschitz's characterization, were the basis for the claims and therefore the source of applicable law. With this in mind, she took the offensive and accused U.S. museums more broadly of failing to take claims for restitution seriously and thereby breaching their implicit promises to the public as nonprofits. In this vein, she argued, the court should not apply strictly the three-year statute of limitations. Rather, she suggested, the court should apply a flexible standard by invoking principles of equity (and thus ruling out the application of a laches defense, which is an equitable defense).

As to the application of the three-year statute of limitations, however, Seger-Thomschitz faced her greatest, and ultimately fatal, hurdle. She argued in her opposition that she could not have known, and did not know, of the existence of her claims, until 2003, and promptly retained counsel to investigate. But, she did not articulate any explanation for the correspondence involving Raimund, her predecessor, in the years before 2003. Nor did she provide context for the timing of her discovery of her claim relative to the filing of a claim (or counterclaim). She did not make a formal demand or reach the tolling agreement with the MFA until 2007, by any measure more than three years after the discovery in her version of events in 2003.

Ultimately, the court sided with the MFA. The court issued a Memorandum of Decision and Order on the MFA's motion on May 28, 2009. It did not reach a conclusion on whether the 1939 sale was legitimate, rather, it decided the motion entirely on statute of limitations grounds. *See Museum of Fine Arts v. Seger-Thomschitz*, Civil Action No. 08-10097-rwz, 209 U.S. Dist. LEXIS at 26–27 (D. Mass May 28, 2009). It did, however, incorporate into the decision reference to the 1982 and 1985 correspondence from Raimund about his father's Kokoschka paintings. First, the court rejected Seger-Thomschitz's request to ignore the Massachusetts statute of limitations and apply some federal common law standard because the court disagreed that the 1939 transaction was so obviously coercive. Although perhaps a slight distinction, this conclusion, while not ultimately a ruling on the title transfer itself, is clearly informed by the MFA's explanation of the history and claim to legitimacy. However, unconvinced of a compelling reason to set aside the statute of limitations, the court declined to do so.

Similarly, the court did not accept Seger-Thomschitz's creative theory that her claims were contract-based rather than torts. Seger-Thomschitz pleaded no agreement between her and the MFA that was allegedly breached, rather she alleged the MFA's wrongful possession. Instead, the court concluded, "[s]uch claims clearly sound in tort, not contract, and thus is subject to the three-year limitations period." *Id.* at *21. Under that limitation, the court concluded that the claim was time-barred even under the discovery rule. First, it held, the Reichel family "had sufficient knowledge of Reichel's ownership and transfer of the painting to put them on notice of a possible injury." *Id.* at *23. The court was also swayed by the request by Reichel's son for restitution for some property but not the painting at the center of the lawsuit. That conclusion would be dubious on a summary judgment posture if standing alone. It does not necessarily follow that because the family knew of specific, personal property later identified for restitution that the family also knew of other specific, personal property, which could easily have been obscured or unknown.

Raimund Reichel was subjectively aware of the Kokoschka paintings and discussed them specifically decades after the war. Combined with the frequent exhibition of the paintings over the years, the court held Raimund—and thus Seger-Thomschitz as his successor—to that duty of inquiry, and that if he or they believed they were aggrieved they could have known sooner than 2003 had they exercised the diligence required by the court. The court made a point to underscore the justification for limitations periods, citing the diminishing availability of evidence. *Id.* at *28, *citing Am. Pipe & Constr. Co. v. Utah*, 414 U.S. 538, 554 (10742). Indeed, the court took the occasion to contrast the Reichel family's approach to the one used by Max Stern's Estate.

Lastly, even if any of the foregoing were sufficiently disputed as a matter of fact to warrant summary judgment (which, to be clear, the court did not accept), the court held that the claim was still too late because Seger-Thomschitz waited more than three years to make a demand and/or secure a tolling agreement. By the time the MFA filed suit, let alone by the time she counterclaimed, Seger-Thomschitz could not claim to have discovered the basis for her claim within three years. Summing up, the court stated:

> The conclusion is inescapable that, in 2003, [Seger-Thomschitz] knew or should have known of Reichel's previous ownership of the Painting, his transfer of the Painting to Kallir and the MFA's current ownership, all of which was public knowledge and easily discoverable. Because she did not make a demand on the MFA until 2007, Seger-Thomschitz's claims are time-barred, even if the cause of action were tolled until 2003.

Id. at *830*. The court was no more persuaded by Seger-Thomschitz's allegations concerning Kallir and fraudulent concealment that would toll the statute of limitations because, it noted, any alleged misdeeds by Kallir preceded the MFA's predecessor in title and Seger-Thomschitz's knowledge no later than 2003.

The court repeatedly referenced and contrasted the *Vineberg* decision, comparing the Stern estate's efforts over the years to find the subject of that litigation from the Reichel's silence over the years about the Kokoschka painting at the MFA. Although the question of title or the validity of the 1939 transaction were never explicitly reached because of the timeliness question, it is difficult to avoid the conclusion that the court agreed with the MFA in the view that the painting had not actually been stolen from Reichel or taken under duress.

Seger-Thomschitz appealed the dismissal, but the First Circuit saw no reason to disturb the District Court's ruling. *Museum of Fine Arts v. Seger-Thomschitz*, (23 F.3d) (1st Cir. 2010). The First Circuit was more circumspect about how to view the 1939 transaction, summing it up by saying "details of this transaction are sketchy." *Id.* at 4. Noting that the only question before it was the question of timeliness, the First Circuit expressly observed that the question of the validity of the 1939 conveyance is not "clear cut." *Id.* at 6. Seger-Thomschitz apparently abandoned the contract theory of statute of limitations on appeal and pressed the applicability of the discovery rule to argue that she was within the applicable period. The First Circuit removed any doubt as to what the outcome would be with this passage:

> The party seeking the benefit of the discovery rule has the burden of showing (1) that she lacked actual knowledge of the basis for her claim and (2) that her lack of knowledge was objectively reasonable. *Koe v. Mercer*, 876 N.E.2d 831, 836 (Mass. 2007). Courts applying the discovery rule in missing art cases have tested the reasonableness of the claimant's lack of knowledge by asking whether the claimant "acted with due diligence in pursuing his or her personal property." *O'Keeffe v. Snyder*, 416 A.2d 862, 872 (N.J. 1980); *accord Autocephalous Greek-Orthodox Church v. Goldberg & Feldman Fine Arts, Inc.*, 917 F.2d 278, 288–89 (7th Cir. 1990); Erisoty v. Rizik, No. 93-6215, 1995 WL 91406, at *10 (E.D. Pa. Feb. 23, 1995).
>
> In contrast to many missing art cases, the location of the Painting has been no secret in this case. The Painting has long been on public display at the MFA, a major international museum. Since 2000, the MFA has listed the Painting in a provenance database on its publicly accessible website. Several published books and at least one catalogue raisonné of Kokoschka's works identify the MFA as the current holder of the Painting.

Id. at 7.

Under this standard, the First Circuit also found the correspondence from 1980s to be dispositive of the question of whether a dispossessed claimant *could* have known sooner of the claim. That is to say, assuming for the sake of argument that the paintings were stolen, the letters showed Raimund's subjective awareness of their existence and location in the United States. Given that, a properly motivated claimant would have investigated further, and, more important, could have located the painting at the MFA with a reasonably diligent search. The discovery rule does not require the possessor to prove any more.

In any event, as noted by the District Court, even under Seger-Thomschitz's version of events, she knew of the painting's location no later than 2003, making the application of the discovery rule more or less irrelevant. Again, assuming for the sake of argument that the painting had been stolen and neither Raimund nor Seger-Thomschitz could possibly have known where it was, Seger-Thomschitz *did* know in 2003, more than three years before the MFA's lawsuit and therefore, by definition, more than three years before Seger-Thomschitz's Counterclaim.

At the time, the MFA's strategic decision to dismiss the case on statute of limitations grounds provoked some controversy. Notwithstanding the District Court's pronouncements regarding the purpose of limitations periods, the assertion of a timeliness defense is seen as inconsistent with the prevailing view espoused since the Washington Principles, *i.e.,* reaching what could be deemed fair and just solutions with respect to claims for stolen art. From that perspective, the MFA's litigation tactics prevented the fundamental question about whether the 1939 conveyance was valid. Although the District Court's opinion was perhaps more open regarding its view of the transaction, not surprisingly the First Circuit was more cautious when stating that that particular question was not before it, and thus no inferences about it should be drawn from the decision on timeliness.

From the other perspective, however, the MFA's rationale was straightforward. It believed that the 1939 sale was not coerced and that all transfers thereafter were legitimate. Winning the case and quieting title to the paintings through the statute of limitations was therefore the quickest way to confirm what it had subjectively concluded: that the painting was not looted art. Additionally, there is no question that the MFA drew its conclusion from a substantial investment of time and resources. Were it not for the 1980s correspondence, the 1939 transaction would look very different, and the gaps in information would have to be held to support a finding of duress. The gap between the *Anschluss*, the forced property declarations just months later, and the complete chaos that befell Vienna's Jews do not permit any other rational conclusion in the abstract. However, in this case, those letters address a subjective understanding of the fate of the paintings and do not address the concern that the conveyance had been other than what Reichel wanted. The timeliness defense was the shortest route to that result. As later litigations will reveal, the assertion of nonsubstantive defenses is not always supported by this use of exhaustive effort and the presence of evidence to legitimize the transaction. The MFA's belief that it was warranted in retaining the painting goes a long way to distinguishing it from other museums that seem indifferent to their collections' looted past.

Chapter 10

Prescriptive Law in Louisiana

Things went little better in Louisiana in a dispute that Seger-Thomschitz had with Sarah Blodgett Dunbar concerning a painting of one of the Reichel family members (Hans) by Oskar Kokoschka: *Portrait of a Youth* (1910). Dunbar is the daughter of the same Sarah Reed Blodgett (also referred to as Sarah Reed Platt). Reed Blodgett bequeathed the 1913 painting to the MFA; the painting was later the subject of the lawsuit in Boston. *Portrait of a Youth* was one of the paintings sold in the 1939 sale from Dr. Reichel to Kallir. Reed Blodgett purchased the painting from the Galerie St. Etienne in February 1946. She later lent the painting to an exhibition in 1948 entitled "Oskar Kokoschka: A Retrospective Exhibition" (Boston, New York, Washington, St. Louis, and San Francisco).[66] The provenance at the show was listed as Dr. Reichel, Vienna, followed by Galerie St. Etienne, New York, and stated that the painting had been lent by Mrs. John W. Blodgett, Jr., Portland, Oregon.[67] The 1948 show was reviewed in *ARTnews* and *Art Digest*. Over the years, Dunbar later alleged, the painting was shown publicly in a number of exhibitions:[68]

- Oskar Kokoschka Retrospective Exhibition, ICA, Boston; MOMA, New York.

- Phillips Gallery, Washington, D.C.; City Art Museum, St. Louis, and De Young, San Francisco, 1948-1949 Nr. 4.
- Oskar Kokoschka, Tate Gallery, London, June 11 – August 10, 1986, Cat. No. 15.
- Oskar Kokoschka: Guggenheim, Guggenheim Museum, New York, December 9, 1986 – February 16, 1987, Cat. No. 5.

In addition, the authors of the catalogue raisonné on Oskar Kokoschka interviewed Raimund Reichel in 1953 regarding the Reichel Family's Kokoschka paintings. *See Oskar Kokoschka Die Gemaelde 1906-1929*, Salzberg: Galerie Welz by Winkler and Erliny.

By all accounts Blodgett retained ownership of it for the remainder of her life, whereupon she bequeathed it to Dunbar (her daughter), who likewise kept it as personal property. As Dunbar recounted it, she received a demand letter dated April 12, 2007, from Seger-Thomschitz's attorney.[69] The letter demanded the immediate return of the portrait of Hans Reichel and characterized the 1939 sale as coercive and/or occurring under duress. Rather than await a lawsuit from Seger-Thomschitz, Dunbar seized the initiative and sued Seger-Thomschitz in the U.S. District Court for the Eastern District of Louisiana, seeking to quiet title to the work. Anticipating a possible defense, Dunbar alleged that Seger-Thomschitz (an Austrian) was subject to the jurisdiction of the court by virtue of sending the demand for the return of the Kokoschka painting.

Substantively, the Complaint invoked an idiosyncrasy of Louisiana law: prescription. In every state in America, there is some version of the adverse possession doctrine, also known as title by prescription. Adverse possession of land is a concept by which someone can acquire title to a parcel he or she does not own by using it for a prescribed period of time in a manner that is obviously at odds with the true owner's rights, such that the true owner would presumably object to it. In the absence of such an objection, the trespasser can become the true owner.

Common-law states do not extend this doctrine to moveable personal property. Much like the inability to acquire a title in good faith from someone who does not legally have it, this policy choice not to allow prescription of personal property is rooted in the concept of the relative risks and equity. Whereas using land is necessarily observable by the person who owns it, that is not necessarily or even likely the case with moveable personal property. Hanging a stolen painting on one's wall is adverse to the title of whoever truly owns it, but it is far messier as a factual matter to determine when the true owner would have reason to know about it.

Because of its Napoleonic Code antecedents, Louisiana law does allow the acquisition of title to personal property by prescription. So, rather than litigate the question of whether the 1939 transaction was valid, Dunbar's claim assumes for the sake of argument that it is invalid, but that she nonetheless would have acquired good title since then. Remarkably, where most adverse possession statutes for real property are about twenty years, Article 3490 of the Louisiana Civil Code sets the prescriptive period at only three years. Raising the temperature still further, Dunbar initially brought a claim for slander of title, which is the disparagement of one's property ownership, though she later dropped that claim before the case was over.

Seger-Thomschitz answered and counterclaimed under theories of quasi-contract, unjust enrichment, and declaratory judgment as to the true ownership. Seger-Thomschitz set forth a similar version of the 1939 transaction that she would later allege in the MFA case. Directly to the point of ownership, she alleged that the escalating persecution and closing of Dr. Reichel's business, culminating in the property declaration of 1938, itself amounted to a confiscation. As a result, Seger-Thomschitz argued, there was really no inquiry to be performed regarding the 1939 transaction because under her theory, the painting had already been expropriated by the Nazis, and Kallir could not have acquired good title no matter how Dr. Reichel (or later Raimund) felt about it. It was a creative theory designed to deflect the importance of the 1939 sale, of which there was no contemporary evidence as to Dr. Reichel's state of mind (as opposed to the inferential evidence adduced by the MFA that Raimund would have objected if the family considered the painting to be stolen). Indeed, she alleged specifically that the Nazi persecution of Reichel made him legally incapable of conveying title unilaterally.

Seger-Thomschitz also made a number of affirmative allegations about Blodgett-Pratt's 1946 acquisition in her Answer and Counterclaims.[70] Seger-Thomschitz described the sale as a "prototypical 'ask no questions' purchase without investigating its provenance" and that Blodgett-Pratt had "ignored warnings that the U.S. government made to the art world to exercise appropriate precaution against acquiring Nazi-confiscated and other looted artworks."[71] Her Counterclaim sets forth the same articulation of U.S. military policy, government policy, and the Tate letter that she argued in the MFA case.

In response to the prescriptive acquisition theory, Seger-Thomschitz invoked in her Counterclaim the doctrine of *contra non valentem agere mulla currit praescriptio,* which "prescribes that a claim to recover a particular artwork will not accrue and the relevant period of prescription will not begin to run until the plaintiff knew—or in the exercise of reasonable diligence under the specific facts and circumstances of the case could or should have known—that the particular artwork was stolen or converted and could locate such artwork and identify the current owner."[72] She once again argued that until they could see the property declaration, no one in the family (Seger-Thomschitz's predecessors in title) could have known that this particular painting was confiscated, and the statute of limitations therefore could not have begun. Moreover, she alleged that the property declaration came first and thus theoretically available in 1998, whereas, in fact, it was not available until she heard from the Vienna museums in 2003. Without explaining why four years had elapsed before making her demand, she tried to contrast what she described as the Blodgett-Dunbar family's failure to inquire about the painting's history before they acquired it.

Dunbar moved for summary judgment in October of the year in which the case was filed (2008). Specifically, she sought partial summary judgment on the original claims in her Complaint(s), and for full summary judgment on Seger-Thomschitz's two Counterclaims. The argument was premised entirely on the doctrine of prescription. Again, without actually conceding anything had the motion failed, Dunbar's motion assumed for the sake of argument that the 1939 sale was sufficiently coercive and that it failed to pass title to Kallir, and thus to Kallir's successor, Blodgett-Platt. In an area of law in which seventy-five pages of briefs are common, Dunbar's lawyers played what is often the best card: brevity. Their brief in support of the motion was a mere eleven pages. Under Louisiana law, Dunbar pointed out,[73] the possessor in good faith of personal property can obtain title that was not available at the time of acquisition once she has possessed the property for three years:

> Article 3490 provides that "[o]ne who has possessed a movable as owner, in good faith, under an act sufficient to transfer ownership, and without interruption for three years, acquires ownership by prescription." La. Civ. Code art. 3490. Thus, a putative owner must satisfy four requirements: (1) possession as the owner, (2) possession in good faith, (3) possession as a result of an act sufficient to transfer ownership, and (4) possession without interruption for three years.

Dunbar took the position, not surprisingly, that her mother had acquired the painting in good faith and that she therefore only had to show possession without interruption for three years, the latter of which was clearly the case. As evidence of her good faith, Dunbar pointed to her mother's acquisition of the painting from Kallir, a known and reputable dealer. The chain of possession was undisputed, and she suggested that no facts could support an inference that Blodgett-Platt had any subjective concerns about Kallir's right to sell the painting.

Even if there were facts to contest the good faith of the 1946 acquisition, Dunbar highlighted that Louisiana still has a ten-year prescriptive period, regardless of the good faith of the possessor. La. Civ. Code art. 3491. It is surprising that such a law exists in the United States, but Dunbar was correct. It is hard to conceive of a stronger incentive to conceal stolen property than such a law (which is not to suggest that the Blodgetts or the Dunbars did so, only that such a response on a larger scale is inevitable). Thus, because more than ten years had passed since 1946, Dunbar argued, she was now the owner of the painting regardless of what had happened in 1939.

Seger-Thomschitz's opposition argued in the first instance that the prescriptive acquisition argument did not address her quasi-contract and unjust enrichment claims. Seger-Thomschitz described an action in quasi-contract as "based on an implied contract of a person in wrongful possession of property to return it whenever the retention of the disputed item would result in unjust enrichment." *Kramer v. Freeman*, 198 La. 244, 252 (1941). The challenge is that Seger-Thomschitz's brief, while accurately pointing out that her Complaint specifically invoked quasi-contract and unjust enrichment, did not clearly explain the implied contract. From a neutral perspective, the case involves complete strangers who are unaware of each other's existence until at least 2003. It is not obvious when any implied or express agreement could have arisen between them. Although Seger-Thomschitz accused Dunbar of mischaracterizing the nature of her claims, she did not, in the end, clearly explain what she argued had been mischaracterized. Without that explanation, all that was left was the prescription analysis.

With regard to prescription, Seger-Thomschitz first suggested that there were disputes of fact regarding the 1946 good-faith acquisition from Kallir. Good faith cannot be conclusively determined, she argued, if there are facts in dispute about whether the possessor "ignore[d] a fact or circumstance that suggests the need for further inquiry." *Thibodeaux v. Quebodeaux*, 282 So.2d 845, 851 (La. App. Ct. 3rd Cir. 1969). As Seger-Thomschitz argued:[74]

> Several considerations made it imperative for [Blodgett-Pratt] to investigate the background of the Painting before she bought it in 1946, and that correspondingly put Dunbar on notice of the need for further inquiry when she putatively acquired the Painting by bequest in 1973.

Interestingly, Seger-Thomschitz argued that the New York art market itself was a red flag. For Seger-Thomschitz to describe what is one of the largest and most important places of art commerce as facially cause for suspicion is hard to accept. Although Seger-Thomschitz was correct to cite a variety of New York court decisions that stressed the importance of diligence, those decisions all state that their holdings are for the purpose of ensuring that New York not become a haven for illicit art trade. For Seger-Thomschitz to argue that New York courts like the one that decided *Lubell* have gone out of their way to enforce the premise that New York should not become a center of stolen art trade on the one hand for the point on the other hand that the trade of art in New York *itself is a red flag* does not follow as a logical matter. Otherwise, any protection or prohibition could be viewed as proof that the activity protected against had in fact taken place.

Somewhat more persuasively, Seger-Thomschitz invoked the postwar climate itself as imposing a heightened duty of inquiry—and with solid foundation. Submitting an affidavit from Jonathan Petropoulos, Seger-Thomschitz argued that the international art market was sufficiently aware of the Nazis' looting of art such that the market's participants should have been on heightened alert when considering the circumstances of any works that had passed through affected areas of the war. This is a far stronger argument than the disparagement of the New York art market generally, with which she led. As evidence of that contemporaneous climate, Seger-Thomschitz cited cover stories in both *Time* and *Life* magazines, the proceedings at the International Military Tribunal in Nuremberg, the activities of the American Commission for the Protection and Salvage of Artistic and Historic Monuments in War Areas (the Roberts Commission), and circulars distributed by the Roberts Commission in 1946. Seger-Thomschitz also argued, supported by an affidavit from Petropoulos, that Kallir had a reputation for having worked closely with Nazi authorities in dispossessing persecuted Jews such as Oskar Reichel of artworks.[75] Presumably to blunt the anticipated defense offered by Dunbar (and the MFA) that Kallir was Jewish, Petropoulos stated in his affidavit that in 1938 Kallir even sold an artwork belonging to a Jewish family to Adolf Hitler, and then delayed payment to the family.[76] For any or all of these reasons, Seger-Thomschitz argued, it could not be said that Blodgett-Platt's good faith (clearly material to the three-year prescriptive period) was an undisputed fact.

Lastly, Seger-Thomschitz argued that even if the prescriptive period would otherwise apply under Louisiana law, the court should invoke federal common law and refuse to apply the ten-year prescriptive period that would apply even if the acquisition was in bad faith (because it had clearly been at least ten years since the 1946 acquisition). To make this argument, Seger-Thomschitz stated the proposition that "federal courts supplant otherwise applicable state law whenever it conflicts with or frustrates important federal interests or policies." *United States v. Kimball Foods, Inc.*, 440 U.S. 715, 728 (1979). Citing *Wright & Miller*, she went on to suggest that "[t]o some extent, each exercise of federal common lawmaking is sui generis in that it is the product of the unique interplay of specific statutory language, case-sensitive policy concerns, and other case-specific matters." 19 *Wright & Miller*, § 4514 3rd ed. (2007). Where state law statutes of limitations are not "devise[d] . . . with national interests in mind." *Occidental Life Ins. Co. v. EEOC*, 432 U.S. 355, 367 (1977). As such, "in some circumstances . . . state statutes of limitation can be unsatisfactory vehicles for the enforcement of federal law." *DelCostello v. Int'l Brotherhood of Teamsters*, 462 U.S. 151, 161 (1983).

With this possibility in mind, Seger-Thomschitz argued that allowing an allegedly stolen painting's title to be quieted would conflict with federal law, and therefore should not be dismissed based on a state's statute of limitations law. To spotlight this conflict, Seger-Thomschitz cited the above-repeated history of national policy and awareness, as well as the 1998 Holocaust Victims Redress Act (HVRA), P.L. 105–158, under which Congress expressed that:

> consistent with the 1907 Hague Convention, all governments should undertake good faith efforts to return private and public property, including works of art, to the rightful owners in cases where assets were confiscated during Nazi rule and there is reasonable proof that the claimant is the rightful owner.

Seger-Thomschitz did not address the act's explicit reference to looted gold rather than looted art. Nevertheless, she argued that the contrast between what she described as national-level policy on Nazi looted art on the one hand and the Louisiana law's potential to undermine it justified setting aside the statute of limitations.

In the end, the court sided with Dunbar. Addressing the dispute over the nature (contract or tort) of the action, the court said that a possessor seeking to establish ownership need only show possession for ten years and that:

> [C]laims, actions seeking ownership of property or enforcement of rights thereof, whether movable or immovable are real actions. Yiannopoulos, 2 *Louisiana Civil Law Treatise,* § 241, 476 (1991).

Such real actions, otherwise known as "revidicatory actions," are expressly authorized by the Louisiana Civil Code. La. Civ. Code art. 526.... [T]here are two kinds of revidicatory actions, depending on the object seized: (1) a "petitory action" for the recovery of immovable property, and (2) an "innominate real action" for the recovery of movable property. Yiannopoulos, *supra,* § 242, 477.

It follows from this basic dichotomy that, as the Civil Code specifically provides, liberative prescription periods for all manner of personal actions, including delictual, contractual, and quasi-contractual would not bar real actions seeking to protect the right of ownership. La. Civ. Code. Art. 3492–3502; Yiannopoulos, *supra,* § 249, at 487. The rationale for this distinction is that "[u]nder our Civil Code, ownership can never be lost by the failure to exercise it—only by the acquisition of ownership by another through possession sufficient to acquire it through acquisitive prescription." *All-State Credit Plan Natchitoches, Inc. v. Ratliff,* 279 So.2d 660, 666 (La. 1972). Pursuant to article 3491 of the Louisiana Civil Code, "one who has possessed a movable as owner for ten years acquires ownership by prescription. Neither title nor good faith is required for this prescription." It is well established that the burden of proof of establishing the facts of acquisitive prescription rests on the party who makes the plea. *Humble v. Dewey,* 215 So.2d 378 (La. App. 3rd Cir. 1968). However, the possessor is aided in this burden by a presumption that the Louisiana Civil Code article 3488 provides:

> [A]s to the fact itself of possession, a person is presumed to have possessed as master and owner, unless it appears that the possession began in the name of and for another.

Dunbar v. Seger-Thomschitz, 638 F. Supp. 2d 659, 662-63 (E.D. La 2009). This passage is almost impossible to understand, and seems unconcerned with its obvious consequence, even incentive, regarding illicit property. Possession turns out to be nine tenths of the law, perhaps.

Even if the claims were grounded in quasi-contract, the court held, the result is the same because those actions have a prescriptive of the same outside length: ten years. As to whether the period should be tolled, the court was clearly persuaded by Dunbar's argument with respect to diligent search, noting the Reichels' claims for other paintings and property—but not this painting.

Lastly, the court summarily rejected the federal common law argument. Citing *Erie v. Tompkins*, the court was dismissive of the idea that there is any federal common law. *Erie v. Tompkins*, 304 U.S. 64, 78 (1938). In addition, while as every law student knows, that case provides the rule of decision for diversity actions in federal court, it does not mean that there is no such thing as federal common law. In any event, Seger-Thomschitz cited ample, colorable precedent in support of not applying the state law's statute of limitations.

With regard to the HVRA, the court held that the statute does not create a private cause of action, citing *Orkin v. Taylor*, 487 F.3d 734, 739 (9th Cir. 2007). Further, the court held:

> [T]he plain language of the statute indicates it was meant to encourage return of works of art where (1) the art was confiscated from claimant during the period of Nazi rule; and (2) the claimant has reasonably proven she is the rightful owner.

Dunbar, 638 F. Supp. 2d at 664. Regarding the allegations of the Complaint and Seger Thomschitz's Counterclaims, it is somewhat difficult to understand how the court could have viewed Seger-Thomschitz's claim any other way. Thus, while (thanks to the MFA) there is a powerful and indeed persuasive explanation for legitimizing the 1939 sale, that is an argument, not an answer. It is certainly not illogical to conclude otherwise. If the 1939 sale's legitimacy were in dispute, then summary judgment would be premature. Instead, the court cast Seger-Thomschitz's arguments that the 1939 sale was coercive and invalid as "suppositions,"[77] but those inferences are the very heart of summary judgment. Are there competing conclusions a rational fact-finder could draw? On this point, the answer would seem to have been yes, partially because Dr. Reed's thorough investigation was not, at that time, available.

Seger-Thomschitz appealed this rather cursory ruling to the U.S. Court of Appeals for the Fifth Circuit, which affirmed the result. *Dunbar v.*

Seger-Thomschitz, 615 F.3d 574 (5th Cir. 2010). The Fifth Circuit did walk back the District Court's overstatement about the nonexistence of federal common law, observing more precisely:

> [A]bsent some congressional authorization to formulate substantive rules of decision, federal common law exists only in such narrow areas as those concerned with the rights and obligations of the United States, interstate and international disputes implicating the conflicting rights of States or our relations with foreign nations, and admiralty cases.

Id. at 577. Texas Indus., Inc. v. Radcliff Materials, Inc., 451 U.S. 630, 640–41 (1981). The Fifth Circuit agreed with the lower court that HVRA created no private right of action, and that "no interstate or international disputes are implicated in this controversy." *Dunbar*, 615 F.3d at 577. Given that the lawsuit was between a Louisiana resident and an Austrian, this is somewhat difficult to understand, but the Court of Appeals thought otherwise.

Most significantly, Seger-Thomschitz abandoned the argument that the HVRA provided a basis to set aside the statute of limitations. Instead, she raised a theory that had not been argued in the lower court: that the Terezin Declaration in 2009 preempted the state law. She defended the nonarticulation of this theory (which would ordinarily bar raising an appeal for the first time as a matter of course) by pointing out that the declaration preceded the District Court's ruling by a matter of days. The appellate court was willing to indulge this point, but held that in any event the Terezin Declaration "is not crucial to the Appellant's preemption argument," *Dunbar*, 615 F.3d at 578, because, had the 2009 declaration never been created, its principles were embodied in earlier undertakings, the Washington Principles chief among them. Seger-Thomschitz had cited *American Insurance Association v. Garamendi*, 539 U.S. 396, 123 S. Ct. 2374 (2003) in defense of this theory. In *Garamendi*, the Supreme Court struck down a California law that required insurers that did business in California and that sold insurance policies to Europe during the Holocaust era to disclose information about those policies to the California State Insurance Commissioner.

This law, the Supreme Court eventually held, was preempted by the implied foreign affairs power of the president. *Id.* Thus, Seger-Thomschitz argued, any state law (such as Louisiana's statute of limitations) that impaired the restitution of Nazi-looted art impinged on the president's power and commitments in that regard and was thus preempted. The Fifth Circuit distinguished *Garamendi*, however, noting that:

> California was essentially pursuing independent policy objectives in favor of Holocaust victims. The existence of its law limited the President's ability to exercise his preeminent foreign affairs authority. In this case, Louisiana has not pursued any policy specific to Holocaust victims or Nazi confiscated artwork. The state's prescription periods apply generally to any challenge of ownership to movable property.

Id. at 579.

Chapter 11

The Nathan Heirs, the Detroit Institute of Arts, and the Toledo Museum of Art

A different theory of involuntary sale was advanced by the claimant in a case involving a Van Gogh painting in the Detroit Institute of Arts (DIA). Martha Nathan was a German Jewish woman who owned the Van Gogh painting, *The Diggers*, which was painted in 1889. Nathan's travails were largely undisputed but were somewhat unusual compared with many other cases, because she had immigrated to France and, in the DIA case, the painting was in Switzerland at the time of its sale.

Nathan was born in Frankfurt am Main as a member of the Dreyfus family. She married Hugo Nathan, who was also an art collector, in Frankfurt. He already owned *The Diggers* when they married, and she inherited it upon his death in 1922. While still living in Frankfurt during the Weimar era, Nathan met the Thannhauser family and lent some of her collection to Thannhauser galleries in Berlin, and in Basel (Switzerland), and to the Frankfurter Kunstverein. In 1930, Nathan shipped a number of her paintings to the Dreyfus (her family) bank in Basel. The Van Gogh was among them, and it remained there but for a brief loan in 1931 to the Städelsche Kunstinstitut (Städelsche Museum) in Frankfurt.

The decade that followed went poorly for Nathan. According to the DIA's published research, Nathan formally immigrated to France in 1937 and became a French citizen. In August 1939, whether by prescience or good luck on the eve of the outbreak of World War II, Nathan moved to Switzerland permanently. The DIA later argued that Nathan had transferred most of her assets out of Germany before her emigration and paid the Reichsfluchtsteuer (flight taxes) before being allowed to take her household effects out of Germany. After immigrating to France, Nathan contacted Georges Wildenstein, the legendary art dealer in Paris, and Justin Thannhauser, by then also in (still-unoccupied) Paris. The DIA claimed that its research showed that Wildenstein, Thannhauser, and Alex Ball offered to buy the Van Gogh for CH 40,920 and CH 30,000 for a Paul Gauguin painting that Nathan had previously loaned to Thannhauser. In December 1938, Wildenstein, Thannhauser, and Ball viewed the paintings and Nathan supposedly agreed (this was the disputed part) to the prices they offered. In March 1941, Wildenstein, Thannhauser, and Ball sold the Van Gogh to Robert H. Tannahill in Detroit for $34,000 (roughly three and a half times what they paid for it). Tannahill bequeathed the Van Gogh to the DIA in 1969, and the DIA transferred ownership to the City of Detroit in 1970.[10]

After the war, Nathan pursued claims for lost property to an extent that was also disputed. According to the DIA, however, the Van Gogh was not among the property whose return she pursued. She lived in Switzerland until she died in 1958. At some point in or around 2006, a group of heirs made a demand on the DIA that it convey the Van Gogh to them as restitution for a wrongful transfer. The DIA maintains that it considered their claim in view of the AAMD and AAM policies and the Washington Principles. After reaching a conclusion that it had no obligation—legal, moral, or otherwise—to return the painting, the DIA took the first initiative and sued the Nathan heirs in the action captioned as *Detroit Institute of Arts et al. v. Claude George Ullin et al.*, 2:06-cv-10333-DPH-MKM. The DIA and the City of Detroit sought declaratory judgment and quiet title action regarding the Van Gogh on the argument that the painting was not looted and was rightly in its collection.

The Complaint set forth much of the uncontested history, but as in many cases brought by a current holder of a painting on the offensive against someone claiming ownership, the Complaint went to great lengths to establish the publicly available location of the work since the war. The Complaint listed publications stretching from 1939 to 1996 that named the current location of the painting for the point that someone who believed it was theirs could and/or should have known where it was and thus made a timely claim. The Complaint also stressed the DIA's view that it had observed and complied with the applicable AAM and AAMD policies, as well as reiterating its commitment to those policies.

The initial defendants answered the Complaint and made a Counterclaim for the return of the Van Gogh. Defendants Claude George Ullin, Albert Henry Ullin, Peggy Dreyfus-Kaufman, Christopher Georges Dreyfus, Dominic Georges Dreyfus, Coralie Cowper f/k/a Coralie Eve Dreyfus, Brigitte Bernard-Salin, Elizabeth Cronk Salin, Francois Birman, Isabelle Williams, Stephane Birmant, and Brigitte Amzalac alleged similar background facts with respect to Nathan's family history. They alleged that although Nathan had indeed managed to leave Germany in 1937, the mere fact or the payment of the flight tax did not presuppose that she (or anyone else in that circumstance) was simply free to take her assets with her. As conditions worsened in Germany, Nathan loaned her brothers considerable amounts of money to keep the Dreyfus bank in operation.

With regard to the retrieval of Nathan's personal effects from Frankfurt, the defendants/counterclaimants agreed that she had been permitted to do so. However, they alleged that the permission had been extracted at a cost of an agreement to donate six paintings to the Städelsche Museum.[78] These paintings consisted of a Gustave Courbet, two by Fritz Boehle, one by Wilhelm Trübner, one by Anton von Burger and a Max Slevogt. In addition, her remaining property was sold following the April 26, 1938, law that required declaration of all Jewish property, and the proceeds paid into blocked accounts, nominally owned by Nathan but inaccessible to her. The remaining contents of her Frankfurt home were shipped to then-unoccupied Paris. Eventually following the German occupation, those items were seized by the Nazis in June 1942.

The Nathan heirs described at great lengths the horrors that followed in German and other occupied areas as she witnessed them. By the end of 1938, they alleged, the money Nathan had been allowed to keep was essentially gone. The heirs pointed out that wherever Nathan lived, her financial desperation had only one cause: her persecution as a Jew. The defendants disputed that it was clear whether Nathan had approached Wildenstein et al., or vice versa, but acknowledged that at some point they made contact. At whatever point the transaction was consummated, the defendants alleged that there was no evidence that Nathan had actually received the money referenced.

Relying on the trail of misery that brought Nathan to the point of sale, the defendants argued[79] not that the sale was under duress by virtue of where and when it took place, but that the agreement for sale was unenforceable because it was unconscionable. Specifically:

> Georges Wildenstein, Justin Thannhauser, and Alexander Ball also knew of the inequality of the bargaining positions and the substantial disparity between themselves and Martha Nathan. They knew that the purported sale would not have occurred in the same form and manner without the continuing result of Martha Nathan's suffering from Nazi persecution.

This was evidenced, they alleged, by the fact that the transaction price was less than half the insured value of the painting and one quarter of what Tannahill paid in 1941. They argued that Swiss and German law would make the transaction voidable. In addition, the Counterclaims alleged[80] that:

> [t]he United States, as a matter of public policy confirmed by the office of the Secretary of State, considered transfers of property from January 30, 1933 to May 8, 1945 to have been presumptively made under duress, and therefore void, if the transaction involved any person who was directly exposed to persecutory measures by reasons of race, religion, nationality, ideology, or political opposition to the Nazis.

This is only partly true, however. That was the policy of the United States but only for transactions with a nexus to occupied areas or to Germany itself. Otherwise, the same presumption would have applied to a transaction in New York in 1941.

With regard to Tannahill, the defendants alleged that the outbreak of war and the depravity of the Nazis' conduct meant that "[c]ollectors of art during the period from December 1938 to March 1941 undoubtedly knew that Jews were continuing to be persecuted by the Nazis."[81] The defendants extrapolated from there to argue that the fact of Nathan's appearance in the provenance triggered a duty of inquiry into the potentially coercive circumstances of such a transaction in Frankfurt. Therefore, they argued, Tannahill was not a bona fide purchaser. Thus, when the DIA acquired the painting from Tannahill's estate, they argued, the DIA could not and therefore did not acquire valid title to *The Diggers*. Lastly, the defendants argued that the DIA had waived any application of the statute of limitations or a laches defense when it agreed to review the provenance of the painting in response to the claim.

The DIA, without seeking any additional discovery, moved to dismiss the Counterclaims. This allowed the DIA to attack the defendants' and/or counterclaimants' best-case scenario: assuming every fact alleged by the claimants to be true, the DIA argued that nonetheless, the Nathan heirs could never prevail in their effort to prove they (and not the DIA) had title to the Van Gogh. Ultimately, the court agreed. The DIA made a two-pronged argument: The claim to *The Diggers* was barred by either the Michigan statute of limitations or the doctrine of laches. Like most states, Michigan's statute of limitations' conversion or replevin is three years. At the outset, however, the DIA pointed out that the defendants/counterclaimants did not even allege that the Nazis stole the painting. In any event, assuming the agreed-upon date of sale in 1938, the claim would have expired under Michigan law in 1941. Moreover, and somewhat unusually, Michigan does not have a discovery rule under which statutes of limitations are tolled for conversion claims. Instead, "the Counterclaims accrued to the [Counterclaimants] or to someone through whom the [Counterclaimants] claim," M.C.L.A. § 600.5805, "at the time the wrong upon which the claim is based was done regardless of the time when damage results." M.C.L.A. § 600.5827.

The statute of limitations argument, articulated thusly, does raise a few questions of logic and/or policy (not specific to DIA or Michigan). Specifically, what relationship would Michigan law have to a transaction in

Switzerland in 1938? For example, assume a different scenario of outright and overt theft: At gunpoint, Party A robs Party B of a painting in Geneva and successfully conceals it. Five years later, Party B sells the painting to Party C in Detroit. Three years after this theft, the Michigan statute of limitations would have run before the property had any relationship to Michigan or to Party C. Specific to (and problematic with regard to) Michigan, that is the reason for the discovery rule; otherwise, Party A would never be able to recover the property.

In any event, the DIA anticipated and addressed alternative theories of when the statute of limitations would have begun to run. Specifically, if the statute of limitations began when Tannahill bought the painting, then the statute of limitations would have expired by 1944. The same result would follow if the statute began to run when the war ended (1945), or when Tannahill left the painting to the DIA (1968). Shrewdly, the DIA also cited to Michigan's borrowing statute, M.C.L.A. §600.5861, which dictates that even if a statute of limitations other than Michigan's applies, a Michigan forum court should apply the *shorter* period as between that other law and Michigan's. The upshot is that if Ullin et al., could point to a law that should apply other than Michigan's and that jurisdiction's statute of limitations were longer than three years, then the three-year time bar would still apply. The DIA's brief did not address the critical link between those concepts: namely, what if that other jurisdiction's statute did allow for a discovery rule or tolling? In such an event, wouldn't the forum court have to combine the rules and limit the statute of limitations to three years but toll it until the plaintiff knew or could have known of the claim? If that were the case, then Ullin's claims would have to be sorted out based on the discovery rule, which is a more complicated question of fact, but which was never litigated.

As noted above, the DIA also asserted a laches defense. As articulated under Michigan law (similar to most in this respect):

> Laches "denotes 'the passage of time, combined with a change in condition which would make it inequitable to enforce a claim against the defendant.'" *Lothian v. City of Detroit*, 414 Mich. 160, 168, 324 N.W.2d 9, 13–14 (1982) (citations omitted); *see Sobocinski v. Quinn*, 330 Mich. 386, 391, 47 N.W.2d 655, 657–658 (Mich. 1951).

The DIA began the argument by suggesting that Nathan would have had no excuse to wait so long if she believed she had been robbed. Not only did Nathan not file suit or make a claim, her claims would have passed after her death in the first instance to her brother, Willy. He did pursue litigation regarding the Nazi-looted property but did not make any claims for the Van Gogh.

Delay is only half of the laches equation, however. The defendant asserting the defense must show that the claimant's delay prejudiced the current possessor. In this regard, the DIA argued that particular prejudice by the death of witnesses who had actual knowledge of the transaction, which included Thannhauser, Ball, Wildenstein, and Tannahill.

Lastly, the DIA argued that either the AAMD and/or AAM guidelines or the offer to consider the claim constituted a waiver of the statute of limitations. A waiver is not ordinarily an acquiescence to something, it is a conscious and explicit abandonment of a right that one otherwise has. *Roberts v. Mecosta County Gen. Hosp.*, 466 Mich. 57, 65 n. 4, 642 N.W.2d 663, 668 (2002). DIA disputed that its "decision to provide full public disclosure of any provenance information it may have regarding a painting's Nazi/World War II era (1933–1945) provenance does not constitute an intentional waiver of its statute of limitations and laches defenses."[82] The DIA clearly believed, with good reason, that Nathan's 1938 sale was not theft or a coercive sale. However, its position on waiver does raise questions. What if, as we shall see with respect to the Kingdom of Spain, there is no question that a painting was looted but a time bar or prescription has run? It hardly seems equitable to invite claimants to review the provenance only to tell them it has been too long.

The defendants/counterclaimants opposition led with the waiver theory:

> [DIA] engaged in actions and conduct clearly indicating its intentional and voluntary relinquishment of its statute of limitations and laches defenses with respect to claims, such as Defendants' claim, asserted in artworks it holds in its collection that have a Nazi-era provenance.[83]

Yet, the facts that the Counterclaims alleged to support that argument had mostly to do with federal efforts in the United States to address and support restitution, not with respect to any specific conduct by DIA. The exception to that was DIA's adoption of the AAMD guidelines, according to defendants. That act constituted a waiver of the DIA's right to assert the statute of limitations. The defendants put it this way:

> [T]he question has to be asked as to whether Plaintiff intended to adopt the Guidelines in anything but name only. Yet, as Plaintiff repeatedly asserts, the DIA is profoundly committed to the highest legal and ethical standards for resolving Nazi-era claims. The only way in which this potential inconsistency can be resolved is by finding that Plaintiff necessarily waived the invocation of procedural defenses such as the statute of limitations and laches so that substantive claims could be decided on the merits.

The defendants characterized the DIA's adoption of the guidelines as an intention to fulfill public policy that waived the defenses it later asserted. The defendants' argument is that the invitation to the general public to examine the results of its Nazi-era provenance research was an implicit acceptance that claims might follow, but that it would also be counterintuitive for the DIA to then try to bar such claims based on something other than the merits. This argument does make some sense. Taking it a step further, the defendants dropped a biting footnote[84] (emphasis added):

> [I]t is, at best, ironic that Plaintiff would contend, as it did at page 19 of its Brief, that it had not waived its statute of limitations and laches defenses because the Guidelines do not mandate its waiver. It should not be necessary for the Guidelines to do so because *in the absence of a waiver of such defenses, the Guidelines are substantively meaningless, save for the public relations benefit to museums such as Plaintiff that would take such cynical advantage*—a stance at odds with Plaintiff's oft-professed fidelity to the highest ethical and legal standards.

The defendants/counterclaimants argued that the DIA had not investigated anything about the painting's provenance, which by 1998 included a transfer during a period of time (the Nazi regime) and involving a persecuted party that were themselves a red flag requiring further scrutiny—until someone contacted the museum. Defendants/counter-claimants ended the waiver argument as follows:[85]

> Plaintiff cannot have it both ways (or all ways): either it is serious about its oft-stated commitment to the highest legal and ethical standards, either it is serious about its commitment to the obligations that it voluntarily assumed when it adopted the Guidelines or it is not. Even if Plaintiff now wishes to affirmatively and openly renounce its adoption of the Guidelines, a genuine issue of material fact exists as to whether it waived any defense claiming the expiration of the applicable statute of limitations concerning Defendants' counterclaims.

Addressing the actual application of the statute of limitations, the defendants argued somewhat less persuasively that the causes of action were not all governed by the same limitations period. In particular, they argued, the declaratory judgment claim was not ripe (because there was no dispute) until 2004, and therefore, the declaration request was within three years. Further, given the assertion of waiver, the timing of that waiver was at least a dispute of fact, and they suggested the date of accrual of a statute of limitations is a factual question for a jury.

Finally, the defendants/counterclaimants took aim at the laches defense in broad strokes in a section entitled "THE COUNTERCLAIMS ARE NOT BARRED BY THE DOCTRINE OF LACHES AS THE PUBLIC POLICY INITIATIVES BEHIND THE RESOLUTION OF CLAIMS TO NAZI-ERA ASSETS WOULD BE RENDERED MEANINGLESS."[86] Putting it another way, the defendants/counterclaimants challenged the idea that there was any unreasonable delay. Instead, they claimed, it was the very adoption of the guidelines (*i.e.,* the DIA's conduct) that brought the issue to their attention.

Ultimately, however, the court sided with the DIA. It took some issue with the breadth of the DIA's argument about the unavailability of the discovery rule but agreed that it was not available in this case because Nathan was the one who sold the painting in 1938 and would have known immediately that she had a claim. Even if the court entertained tolling the statute of limitations, it concluded that it would still have to find the claims time barred because of the claims made in 1973 by Nathan's executor. That would have triggered the duty to investigate further, at the very least. The court was not swayed by the argument that the disagreement that gave rise to the declaratory judgment claim was more recent and therefore timely:

> "[B]ecause a declaratory judgment action is a procedural device used to vindicate substantive rights, it is time-barred only if relief on a direct claim would be barred." *International Ass'n of Machinists and Aerospace Workers v. Tennessee Valley Authority*, 108 F.3d 658, 668 (6th Cir. 1997).

The court was no more moved by the waiver argument, either (emphasis in original):

> The Guidelines further state that "in order to achieve an equitable and appropriate resolution of claims, museums *may* elect to waive certain available defenses." (Id.) Plaintiff/Counter-Defendant has sought to achieve resolution of this claim by initiating the instant quiet title action. This act alone is inapposite to waiving its right to assert defenses it may have available to it.

The claimants appealed the judgment of dismissal of the U.S. Court of Appeals for the Sixth Circuit but dismissed the appeal only three days after it was docketed, bringing the case to an end.

What is perhaps most interesting about this case is how unusually hostile Michigan law turned out to be with respect to stolen property claims. Apart from Louisiana's prescriptive acquisition law, one can scarcely imagine a better forum to retain stolen property. That is not to say that *The Diggers* was stolen, it is to say that as a matter of substantive policy the incentives created by Michigan law are troubling.

The other problem is that the DIA decision effectively gutted the AAMD guidelines from any broader meaning. They have never recovered, and the AAMD has not tried to reverse that. The Ullin parties' observations that museums cannot have it both ways were well put.

The Nathan heirs' case involving the Toledo Museum of Art (TMA) followed a similar course to a significant extent; the adversaries were represented by the very same counsel who squared off in the DIA case. The case involved the painting referenced in the course of the DIA case: *Street Scene in Tahiti* by Paul Gauguin (1891). Indeed, the Complaint, filed by the Toledo museum against the same heirs of Nathan, contains large passages of the same text about the history of Nathan's collection and her life in Europe, except targeted to the Gauguin rather than the Van Gogh. The Gauguin was purchased by the same consortium (Thannhauser, Ball, and Wildenstein), which then sold it to the Toledo museum in 1939 for $25,000. The museum laid claim to the same respect for and adherence to the AAM guidelines, and argued that it had, in response to the heirs' claim, examined the provenance of the work pursuant to the guidelines.

Specific to Toledo and the Gauguin, the Complaint listed dozens of public exhibitions in the intervening decades at which, the museum alleged, a reasonably prudent owner would have discovered its whereabouts, all other things being equal as to title. It similarly alleged that the 1938 price was consistent with a fair market value at the time as a French citizen living in neutral Switzerland. As the DIA had, the Toledo museum pointed to claims that Nathan had made for property and artwork that made no claim to the Gauguin. The TMA sought to quiet title to the painting and for a declaratory judgment that the Nathan heirs had no title to the painting.

The Nathan heirs answered and filed a Counterclaim nearly identical to that asserted in the DIA case. The theory of the case was also the same at its core: that the motivation to sell the Gauguin was indistinguishable from the persecution that Nathan had suffered and witnessed, and that Wildenstein, Ball, and Thannhauser, at the very least, took advantage of that desperation.

The TMA moved to dismiss the Counterclaims even more swiftly than the DIA had. Naturally relying on Ohio (which has a four-year limitations period rather than three years) instead of Michigan law, structurally the argument was the same: That no matter how one construed the timing of the alleged deprivation of title, the claims were time barred. Ohio does have a discovery rule (unlike Michigan), but the TMA made the same argument that the DIA had made in the abstract—that even a discovery rule would have started to run at some point in the intervening decades:

> [E]ven assuming, *arguendo*, that a claim to the Painting began to accrue at various possible dates later than 1938, the claim is still time-barred by Ohio's statute of limitations. *If* a claim began to accrue when the Painting was purchased by TMA in 1939, *id.* ¶¶ 149, 150, such claim would have been time-barred by 1943. Alternatively, *if* a claim began to accrue in 1945, after World War II, such a claim would have been time-barred by 1949. Alternatively, *if* a claim began to accrue after Mrs. Nathan's death in 1958, *id.* ¶ 78(e); Ex. A. (TMA Complaint) ¶ 84, such claim would have been time-barred by 1962.

The TMA made the same arguments with respect to laches and waiver that the DIA successfully made in its case, as well as the counter to the claimants' arguments about the AAM guidelines and changes in policy. In response, the claimants advanced their same theories.

In the end, the United States District Court for the Northern District of Ohio ruled the same way, dismissing the Counterclaims as time barred and defeated by laches regardless. This time, however, the opinion was more pointed as to the central theory of the claimants' case:

> In short, this sale occurred outside Germany by and between private individuals who were familiar with each other. The Painting was not confiscated or looted by the Nazis; the sale was not at the direction of, nor did the proceeds benefit, the Nazi regime.

Toledo Museum of Art v. Ullin, 477 F. Supp. 2d 802, 805 (N.D. Ohio 2006). Given that the holding turned on the statute of limitations and laches, this is dicta, but it is a harsh pronouncement nonetheless.

The claimants appealed the judgment, but in the end, the appeal from the Toledo case was also dismissed by the appellants/claimants.

Chapter 12

The Knives Come Out

By the time that the DIA and the TMA disputes were developing, the problem of timeliness assumed greater prominence. The MFA and other cases at least underscored that the manner of defending a case was often as important as whether or not to do it. Unfortunately, that manner took a darker turn in cases involving some of New York's most prominent museums.

One of the litigations involved the intersection of the artist George Grosz, who was himself persecuted as a degenerate artist (though not as a Jew) and the renowned dealer Alfred Flechtheim, who was targeted so swiftly and ruthlessly that he had to flee Germany before 1933 was even half over. The paintings involved were Grosz's *The Poet Max Herrmann-Neisse* (1927), *Self Portrait with Model* (1929), and *Republican Automatons* (1920). The dispute pitted MoMA against Lilian, the painter's daughter-in-law (as widow of his son Peter), and Martin Grosz, the painter's last surviving son (and Lilian's brother-in-law).

Grosz is now known as one of the paragons of German Expressionism. Many of the expressionists' work captured the disaffection of late imperial Germany and the desolation and desperation of the inter-war period. In particular, painters such as Grosz and Otto Dix (*Kriegskrüppel,* 1920) excoriated what they perceived as the militaristic aspects of German society that had allowed the country to plunge so headlong into the First World War and to be left in such a disastrous state as a result of it.

Not surprisingly, the Nazis found the expressionists' message intolerable. It conflicted with their advocacy of the *Dolchstoßlegende* (the stab-in-the-back legend) that held that Germany's loss in the war was the result of politicians who had betrayed the army in the field; otherwise, Germany would have won the war. This idea was not only causally absurd—the failed springtime offensives of 1918 that completely ended Germany's ability to wage war say otherwise—but was also historical fiction. In any event, throughout their simmering resentment and plots of the 1920s, the Nazis were watching the Expressionists with rage.

Grosz had his first major exhibition at Flechtheim's gallery in 1923. According to Grosz's heirs' 2009 Complaint, by 1925 Flechtheim was paying Grosz a monthly advance of between 300 and 800 Reichsmarks on consignment sales of his paintings. The Hermann-Neisse portrait was created in 1927 and consigned to the Galerie Flechtheim in 1928. Flechtheim loaned the painting to MoMA in 1931 for an exhibition of German painting and sculpture. The self-portrait now at MoMA was similarly painted in 1928 and consigned in 1929.

According to the Grosz heirs, the Galerie Flechtheim terminated the consignment agreement in December 1931, but the works remained physically in Flechtheim's custody. Negotiations followed over the next year, with Curt Valentin acting as Flechtheim's agent. Grosz declined to renew the exclusive agency, but agreed to a further nonexclusive consignment relationship. Throughout this period immediately prior to the Nazi seizure of power, the heirs alleged, the Grosz paintings remained at the Galerie Flechtheim.

Flechtheim sadly did not have to wait until after the Nazis seized power to attract their attention, as evidenced by a now-infamous 1930 issue of the Party propaganda paper *Illustrierter Beobachter* in which Flechtheim's exaggerated Semitic features are portrayed with an illustration that stated "Die Rassenfrage ist der Schlüssel zur Weltgeschichte" ("The race question is the key to world history"). Not content with that level of subtlety, the image superimposes Flechtheim's face on a globe as a star of David rises over it like the sun.

After January 1933, Flechtheim simply could not stay in Germany. He fled and left his galleries in the hands of his longtime employees. In

April 1934, Flechtheim wrote to Grosz in New York to tell him the whereabouts of his paintings. He listed *Self Portrait with a Model* as in Paris and included a price, but did not mention *Hermann-Neisse*. The RBK wrote to Valentin on November 14, 1936, and told him to:

> . . . make use of your connections with the German art circle and thereby establish supplementary export opportunities, if [this is done] outside Germany. Once you are in a foreign country, you are free to purchase works by German artists in Germany and make use of them in America.

As the forced liquidation of Flechtheim's company neared its conclusion that year (the gallery space in Düsseldorf itself having been appropriated by another Flechtheim assistant, Alex Vömel, in 1933), Flechtheim authorized the loan of *Self Portrait with a Model* to the Kunstzaal van Lier, an Amsterdam art dealership run by Carel van Lier, for a July–August 1936 sales exhibition. The final dissolution of Galerie Flechtheim GmbH was on February 20, 1937. Less than a month later, Flechtheim died in London. His widow, Betty, died in 1941, committing suicide after learning that her deportation to a camp in the east was imminent. The Grosz heirs argued that there was no evidence that Flechtheim ever sold either *Self Portrait with a Model* or *The Poet Max Hermann-Neisse* before his death.

Shortly after Flechtheim's death, Van Lier arranged for an auction in early 1938. Van Lier was the high bidder on both *Self Portrait with a Model* and *The Poet Max Hermann-Neisse*. Thereafter, *Self-Portrait with a Model* was sold two months later to Leo Lionni, later the director for *Fortune* magazine from 1948 to 1960. In 1954, Lionni gave the painting as a gift to MoMA.

With regard to *Hermann-Neisse*, it followed a stranger path. Charlotte Weidler was a German art critic, dealer, and curator for the Carnegie Institute in Pittsburgh. On April 12, 1937, she wrote to Paul Westheim, another German critic. The letter, quoted at length in the Grosz heirs' Complaint,[87] bears review (emphasis added):

> I almost forgot something. *To my big surprise I inherited something.* Unfortunately no money. But paintings. As a token of gratefulness.

> This surprised me particularly, because I have long since gotten rid of the habit to count on gratefulness. *It is, which I would never have thought for my life, from Alfred Flechtheim*. I once did him a favor. In his carefree ways, he had spent foreign currency for paintings that were from here, and he would have had to hand in that currency because of the foreign currency laws. They found out about this and it would have caused him and his wife many difficulties. So we made an exchange, I gave him my dollars and got deutschmarks. It helped him and was no big deal for me and quickly forgotten. Also he wants to thank me for spending time with his wife, who suffered under the life in Germany and the persecution. Betty Flechtheim, a fabulous being, Lotte Fürstenberg, Else Schiffer and I are together a lot. Now he wants to thank me that I did not withdraw like so many of those so-called "good friends", but that I, what I've always taken for granted, always stood by her. It really touched me, deeply. In any case, I now have 9 paintings by George Gross [sic], amongst those former museum-property, the big artist-painting, an early, very exquisite one, the [Portrait of the Poet] Max Herrmann-Neisse, the Marseille Girl, the landscapes in Marseille and a still-life, that I admittedly find only moderate. Then a drawing by George Gross [sic] and an important early Pechstein: the women's house on Palau. A Serna wasn't good and I declined to take it. Now the question is what to do with all these pictures. Selling will hardly be an option. Anyways, it really pleased me. Please don't publish this, because otherwise I will only get in trouble, will have to pay inheritance taxes and they will say, how come you are still in contact with the Flechtheim Family.

MoMA founder Alfred Barr later cited the *Hermann-Neisse* as an early Grosz that had been taken from the Kronprinzenpalais in Berlin. Barr's assertion that the painting had been taken from the museum was not true. However, under the circumstances, could Barr have checked the Degenerate Art register to see if the painting had indeed been taken from the German museum, given that Grosz was a prime target in the Degenerate Art auction because of his politics? In any event, Valentin sold the painting to MoMA in 1952 without revealing Weidler's name.

Ironically, Grosz was himself living in New York at the time, but according to his son and daughter-in-law, MoMA never contacted him. It nonetheless came to his attention, however, because he wrote on January 8, 1953, that MoMA "exhibited a painting that was stolen from me (I am powerless against that) they bought it from someone, who stole it."

Over the decades that followed, Germany's federal government and courts recognized its persecution of Grosz both in response to his heirs' restitution claims and as a matter of public recognition. At least as far as his family was concerned, however, the Grosz's claimed not to know about *Portrait of a Model* or *Hermann-Neisse* until 2002 when art historian Ralph Jentsch made the connection while conducting research. Jentsch made demand on behalf of the Grosz heirs on MoMA on November 24, 2003, for their return. On April 12, 2006, MoMA formally refused.

Three days short of the three-year anniversary of that refusal, the heirs filed suit. It is interesting that with the *Schoeps* case behind it, MoMA elected not to follow the same strategy. In other words, it did not sue the Grosz heirs to quiet title in the face of their demands as it had with *Schoeps*. Was this in response to public criticism of the *Schoeps* litigation? It is impossible to know. The heirs made the argument that Galerie Flechtheim had never owned the paintings, so any subsequent transferee tracing its ownership to Flechtheim could not own the paintings, and, in any event, under the circumstances, could not claim to have acquired it in good faith, innocent of its appropriation. In any event (and that assertion was never litigated), the heirs pointed out, the Weidler-based provenance certainly could not be true, and therefore must be disregarded.

After this detailed recitation, the Complaint addresses[88] *Republican Automatons* in only a single paragraph:

> The MOMA acquired Republican Automatons through a source with void title. Title resides in the Heirs.

The heirs sought the return of the paintings and/or compensation for their lost value.

MoMA swiftly moved to dismiss, arguing that the claims were time-barred under New York's statute of limitations. After flatly denying that the paintings had ever been stolen, MoMA pointed the court to New York's choice-of-law rules, advocated for the application of its three-year statute of limitations, and that there was an earlier accrual date that compelled the conclusion that the limitations period had passed. MoMA argued that the cause of action accrued under either Dutch or German law decades earlier and that was governed by statutes of repose there that barred the claims in contemporary times. This distinction is critical, MoMA argued, because New York's demand and refusal rule would apply only if New York substantive law applied to the claims themselves. MoMA argued that even under that rule the Complaint was filed more than three years later.

Under New York law, as MoMA correctly argued, the statute of limitations analysis distinguishes among good-faith actors and bad-faith actors. The demand and refusal rule, it suggested, applies only to good-faith possessors. Yet, the Complaint goes out of its way to criticize the circumstances under which the paintings were acquired, MoMA argued, as a result of which the statute would have run from the date of acquisition in the 1950s. If the acquisition were in good faith, MoMA posited that *Lubell* still requires that the demand not be unreasonably delayed. MoMA argued that even accepting the allegations of the Complaint as true, the Grosz heirs' delay was unreasonable and the claims were too late. This is as a matter of the statute of limitations—not laches, which the motion mentions but explicitly does not advance as a basis for dismissal. *Lubell*, of course, says precisely the opposite with regard to demand and refusal.

With regard to the refusal, MoMA disputed the date and argued that the refusal came no later than 2005, four years earlier. It offered several letters in which MoMA articulated its conclusion that its ownership was justifiable, all outside the three-year limitations period. MoMA argued that the April 12, 2006, letter was selectively chosen and was in fact after the final and effective refusal.

As far as *Automatons* and *Self Portrait with Model* are concerned, MoMA argued that German or Dutch law applied to govern the claims for restitution, but that those laws (either of them) create title by prescription. Unlike Louisiana's short prescription period, German and Dutch law, like many civil law countries, have a longer period that is a hybrid of a statute of limitations and a statute of repose. These, argued MoMA, made the claim to the latter two paintings untimely because of either (1) the van Lier auction, or (2) the end and/or breach of the consignment agreement in Germany, both of which were longer ago than the prescriptive period.

Not surprisingly, the Grosz's opposition leaned heavily on the demand and refusal rule. In addition, they pointed out, their claims for replevin (return) were New York state law claims, not German or Dutch claims. As the opposition[89] framed the issue:

> The Heirs have pleaded (1) Grosz owned the Paintings when he fled Germany; (2) Grosz did not abandon the Paintings; and (3) the Paintings were never returned to Grosz or one of his legal heirs (Complaint ¶ 17, 38-39). Grosz's actions for conversion accrued only at the moment MoMA refused the Heirs' demand.

The claims were New York claims, they argued, because Grosz had never lost ownership. The wrongful act to be adjudicated was not the theft or wrongful sale in Europe during the Nazi era, but the museum's refusal to return a work it did not own, which only occurred in New York. In that sense, the motion strongly implies, the case is no different under the law than a run-of-the-mill, wrongful possession issue. In addition, the Grosz heirs pointed to New York Civil Practice Law and Rules (CPLR) 209, enacted specifically in 1948 to toll claims arising in foreign countries during periods of occupation during the war.

The heirs also took aim[90] at the argument that the statute of limitations tolled from the moment of the alleged theft:

> In every case of stolen property, there is an original thief. If the expiration of a conversion claim cut off rights of a true owner, that would void New York's entire statutory scheme of demand and refusal against subsequent good faith purchasers.

In any event, they suggested, the question of what the final refusal had been was at the very least a question of disputed facts that existed regarding whether the 2005–2007 correspondence had foreclosed any return definitively or was rather a discussion of the available evidence. A fact finder could conclude that the April 12, 2007, letter was the final refusal, just as a fact finder could conclude that it was earlier. However, that is the point: only a fact finder could determine that, and a motion assessing the legal sufficiency of the pleadings cannot resolve factual disputes. In addition, the letters cited by MoMA certainly reference continued conversations, not a flat refusal to discuss further. Most important, MoMA director Glenn Lowry wrote to the heirs on January 18, 2006, stating that the decision had to be considered by the board of trustees—implying that the decision had not yet been made because only the trustees could make it.

With regard to the timeliness defenses, the heirs argued that they are just that: defenses, to be pleaded in an answer and proven. It supported this argument with some colorful diction:[91]

> MoMA's howls about purported missing evidence only increases the likelihood that the Heirs will prevail on the merits. The Court can take judicial notice of the fact that MoMA has not been hit with any earthquakes or floods since its inception. The burden is now upon MoMA to prove a valid legal transaction that would give MoMA good title.

The Grosz heirs also challenged the museum's argument that they had alleged they were bad-faith purchasers. The bad-faith acquirers, they countered, were van Lier, Weidler, and/or Valentin.

The motion sat pending for several months while the parties engaged in a variety of discovery disputes. In particular, the heirs sought discovery about MoMA's acquisition of other works from Valentin, arguing that it would bear on the state of MoMA's knowledge. The magistrate judge assigned to the case denied[92] the discovery dismissively:

> Plaintiff's application to appeal production of addition documents relating to paintings that are not in issues is denied. The discovery plaintiffs seek is at most, highly tangential to the matters in issue. They will shed no light on whether MOMA legitimately acquired title to the paintings in issue. Moreover, the burden entailed in responding to the request far exceeds the probative value of the material being sought.

During this interval, the Honorable Colleen McMahon also disclosed her acquaintance with an associate general counsel not involved in the dispute. The heirs made no request for recusal.

On January 6, 2010, Judge McMahon allowed the motion to dismiss on the grounds that the claims were barred by the statute of limitations. The opinion is interesting, particularly with respect to its analysis of the historical background. Put another way, it drips with contempt for both the claimants and for their theory of Nazi persecution. There is no question that, given the dismissive description of the Flechtheim gallery, the court did not believe anything untoward had led to the painting's sale in the 1930s. For example, the court referred to Flechtheim's involvement and held (emphasis added):

> Flechtheim [sic] *apparently* went out of business at some point. The plaintiffs speculate that his liquidation was the result of Nazi coercion, but that theory is contradicted by certain documents they have attached to their Complaint.

Grosz et al. v. Museum of Modern Art, 772 F. Supp. 2d 473, 478 (S.D.N.Y. 2010). This is a stunning passage, though it is dicta. Flechtheim's persecution is beyond dispute. His financial ruin was not a casual or coincidental event. Even the German Advisory Commission (see Chapter 20), which has shown a willingness to look at the early 1930s with rather rose-tinted glasses, accepted the fact of Flechtheim's persecution categorically and without qualification. The man's face was the focus of Nazi propaganda, after all. It proved to be a telling insight into the court's perspective. The further reference to Flechtheim's affairs "notwithstanding his financial missteps" (*id.*) is, frankly, shocking.

With regard to the applicable law of conversion, the court concluded that an argument of unreasonable delay applied only to a defense of laches, an issue that was not yet ripe for decision. There is little question, however, that the court was displeased with what it described as a lengthy delay in seeking the paintings. That left only the question of when the statute of limitations had begun to run. Assuming a good-faith acquisition by MoMA, when did the Grosz heirs make the demand and when did MoMA refuse to return it? In this respect, the court had no patience at all for the

Grosz heirs' description of the correspondence between the parties and stated flatly, "plaintiffs' claims against the museum accrued on the date when MoMA rejected plaintiffs' November 24, 2003 demand." *Id.* at 483.

The court surveyed several cases involving refusal, pointing to the *Feld v. Feld*, 279 A.D.2d 393, 395 (N.Y. App. Div. 1st Dep't 2001), in which the Appellate Division defined the requirement: "A refusal need not use the specific word 'refuse' so long as it clearly conveys an intent to interfere with the demander's possession or use of his property." In *Borumand v. Assar*, No. 01 Civ. 6258, 2005 WL 741786m, at *14 (W.D.N.Y. Mar. 31, 2005), the U.S. District Court for the Western District of New York took it a step further, holding that "[a]ctions may be sufficient to constitute refusal if they amount to 'an overt and positive act of conversion.'" Based on this, the court held that the July 20, 2005, letter, which followed more than two years of discussion and the retention of former U.S. Attorney General Nicholas Katzenbach to investigate, "was an act utterly inconsistent with plaintiffs' claim of right. It thus constituted the sort of refusal contemplated by the demand and refusal rule." *Grosz*, 772 F. Supp. 2d at 485. Lowry's letter to Jentsch pointed out that the parties agreed that the available information had been exchanged but that they had reached different conclusions about it: "[W]e believe that the available evidence does not lead to any definitive conclusion that challenges the museum's ownership of the picture. In fact, much of what we know argues in favor of MoMA's clear title." *Id.* Thus, that statement, "coupled with the museum's continued retention of the works after it was sent, indicates its continuing intent to interfere with the rights asserted by plaintiff in their demand. . . . After reading the July 20, 2005 letter, no reasonable person could have concluded that MoMA agreed with plaintiffs' assertion that they were the rightful owners of the Paintings." *Id.* at 486.

The court further rejected what it called Lowry's "temporizing" (*id.*) language, describing as "almost certainly designed to entice plaintiffs to continue negotiating and to prevent the dispute from becoming public or escalating into litigation." *Id.* at 487. The interesting part is that the court rejected the idea that Lowry's expressed willingness to consider new evidence meant the demand had not been rejected. Considering that very example, the court ruled that the Grosz's claims were time barred; if hypothetically new evidence came to light the very next day that definitively proved the Grosz heirs' ownership, they would have no recourse whatsoever because their claim was already dismissed. They would be left to argue that MoMA's stated willingness to discuss new evidence somehow constituted waiver of a defense on which it had already prevailed. That is illogical. Lastly, the court rejected the plaintiffs' equitable tolling arguments. That turns, as the court noted, not on an overall argument of fairness, but that something affirmatively prevented the plaintiffs from filing suit in the period during which they sought to toll the limitations period.

The plaintiffs moved for reconsideration, but this was denied, as it usually is absent some compelling, and more recently available information. The plaintiffs then appealed to the U.S. Court of Appeals for the Second Circuit. The case attracted amicus curiae filings that urged the appellate court to overturn the dismissal by the Commission for Art Recovery, and the American Jewish Congress. In the end, however, the Second Circuit summarily affirmed the dismissal:

> As the District Court explained in its thoughtful and comprehensive opinion, the record indicates that refusal took place, at the latest, in a letter from the Director of MoMA to the Grosz heirs' agent on July 20, 2005, and that the agent of the Grosz heirs' confirmed his understanding that refusal had taken place in at least two subsequent letters to MoMA. Because plaintiffs did not file suit until April 10, 2010, more than three years after refusal took place, the District Court correctly dismissed the action as falling outside the statute of limitations.

Grosz v. Museum of Modern Art, Docket No. 10-257, Summary Order and Judgment, at p. 3 (2d Cir December 16, 2010). This is an interesting description of the District Court's caustic opinion. The Second Circuit had no greater interest in the equitable tolling argument: "The mere existence of settlement negotiations is insufficient to justify an estoppel claim." *Id.* Estoppel simply means that a party is prohibited from making a certain argument based on prior conduct that would have induced the other party into acting in a way otherwise detrimental to its interests.

The last few procedural events were interesting after the appellate court's affirmance. On October 20, 2011, after the Groszes' petition for a writ of certiorari was denied, MoMA submitted a letter of motion. MoMA referenced a Confidentiality Order that had been entered earlier in the case. These orders are routine in the course of litigation where parties cannot resist the exchange of information because it could bear on the dispute, but the court restricts or at least slows down the manner in which it can be made public. Such confidentiality orders often have provisions to return information designated as confidential at the end of the case. In this instance, MoMA argued that the Grosz heirs had not returned information designated as confidential. Further, the letter motion stated (emphasis in original), "Plaintiffs' counsel instead has stated that he will neither return nor destroy the designated material, but instead intends to disclose immediately the material to third parties" (emphasis in original).[93] That initial designation had apparently been the subject of motion practice earlier in the case that was unresolved before the case was dismissed. The plaintiffs had challenged the designations and the magistrate judge assigned to hear discovery disputes had directed MoMA to provide more detailed explanations. The case ended before any judge had occasion to rule on the designations. The letter motion stated that plaintiffs had taken the position that absent the court's blessing of confidentiality, none of the materials was confidential. The plaintiffs argued that they intended to provide the materials to the United States Holocaust Memorial Museum and the Yad Vashem Holocaust Memorial Museum in Israel.

The court again referred the dispute to the magistrate judge. The magistrate judge discussed at length the basis for the dispute but noted that at the time, he had assumed that the documents were being exchanged for litigation purposes. Now that the litigation was over, he held, there was no way to allow the information to remain with plaintiffs under the terms of the Confidentiality Order—even though he noted his sympathy to many of the plaintiffs' arguments about the actual designations.

Professor Jennifer Kreder, a scholar at the Chase College of Law at Northern Kentucky University, sought a stay of the discovery ruling until "such time as the Court deems appropriate under the exigent circumstances of allowing two of the premier institutions in the world fostering advanced studies related to the Shoah—the United States Holocaust Memorial Museum and Yad Vashem to deliberate on the most effective way of preservation of records relating to the Shoah."[94] MoMA opposed substantively and procedurally, suggesting that the law professors had no standing to object nor a right to seek to intervene to gain such standing. The magistrate judge denied this request in a handwritten order on the letter opposition "for substantially the same reasons set forth above,"[95] *i.e.*, MoMA's position. That was the end of the case.

Taking a step back, what was this really about? Why did the museum fight so hard to keep documents a secret in a case it had already won? No doubt, as the magistrate judge observed, the museum had been unhappy about turning them over in the first instance. From the perspective of the magistrate judge, once MoMA relied on the Confidentiality Agreement, he probably had no choice. It is hard not to be troubled, however, by the very assertion of that argument. By 2011, the AAMD guidelines were settled museum ethics and encouraged greater transparency among the most important courses of action consistent with those principles. Is it unreasonable to assume that the confidentiality fight was premised on a concern that the documents might prompt other claims? If so, it begs the question, should museums be looking for art or defending against claims to it? At least one museum is clear about where it stands on that issue.

PART FOUR

Back and Forth

Chapter 13

Paul von Mendelssohn-Bartholdy

Paul von Mendelssohn-Bartholdy (1875–1935) was a Jewish banker in Berlin. He was member of the illustrious Mendelssohn extended family, with ancestors and relatives that include the family patriarch and philosopher Moses Mendelssohn, the renowned composer Felix Mendelssohn (von Mendelssohn-Bartholdy's great uncle, born Jakob Ludwig Felix Mendelssohn-Bartholdy) and Felix's sister Fanny, and his banker grandfather (also named Paul Mendelssohn-Bartholdy). The Mendelssohn & Co. bank was established in 1795 by Joseph Mendelssohn, the eldest son of Moses, in collaboration with Joseph's brother, Abraham. Starting in 1815, the Mendelssohn bank was located at Jägerstrasse 49-50 in Berlin until its Aryanization in 1939. Adding to the confusion are the multiple Pauls within the family. Paul Mendelssohn-Bartholdy (1841–1880) was a chemist and a co-founder of the Aktiengesellschaft für Anilinfabrikation (AGFA), son of Felix and cousin to Paul von Mendelssohn-Bartholdy.

Von Mendelssohn-Bartholdy was born in 1875, the oldest son of his parents Ernst and Marie (née Warschauer). He studied at Balliol College in Oxford, and later studied law in Berlin and Bonn. In 1902, he became a shareholder in the family bank, and in that same year married Charlotte Reichenheim. Paul and Charlotte had no children but assembled a remarkable collection of artifacts and paintings, notably by Picasso in particular. They divorced, and Paul remarried to Elsa Lucy Emmy Lolo von Lavergne-Péguilhen, whom he named as his heir (and who, after being widowed, married the Austrian earl Max von Kesselstatt).

Among his collection were Picasso's works *Boy Leading a Horse* (1906), *Le Moulin de la Galette* (ca. 1900), and *Madame Soler* (1903). When he died in 1935, von Mendelssohn-Bartholdy was survived by his second wife and his sisters, Kathe Wach, Enole von Schwerin, Charlotte Hallin, and Marie Busch. Busch's grandson, Dr. Julius Schoeps, son of Hans-Joachim Schoeps, was to become the focal point of the disputes over von Mendelssohn-Bartholdy's Piscassos.

After rising to prominence within the family bank, von Mendelssohn-Bartholdy lived in a home at Alsenstrasse 3, near the Reichstag in Berlin. He also had a country estate known as Gutshaus Börnicke. He was Royal Consul General for Denmark. In addition to the Picassos referenced above, his remarkable collection at the time of the Nazi seizure of power in 1933 included works by Vincent van Gogh, Edouard Manet, Pierre-Auguste Renoir, Claude Monet, Edgar Degas, and Giovanni Battista Tiepolo. He had, according to his later heirs, never attempted to sell any of his collection before the pivotal events of 1933. As with so many prominent German Jews, von Mendelssohn-Bartholdy's visibility and commercial success made him an immediate target of Nazi attention and persecution. First, municipalities throughout Germany boycotted the family bank, undermining its previously successful municipal bond work. This was accompanied by the usual litany of abandonment by German friends and employees and, in January 1934, a designation as an alien under citizenship laws.

As this persecution took effect and with his livelihood under threat, von Mendelssohn-Bartholdy began selling parts of his art collection. In October 1934, he consigned to Justin Thannhauser in Berlin several Picasso paintings including *Madame Soler* (1903), *Head of a Woman* (1903), and *The Absinthe Drinker* (1903), along with *Moulin de la Galette* and *Boy Leading a Horse*. Thannhauser attempted unsuccessfully to sell the works at an exhibition in Buenos Aires. As his later heirs described it, Thannhauser then either stole the paintings or purchased them from von Mendelssohn-Bartholdy for a price far below their fair market value.

In 1936, Thannhauser sold *Boy Leading a Horse* to William S. Paley in Switzerland. Thannhauser used Albert Skira as an agent, whom the heirs later accused of being a well-known trafficker in Nazi-looted art. When Paley asked, Skira allegedly refused to tell Paley to whom he had sold the painting. In approximately 1964, Paley gave *Boy Leading a Horse* to the Museum of Modern Art in New York, retaining a life estate for himself. It remains at MoMA today.

Thannhauser immigrated to the United States in 1940. He brought *Le Moulin de la Galette* with him, or arranged for its delivery to follow him shortly after he arrived. In 1978, he donated the painting to the Solomon R. Guggenheim Museum.

On March 28, 2007, Julius Schoeps's counsel (who also represented Claudia Seger-Thomschitz) wrote to both museums asserting that the 1935 sale was coercive and invalid. On November 1, 2007, he asserted that Schoeps held title and demanded that the Guggenheim and MoMA return each of them to him. Following the museums' internal investigation regarding the provenance and their respective subsequent conclusion that the 1935 sale to Thannhauser was valid, they preemptively sued Schoeps together for a declaratory judgment that they held valid title.

To a startling extent, the museums began aggressively. "[C]ontrary to Schoeps' contention, there is no legal or factual basis for a presumption of duress."[96] Even now, this is a shocking statement; a sale by von Mendelssohn-Bartholdy in 1935, in Germany, is entitled to a presumption of duress under both U.S. law and any sense of morality. The implicit assertion is that the presumption should not apply because Thannhauser was also Jewish. The museums would later make this dubious assertion explicit, as will be seen in the motion papers that followed. In any event, the museums argued, even if a presumption of duress existed, it was rebutted by the available facts in the case. Lastly, the museums rolled out the laches defense that Schoeps had not done enough to look for the paintings such that the museums were prejudiced. MoMA and the Guggenheim also raised an argument not seen in other contemporary cases, even where the familial connection was evident on its face (as was the case in Dr. Seger-Thomschitz's claim to be the sole heir of the Reichel family in the

Dunbar and *Museum of Fine Arts, Boston* cases discussed above); in other words, Schoeps lacked the legal right and was not the proper plaintiff to bring the claim.

The museums' recitation of facts is alarmingly self-serving. MoMA is "the largest and finest museum of its kind,"[97] which, although true, is irrelevant. As in other cases, the museums went to great lengths to describe the extent to which the paintings had been exhibited throughout the world in the decades that followed the museums' acquisition of them. (*Boy Leading a Horse* was the cover illustration for a traveling exhibition of the Paley collection.) Curiously unmentioned is the notorious extent to which Alfred Barr, MoMA's founder, relied on Curt Valentin as a pipeline for degenerate art (now nearly priceless works of expressionist and modernist art) out of Germany in the late 1930s and 1940s. Both museums' incorporation as nonprofits—a fact not at all in dispute—is belabored in the Complaint. The Guggenheim crowed:[98]

> The Guggenheim is a world-class institution with a global reach that realizes its mission through its exhibitions, education programs, research initiatives and publications. Last year, over 2.4 million visitors came to view the art on display in the network of museums that are operated by the Guggenheim in New York, Venice, Bilbao, Berlin and Las Vegas.

The museums' Complaint acknowledges the breadth and importance of the von Mendelssohn-Bartholdy collection, as well as the prominence of the family for generations. It also touts his "longstanding relationship with Thannhauser, from whom he purchased a number of his works, including *Le Moulin de la Galette*."[99] With regard to Thannhauser's history:[100]

> Thannhauser became a leading force in the German and international art community, and the von Mendelssohn-Bartholdys and their extended family became regular and important clients. Due to the rise of the Nazi regime, Thannhauser emigrated to Paris in 1937. He was then forced, in 1939, to remain in Switzerland when the borders with France closed. In 1940, he emigrated to New York.

Acknowledging the persecution faced by von Mendelssohn-Bartholdy, the museums nonetheless focused on the ethnicity of his widow (emphasis added):[101]

> Under these laws von Mendelssohn-Bartholdy, were he still alive, would have been considered Jewish, but his second wife, Elsa, would not. Up until the time of von Mendelssohn-Bartholdy's death in May *1935,* the prominence and social and economic standing of the von Mendelssohn-Bartholdy family, and the prevalence of Protestantism among the family since the mid 1800s, *mitigated the impact of Nazi anti-Semitism on von Mendelssohn-Bartholdy.*

In this view, socially prominent, intermarried Jews were less vulnerable to Nazism. The reality, of course, is the opposite. Prominent Jews, particularly with assets desired by the Nazis for either their monetary worth or their propaganda value, were among the first, not the last, to be targeted.

After discussing for innumerable pages the museums' view regarding the relatively minimal impact that early Nazi terror supposedly had on von Mendelssohn-Bartholdy, the Complaint argues that von Mendelssohn-Bartholdy's ability to send the five paintings for exhibition as evidence that his life was not dramatically affected (One tactic was to minimize time into smaller units like "1930–34" thus creating the impression that a shorter period of time had elapsed when in reality, it spanned the Nazi seizure of power itself.). However, the date of that shipment was March 1933. While easily within the period in which discrimination and Nazi persecution had taken hold, it was still only two months removed from the takeover. Not only that, the Complaint actually *touts* that shipment and its receipt for exhibition by Christoph Bernoulli, a name that appears too often in the postwar chain of title in stolen art cases to be just coincidence (that is, going to the inevitable arguments about good-faith acquisition).

As the Complaint rightly points out, von Mendelssohn-Bartholdy wrote a letter in July 1934 that stated that he would be willing to sell the five Picassos "eventually, for a good offer."[102] Again eliding over significant portions of time in an era in which every passing month brought increasing hardship to Germany's Jews, it casually observes that *Boy Leading a Horse* and *Le Moulin de la Galette* were in Thannhauser's hands by the end of August 1935.

The Complaint argued that it is not actually known when Thannhauser acquired the paintings, whether before or after von Mendelssohn-Bartholdy's death of a heart attack on May 10, 1935. The implication is clear: If he died before August, then Thannhauser may have acquired the paintings from the widow, who was not Jewish and who would therefore enjoy no presumption of duress. Adding to this, the museums cited what they said was the outright transfer of the entire collection in 1927 to Elsa:[103]

> Immediately following the funeral, the beneficiaries of von Mendelssohn-Bartholdys will, including his four sisters, met at Schloss Börnicke in the presence of von Mendelssohn-Bartholdy's pastor and lawyer, and signed a legal protocol representing their official acceptance of the February 1935 will as valid and legally binding and expressly ratifying the 1927 inter vivos gift of von Mendelssohn-Bartholdy's art collection to Elsa and confirming her right to dispose of that collection.

To complete the addition of insult to injury, the Complaint alleges the continued existence of the family bank until 1938, before:

> In December 1938, the three Mendelssohn family members considered Jewish under the Nuremberg laws stepped down as owners, and the process of liquidating the bank began in January 1939 under the leadership of the non-Jewish family members, including Robert von Mendelssohn, and longstanding bank staff member, Dr. Ferdinand Kramer.[104]

This, of course, was less than a month after Kristallnacht. The bank was acquired by Deutsche Bank sometime around 1941–1942.

From there the museums' Complaint takes aim at the very idea of coercive sales, alleging that MGL 59 is no longer in effect—ignoring that whether MGL 59 was in effect in 2007, or 1987, or 1967, is irrelevant. What matters is whether it applied retroactively to sales during the Nazi period. The answer is that of course it did, otherwise MGL 59 would make no sense. Worse, it argues that a sale to a private person enjoys no such presumption, only had the counterparty been the Nazi state itself. This too ignores the logic of the presumption itself: the unconscionable disparity of bargaining power under which an arms' length negotiation is literally impossible.

As to the laches defense, the museums argued that:[105]

> there is no evidence of any steps taken by him or any members of his family to recover the Paintings until 2005, when Schoeps allegedly discovered information on the Nazi-Era Provenance Internet Portal and on MoMA's website that Schoeps claims suggests the Paintings were sold to Thannhauser in Germany in 1935.[105]

But, why would a person assume a painting was stolen in the absence of indications that it was? Why would a person look for a painting that he had no objective reason to believe was stolen—until he did believe that it was stolen? This, it appears, is precisely what Schoeps did, and made prompt inquiry and demand for its return.

Lastly, the museums relied on the intervening ownership of Thannhauser and Paley:[106]

> Here, the available facts show a strong probability that the Paintings were in Switzerland when they were sold to Thannhauser. The subsequent sale of *Boy Leading a Horse* to Paley in 1936 definitely occurred in Switzerland. Even if, as Schoeps claims, the Paintings were sold when they were located in Germany, then under New York choice of law rules, the governing law would be the law of Germany.
>
> Both German and Swiss laws permit good faith purchasers to acquire valid title to art even if the seller did not have proper title.

This latter sentence is a true statement of Swiss and German law in the abstract, but it hardly answers the question of whether museums that enjoy tax subsidies assert it to retain allegedly stolen property. Indeed, the museums defended their decision to sue Schoeps as warranted for the some public benefit.

Schoeps first moved to dismiss the Complaint, arguing that the validity of whether he could be sued as an individual as opposed to being a representative of other heirs. Schoeps was in this position because of an intermediate result in a case to recover the other Picasso that passed through Thannhauser's hands. In *Schoeps v. The Andrew Lloyd Webber Foundation*, 2007 NY Slip Op. 52183U, 2007 WL 4098215 (N.Y. Sup. Ct. Nov. 19, 2007), the New York Supreme Court (the trial court) ruled that Schoeps lacked capacity to sue as an individual; rather, a personal representative of the estate had to be appointed by the Surrogate's Court. Although Schoeps contested that argument and had appealed the *Webber* decision at the time he moved to dismiss the MoMA and Guggenheim Complaint, he effectively argued that until if and/or when that decision was reversed in his favor, there was no proper dispute between him and the museums. The museums countered that he was being sued individually for his assertion of personal rights to the paintings, which made the dispute ripe for adjudication.

A subsidiary dispute then arose over whether German or New York law should govern the question of whether Schoeps had standing to sue or be sued. As the court noted, "Federal Rule of Civil Procedure 17(b)(1) provides that the capacity to sue or be sued of 'an individual who is not acting in a representative capacity' is determined 'by the law of the individual's domicile'"[107]—in Schoeps's case, Germany. The court thus solicited the parties' views as to what that law holds. The museums submitted an opinion by Dr. Wolfgang Ernst, who opined, "[A] single co-heir can be sued for a negative declaration, since the defendant could 'comply' with the judgment without the assistance of his co-heirs."[108] Schoeps did not offer German authority to the contrary but argued that the extent of what the museums could achieve in the lawsuit was not that they owned the painting, but only that he could not sue as an individual to answer that question.

The court denied the motion, concluding that "to require the Museums to wait to file an action to quiet their title while Schoeps takes steps (or not, as he chooses) to be appointed estate representative would grant to Schoeps the unilateral power—to refuse to initiate a lawsuit while hanging the threat of one over the Museums—that the declaratory judgment remedy is designed to temper."[109] The court further stated:

> As the Museums repeatedly have emphasized, however, they seek in this action declarations of their property rights in the paintings

only vis-à-vis Schoeps as an individual, rather than a final adjudication that they hold title to the paintings. They do so because it is Schoeps who has challenged their ownership.[110]

The court also rearranged the captioning of the parties with Schoeps as the plaintiff. Schoeps then answered the Complaint to deny the museums' arguments and asserted a Counterclaim for the return of each of the paintings and a declaration that he owned them. He later amended the Counterclaims to add additional heirs, Edelgard von Lavergne-Péguilhen and Florence von Kesselstatt. The latter two are the sole heirs of Paul's widow Elsa; Kesselstatt is her adopted daughter, and Lavergne-Peguilhen is Kesselstatt's niece. The counterclaimants accused Thannhauser of deliberately concealing the fact of the consignment from the Mendelssohn-Bartholdy family such that they were unaware of it. He stressed that Mendelssohn's decision to sell any of his works only came about after the Nazi seizure of power. The Counterclaim characterized the entire Paley sale as inherently suspicious such that no purchaser could claim to take title in good faith.

After a period of discovery, the museums moved for summary judgment. As with their initial Complaint, the summary judgment motion stands out among other restitution cases for its stridency and aggressiveness. It raised the same arguments outlined in the Complaint: (1) challenging Schoeps's right to be a plaintiff, (2) arguing that the additional plaintiffs had repudiated their claims, (3) arguing that the family's claims were barred by laches, (4) that Paul was affluent in 1935 and therefore was not under duress, and (5) Paley acquired a good-faith title even if Thannhauser didn't have it and passed that title to the museums.

The first argument was premised on the contention that Paul von Mendelssohn-Bartholdy gave his entire art collection to Elsa while he was alive such that Schoeps (who was not a descendant of Elsa's) could not have inherited any claim to Paul's rights. The museums pointed to a contract dated February 8, 1935, as confirmatory of that prior gift. This contract was appended to the motion in the original German, along with multiple translations. The contract states that Elsa would receive the household items and wedding gifts but that "Dabei wird bemerkt, dass die Gemälde Frau von Mendelssohn-Bartholdy bereits bei der Hochzeit von ihrem Gatten geschenkt geworden sind" ("Here it should be remarked that the paintings of Mrs. Mendelssohn-Bartholdy had already been given to her by her husband at the wedding").[111] According to the museums, this was proof that Paul did not own the paintings when he died, which meant Schoeps was not an heir to any claim to the paintings. They did not address or explain the fact that the contract between Paul and Elsa says nothing about which paintings.[112] It certainly does not say these paintings. Moreover, if Paul had given the paintings to Elsa, *he could not have sold them to Thannhauser.*[11] The museums argued that the notary who executed the agreement with the couple (Dr. Ernest Wolff) made some handwritten notes that were kept and filed. The museums argued that these notes "prove . . . that Paul gave the paintings to Elsa, without any encumbrance, upon their marriage in 1927."[113] Yet, the passage cited by the museums merely paraphrases what is in the final document with no mention of which paintings it means. It says nothing about Paul giving all of his paintings to her and is certainly not an available inference on summary judgment. This undermines the argument that the Mendelssohn-Bartholdy family ratified the fact of the gift because all they affirmed was the existence of the contract.

With regard to attacking the rights of Elsa's heirs, the museums argued that because Lavergne-Peguilhen and von Kesselstatt agreed with Schoeps that he was among the rightful owners, they had repudiated Elsa's ownership of the paintings and therefore the rights that they inherited. This too fails as a matter of logic. Lavergne-Peguilhen and von Kesselstatt denied that Paul had given the Picassos to Elsa before he died. Assuming that were true (as this argument did), then Paul owned the Picassos when he sold them under duress and then died. His claim for the return of the painting would have passed to his estate, of which Elsa was the primary heir. Indeed, in that case Elsa's heirs would be the only plaintiffs. Their acceptance of Schoeps as a proper claimant certainly does not repudiate anything about their own rights.

Thereafter the museums motion pressed the theory of laches. First, however, they reiterated their argument that the sale was free from coercion. Most noxiously, the museums' motion pleads Paul's relative affluence as definitive proof that he was under no duress when he sold the Picassos to Thannhauser. This has nothing to do with laches, however. The more relevant point to the argument was the allegation that the claimants could have pressed the claim any time in the sixty years that preceded the dispute.

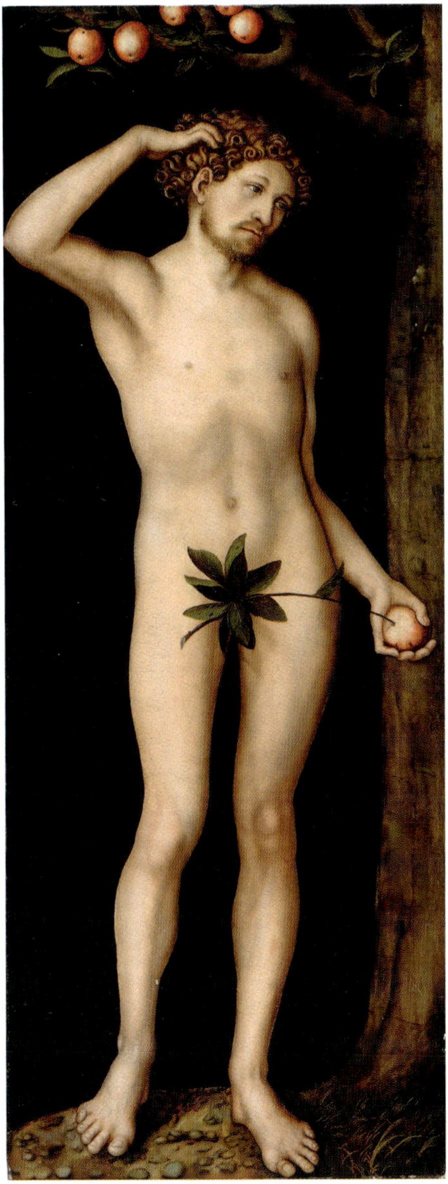

Cranach, Lucas the Elder, German,
1472–1553
Adam, c. 1530
Oil on panel (one of a pair),
75 x 27½ in. (190.5 x 69.9 cm)
Norton Simon Art Foundation

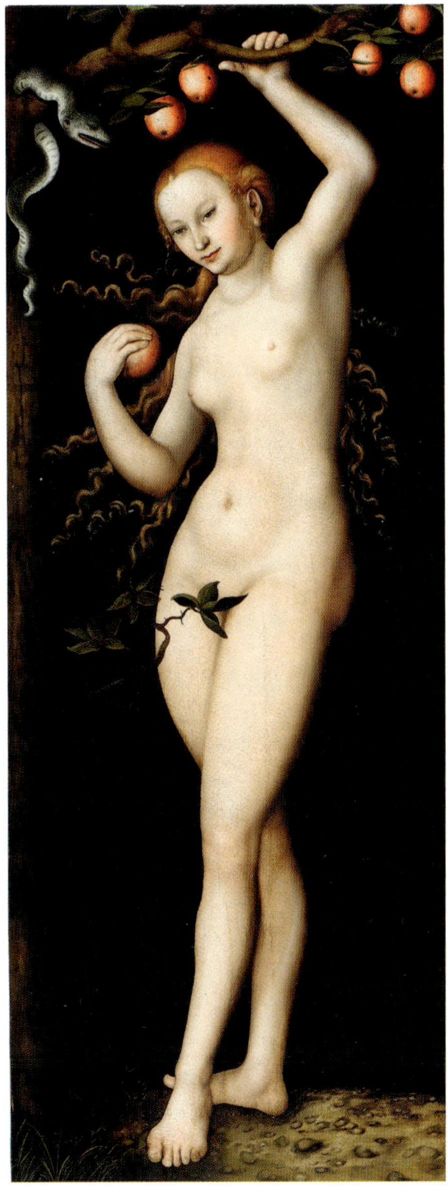

Cranach, Lucas the Elder, German,
1472–1553
Eve, c. 1530
Oil on panel (one of a pair),
75 x 27½ in. (190.5 x 69.9 cm)
Norton Simon Art Foundation

Adam *and* Eve *were among the assets of Jacques Goudstikker's gallery when it was expropriated by Hermann Goering and Alois Miedl. Goudstikker's daughter-in-law and heir Marei von Saher has been in litigation with the Norton Simon Museum at Pasadena over their return.*

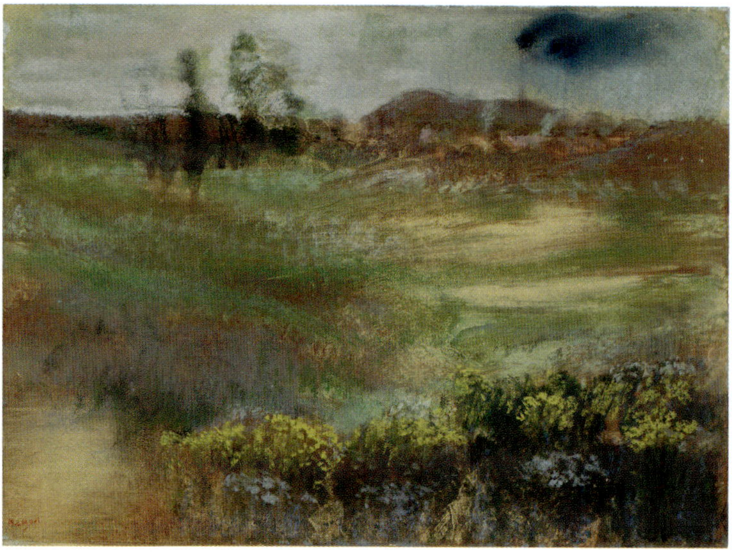

Edgar Degas, French, 1834–1917
Landscape with Smokestacks, c. 1890
Pastel, over monotype, on textured cream wove paper, edge-mounted on board, 317 x 416 mm
Purchased from the collection of Friedrich and Louise Gutmann and gift of Daniel C. Searle
1998.915
The Art Institute of Chicago

Landscape with Smokestacks *was one of the first public restitution disputes in the 1990s. After a period of litigation, the Art Institute of Chicago restituted the work and purchased back a share, after which the heirs of Friedrich and Louise Gutmann donated the remainder.*

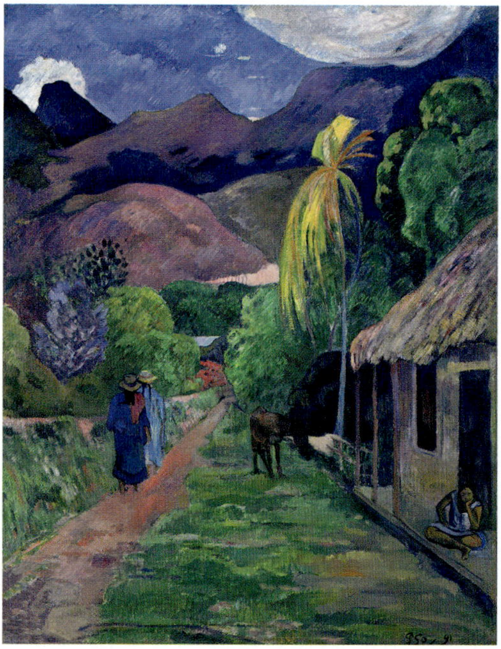

Paul Gauguin, French, 1848–1903
Street in Tahiti, 1891
Oil on canvas, 45½ x 34⅞ in. (115.5 x 88.5 cm)
Toledo Museum of Art,
Purchased with funds from the Libbey Endowment,
Gift of Edward Drummond Libbey
1939.82

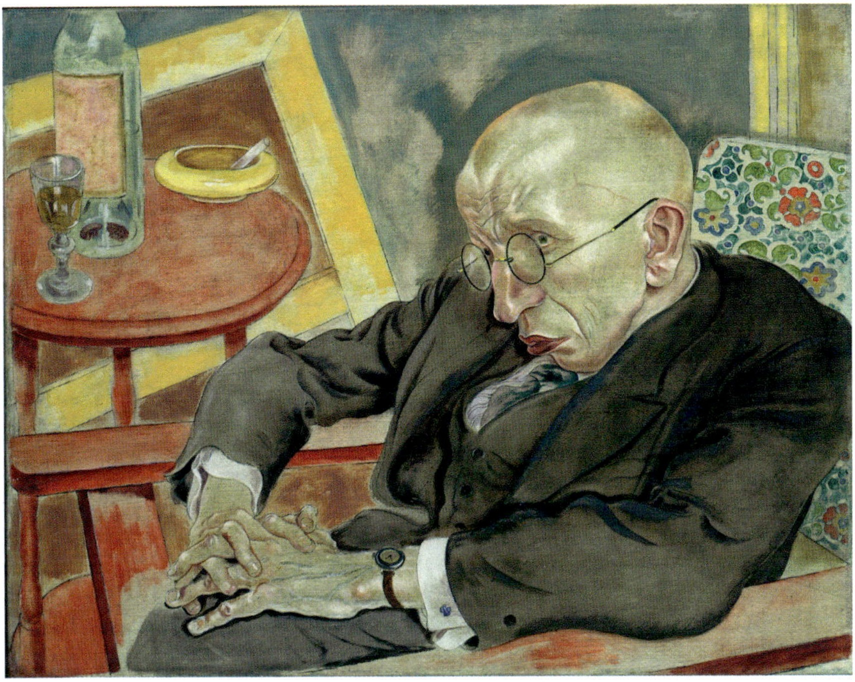

George Grosz, German, 1893–1959
Portrait of the Poet Max Hermann-Neisse (1927/1928)
Oil on canvas, 59.4 x 74 cm
Museum of Modern Art, New York, USA © Leemage/Bridgeman Images

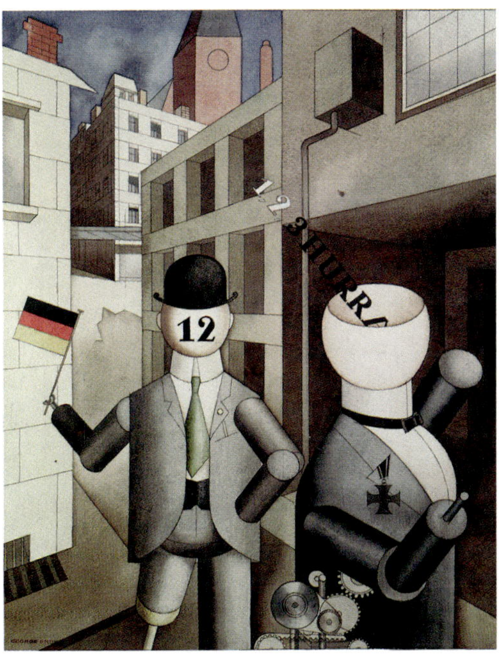

George Grosz, German, 1893–1959
Republican Automatons (1920)
Watercolor and pencil on paper, 60 x 47.3 cm
Museum of Modern Art, New York, USA
Bridgeman Images

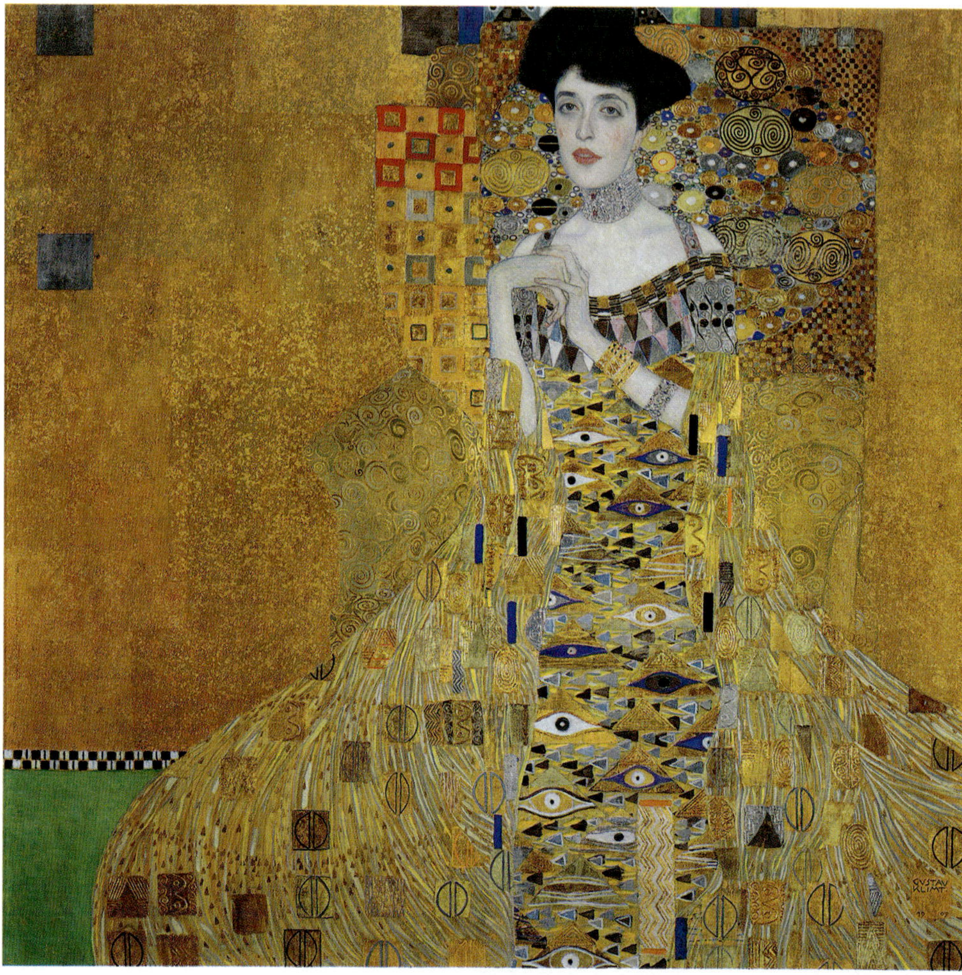

Gustav Klimt, Austrian, 1862–1918
Portrait of Adele Block Bauer I (1907)
Oil, silver, and gold on canvas, 138 cm × 138 cm
Neue Galerie, New York
De Agostini Picture Library/E. Lessing/Bridgeman Images

Maria Altmann, the niece of the subject of the painting, made world headlines when she sued the Republic of Austria over several paintings once owned by her uncle, Ferdinand Bloch-Bauer. The case went to the Supreme Court in 2004 and the portrait was eventually returned to her.

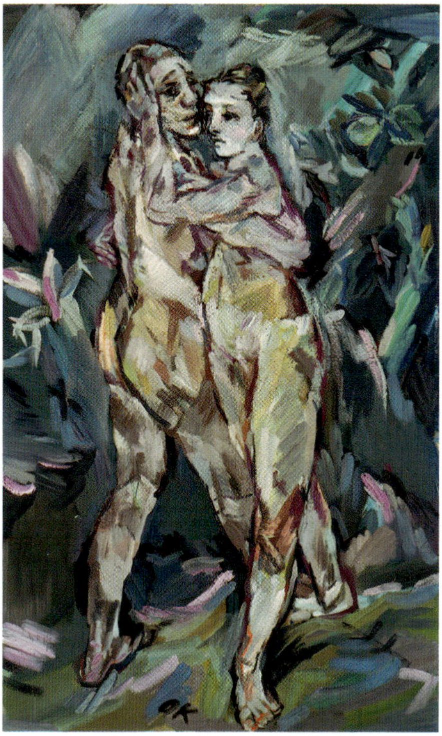

Oskar Kokoschka, Austrian, 1886–1980
Two Nudes (Lovers), 1913
Oil on canvas, 163.2 x 97.5 cm (64¼ x 38⅜ in.)
Museum of Fine Arts, Boston
Bequest of Sarah Reed Platt, 1973.196

The Museum of Fine Arts, Boston brought a preemptive declaratory judgment action over title to this painting that had been owned by Oskar Reichel of Vienna. The museum prevailed in arguing that Reichel's heir, Dr. Claudia Seger-Thomschitz, had pressed her claim too late.

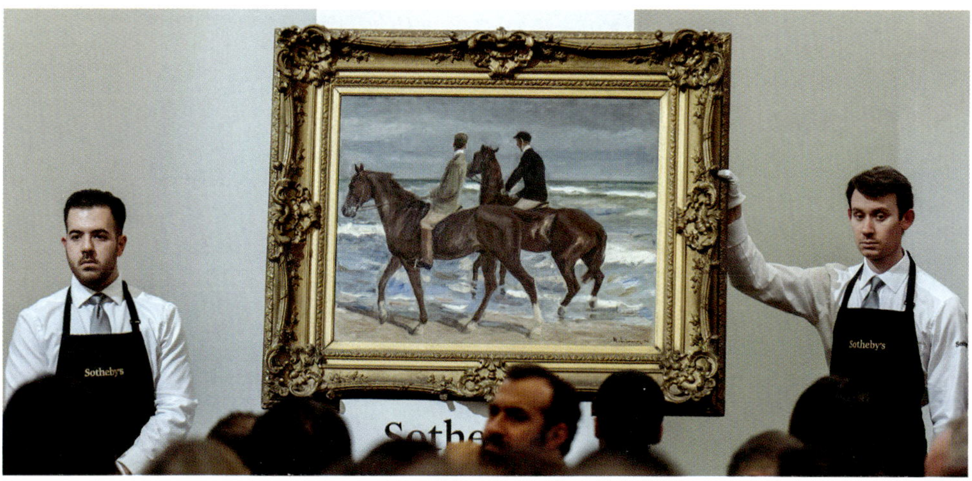

Max Liebermann, German, 18471935
Two Riders on the Beach (*Zwei Ritter am Meer*), 1901
Oil on canvas, 71 cm x 91 cm, private collection

This image became an icon of the Gurlitt saga as one of those immediately circulated with coverage in November 2013 of the bizarre discovery of hundreds of works of art in the Munich apartment of Cornelius Gurlitt, many of which are suspected to have been looted by the Nazis before passing into the hands of Cornelius's father, Hildebrand Gurlitt.

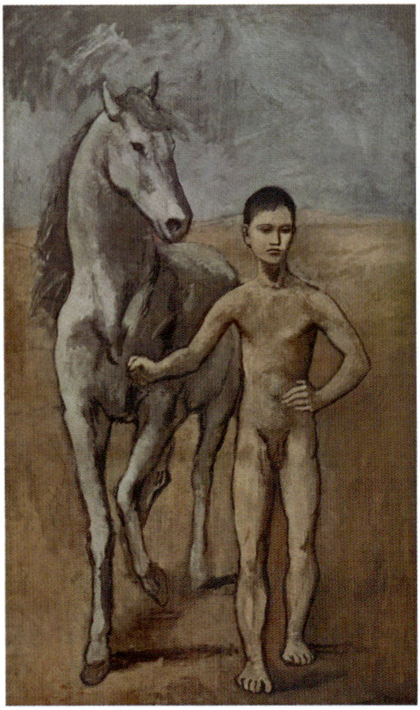

Pablo Picasso, Spanish, 1881–1973
Boy Leading a Horse, 1906
Oil on canvas, 220.6 cm × 131.2 cm
Museum of Modern Art, New York/
Bridgeman Images

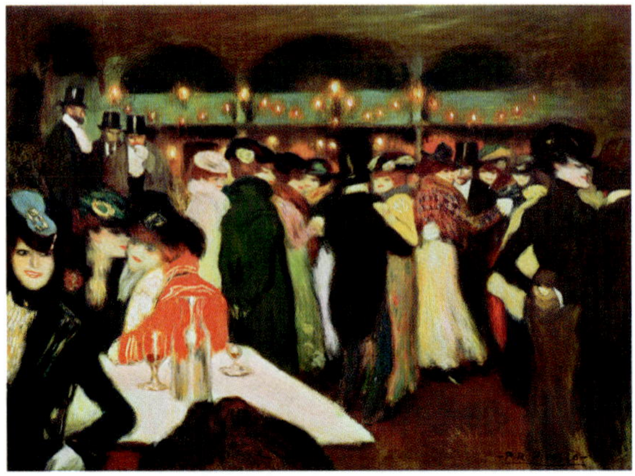

Pablo Picasso, Spanish, 1881–1973
Le Moulin de la Galette, ca. 1900
Oil on canvas, 88.2 x 115.5 cm
Solomon R. Guggenheim Museum, New York/Bridgeman Images

*The heirs of
Paul von Mendelssohn-Bartholdy
battled two New York museums over
these Picasso paintings before reaching
a settlement on the eve of trial.*

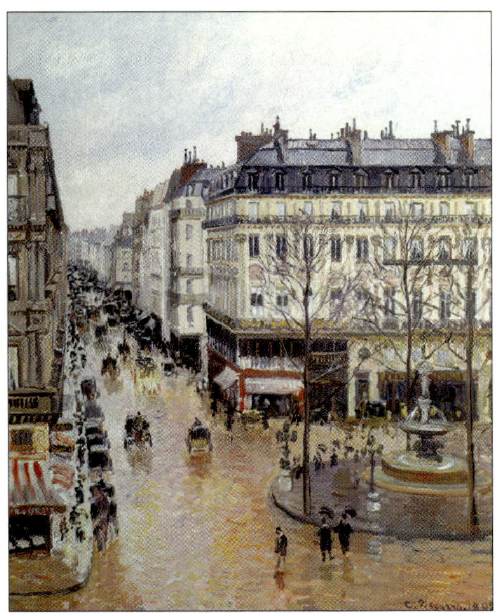

Camille Pissarro, Danish-French, 1830–1903
Rue Saint-Honoré, après-midi, effect de pluie
(*Rue St. Honoré, Afternoon, Rain Effect*), 1892
Oil on canvas, 81 x 65 cm
Thyssen Bornemisza Museum, Madrid
De Agostini Picture Library/G. Nimatallah/
Bridgeman Images

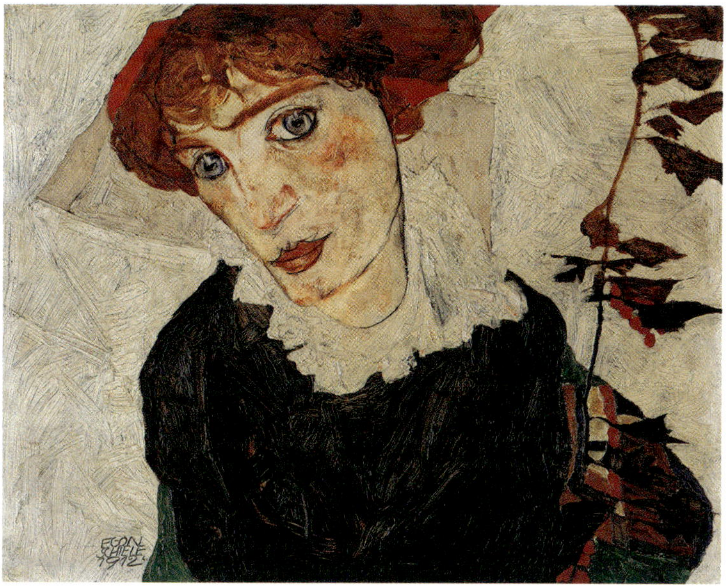

Egon Schiele, German, 1890–1918
Portrait of Wally, 1912
Oil on panel, 32 cm × 39.8 cm
Leopold Museum, Vienna, Austria
De Agostini Picture Library/G. Nimatallah/Bridgeman Images

Few works are as emblematic of restitution battles as this Schiele painting. Seized in New York in 1997 while on temporary loan, the litigation lasted until 2010, when the painting was returned to Vienna's Leopold Museum and the heirs of Lea Bondi were compensated for its seizure during the Nazi era.

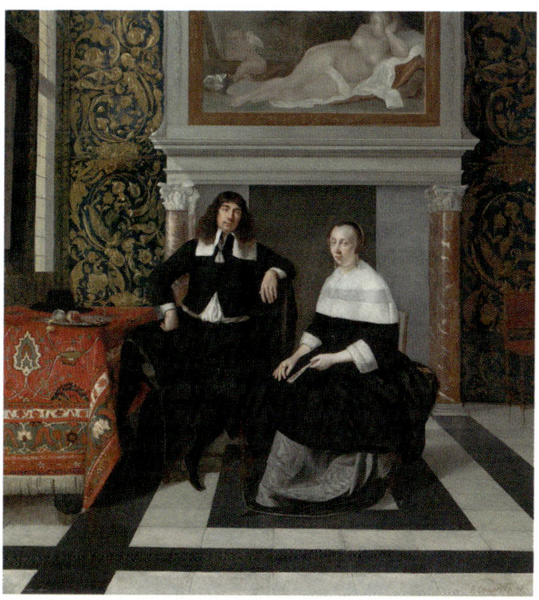

Eglon van der Neer, Dutch, 1634–1703
Portrait of a Man and Woman in an Interior, 1665–1667
Oil on panel, 73.9 x 67.6 cm (29⅛ x 26⅝ in.)
Museum of Fine Arts, Boston
Seth K. Sweetser Fund, 41.935
Photograph © 2016 Museum of Fine Arts Boston

Although the heirs of Walter Westfeld could not obtain the return of works of art that had been auctioned at a forced sale, the Museum of Fine Arts, Boston did agree to a settlement with them about this painting without any litigation.

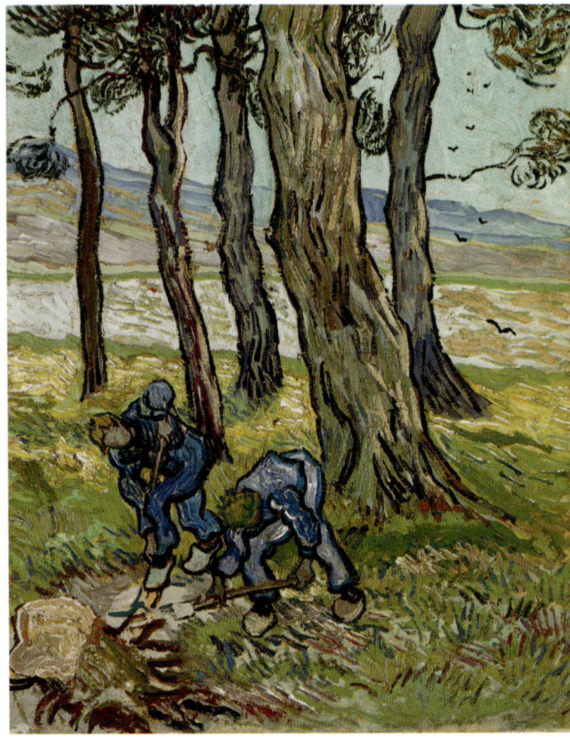

Vincent Van Gogh, Dutch,
1853–1890
The Diggers, 1889
Oil on paper, 65.1 x 50.2 cm
Detroit Institute of Arts
Bequest of Robert H. Tannahill/
Bridgeman Images

Martha Nathan owned this painting and the Gaugin in Toledo. Her heirs unsuccessfully sought to compel their return, but both museums successfully argued that their claims were time-barred under Michigan and Ohio law.

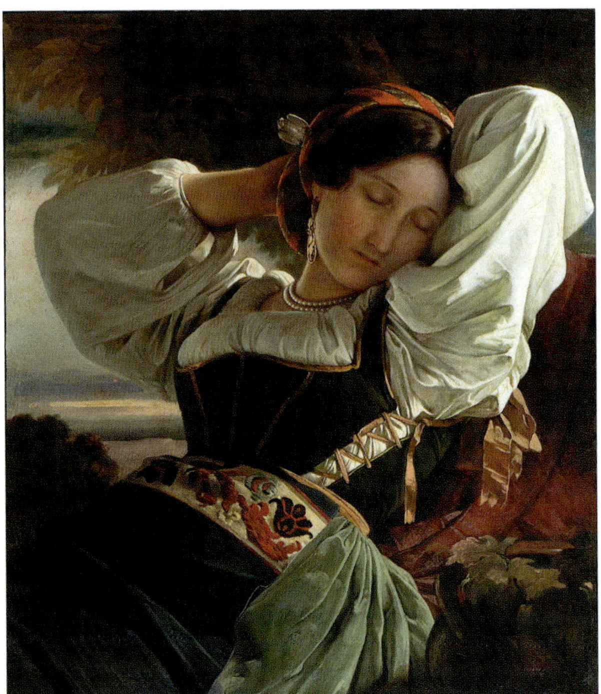

Francis Xaver Winterhalter
Mädchen aus den Sabiner Bergen (Girl from the Sabine Mountains)
Oil on canvas, 74.5 x 63 cm
Iris and Max Stern Foundation,
Montreal, Canada

This recovery by the heirs of Max Stern remains the only final judgment from a U.S. court compelling the return of a Nazi-looted work of art (though many others have been restituted before or during litigation pursuant to settlement agreements).

Lastly, the museums contested the assertion of duress at all. Despite acknowledging that *Menzel v. List* endorsed the proposition that property left in flight to avoid persecution could be considered conveyed under duress, the museums again challenged that Paul had been in any distress:

> It is important, difficult as it may be, to avoid assessing Paul and Elsa's circumstances when the Paintings were sold in 1934 or early 1935 in light of what we now know about the horrendous events that followed. The Museums do not dispute that persons considered Jewish by the Nazis would have been aware of the acts of invidious discrimination and sporadic violence perpetrated by the Nazi Party and the Third Reich before Paul's death.[114]

One needs no hindsight to be shocked at the suggestion that violence against Jews was "sporadic."

The claimants opposed the museums' motion. Principally, the task of one opposing summary judgment was to point out the facts that would have to be resolved to reach a legal conclusion, and Schoeps et al. did just that. Interestingly, their first response to the laches defense was to argue the defense known as "unclean hands." Laches is an equitable defense, meaning it is fundamentally an appeal to fairness. But, to seek equity, one must do equity. As it is often put, one cannot come to a court with unclean hands and plead for fairness. The claimants argued that the museums had recklessly acquired the paintings without the required diligence and were ineligible for these equitable defenses.

The court denied the motion. While acknowledging that a sixty-year gap in pursuing a claim might often be a basis to consider a claim to be too late, it turned on its head the museums' defense that they deserved sympathy because of a lack of witnesses:

> The combination of unique historical circumstances that form the backdrop to this case and the absence of living witnesses to most of the events in question persuades the Court that, at least at the summary judgment stage, greater liberty must be accorded to the drawing of extended inferences than might ordinarily be the case.[115]

The museums moved to reconsider, which the court likewise denied.[116]

With no other issues to sort out, the parties prepared for a jury trial. They submitted jury questions, motions to exclude certain evidence, and other pretrial motions. On the day the trial was to begin, however, the parties reported that the case had settled. The terms were not disclosed, though the paintings remained in the museums. The court was not pleased. It first framed the trial that was to have commenced thusly:

> At the heart of this action are issues of considerable public import. Plaintiffs, heirs of Paul von Mendelssohn-Bartholdy and his wife, claim that two of New York's foremost cultural institutions turned a blind eye to the fact that great works of art in their collections—Pablo Picasso's *Boy Leading a Horse* (1905–1906), now owned by the Museum of Modern Art, and Picasso's *Le Moulin de la Galette* (1900), now owned by the Solomon R. Guggenheim Collection, were sold by von Mendelssohn-Bartholdy against his will because of Nazi duress in the 1930s. The defendant museums, for their part, originated this action (in the form of a declaratory judgment action) to clear their names (or so they said) and to combat what they alleged, in effect, was an effort by plaintiffs and their counsel to use the facade of Nazi iniquities to extort monies from public institutions that were vulnerable to bad publicity.[117]

It was with this at stake that the parties announced a settlement but also an agreement not to disclose its terms. The court was concerned:

> The Court finds the confidentiality provision of the settlement agreement and the plaintiffs' objection to disclosure to be against the public interest and a troubling reversal of the parties' previously stated positions on this issue. From the outset, the parties on both sides portrayed this lawsuit as of considerable public interest because of the importance of establishing the truth concerning the sensitive issues involved. The Museums, when they first brought this action seeking declaratory judgment, stated that they were "prepared to have all factual and legal issues surrounding [plaintiffs'] claims to the Paintings resolved by this Court," Compl. ¶ 8, and they have

> subsequently reiterated that "they are and remain committed to transparency in their actions."[118]

The court clearly pressed the parties to release the terms: "It is hard to see why institutions that proclaim their public status and that seek and receive public support should view themselves as not owing a similar obligation, even if one is not imposed by law."[119] The museums subsequently withdrew their objection. The plaintiffs, however, did not, and the judge responded:

> Plaintiffs, however, for reasons wholly unexplained and seemingly no more compelling than concealing the amount of money going into their pockets, remain opposed.[120]

After reviewing relevant second circuit precedent, however, the court concluded that it was bound to honor the parties' confidentiality agreement. It issued a final parting shot:

> Nonetheless, the Court will docket a copy of the settlement agreement, under seal, in the hope that the plaintiffs, after they have had a greater opportunity to reflect on their public responsibilities, not just to the courts of the United States that have made judicial process so freely available to them, but to the public generally, may yet move to unseal it.[121]

It is easy to understand the court's frustration on the one hand, given the preamble and the case's public importance. However, within the reality of civil litigation settlements, it is hard to square this aspiration with what the agreement might reveal. The museums surely denied liability, and the agreement—like most—is undoubtedly couched as a practical resolution rather than as an adjudication. But, Judge Rakoff's disappointment was to have a lingering importance in the last of the Mendelssohn-Bartholdy cases filed, as will be seen further on.

Chapter 14

Léone Meyer and the University of Oklahoma

A more recent example gives pause to the discouragement that many claimants have expressed, and rebuts the often cynical, hands-in-the-air assertion that litigation serves no purpose. Indeed, only after categorical refusal and litigation did the story find a resolution.

Léone Meyer is the daughter of Raoul Meyer and Yvonne Bader Meyer. Yvonne was the daughter of Théophile Bader, the founder of the Groupe Galeries Lafayette. The Meyers owned a painting by Camille Pissarro, *La bergère rentrent des moutons*. Sometime before 1940, the painting had been sold to Théophile, who then conveyed it to Yvonne. The Meyers were Jewish. After Germany invaded France in 1940, the two countries signed an armistice on June 22, 1940, and the so-called Vichy regime was created, in which Germany occupied part of France and a nominally independent but functionally servile French government administered the remainder of the country. As in other occupied countries, both the German occupiers and the Vichy government passed a series of laws designed to discriminate against Jews and deprive them of civic, political, and economic rights. Amidst this legislative activity, Raoul, Yvonne, and their families entrusted their art collections to the Bank Crédit Commercial de France in Mont-de-Marsan. Shortly thereafter, the German Financial Exchange Protection Commando, better known by its German name, Devisenschutzkommando (DSK), seized a collection of art registered to those same families from the Bank Crédit Commercial and transferred the collection to the Einsatzstab Reichsleiter Rosenberg (ERR); the ERR was the task force that oversaw the looting of many cultural objects in German-occupied areas. The ERR had a depot at the Jeu de Paume in the Louvre. The Pissarro entered the Jeu de Paume sometime around 1941 or thereafter and was assigned a code, *Meyer 13*.

After the war ended, the French government's Commission de Récupération Artistique (CRA) was charged with researching artworks and collections that had been looted during the Vichy regime. Raoul submitted an inventory of his lost collection to the CRA, which included a work entitled, *Petit tableau: la Bergère*. Raoul recovered some works of art through the CRA, but not the painting. In addition, the French *Office des biens et interêts privés* (OBIP) was created in 1944 to gather works recovered from Germany but whose owners were unknown. Raoul also submitted claims to the OBIP.

Later, the French Ministry of Culture published its Registry of Assets Looted in France During the War of 1939–1945 (the *Répertoire des Biens Spoliés en France Durant la Guerre de 1939–1945,* or the "Répertoire"). The Pissarro is listed in the Répertoire. Pursuant to a July 8, 1946, tripartite agreement, the Répertoire was circulated amongst its signatories (France, the United States, and the United Kingdom), as well as countries that might have received looted art (including Switzerland).

Thereafter, in 1953, Raoul found the painting in Switzerland in the possession of Christoph Bernoulli. Bernoulli was listed on a 1946 "Index of enemy and collaborationist personnel involved in art looting recommended for exclusion from the United States,"[122] compiled by the Art Looting Investigation Unit of the Office of Strategic Services (OSS). Raoul unsuccessfully attempted to acquire the painting from Bernoulli, including seeking judicial recourse in Switzerland.

By 1947, the Répertoire had been distributed to major U.S. museums, such as the Metropolitan Museum of Art and the Frick Collection, and to various art galleries including M. Knoedler & Co. The Pissarro was included in an exhibit in the fall of 1956 in New York City at the David Findlay Galleries, French Paintings from the XIXth and XXth Centuries,[123] from the collection of E. J. van Wisselingh & Co., an Amsterdam art dealer. The painting was sold in 1956 to Aaron and Clara Weitzenhoffer, an Oklahoma couple. In 2000, the Weitzenhoffers bequeathed the Pissarro to the Fred Jones Jr. Museum of Art at the University of Oklahoma.

Léone Meyer filed suit on May 9, 2013, seeking damages for conversion and unjust enrichment from the museum, the university, its president, and several New York galleries that she alleged were affiliates or successors of the David Findlay Gallery.[12] The case was assigned to Judge McMahon, who had decided the *Grosz* case against the Museum of Modern Art as well. The Oklahoma defendants quickly moved to dismiss for lack of personal jurisdiction, arguing that they had insufficient contact with New York to be hauled into court there. The motion practice centered on the activities within New York's borders of the university analyzed under New York's long-arm statute. As the Oklahoma defendants correctly pointed out, even seemingly regular activities like recruiting students in New York do not make a foreign defendant necessarily amenable to suit there.

Meyer then amended the Complaint to add the AAMD and the AAM, alleging that she was a third-party beneficiary of their respective guidelines. Specifically, she alleged that the Fred Jones Jr. Museum had a contract with the AAM and AAMD (the guidelines), of which she and other claimants were the intended beneficiaries. According to her theory, those organizations had breached their own guidelines by failing to punish the Oklahoma museum. This was a creative theory, though ultimately one that would not have sustained the New York gallery defendants' presence in the action. The AAMD is an association of people (directors), not museums, and the Fred Jones Jr. Museum's president was not a member. Although the AAM guidelines apply more broadly—and notwithstanding the issues that the guidelines create about whether they have any teeth or force—it is another step entirely from there to an enforceable beneficiary theory. As noted below, this theory was never adjudicated, because Meyer released these defendants voluntarily as well.

Judge McMahon, who had presided over the *Grosz* case, drew the *Meyer* case. She once again issued a caustic dismissal. She noted the factors at issue under New York's long-arm statute and held that Meyer had not satisfied them. The court first noted that:

> The Court long ago concluded that the Findlay Defendants were sued as window dressing, in order to try to site the case in New York rather than in Oklahoma.[124]

With no New York defendants, the court saw no connection to the forum. Most relevantly:

> No allegations in the First Amended Complaint would render the Oklahoma Defendants amenable to specific (long-arm) jurisdiction in New York pursuant to N.Y. Civ. P. Law & Rules § 302. The Oklahoma Defendants allegedly came into the possession of the Pissarro painting in 2000, when it was gifted to the University by the Weitzenhoffer family—who, according to publicly available materials, lived in Oklahoma City. Since then, the painting has been housed on the campus of the University. The First Amended Complaint pleads not a single New York-based activity by the Oklahoma Defendants in connection with either the University's acquisition or its subsequent maintenance of the painting—all of which allegedly took place in Oklahoma.[125]

Analyzing the then-recent Supreme Court case of *Daimler AG v. Bauman*, 134 S. Ct. 746, 760 (2014), the court considered whether even if New York's long-arm statute were applied or satisfied, the Oklahoma defendants were generally present enough that being sued in New York would be consistent with due process. She concluded that they were not:

> So the question is whether the Oklahoma Defendants are amenable to general jurisdiction in the State of New York.
>
> The question answers itself.
>
> The University (sued through its trustees) is located in Oklahoma (indeed, it is an arm of the State of Oklahoma, which raises issues of sovereign immunity); its Trustees govern it in Oklahoma; President (former Senator) Boren resides on the campus in Oklahoma and his

> office is in Oklahoma. The University, its Board and its President are quintessentially "at home" in Oklahoma—not New York.[126]

The court was not finished with Meyer, however. With regard to the AAMD/AAM claims, the court stated:

> Finally, as noted at the top of this opinion, the American Alliance of Museums and the Association of Art Museum Directors were added as defendants when the First Amended Complaint was filed and have recently acknowledged receipt of process. Having read the First Amended Complaint, I assume that a motion to dismiss is forthcoming. Again, I remind counsel for Meyer of their obligations under Rule 11 as signatories of pleadings.[127]

Meyer obliged and dismissed the remaining defendants voluntarily.

A funny thing then happened. Meyer appealed the case to the U.S. Court of Appeals for the Second Circuit. The Court of Appeals never ruled on the judgment of dismissal. It chose instead to remand the action for consideration of whether the case should be transferred to Oklahoma. This may seem like semantics, but it was the safest course to ensure that no statute of limitations could elapse between the judgment of dismissal and the refiling. A dismissal on jurisdictional grounds, of course, does not affect the merits of the case, and the plaintiff can refile in a place where the defendant can properly be sued (although it restarts the clock for any statute of limitations). Clearly, Oklahoma was a more appropriate place to file suit, at least as far as the forum is concerned.

On remand, the District Court reluctantly agreed to transfer the case, albeit defensively:

> The Court of Appeals indicated that this court had "not had an opportunity" to consider Meyer's transfer request because the case "was dismissed before the question of transfer *could* be argued." (Emphasis added.) I must take issue with that statement. The question of a transfer *was not* argued before the complaint was dismissed, but it *could very well have been* argued.[128]

Nonetheless:

> I have great sympathy for plaintiff in her quest to retrieve a painting that meant a great deal to her family, and that was apparently stolen from them in the most heinous circumstances. However, it is difficult for this busy court not to feel put upon by plaintiffs litigation strategy. Her decision to sue the New York Defendants (against whom she had no claim that was not on its face time barred, *see Grosz v. Museum of Modern Art*, 772 F. Supp. 2d 473, 476 (S.D.N.Y.) aff'd, 403 F. App'x 575 (2d Cir. 2010), was a transparent gambit to get this lawsuit out of Oklahoma, which she obviously viewed as an inhospitable forum. Any doubt on that score was eliminated when Meyer discontinued the lawsuit against those parties with prejudice once this court concluded that it lacked personal jurisdiction over the Oklahoma Defendants.
>
> However, I can read between the lines, and I would like to spare the taxpayers of Oklahoma the expense of briefing the issues relating to the never-made motion for transfer. So, after noting that the traditional factors in a transfer analysis overwhelmingly favor transfer, I will *sua sponte* examine the Oklahoma Defendants' four arguments against transfer as presented in the first instance to the Court of Appeals.[129]

That transfer, with the case hanging by a thread, would turn out to be the most important decision in the case.

There had already been important public interest in the case before it was transferred to Oklahoma. On May 13, 2014, the Oklahoma House Conference Committee on Government Modernization and Accountability met to discuss the painting. Representative Mike Reynolds read an opening statement:

> The story of this painting has echoes all over the world right now. At issue is whether or not people who own a piece of property can trust that title to that property will be honored anywhere, under the rule of law.

> We take as our guidance the Constitution and the law, which guarantees that you can trust the value of the title of the property you own.
>
> Moreover, as elected representatives of the state of Oklahoma, we have a fiduciary responsibility to see that not only are state funds honorably spent but that property held within our jurisdiction isn't stolen, however acquired.
>
> That means that today is, underneath it all, about trust.
>
> Trust that the people of Oklahoma know their museums aren't safe havens for stolen art.
>
> Trust that the governance of our universities and museums hasn't been shortchanged: that those empowered to do their duty are in fact doing their duty before the law.
>
> Trust that people of Oklahoma have invested in us as their representatives, to see our tax dollars spent wisely and that the standard of due process has been met—in every respect.
>
> So why the difference of opinion over what's stolen and what isn't?
>
> Some people believe a piece of stolen art isn't like a stolen car—an open and shut case.
>
> If the pickup in your driveway comes up stolen, you're facing criminal charges if you don't return it. It doesn't belong to you and due process demands the right owner get the property back.
>
> Here's my bottom line: why is a piece of art that everybody agrees was stolen in 1941 any less stolen today?[130]

Roughly a year later, the case was transferred to Oklahoma, renewing attention that had flagged. This caught the attention of, among others, the University of Oklahoma (OU) students. In early September 2015, a hired plane flew over tailgaters at a Sooners football game with a banner exhorting "return the stolen art."[131] "We want people to understand that something is happening," said OU sophomore Eric Sundby. "We're not trying to bash anyone. We're not trying to hurt anyone. What we're trying to do is raise awareness."[132] Publicly, the university and President David Boren were unmoved, stating a reluctance to set a bad precedent for the university by "automatically giving away other people's gifts to anyone who claims them,"[133] which is a slightly creative description of a painting that no one was disputing had been stolen.

Behind the scenes and with the apparent mediation of Ronald Lauder, the parties were actually talking, because in February 2016 they announced that they had reached an agreement.[14] As reported by Graham Bowley at the *New York Times*, title to the painting was confirmed as Meyer's, and the work would be displayed on a rotating basis in France (where Meyer lives) and the Fred Jones Jr. Museum of Art until Meyer donates it to a French museum (either during her lifetime or in her will). Meyer's attorney said, "Léone Meyer has agreed that, rather than getting the painting back for her own living room, to continue the public display of the painting for the public."[134] For his part, David L. Boren said, "The University is pleased that a constructive agreement has been reached. The rotating display of the work meets the University's long-stated goal to ensure the painting remains available to Oklahomans and that it continues to be available for educational purposes."[135]

As has been the case often before, a settlement is just that: a settlement, not an admission or concession of what the result would have been. Indeed, the defendants had a powerful legal argument that the Swiss judgment extinguished any claim to title by the Meyer family. Bernoulli is a notorious name that should be a red flag in any provenance, but the finality of a Swiss judgment that found him to be a good-faith purchaser is something that Meyer would have had to contend with. In addition, the Oklahoma defendants reportedly extracted an acknowledgement that the Weitzenhoffers had purchased the painting in good faith as part of the agreement, honoring the university's benefactors.

This was a remarkable development in a case that the Oklahoma defendants had defended vigorously. Giving credit where it is due, like the Degas settlement in Chicago, it is a credit to the participants and lawyers involved on both sides that they were able to bridge the gap and reach an agreement. Bizarrely enough, a number of comments lauded Oklahoma's settlement as proof that agreed resolutions were better than litigation, ignoring entirely that the litigation—above all else—was what led to the willingness to give back the painting.

Chapter 15

Legally Present: A Jurisdictional Hook

The U.S. Supreme Court may have confined *Altmann* to a narrow holding about retroactivity, but the implications of the case were far reaching. Now, art hanging on the walls of European museums was in play. Into the breach stepped the heirs of Kazimir Malevich (born Malewicz), the Russian Suprematism Movement painter. His heirs filed just a few weeks after *Altmann* was decided in the United States District Court for the District of Columbia, concerning fourteen paintings in the possession of the Stedelijk Museum in Amsterdam.

Malevich brought more than 100 paintings to Berlin as part of the exhibition *Berliner Kunstausstellung* in the late 1920s. He had to return unexpectedly to Leningrad and entrusted the paintings to several friends in Germany: Gustav von Riesen, with whom he had stayed in Berlin; Hugo Häring, an architect whom Malevich had met in Berlin; Hans Richter, with whom Malevich apparently meant to make a motion picture; and Dr. Alexander Dorner, director of the Landesmuseum in Hannover. The exhibition closed in September 1927. All of the Malevich works were crated and sent to Dorner at the Landesmuseum. As the Malevich heirs would allege later, returning the works to the Soviet Union was pointless because "Stalinist condemnation of abstract art would undoubtedly have led to their confiscation and destruction."[136]

Dorner exhibited the paintings in Hannover for the remainder of the decade and into the next. Not surprisingly, the paintings attracted the attention of the Nazi authorities as modernist and degenerate art. Alfred Barr, the founder of MoMA, visited the museum in 1935 and expressed an interest in the paintings. Dorner arranged to ship some of the works to MoMA on loan. Malevich died in 1935. Dorner himself later fled Germany in 1937 and brought two other Malevich works with him. He bequeathed those two works to the Busch-Reisinger Museum at Harvard on loan for the benefit of "the rightful owners."[137] Both MoMA and Harvard came to an agreement with the Malevich heirs in 1999. MoMA returned one of the works; Harvard returned all of the paintings in its possession.

By the time the Nazis were in power, the Germans with whom Malevich had left the paintings had scattered, except Hugo Häring. Dorner thus decided to leave the remaining paintings with Häring before leaving Germany. Häring accepted the entrustment and looked after the paintings in Berlin until the Allied bombardment drove him out in 1943. He returned to his hometown, Biberach, where he lived until his death in 1958. Häring had an indirect connection to the Stedelijk Museum. Naum Gabo was a mutual friend of Häring's and of Dr. W. J. H. B. Sandberg, the director of the museum after the war. Gabo led an effort to move the paintings to a more permanent and secure location.

Seeking the works, Sandberg visited Häring in 1951 and continued to visit him until 1956. Häring emphasized that he did not own the works but was merely safeguarding them. He eventually agreed, however, to loan them to the Stedelijk. The Malevich heirs characterized that loan, however, as the result of Häring's "early senectitude, coupled with pressure from his wife and family."[138] On February 29, 1956, Sandberg signed a proposal memorializing the contemplated loan. It provided that the paintings would be loaned to the Stedelijk in exchange for an annuity of 12,000 Deutschemarks, with an initial term of one year followed by the possibility of extension. The uncertainty of the Stedelijk's present ability to pay was also referenced. Sandberg left the proposal with Margot Aschenbrenner, Häring's longtime secretary. Aschenbrenner responded with a memo dated May 8, 1956, that suggested the possibility of purchasing the works for 120,000 DM less the sum of the accrued rental payments.

Sandberg accepted the loan but questioned the purchase scenario, explicitly referencing the fact that Häring did not own the collection. Gabo, too, wrote a letter underscoring what amounted to a bailment, or agreement, to keep something in custody for later return. Gabo also stressed what he described as the "pack of wolves"[139] waiting to take advantage of Häring, as well as the desperate straits the Malewich family found itself in when the painter died. Yet in response to Sandberg's letter questioning Häring's legal capacity, a letter arrived on Häring's behalf. The letter claimed that under German law, Häring had actually become the owner of the paintings. The Malevich heirs accused Ernst Böhme, a notary, of being the author. It also included a purportedly sworn declaration by Häring. The Malevich heirs alleged that these documents were blatant forgeries created by Böhme. As a result, they argued, when the Amsterdam museum exercised its option to purchase the works from the loan, it was knowingly at odds with what Sandberg et al. knew to be the truth.

Over the intervening years, the heirs argued, the museum failed to exhibit, or certainly be transparent about, the history of the paintings. Consequently, none of the purported compensation went to the Malevich heirs; it went to Häring's estate. The Malevich heirs began seeking the assistance of their own government—the Soviet Union—in 1972, but without success. Not until several years after the fall of the Soviet Union, they alleged, were they able to locate the paintings in Amsterdam. In 1996, they sought the return of the paintings, which was supposedly met with statements from the Amsterdam government and the Stedelijk that they were considering the claims. In September 2001, the museum announced it would not return the paintings.

The heirs' suit was filed while the paintings were in the United States for an exhibition at the Menil Collection in Houston that was about to end. The Complaint invoked the same exception to sovereign immunity as *Altmann:* the expropriation exception of § 1605(a)(3) against the City of Amsterdam, a political subdivision of the Kingdom of the Netherlands.

Quite unlike *Portrait of Wally* or *Dead City III,* however, the paintings in question had received immunity from seizure under IFSA, 22 U.S.C. § 2459, which states:

> (a) Whenever any work of art or other object of cultural significance is imported into the United States from any foreign country, pursuant to an agreement entered into between the foreign owner or custodian thereof and the United States or one or more cultural or educational institutions within the United States providing for the temporary exhibition or display thereof within the United States at any cultural exhibition, assembly, activity, or festival administered, operated, or sponsored, without profit, by any such cultural or educational institution, no court of the United States, any State, the District of Columbia, or any territory or possession of the United States may issue or enforce any judicial process, or enter any judgment, decree, or order, for the purpose or having the effect of depriving such institution, or any carrier engaged in transporting such work or object within the United States, of custody or control of such object if before the importation of such object the President or his designee has determined that such object is of cultural significance and that the temporary exhibition or display thereof within the United States is in the national interest, and a notice of that effect has been published in the Federal Register.

Altmann and *Malewicz* both concerned the broader questions of immunity from suit: whether the sovereign defendants could be sued in a U.S. court. That in turn relates to the power of a U.S. court to extend over a certain class of defendants. Immunity from seizure (like the *Portrait of Wally* arguments), by contrast, concerns property, not potential defendants. A painting that is immune from seizure cannot be seized by the government or to satisfy a judgment in a civil lawsuit. IFSA immunizes an object, not a defendant, from seizure, if it has been previously cleared by the State Department. Without that immunity, such seizures or executions (after final judgment) happen as a matter of course; it is how judgments are commonly paid for. If a painting or cultural object has IFSA immunity, it cannot be seized for any reason. IFSA has been the law since 1965 and plays an important role in the willingness of foreign lenders to loan works in an uncertain world.

The filing of suit in relation to the Menil Collection exhibition was not merely a coincidence, however. Amsterdam's Motion to Dismiss focused on the expropriation exception that had probably received the least attention: the commercial activity. The Amended Complaint does not address Amsterdam's commercial activity apart from the Menil show; thus, in assessing the plaintiffs' claims, Amsterdam challenged whether that allegation alone was enough. Amsterdam's initial motion to dismiss the case pulled no punches. It argued that (1) the expropriation exception did not apply, (2) the paintings were neither present in the United States nor present in connection with commercial activity, (3) the claims were barred by the statute of limitations, (4) the claims were barred by the Act of State doctrine, and (5) *forum non conveniens* compelled dismissal.

Amsterdam first argued against the applicability of the expropriation exception. The motion was filed on April 30, 2004, still several months before the Supreme Court's decision in *Altmann,* but still with the benefit of that case's decisions in the District Court and the Court of Appeals (neither of which is even mentioned in Amsterdam's opening brief, not surprisingly). Amsterdam made the threshold argument that exhaustion of remedies abroad was required, citing countries like Iran as the sort of forum that courts would consider futile.

Next, Amsterdam pointed out that by the time of the briefing, the paintings were not actually in the United States. Even though they had been in the country, the paintings had been returned to Amsterdam, before the defendant was served with the Summons and Complaint. In any event, Amsterdam argued that prior presence was not "in connection with commercial activity" (28 U.S.C. § 1605(a)(3)) within the meaning of the FSIA. Here, Amsterdam made a creative argument about circumstances that, by all accounts, had never happened before. Namely, Amsterdam suggested that the paintings were not here "for legal purposes"[140]—suggesting distinction between legal and physical presence—because of the grant of IFSA immunity. Given the grant of immunity from seizure, the paintings' "temporary former presence here could not provide any basis for any claim by the heirs (or anyone else) for their recovery."[141]

Amsterdam then turned to the nature of commercial activity, which would turn out to be the most important legacy of the case. Amsterdam argued that "the Stedelijk Museum's loan of the Malevich artworks was not the type of activity by which a private actor would engage in trade and traffic or commerce,"[142] relying on *Aschenbrenner v. Conseil Regional de Haute-Normandie,* 851 F. Supp. 580, 585 (S.D.N.Y. 1994) (exhibition "[t]aken as a whole . . . were not a type that a private entity would carry on for profit."). Extending this principle, Amsterdam contended that the educational purpose of the exhibition loan, as underscored and confirmed by the State Department IFSA grant, was thus:

> A museum loan is a cultural exchange "granted as a courtesy to other institutions abroad as a means of promoting a greater understanding and enjoyment of art, and advancing the interest of scholarship." Int'l Art Exhibitions Group, GENERAL PRINCIPLES ON THE ADMINISTRATION OF LOANS AND EXCHANGE OF WORKS OF ART BETWEEN INSTITUTIONS § 1.5 (Lisbon 1995), reprinted in NORMAN PALMER, ART LOANS 415, 417 (1997) ("GENERAL PRINCIPLES"). . . . Museum loans are not the type of activity by which a private party engages in "trade and traffic or commerce."

The motion leaned further on the International Council of Museums (ICOM) Code of Ethics: "[A] museum director's task is primarily cultural, allowing certain priorities to operate concerning the promotion of works of art to the widest possible audience, and the care and preservation of those works for posterity."[15] Summing up:

> the Stedelijk Museum Director's decision to loan the fourteen Malevich works to the American museums was based on cultural and educational criteria, not commercial ones. Imanse Decl. ¶¶ 5, 6, 9. Indeed, as expected and intended in such an act of courtesy, the loan-handling fees received from the American museums were nominal and did not cover even the administrative and other costs incurred by the Stedelijk Museum, causing the Stedelijk Museum to lose money.[143]

Whether exhibition loans are commercial activity within the meaning of the expropriation exception was an unsettled question, and Amsterdam made an eloquent and forceful case that the loan of the paintings simply didn't fit within the statute.

Building on that, Amsterdam argued that the claims were too late. Looking to the forum's statute of limitations, Amsterdam noted that under D.C. law, the statute of limitations for claims "for the recovery of personal property or damages for its unlawful detention" is three years after accrual. D.C. Code § 12-301(2) (2001 ed.); *see also Dayton v. Czechoslovak Socialist* Republic, 672 F. Supp. 7, 13 & n.6 (D.D.C. 1986) (applying D.C. Code § 12-301 to property claims in FSIA case), *aff'd,* 834 F.2d 203 (D.C. Cir. 1987). Addressing the heirs' allegations that the Stedelijk had an indefinite loan, Amsterdam cited that in a loan or bailment situation, the claim accrues when "demand has been made and refused, or the bailee takes some action inconsistent with the bailment." *Estate of McCagg v. Indus. Nat'l Bank,* 450 A.2d 414, 416 (D.C. 1982). Thus, according to Amsterdam, the claim accrued in 1958 when Amsterdam proceeded outside the terms of the original loan. At the very least, the Dutch museum contended, the claim accrued in 1996 when Amsterdam's Dutch lawyer, Mr. W.D.T.D. Wiarda, rejected the plaintiffs' demand to return the artwork. Anticipating the plaintiffs' response, Amsterdam argued that "lulling" by the defendants would toll the statute of limitations only where (1) there was "affirmative inducement" by the defendant causing the plaintiff to delay bringing suit, and (2) the defendant acknowledged indebtedness and made a "promise to pay." *Jones v. Government Employees Insurance Co.,* 621 A.2d 845, 847 (D.C. 1993); *see also Bailey v. Greenberg,* 516 A.2d 934, 937–40 (D.C. 1986).

Next, Amsterdam maintained that the Act of State doctrine barred the claims. This argument was harder to accept. The doctrine, as reviewed above, immunizes from review a sovereign's official acts within its own territory. However, it also requires the involvement of one of its citizens, which Häring plainly was not. Moreover, if the Häring loan fit within the Act of State doctrine, then any taking outside a sovereign territory (where the paintings were first taken, it would seem) would become an official act when the property arrived back within the territory. Amsterdam attempted to counter that problem by pointing to the exercise of the option in 1958.

This is a fair point, but still stretches the logical underpinnings of the doctrine.

Lastly, Amsterdam pleaded forum non conveniens, which holds that even where there is jurisdiction over the claims and parties, dismissal is warranted under certain circumstances where the case should be dismissed so it can be litigated in a more convenient forum. As most defendants do, Amsterdam downplayed the plaintiffs' agency in choosing where to sue. Instead, Amsterdam framed the question as one of choice: a court could dismiss if there were an adequate alternative forum. This tilted the presumption slightly outside the normal course, but Amsterdam's argument focused on the relevant factors: the balance of the private interests of the litigants and the interests of the public. Amsterdam noted that the plaintiffs had gone so far as to draft a Dutch Complaint, conceding the availability of the Netherlands as a forum. The private convenience, the museum argued, favored the Netherlands because of the location of the paintings, the availability of compulsory process, and the last remaining live witness (a rarity in these cases). Relying on a case involving Brazilian sources of proof, the museum argued that the need to translate documents favored dismissal. This argument is often made and frankly hard to understand. Claimants against a forum institution, unless they are native speakers, will necessarily have to translate relevant documents even to make sense of them. To ignore their choice of forum on that basis does them no good; they are still put to that burden.

With respect to the public interest, Amsterdam argued that there was no connection at all to the District of Columbia. In contrast, the Netherlands had its own public interest in the fate of the paintings. The need to interpret Dutch and German law, Amsterdam argued, was better left to Dutch courts than an American one.

Still without the game-changing precedent of *Altmann,* the plaintiffs responded by starting with the presumption that the defendant bears the burden to disprove the statutory exception to sovereign immunity. The expropriation theory was simply and elegantly put: "Defendant took the Malevich artwork without compensation to [plaintiffs], their true owners, none of whom was then or thereafter a citizen of the Netherlands is, under 'well settled' principles, 'sufficient for purposes of alleging that the taking violated international law.'"[144] The heirs noted that the exhaustion requirement does not apply where the local remedies are "plainly inadequate," citing *Millicom Int'l Cellular v. Republic of Costa Rica,* 995 F. Supp. 14, 23 (D.D.C. 1998); *McKesson v. Islamic Republic of Iran,* 1997 Dist. LEXIS 8903, *53 n. 25 (D.D.C. June 23, 1997).

The real dispute was over the IFSA question. There was no dispute that the property was physically present in the United States when the case was filed, even if not when process was served. Plaintiffs sensibly pointed out that IFSA relates to seizure and not to any legal fiction about the property's presence in or absence from the United States. They distinguished between the provisions that Amsterdam had cited against seizure within the FSIA—which has its own hierarchy of what may or may not be seized in a case brought under that statute—from the separate regime created by IFSA. As they noted, seizure was not the issue in *Malewicz,* jurisdiction was.

With that said, plaintiffs turned to the issue of commercial activity. Disputing Amsterdam's interpretation, plaintiffs deemed the loan of artwork to be commercial activity, activities defined as "powers that can also be exercised by private citizens, as distinct from those powers peculiar to sovereigns."[145] The very same exhibition, plaintiffs pointed out, included procedurally identical loans from numerous private entities from around the world. Thus, not only could a private citizen engage in the activity in question, but, in this specific case, private citizens did engage in such activity. The Supreme Court had something to say about this in the *Weltover* case as well, on which Plaintiffs relied:

> Because the FSIA provides that the commercial character of an act is to be determined by reference to its 'nature' rather than its 'purpose,' . . . the question is not whether the foreign government is acting with a profit motive or instead with the aim of fulfilling uniquely sovereign objectives.

Republic of Argentina v. Weltover, 504 U.S. 607, 614 (1992). Thus, plaintiffs argued, Amsterdam's educational motives are irrelevant; it is instead the nature of the act that must be considered. Plaintiffs then listed a number of examples of private loans that generated substantial fees, including, ironically, the payment to Baron Hans Heinrich Thyssen-Bornemisza that would later feature in the *Cassirer* case.

Plaintiffs argued that their action was timely first by pointing out the rarity with which a statute of limitations defense will be considered, let alone granted, at the Fed. R. Civ. P. 12(b)(6) stage at which all allegations in the Complaint are assumed to be true:

> A motion to dismiss on statute of limitations grounds . . . is particularly disfavored in this Circuit, as shown by the 'overwhelming line of authority':
>
> There is an inherent problem in using a motion to dismiss for purposes of raising a statute of limitations defense. Although it is true that a complaint sometimes discloses such defects on its face, it is more likely that the plaintiff can raise factual setoffs so such an affirmative defense. The filing of an answer, raising the statute of limitations, allows both parties to make a record adequate to measure the applicability of such a defense, to the benefit of both the trial court and any reviewing tribunal.

Richards v. Mileski, 662 F.2d 65, 83 n.13 (D.C. Cir. 1981); *see also Firestone v. Firestone,* 76 F.3d 1205, 1208-09 (D.C. Cir. 1996); *Allen v. Beta Constr.,* 309 F. Supp. 2d 42, 48 (D.D.C. 2004). Against this, plaintiffs cited what they said were the Complaint's allegations of deceit and concealment to warrant denial of a statute of limitations argument on a motion to dismiss.

Plaintiffs also took issue with Amsterdam's contention about *when* the refusal occurred. They argued that the selection of the 1996 letter in the course of ongoing negotiations was not a final refusal. Taking issue with precisely the kind of analysis that would later doom the Grosz heirs, the Malevich plaintiffs took issue with the idea that an exchange of information can be considered a refusal even if the possessor never indicates an actual willingness to return the painting. It is striking (and fortuitous) given the contempt that the Grosz heirs received, to read a cogent argument such as this:

> The Heirs' American counsel subsequently advised Defendant that it had carefully reviewed the facts related to the Malevich artworks

> possessed by Defendant and had consulted with Dutch counsel, and conveyed the Heirs' continuing demand that the artworks be returned, offering to discuss the case at a meeting in New York or Amsterdam.[146]

In other words, the museum was at least giving consideration to returning the works. Only on September 5, 2001, did the museum issue a formal statement that the city officials had rejected the claim—just like the board resolution that the court brushed aside in *Grosz.* Plaintiffs cleverly began with the more recent timeframe and the demand and refusal requirement. They next responded to the idea that the claim accrued in 1958. They pointed out that the Complaint squarely alleges an instance of fraud and concealment at a time when the heirs were all behind the Iron Curtain.

With respect to the Act of State doctrine, plaintiffs argued that the theft was by the City of Amsterdam, which while a sovereign subdivision, is not a national sovereign government, and therefore, the doctrine was not relevant. The requirement forbids application of the doctrine to a subdivision of the national government. A city cannot engage in foreign relations at the national level, so it requires no deference to matters of state.[16]

Lastly, the plaintiffs challenged the *forum non conveniens* argument. The Netherlands were not an adequate alternative forum, plaintiffs argued. Indeed, the preparation of a draft of a Dutch Complaint but the decision not to file it was in large part due to the realization that no such claim was available because Amsterdam's lawyer articulated why the claim would be barred by the statute of limitations. This made it clear, plaintiffs argued, that the museum intended to raise the Dutch statute of limitations in the city lawyer's letter:

> Your clients are of the opinion that reliance on a limitation period is "unacceptable", which I do not understand. I cannot find any support in legal literature or in case law for your argument that a higher standard should apply to the Municipality, as a government organ, than to private parties. I would remind you that, pursuant to the 31 October 1924 Act and until 1 January 1992, claims against the government became time-barred after a period of 5 years.[147]

Further, plaintiffs challenged the contention that the balance of the parties' private interests analysis favored dismissal. A plaintiff's U.S. citizenship or residence is entitled to consideration in favor of retaining jurisdiction. *Wiwa v. Royal Dutch Petroleum Co.,* 226 F.3d 88, 102 (2d Cir. 2000), *citing Guidi v. Inter-Continental Hotels Corp.,* 224 F.3d 142 (2d Cir. 2000). Plaintiffs also raised the very point alluded to above: The documents that supposedly needed to be translated were actually in the city's possession, undermining any claim of hardship. A home forum for a U.S. resident or citizen does not have to be the one where the plaintiff lives. *Iragorri v. United Techs. Corp.,* 274 F.3d 65, 73 (2d Cir. 2001). "There is very little inconvenience," plaintiffs argued, "in shipping documents from the Netherlands to the District of Columbia."[148] Two plaintiffs spoke English but none spoke Dutch. In addition, the claim of compulsory process was not right, given the Netherlands' hostility to U.S.-style discovery. Lastly, plaintiffs noted that wherever the case was tried, that court would have to apply and interpret laws other than its own. Balanced against the defendant's assertion of foreign interests, plaintiffs asserted the District of Columbia's own interest in the case:

> The FSIA's expropriation exception, in favor of our courts hearing cases involving the alleged expropriation of property in violation of international law, which stands in stark contrast to the policy of The Netherlands, which, as discussed above . . . has helped create a haven for stolen art.[149]

After the briefs were submitted, *Altmann* was decided by the Supreme Court. The District Court issued its ruling about four months later. The court determined that it did not have a complete enough record to rule on the extent of Amsterdam's commercial contact with the United States. The court reviewed the factual allegations and the text of the FSIA and IFSA; they also noted that it need not make a threshold determination of whether the rights in property were taken in violation of international law, only that "[t]he claim must merely be substantial and non-frivolous to provide a sufficient basis for jurisdiction" *Malewicz v. City of Amsterdam,* 362 F. Supp. 2d 298, 307 (D.D.C. 2005). The court ruled that unless Amsterdam waived its statute of limitations defense under Dutch law, it could not determine that there was a clearly adequate remedy in the Netherlands that would have required plaintiffs to exhaust their remedies there. *Id.* at 308.

The court rejected Amsterdam's interpretation of the FSIA to require the physical presence of the property in the United States. *Id.* at 309. It acknowledged the codification in the FSIA of the restrictive theory of sovereign immunity, as explained in *Altmann.* That history was more than a preface with regard to the particularities of the property's location in *Malewicz:*

> Critically for this point, FSIA intentionally overrode the common-law requirement that a plaintiff obtain *in rem* jurisdiction over property before suit could be filed against a foreign sovereign. *See* U.S. Statement at 6 ("Section 1605(a)(3) of the FSIA, first effective in 1977, provides for the possibility of *in personam* jurisdiction over foreign states in expropriation cases without the need for the prior attachment of the property in question.") (citing H.R. Rep. 94–1487, 94th Cong., 3d Sess. at 8, *reprinted in* 1976 U.S.C.C.A.N. 6604, 6606). It would be anomalous to re-insert the jurisdictional requirements of an *in rem* action when Congress so clearly intended to remove them from consideration. The Court concludes that Plaintiffs' filing of the complaint while the artworks were physically present in this country was sufficient to meet the "present in the United States" factor of FSIA without regard to later service of the complaint.

Id. at 309-10.

The status of the paintings as possibly affected by IFSA, however, posed a question that intrigued the court. The United States Department of State had filed a statement of interest. That statement pejoratively described the case as "Plaintiffs are therefore using the window of opportunity afforded by the Malevich exhibition[s] as the jurisdictional hook for their claims,"[150] a characterization with which Plaintiffs did not disagree. The United States argued that § 1605(a)(3) requires a sufficient nexus such that the foreign sovereign would have fair notice that it was submitting to the jurisdiction of the courts. The United States had taken the position that a sovereign would have had no such expectation by lending to a temporary exhibition. The United States did not take a position on the specific case, but nonetheless asked the court to give "great weight" to its opinion about commercial activity.[151]

The court, however, found no inconsistency. IFSA and the FSIA were neither inconsistent nor contradictory. A plaintiff cannot seize a painting with immunity, and it cannot serve the defendant in a way that would interfere with the physical custody or control of the artworks. Amsterdam's reliance on IFSA was thus misplaced because immunity from seizure is not immunity from suit for a declaration of rights.

The court then turned to the extent of the commercial contact by considering another section of the FSIA that contains reference to a "substantial" contact. 28 U.S.C. § 1605(e). Here again the nature of the act was critical. The court looked to *Practical Concepts, Inc. v. Republic of Bolivia,* 811 F.2d 1543, 1549 (D.C. Cir. 1987): "[I]f the activity is one in which a private person could engage, it is not entitled to immunity." The court went on:

> In large measure, the terms "commercial" and "sovereign" are merely opposites: if an act is something only sovereigns do, it is not "commercial." Similarly, if an act is something that a private person or entity *can* do, it is not "sovereign." "Commercial" means only "not sovereign," as long as there is some example of private action of a similar type connected with "trade and traffic or commerce."

Id. at 313. In light of this, the court had little trouble concluding that Amsterdam had engaged in such activity by lending the Malevich paintings to the Menil show. Loans occur around the world, and in substance, they do not depend on whether the lender is sovereign or private.

The court was troubled, however, by the prospect of a chilling effect that might be created by finding jurisdiction on the basis of exhibition loans, and whether the loan was substantial enough to warrant that risk. The court denied the motion to dismiss and directed the management of the case to develop the record further on these jurisdictional points.

After discovery, the parties briefed the question again and came before the court. The result was the same: Amsterdam's motion to dismiss was denied. *Malewicz v. City of Amsterdam,* 517 F. Supp. 2d 322 (D.D.C. 007).

The opinion focused on the parties' submissions about the scope of activity within the United States that occurred as part of the Menil exhibition. The loan agreement had been negotiated and executed by correspondence, not in person. The paintings were tendered to the Deutsche Guggenheim in Berlin, not shipped directly from Amsterdam. Stedelijk employees did courier the paintings to America, though that was at the election of the borrowing institution, not the Dutch museum. The court was also interested in the kind of consideration that the Dutch museum received for agreeing to the loan. It received a nominal fee less than the overall cost, making the venture a net cost, not a net profit. Plaintiffs still described that fee as excessive. Many of these factors, the court concluded, seemed minimal, but "The problem with the City's position, however, is that it treats each of these facts in isolation rather than collectively. When the facts are taken together, the City's contact with the United States in connection with this transaction is more significant than it contends." *Malewicz,* 517 F. Supp. 2d at 332.

Unsuccessful with regard to commercial activity, Amsterdam asked the court to reconsider its ruling about the requirement of exhaustion of remedies abroad. In the end, however, the court determined that the plaintiffs' argument was correct: The claims could not proceed in the Netherlands. As with the shorter period in Louisiana in *Dunbar,* the Dutch prescription period ran from possession with no interruption or equitable tolling. The court also returned to the statute of limitations argument, but the procedural posture was still on a motion to dismiss. Discovery had apparently focused on, if not been limited to, jurisdictional issues. The conclusion was thus the same: To reach the issue would have required resolution of too many factual issues. Lastly, addressing the renewed Act of State argument, the court held:

> [T]he City's acquisition of the Malewicz paintings from Hugo Häring in 1956 was not the type of sovereign act that receives protection under the act of state doctrine. The acquisition may have been an "official" act in the sense that it was done by an employee of the City of Amsterdam — the director of the Stedelijk — acting in his capacity as such. But it was not an "official action by a foreign sovereign" as that phrase has been used in the relevant case

> law because it was not an action taken "by right of sovereignty"; any private person or entity could have purchased the paintings for display in a public or private museum.

Id. At 339.

This was apparently sufficient motivation for the parties to resume discussions. In April 2008, they announced that the heirs would be given title to five of the works in dispute.

In response to this case, the U.S. House of Representatives passed the Foreign Cultural Exchange Jurisdictional Clarification Act. Identical bills passed the House in early 2012 and again in 2014 and 2015, but the bills failed to win passage in the Senate and be signed by the president; thus, they expired without becoming law (and remained just a bill sitting on Capitol Hill).

The bills would have amended the FSIA to clarify when a cultural object loaned with immunity from seizure pursuant to IFSA could also constitute the "commercial activity" (28 U.S.C. § 1605(a)(3)) element. They eliminated federal court jurisdiction only when the sovereign defendant has no other commercial activity in the United States, a scenario that has only happened once: in *Malewicz.* In addition, the change still did not apply to claims regarding Nazi-looted art, meaning even a sovereign defendant that lent a painting looted by the Nazis into the United States could be sued, even if the painting could not be seized. The AAMD lobbied heavily for the bill's passage the first time, hardly a surprise given the amicus briefs filed in *Portrait of Wally,* for example. Whatever the merits of the bill, it did not gain sufficient interest to be passed into law in its initial attempt. That changed in 2016. On December 10, 2016, Congress passed the Foreign Cultural Exchange Jurisdictional Clarification Act, and President Obama signed it into law on December 16, 2016, as Public Law No. 114-319.

Chapter 16

The Pissarro of Lily Cassirer

Julius Cassirer, along with his brother Louis, was one of the founding partners of Dr. Cassirer and Co. Kabelwerke Berlin-Spandau, which manufactured electric cables, insulated supply lines, and wires. Julius's son, Bruno, and Louis's son, Paul, joined forces to pursue their passion for art. In 1898, the first cousins founded the Bruno and Paul Cassirer Publishing House. They shared a particular devotion to Impressionism that they had acquired at Paul Durand-Ruel's gallery, art that arrived later in Germany because of the Kaiser's conservative tastes.

Julius died in 1924 and left *Rue Saint–Honoré, après-midi, effect de pluie* (*Rue St. Honoré, Afternoon, Rain Effect*) by Camille Pissarro to his oldest son, Fritz (Bruno's older brother). Fritz was a musician who had worked as conductor of the Komische Oper in Berlin and later in London. He died of a brain tumor just two years after his father. His estate devolved to his wife, Lilly Karolina Cassirer (née Dispecker). Lilly was from the Bavarian town of Oberelsbach. Lilly and Fritz had one child, Eva Charlotte. Eva Charlotte married one of her father's first cousins, Friedrich Wilhelm Cassirer (also nicknamed Fritz). Even a review of these given names confirms the extent of this Jewish family's assimilation within Prussian and German history.

Yet, the younger Fritz was more independent, supposedly joining Carl von Ossietzky's Republican Party in the mid-1920s. Professionally, he worked in the paper industry and advertising business.

They lived in Berlin, on Siemensstrasse in Grünewald, a western suburb, which the city's expansion in the 1920s turned it into the vast, sprawling metropolis for which it was renowned. Their first child was a son, Klaus Wolfgang. Just four months later, Eva Charlotte died of influenza. Klaus grew up in Berlin with his father and near his grandmother, Lilly at nearby Ludwigstrasse 176.

The family's business was forcibly closed on March 30, 1933. Fritz and his twelve-year-old son left their house that night with only two suitcases and fled to Prague, a natural destination for many victims of political persecution. Prague was a traditional Habsburg city with substantial German language history and culture, and many expatriates found refuge there. Together with Franz Höllering, Fritz founded the *Prager Mittag* paper. The *Prager Mittag* was critical of Nazi Germany, and so after the annexation of Czechoslovakia, Fritz could not stay. He went to Paris via Hungary, Yugoslavia, Italy, and Switzerland. Klaus was by then in London.

In 1939, Klaus finished school. His grandmother Lilly, who was by then remarried to Otto Neubauer, was trying to obtain a visa to leave Germany, for obvious reasons. She was eventually able to leave but not until there was a reckoning with the Nazis over her assets. In addition to the Pissarro, she owned an Ernst Barlach sculpture, a Ruysdael landscape, and other artworks. An official of the *Reichskammer der bildenden Künste* (Reich Chamber of the Visual Arts or RBK) obtained a warrant to search Lilly's home. This man, Jakob Scheidwimmer, expressed an interest in buying the Pissarro. Lilly later testified in 1951 that:

> I went along with it, although I knew this price didn't even remotely reflect its true value. Theoretically, I would have the option of trying to sell the painting to another Aryan art dealer. . . . Furthermore, we had to consider the possibility that Scheidwimmer—we weren't sure whether he had connections with the Gestapo—might take offense at our refusal to sell.

On March 16, 1939, they signed a contract for the painting for RM 900. That money, like all assets at that point, went into her blocked account. Scheidwimmer also engaged in a convoluted back and forth with the Ruysdael in which he claimed that experts had declared the work inauthentic, but he believed it was real and wanted to buy it. As Lilly also later said:

> People will wonder why I let this happen and didn't stand up for my rights. In order to understand, you must realize the difficult position we were in at the time. Back then, we weren't living in a state where law and order prevailed; in fact, we Jews in particular were deprived of all rights and ostracized. Day and night we lived in fear of being picked up by the Gestapo for no apparent reason and taken to Dachau.

She and Otto left Germany on July 24, 1939, for England. She was billed RM 136,713 in flight taxes, and RM 104,800 in a Jewish asset tax—more than $4 million today. Klaus was in France in the Pyrénées and was trapped when the war broke out. After a torturous journey through Morocco, he made it to New York, where his father and stepmother had arrived earlier. He changed his named and lived the rest of his life as Claude Cassirer.

The painting followed a complicated path as well. Scheidwimmer had agreed to purchase several other paintings from Jakob Sulzbacher. These included Carl Spitzweg's *Andacht im Freien* (*Outdoor Prayers*), Heinz Bürkel's *Landschaft mit Kühen*, and *Der kranke Dackel* (*The Sick Dachshund*) by Franz von Defregger. Sulzbacher, a department store owner in a borough of Munich, also Jewish, was interned at Dachau after the November 1938 pogroms, and when he was released, Scheidwimmer approached him again. He gave the Pissarro to Sulzbacher for reasons that are unknown—perhaps as consideration for the other paintings—and Sulzbacher fled Germany with the Pissarro in his luggage. It was seized in Rotterdam by the occupying German forces while Sulzbacher was en route to Brazil. The painting somehow made its way from there into the hands of Ari Walter Kampf, son of painter Eugen Kampf and nephew of Nazi-approved landscape painter Arthur Kampf. It was auctioned in 1943 in Berlin at Hans W. Lange auction house for RM 95,000, more than 100 times what Lilly had been paid.

Lilly searched for her property after the war. In 1958, she settled her claims with the German government. The German government confirmed that the painting had been lost due to persecution and paid Lilly DM 120,000. That settlement explicitly referred to the possibility that the Pissarro would surface, although its location was then unknown. In that event, her right to the property would remain unchanged so long as she repaid the settlement. Lilly died in 1962 in Cleveland, Ohio. Claude learned in 2001 where the painting was: Madrid. Baron Hans Heinrich Thyssen-Bornemisza, a Dutch-born Swiss industrialist (and client of Goudstikker), had acquired the painting at some point. The Pissarro had been sold in 1952, in New York, at the Knoedler & Co. Gallery to Sydney Schoenberg in St. Louis, Missouri. Then in 1976, it was purchased by Thyssen-Bornemisza at the Hahn Gallery, again in New York. He sold it, and his vast art collection, to the Kingdom of Spain in 1993, where it has hung ever since in the Museo Thyssen-Bornemisza.

Claude requested the return of the Pissarro from Spain. This request was refused. In 2003, a request from five members of Congress was met with a denial as well. In 2005, with *Altmann* now Supreme Court law, he filed suit in the U.S. District Court for the Southern District of California (the same court in which Maria Altmann had filed her case), in Los Angeles, against the museum as instrumentality and the Kingdom of Spain as a foreign sovereign. Claude Cassirer invoked the expropriation exception of § 1605(a)(3), and alleged that Spain and the Thyssen-Bornemisza Collection Foundation had engaged in commercial activity through:

> borrowing art works from American museums; encouraging United States residents to visit the museum and accepting entrance fees from them; selling various items to United States citizens including images of the painting; and maintaining a web site where United States citizens may buy admission tickets using United States credit cards and view the paintings on display, including *Rue Saint-Honoré, après-midi, effect de pluie*.[152]

The defendants moved to dismiss, and the court permitted some jurisdictional discovery. Among Spain's principal arguments was that regardless of *Altmann*, the FSIA expropriation exception did not apply because Spain had not taken anything in violation of international law, it was merely in possession, now, of the property at issue. After considering that evidence, the District Court denied the motion(s), and the defendants appealed. The initial three-judge panel agreed with Cassirer that § 1605(a)(3) does not require Spain to be the entity that actually engaged in the taking, and that the foundation engaged in sufficient commercial activity to be subject to jurisdiction. It also held that while exhaustion was not required by the statute, a prudential analysis should be conducted, and remanded the case for that determination. The full U.S. Court of Appeals for the Ninth Circuit then agreed to hear the case en banc.

The full court briefly reviewed the history of the FSIA, as the D.C. District Court had under *Altmann*. Neither the Foundation nor Spain argued with the contention that the transaction between Lilly Cassirer and Scheidwimmer was a taking in violation of international law. *Cassirer v. Kingdom of Spain*, 616 F.3d 1019, 1027 (9th Cir. 2010). Because the painting was not in the United States, the Ninth Circuit held that the question was whether the Foundation "is engaged in a commercial activity in the United States. A 'commercial activity' means either a regular course of commercial conduct or a particular commercial transaction or act. The commercial character of an activity shall be determined by reference to the nature of the course of conduct or particular transaction or act, rather than by reference to its purpose." *Id.* The questions for determination on appeal were (1) whether the expropriation exception relied upon in *Altmann* or *Malewicz* covers a claim when neither defendant was the foreign state that took the painting in violation of international law; (2) whether the Foundation was engaged in a sufficient commercial activity in the United States; and (3) and whether exhaustion of remedies was required.

The full Ninth Circuit disagreed with Spain's interpretation. The statutory language is written in the passive voice and "focuses on an event without respect to an actor." *Id.* at 1028. Spain's interpretation would only follow if the statute were rewritten to state, "in which rights in property taken by the foreign state in violation of international law are in issue." *Id.* This was bolstered by considering the underlying policy of the statute: to immunize sovereigns for their sovereign acts but not their commercial, acts. *Id.* at 1030. The court rejected the defendants' concerns that the floodgates of litigation would open, noting that it was bound by the statute as it was written.

As far as commercial activity, the District Court had found that the Foundation was engaged in:

> buying books, posters, and post cards; purchasing books about Nazi expropriation of works of art; selling posters and books, and licensing reproductions of images; paying United States citizens to write for exhibit catalogs; shipping gift shop items to purchasers in the United States, including a poster of the Pissarro painting; recruiting writers and speakers to provide services at the museum; permitting a program to be filmed at the museum that included the Pissarro painting and was shown on Iberia Airlines flights between Spain and the United States; placing advertisements in magazines distributed in the United States, and sending press releases, brochures, and general information to Spain's tourism offices in the United States, at least one of which mentions the Pissarro by name; distributing the museum bulletin, "Perspectives," to individuals in the United States; borrowing and loaning artworks, though not the painting; and maintaining a website through which United States citizens sign up for newsletters, view the collection—including the Pissarro painting—and purchase advance admission tickets through links to third-party vendors.[153]

More important, the Ninth Circuit rejected the argument that the foregoing commercial activity had to have a nexus to the property at issue: "[T]here is no express analogue to the traditional doctrine of specific jurisdiction, nor does it explicitly require any particular level of activity or conduct commensurate to that normally contemplated for general jurisdiction." *Id.* at 1033. Here, the court cited its own decision in *Altmann*.

Lastly, the Ninth Circuit dismissed the argument that the plaintiffs were required to exhaust their remedies in Spain:

> The expropriation exception says nothing at all about exhaustion of remedies. It does not, for example, condition immunity on a claimant's having first presented his claim to the courts of the country

> being sued, or to the courts of the country that did the taking, or to any international tribunal. Spain identifies no language in the FSIA that would obligate Cassirer to exhaust. It follows that exhaustion is not a statutory prerequisite to jurisdiction.

Id. at 1034. Spain gamely cited Justice Breyer's concurrence in *Altmann*, but the Ninth Circuit pointed out that the Supreme Court's holding did not reach the question of exhaustion, and Justice Breyer's concurrence was clearly phrased in the conditional in any event. *Id.* at 1036. The Ninth Circuit en banc reversed the panel and sent the entire case back to the District Court for litigation. The Supreme Court declined Spain's request to review the case.

Back in the District Court, the case was affected by a development in an unrelated case. *Von Saher v. Norton Simon Museum Foundation* had been remanded on the central issue in that case, which was the constitutionality of California's once again amended statute of limitations. In remanding *Von Saher,* however, the Ninth Circuit had noted the possible conflict of the California statute and the restitution litigation it would allow to go forward with a federal issue: the foreign affairs of the United States (raising a potential preemption argument). Shortly after *Cassirer* was remanded, *Von Saher* was dismissed by the (same) District Court. *Von Saher v. Norton Simon Museum of Art at Pasadena*, 862 F. Supp. 2d 1044, 1052-53 (C.D. Cal. 2012). The 2012 *Von Saher* decision conceded that it was in conflict with the Ninth Circuit's holding on conflict preemption but determined that the claim was preempted because Von Saher's "action seeks to trump and interfere with United States foreign policy, by relying on an entirely different remedy for the restitution of Nazi-looted art, i.e., the laws of the State of California." *Id.* at 1053. Spain and the Foundation promptly asked the District Court to dismiss the Cassirer claims on the same basis, which it obligingly did later in 2012.

As noted previously, in 2002, the California legislature had passed Assembly Bill No. 1758, adding Section 354.3 to the California Code of Civil Procedure. Section 354.3 extended the statute of limitations for actions pertaining to the recovery of works of fine art alleged to have been stolen during the Holocaust era (defined as 1929 to 1945) to December 31, 2010, allowing such suits against "any museum or gallery that displays, exhibits, or sells any article of historical, interpretive, scientific, or artistic significance." Cal. Civ. Proc. Code § 354.3. Section 354.3 also barred application of California's "borrowing statute," section 361 of the California Code of Civil Procedure, which provides that if the claim arose in another jurisdiction, and that jurisdiction would bar the claim, such a claim would likewise be barred in California even if otherwise timely. Cal. Civ. Proc. Code § 361. This was the law struck down by the Ninth Circuit in the *Von Saher* case in 2010.

The Foundation's motion argued that the California statute of limitations had expired in 2003 on the Cassirers' claims when the law was amended in 2005. The amendment to make the claims timely, the defendants argued, was something that the state of California had no power to do because the restitution of Nazi-looted art was a subject occupied completely by the foreign affairs powers of the United States:

> Although the statute on its face does not mention Holocaust-era art thefts, the amendments were enacted shortly after the Ninth Circuit overturned a functionally equivalent statute expressly enacted to allow recovery of Holocaust-era artwork.[154]

The analysis, the court held, was to determine the real purpose of the statute, which it held was to facilitate Holocaust restitution claims. With that in mind, the court turned to what it believed the foreign policy of the United States was. It summarized that policy in this way, after viewing the history of the Washington Principles and the Terezin Conference:[155]

> In the years since these principles were adopted, litigation over Holocaust-era art has proceeded in U.S. courts under generally applicable laws. . . . However, in 2011, the U.S. Solicitor General filed an amicus brief supporting denial of the Von Saher petition for certiorari. Brief for the United States as Amicus Curiae, Von Saher Certiorari Petition, May 2011. . . . This was because the *Von Saher* litigation
>
> > concerns artworks and transactions that, consistent with U.S. policies, have already been the subject of both external and internal restitution proceedings, including recent

> proceedings by the Netherlands in response to the Washington Principles. This case does not involve artwork whose existence or provenance has only recently been discovered and had never been the subject of restitution proceedings. The Cranachs were transferred by the United States to the Netherlands in 1946 pursuant to the policy of external restitution. One of the purposes of that policy at the time was to prevent the United States from becoming entangled in difficult ownership questions regarding confiscated property.

> *Id.* at 16. The United States explained that, although "it is United States policy to support both the just and fair resolution of claims to Nazi-confiscated art on the merits and the return of such art to its rightful owner . . . that policy does not support relitigation of all art claims in U.S. courts."

The foreign affairs doctrine generally provides that "[t]he foreign affairs doctrine provides that state laws may not intrude 'into the field of foreign affairs which the Constitution entrusts to the President and the Congress.'" *Mujica v. Occidental Petroleum Corp.*, 381 F. Supp. 2d 1164, 1171 (C.D. Cal. 2005) *Zschernig v. Miller*, 389 U.S. 429, 432 (1968). "The Constitution does not create an express, general power over foreign affairs but rather allocates particular powers related to foreign affairs to particular federal actors." *Deutsch v. Turner Corp.*, 324 F.3d 692, 708 (9th Cir. 2003). The guiding principle is that the individual states of the United States cannot have their own foreign policy, only the United States can.

There are two species of foreign affairs preemption: conflict preemption and field preemption. The former is when a state law conflicts with an existing federal statute. That was not the issue in *Cassirer* or *Von Saher*. The court distinguished the matter from *Von Saher*, which was rooted in a desire to respect a specific Dutch restitution decision after the United States had returned the painting to the Netherlands to do as that nation saw fit. No such U.S. restitution had occurred with the Pissarro, as it had never been in American hands.

Field preemption, on the other hand, is when, in the absence of any conflict, the court has declared state laws incompatible with the federal government's foreign affairs powers. California's abolition of the statute of limitations (§ 354.3) had already been struck down because the court thus concluded that the purpose of California's enactment of Section 354.3 was not to protect the property interests of California residents and to regulate the state's art trade, but to "provide relief to Holocaust victims and their heirs" and to "create a friendly forum for litigating Holocaust restitution claims."

The 2012 companion cases both held that the more neutral revision (§ 338(c)) fared no better. In *Cassirer* the court noted that the newer law was written specifically in response to the invalidation of § 354.1. Further, although the newer law had a shorter limitations period, it was functionally equivalent to the old one because they both revived Holocaust claims that would otherwise be time-barred. While the statute did not mention the Holocaust specifically, the court held that that period encompassed World War II, and that it was not in response to some larger problem of art theft, it was specifically in the context of the pending Holocaust claims. "In the absence of some specific action that constitutes authorization on the part of the federal government, states are prohibited from . . . modifying the federal government's resolution of war-related disputes."[156] The court stated (emphasis added):

> The Ninth Circuit's contemporaneous determination that the federal government has occupied the field with regard to the resolution of Holocaust-era art claims, leaving no room for states to legislate in this area, is binding on this Court. *See Von Saher*, 592 F.3d at 967–68. The resolution of this case then turns on the question whether, by amending Section 338(c), California has sought to legislate in this area. The Court concludes that . . . *[l]ike Section 354.3, Amended Section 338(c) impermissibly intrudes on foreign affairs because its aim is to provide a remedy for wartime wrongs through California courts that would otherwise not exist.*[157]

On this basis, the court dismissed the *Cassirer* Complaint as untimely (without the aid of the newer limitations period).[17]

The Cassirers appealed to the Ninth Circuit, where they prevailed again. *Cassirer v. Thyssen-Bornemisza Collection Found.*, 737 F.3d 613 (2013). The analysis of the dispositive holding in the District Court is actually quite brief. Reviewing the standards of field preemption, the Court of Appeals held that the revised statute did not create an independent remedy for wartime injuries of the sort that would intrude on the federal government's authority in that area, nor was it functionally equivalent to the § 354.3 that was struck down in *Von Saher*. First, the court noted that the extension of limitations for artworks was unrelated to wartime claims on its face. It applies equally to artworks taken under far more mundane circumstances. Indeed, the law is silent on matters of foreign affairs but § 338(c) does not create its own cause of action. *Id.* 737 F.3d at 618–19. Next, the functional equivalence holding was rejected: "But whether a statute of limitations may permit Holocaust era-claims is not the test for preemption." *Id.*

Critically, the court rejected the idea that allowing the claim to proceed was necessarily an adjudication of the fairness of the monies Lilly had been paid by Germany. Had the newer California statute provided a method to attack those German payments collaterally, it might well have intruded on the foreign affairs function, but this law did not, said the court.

The case was revived and returned to the District Court again, albeit eight years after it was first filed. There, the Cassirers scored what seemed like a few significant procedural victories. On October 31, 2014, the court struck several of the Foundation's affirmative defenses. It also denied the Foundation's Act of State argument: "Here Spain did nothing that a private party could not have done. It either directly purchased the Painting as would a private buyer, or indirectly purchased the Painting by providing [the Thyssen-Bornemisza Foundation] the funds to do so." *Cassirer v. Thyssen-Bornemisza Collection Found.*, 2014 U.S. Dist. LEXIS 154774, CV 05-03459 GAF (Ex). There was no official sovereign act by Spain to make such a defense, the court held. The Foundation then moved for a summary adjudication of the impact of a 1958 settlement involving Sulzbacher. It waives Sulzbacher's heirs' rights against Germany, however, not Lilly's rights.

While that motion was still pending, the Foundation continued its onslaught of motion practice and moved for summary judgment. The Foundation argued that (1) under Swiss or Spanish law, the Foundation is the owner of the painting; (2) the California Code of Civil Procedure § 338(c), as amended in 2010, violates the Foundation's due process rights by retroactively depriving the Foundation of its vested property rights; and (3) plaintiffs' claims are barred by laches.

However, to answer these questions, the court had to decide which law applied. The Restatement (Second) of Conflict of Laws (a summary of the prevailing view across jurisdictions) § 222 sets forth the general choice-of-law principle applicable to interests in both real and personal property. The factors relevant to the determination of which state has the most significant relationship to the property in question and the parties include: (1) the needs of the interstate and international systems, (2) the relevant policies of the forum, and (3) the relevant policies of other interested states and the relative interests of those states in the determination of the particular issue, the protection of justified expectations, the basic policies underlying the particular field of law, certainty, predictability and uniformity of result, and ease in the determination and application of the law to be applied. *See* Restatement 2d Conflicts § 222.

The District Court was not even certain of which test to apply, noting a split in recent decisions about choice-of-law rules. Federal common law follows the approach of the Restatement. Applying this rule, the court concluded that, under federal common law, the law of Spain governed. In contrast to Spain's significant relationship to the painting and the Foundation:

> California's relationship to the Painting and the parties is limited to the following facts: (1) Claude Cassirer moved to California in 1980; (2) the Frank Perls Gallery in Beverly Hills, California arranged a sale of the Painting to Sydney Brody in Los Angeles, California in July 1951; and (3) less than a year later, in May 1952, the Frank Perls Gallery in Beverly Hills, California was involved in the sale of the Painting to Sydney Schoenberg in St. Louis, Missouri. Although Plaintiffs' relationship to California is significant, the Painting's relationship to California is not.

Cassirer v. Thyssen-Bornemisza Collection Found., 153 F. Supp. 3d 1148, 1155 (C.D. Cal. 2015).

The same result was warranted, the court believed, under California's test. California applies the three-step "governmental interest" test:

> First, the court determines whether the relevant law of each of the potentially affected jurisdictions with regard to the particular issue in question is the same or different. Second, if there is a difference, the court examines each jurisdiction's interest in the application of its own law under the circumstances of the particular case to determine whether a true conflict exists. Third, if the court finds that there is a true conflict, it carefully evaluates and compares the nature and strength of the interest of each jurisdiction in the application of its own law to determine which state's interest would be more impaired if its policy were subordinated to the policy of the other state, and then ultimately applies the law of the state whose interest would be more impaired if its law were not applied. *Kearney v. Salomon Smith Barney, Inc.*, 39 Cal. 4th 95, 107–108 (2006).

Id. Using this rule, the court held that Spanish law and California differed (Spain allows personal property title by prescription while California does not). Thus, there is a true conflict of laws. Both jurisdictions had an interest in the application of its own laws. Spain's was "applying its law of adverse possession to the Foundation's claim of ownership, especially given that the Foundation is an instrumentality of the Kingdom of Spain and the Painting has been located within its borders for over twenty years." By contrast, the California legislature had stated:

> (1) "California's interest in determining the rightful ownership of fine art is a matter of traditional state competence, responsibility, and concern;" (2) "Because objects of fine art often circulate in the private marketplace for many years before entering the collections of museums or galleries, existing statutes of limitation, which are solely the creatures of the Legislature, often present an inequitable procedural obstacle to recovery of these objects by parties that claim to be their rightful owner;" and (3) "The application of statutes of limitations and any affirmative defenses to actions for the recovery of works of fine art . . . should provide incentives for research and

publication of provenance information about these works, in order to encourage the prompt and fair resolution of claims."[158]

The court therefore had to balance which interest was greater. It chose Spain. The telling passage was:

> Although California has a fundamental interest in protecting its residents and specifically has an interest in protecting its residents claiming to be rightful owners of stolen art, that interest is far less significant where the original victim did not reside in California, where the unlawful taking did not occur within its borders, and where the defendant and the entity from which the defendant purchased the property were not located in California.

Id. at 1159. Instead:

> If Spain's interest in the application of its law were subordinated to California's interest, it would rest solely on the fortuitous decision of Lilly's successor-in-interest to move to California long after the Painting was unlawfully taken by the Nazis and the fact that he happened to reside there at the time the Foundation took possession of the Painting. Subjecting a defendant within Spain to a different rule of law based on the unpredictable choice of residence of a successor-in-interest would significantly undermine Spain's interest in certainty of title.

Id. This overstates the difference considerably. First, describing anything about the fate of Holocaust victims as "fortuitous" is a poor choice of words. Second, it implies that Spain was subject to an uncertainty that would not exist among Spanish litigants—as though Claude had merely happened to rest briefly in an unusual jurisdiction. Is a thief's successor the victim of a "fortuitous" decision by the true owner to move to a common-law country? Such jurisdictions cover a significant part of the world, and is hardly unforeseeable in the way that the decision suggests.

Having sided with Spanish law, the court applied it to find that Spain was the owner. The Foundation had possessed the painting since 1993, publicly and without interruption, for more than the six-year period (Spanish Civil Code Article 433), and the result did not violate the European Convention on Human Rights. ("It is characteristic of property that different countries regulate its use and transfer in a variety of ways. The relevant rules reflect social policies against the background of the local conception of the importance and role of property.") *Id.* at 1167.

The adverse possession ruling decided the case, so the language of the opinion afterwards about the California statute of limitations should be considered dicta (opinion not essential to the holding). However, it is interesting to note that the court gave a sweeping and dismissive treatment of the revised six-year statute of limitations, concluding that it constituted a deprivation of property without due process. This aspect of the decision was hastily composed and not terribly well-reasoned; citing an 1885 case that concludes (uncontroversially) that an after-the-fact amendment to a statute of limitations may deprive the possessor of its property (since absent the amendment, they would face no claim), the court concluded that this statute effects just such a deprivation. However, the logic of this paragraph of the opinion relies entirely on the conclusion that the Foundation had adversely possessed the painting by the time the statute of limitations was extended. This meant the statute of limitations was irrelevant. The Cassirers appealed, and the case was argued before the Ninth Circuit in December 2016.

The Cassirer case embodies the elements of the legal and ethical dilemmas presented by these cases. The Pissarro is a painting that was stolen from a German Jew. Yet, a sovereign government looks at the question from the perspective of a work of art on display for the public, which was not stolen by the government. Bearing in mind all that has come before, have the Washington Principles helped? Spain is a signatory to them yet has no alternative dispute procedure. In what sense is the result fair to the Cassirer family? Absent easy answers, the result is a zero sum game in which Spain has prevailed for the moment. The case also encapsulates the intractable form that so many of these cases take. Spain is clearly immune to whatever ethical opprobrium was directed toward it, resolving that it had the better of the equities. The Cassirers disagree, but have not been able to use a final judgment to compel Spain's adoption of that view. When you have a painting, which all agree was stolen by the Nazis, on public display, what besides a court order would compel the possessor to do act differently?

Chapter 17

Hungary and the Herzog Collection

Baron Mór Lipót Herzog was a Jewish art collector in Budapest, Hungary, in the first half of the twentieth century. Over his lifetime, he assembled a fabled art collection that spanned from Old Masters to the Impressionists. The bulk of that collection, now in the hands of state museums in Hungary, is the subject of a long-running but unresolved dispute filed pursuant to the FSIA. Hungary has moved to dismiss the case three times, occasionally achieving incremental success, but even with the case proceeding, there has been no sign whatsoever of a possible resolution.

Herzog's collection was housed at his home in Budapest and included works by El Greco, Velázquez, Lucas Cranach the Elder, van Dyck, Courbet, and Corot—as well as notable Hungarian artists like Mihály Munkácsy. When Baron Herzog died in 1934, his collection was largely intact and remained with his wife. When she died, the collection was inherited and divided by their children Erzsébet, István, and András. Erzsébet married Alfonz Weiss de Csepel, the son of one of Hungary's leading industrialists. His factories just outside of Budapest produced canned foods, agricultural machinery, and other metal products. During WWI, he expanded into munitions, employing approximately

100,000 workers. András married and had two children. He was sent to do forced labor by the Nazi-sympathizing Hungarian regime and died in 1942. His two daughters, Angela Maria and Julia Alice Herzog, fled Hungary after András's death. The government of Hungary targeted István for deportation to Auschwitz, but he escaped to a safe house under the protection of the Spanish Embassy (an interesting turn of events given Spain's tacit alliance with the Axis powers). He died in 1966, bequeathing his estate to his sons, Stephan and Peter Herzog, and his second wife.

At the time the Nazis rose to power, Hungary was still a relatively young independent state, having broken free from centuries of Habsburg rule only after WWI. Whereas the 1867 compromise, or *Ausgleich*, between the Austrian Emperor and his constituent Kingdom of Hungary (whose crown he held) was seen in Austria as a pragmatic solution to the balance of power in a large empire, for Hungary it was just the beginning of an independent age. Effectively distancing itself from Austria—which with Germany, the victorious powers viewed as the two primary antagonists of the First World War—Hungary became its own sovereign nation again for the first time since the Ottoman occupation after the Battle of Mohács in 1526. Though it ceded substantial territory to Romania, Czechoslovakia, and Yugoslavia, Hungary was nonetheless out from under the shadow of its neighbors. However, national bitterness pervaded the loss of historic territories and the displacement of ethnic Hungarians into newly created foreign countries.

As a result, Hungary in the interwar period was prey to the same economic uncertainty and vulnerabilities that made Germany and Austria such powder kegs. The significant Jewish community was targeted in similar ways as to blame for all manner of social and economic ills. Just as Austria did, Hungary spawned far-right parties that vied for national control. The kingdom of Hungary increasingly allied itself with Nazi Germany and Fascist Italy, though in its administration it remained closer to the latter—repressive and illiberal but not as overtly murderous. Unlike Italy, however, Hungarian Jews represented a meaningful, if still a minority, percentage of the population. Regent Miklós Horthy, an Admiral in the Austro-Hungarian Navy, had served as Regent for the absent king since the end of WWI. Horthy viewed Hitler as an effective buffer against Soviet Communism and as an object of sympathy even if with some ambivalence.

He successfully parlayed his support of German annexation of Czech territories in 1938 into Hitler's assistance with reacquiring disputed former Hungarian territories in Slovakia. Hungary withdrew from the League of Nations in sympathy with Germany, and after the war began, Hungarian troops fought with Germany on the Eastern Front. At the same time politically, Horthy was also fending off his country's own far-right party, the Arrow Cross, headed by Fascist Ferenc Szálasi.

Even in its mildest form, Hungary's alliance with Germany between 1938 and 1944 marginalized Hungary's Jews relentlessly. Jews were excluded from the armed forces in 1941. In that year, an imitation of the Nuremberg Laws was passed, which prohibited all manner of interaction between Jews and ethnic Hungarians. Hungary assented to the deportation of tens of thousands of non-Hungarian Jews in 1941. Most were massacred in Kamianets-Podilskyi (now in Ukraine) after a horrific odyssey by train and foot. The outcry persuaded the government to halt further deportations, but smaller-scale murders in the hundreds still continued. Throughout this period prior to 1944, Jewish men were sent into forced labor as András Herzog was; 27,000 had died under brutal conditions before 1944.

The alliance with Germany turned out to be a miscalculation, of course, after the German loss at Stalingrad (in which Hungary suffered 80,000 fatalities) and the epic battle the following summer at Kursk, which the Germans (and Axis powers, including Hungary) lost. By spring 1944, the Red Army was at the edge of Hungarian territory. On behalf of Prime Minister Miklós Kállay, Admiral Horthy began secret efforts to reach an armistice with the Allies. Hitler invited Horthy to Salzburg, and while he was out of Hungary, German troops occupied their former ally under Operation Margarethe. When he returned to Budapest, German troops met him and gave him the choice to remove Kállay (whose outreach had been discovered by Hitler) or face unknown consequences. Horthy relented and appointed Döme Sztójay.

The results could not have been more catastrophic for Hungary's Jews. The Arrow Cross Party was legalized, and Germany's occupation of the country was facilitated. As the Red Army continued its relentless drive west toward the eventual annihilation of the German army and Germany itself, the Nazi regime still focused its energy on reshaping Hungarian society in its image. In April 1944, Decree 1600/1944 was passed, requiring registration of Jewish property similar to what had been enacted in Austria after the *Anschluss*. The government inventoried and seized Jewish assets. Later, in May, Decree 1930/1944 followed, "On the Recording and Safeguarding of Impounded Art Objects of Jews." This decree created a property commission and required Jews to register with it all art objects in their possession. Those objects were collected by this commission, headed by Dénes Csánky, the director of the Museum of Fine Arts, Budapest. Hungarian Jews were then subjected to decrees forcibly removing them from their homes.

As the storm clouds gathered, the Herzog family tried to protect its collection. According to their heirs, Csánky himself helped them pack and store the art in one of the family's factories. The location was soon revealed, however, and the family later alleged that Csánky was again present when the artworks were unearthed by the authorities. In an article published on May 23, 1944, Csánky boasted that if the Museum of Fine Arts ended up with the paintings (begging a question no one was asking), it would be a world-level collection outranked only slightly by the Museo del Prado in Madrid. The art was then taken directly to Adolf Eichmann's headquarters, who selected a number for shipment to Germany. As the war collapsed around them in late 1944, parts of the remaining collection were moved into Germany itself.

Apart from András, the Herzog family largely managed to escape. This was no mean feat. In barely a year between Operation Margarethe and the Red Army's brutal seizure of Budapest, some 430,000 Hungarian Jews were deported to death camps. At the end of the war, nearly half a million Jews—out of a prewar population of 825,000—were dead. Erzsébet and her children fled Hungary in June 1944, went to Portugal, and then to America in 1946. She became a U.S. citizen in 1952. András's family went to Argentina, then to Italy. Some of István's family stayed in Hungary.

When the war was over, many members of the Herzog family actually returned to Hungary, but did not stay long. Some of the Herzog collection had been recovered by the Allies and returned to Hungary under their standard protocol. Hungary entered into a treaty in 1947 that addressed in part Hungary's role as custodian of heirless works. Hungary did return some of the collection to Herzog family members but only in the form of short-term loans. Under relentless harassment, according to the family, they allowed the works to return to the Museum of Fine Arts for display in 1948.

Hungary was not Austria, however. The Iron Curtain was descending on Eastern Europe. There was no opportunity to investigate or negotiate with the new Communist government and its successors, certainly not after the Soviet invasion of 1956. After the fall of Communism, the family restarted its efforts. Before her death in 1992, Erzsébet negotiated the return of six less significant works. Martha Nierenberg, her daughter, pursued legal action in Hungary. Initially, the Budapest municipal court recognized their claim and awarded ownership of eleven paintings, but in January 2008, an appellate court reversed the decision. The Herzog heirs have consistently characterized that reversal as politically motivated.

At the Washington Conference, Hungary made the following pledge:

> Some of these cultural objects are registered as unclear deposits, some others as part of the basic collection of the museum. In fact, it is one of the museum's most important missions to safeguard its holdings from being sold or alienated until unlawful ownership has not been proved incontestably.[159]

Then:

> The Hungarian Government is fully committed to the restitution or compensation of Holocaust victims concerning cultural assets. For managing this complex task—which includes scholarly research, political decision-making, bill drafting and negotiations... [and] contacts with Holocaust survivors, etc.—a state commissioner will be delegated.[160]

That appointment never happened, however.

In July 2010, David de Csepel, Angela Maria Herzog, and Julia Alice Herzog filed suit in U.S. District Court for the District of Columbia. They invoked the expropriation exception of the FSIA, 28 U.S.C. § 1605(a)(3), as well as the commercial activity exception, 28 U.S.C. § 1605(a)(2) against the Republic of Hungary itself, as well as the Museum of Fine Arts, the Hungarian National Gallery, and the Budapest University of Technology and Economics, as instrumentalities of a foreign state. As to the former, they pleaded an *Altmann*-style taking and a variety of exhibition-related commercial activities. As to the latter, they alleged that the 1945–1948 negotiations and agreements concerning the display of the collection constituted a bailment agreement and that that agreement had a commercial effect in the United States.

Hungary was not intimidated by the prospect of U.S. litigation. If the Herzog heirs had the advantage of recent case law to craft their Complaint (though at the time it was filed, the favorable decision in *Cassirer* was still a few months away, without which many observers considered the entire area of FSIA claims to be in peril), so too did Hungary have the advantage of the arguments (and indeed the same excellent attorneys) as Spain had in asserting sovereign immunity. Following service on defendants and a briefing schedule, the Hungarians filed a seventy-four-page motion to dismiss. The motion contested the applicability of the FSIA (under either exception), the plaintiffs' right to bring their claims under 1947 and 1973 treaties between Hungary and the United States, improper forum, the statute of limitations, the Act of State Doctrine, *res judicata* (the idea that the Nierenberg litigation had resolved the title to at least those eleven works), and payments that David de Csepel's grandmother had received from the U.S. government.

The motion set out in detail the agreements that the United States and Hungary had reached to settle various kinds of claims among states or among the nationals of the United States and Hungary. It also extolled Hungary's transition to western democracy. It noted that on June 26, 1991, Hungary had passed Act XXV of 1991, "On the Partial Compensation for Damages Unjustly Caused by the State to Private Property Owners in Order to Settle Ownership Relations,"[161] for compensation for acts after 1949. On April 7, 1992, the National Assembly then passed Act XXIV of 1992, "On Providing, in Order to Settle Ownership Relations, Partial Compensation for Damages Unjustly Caused by the State of Properties of Citizens through the Enforcement of Legal Rules Framed from 1 May 1939 to 8 June 1949,"[162] to supplement the first law. Herzog family members had received compensation in some amount under these laws, according to the motion. Unsurprisingly, the motion advocated for respecting the outcome of the 1999 Nierenberg litigation.

Hungary first took aim under the 1973 agreement, pointing to the dismissal of analogous claims under agreements between the United States and Czechoslovakia. It then turned to the relevant FSIA exceptions, targeting the commercial activity exception first. Hungary correctly noted that provision's focus on the nature of the act at issue: a sovereign or commercial act, citing *Weltover*, 504 U.S. at 614. The Complaint thus failed, Hungary argued, because it challenged the seizure and/or nationalization of the Herzog collection, acts that are fundamentally sovereign. Any subsequent commercial benefit should be irrelevant. Further, those nationalizations were certainly not in the United States, and in any event had no direct effect in the United States, according to the Hungarian defendants. This request was not a tangential connection, but "an immediate consequence of the defendant's . . . activity." *Princz v. Fed. Republic of Germany*, 26 F.3d 1166, 1172 (D.C. Cir. 1994). As the brief argued, "Just as the U.S. and its sovereign state governments would not expect to be hauled into a foreign court for activities that occurred entirely within the U.S., so too Hungary should not be sued in the District of Columbia for the alleged taking by a former Hungarian government in connection with a nationwide nationalization program."[163]

Similarly, Hungary argued that the expropriation exception did not apply, stressing in particular the point that "expropriation by a sovereign state of the property of its own nationals does not implicate settled principles of international law." *Rong v. Liaoning Province Gov't*, 362 F. Supp. 2d 83, 101 (D.D.C. 2005). As a threshold matter, they argued, the claims did not allege a taking in violation of international law because compensation had been paid in the form of the 1973 treaty. Any subsequent payments or nonpayments by the United States from those proceeds would not implicate Hungary, they argued. Next, they disputed the notion that the museums had "substantial contact"[164] with the United States as discussed in *Malewicz*. Interestingly, they distinguished the contact found sufficient in *Malewicz* as "current loan agreements"[165] from their own alleged contact that was "sporadic or unrelated to the paintings in dispute."[166] This glossed over the fact that the contact alleged by the plaintiffs was unquestionably more significant and frequent than that, though it was correct that it did not directly concern the paintings physical presence in the United States. The allegations did extend, however, to publishing books that concerned the Herzog collection. Hungary rightly portrayed some of the other contacts (*e.g.*, an embassy) as sovereign, not commercial.

The motion argued forum non conveniens under the rubric of improper forum. Citing the now-familiar standard, it argued that Hungary was adequate, and that the presumption of the plaintiff's choice was entitled to no deference because plaintiffs were strangers to the forum, citing *Moscovits v. Magyar Cukor Rt.*, 00 Civ. 0031 (VM), 2001 U.S. Dist. LEXIS 9252, *14 (S.D.N.Y June 29, 2001); and *Dorfman v. Marriott Int'l Hotels, Inc.*, 99 Civ. 10496 (CSH), 2001 U.S. Dist. LEXIS 642, *23 (S.D.N.Y. Jan. 26, 2001; noting that Hungary is an adequate forum). However, *Moscovits* concerned intracompany contracts involving entities that had voluntarily done business in Hungary. In any event, the analysis turns on the public and private factors:

> The events at issue in this action took place in Hungary. To the extent that relevant witnesses are still alive, it is likely that most are located in Hungary and that Hungarian, or Magyar, is their first language. Hungary is a democratic nation, recognized member of the European Union, and is the current President of the European Union—it cannot be reasonably asserted that the Plaintiffs (or their predecessors) could not receive a fair trial in that country.[167]

According to Hungary, public factors, too, weighed in favor of dismissal. "The Hungarian court and the people—not U.S. courts or U.S. citizens—have a better historical and legal understanding of the property confiscation and/or nationalization laws that are alleged to have taken place in Hungary in the Twentieth Century."[168]

Hungary maintained a statute of limitations defense by suggesting that the claims could have accrued no later than 1989—more than three years before the lawsuit—and that the Nierenberg litigation did not toll that limitations period. Returning to the nature of the alleged takings, Hungary also advanced an argument that the Act of State doctrine barred the claims: "In this action, the artwork at issue was taken by the Hungarian government pursuant to various laws and decrees. Whether anyone today agrees with the decisions of the Hungarian government or its laws prior to or after the war, its actions were sovereign in nature and could not have been committed by a private actor."[169]

Lastly, Hungary pleaded for comity and/or *res judicata* (the notion that the claim had already been decided once and could not be litigated again).[170]

> Under claim preclusion, "a subsequent lawsuit will be barred if there has been prior litigation (1) involving the same claims or cause of action, (2) between the same parties or their privies, and (3) there has been a final, valid judgment on the merits, (4) by a court of competent jurisdiction." *Smalls v. United States*, 471 F.3d 186, 192 (D.C. Cir. 2006) (*citing Blonder-Tongue Labs., Inc. v. Univ. of Ill. Found.*, 402 U.S. 313, 323-24 (1971)). The claimant is also precluded from bringing claims that arise from the same nucleus of facts upon which the prior litigation is based. *See Drake v. Fed. Aviation Admin.*, 291 F.3d 59, 66 (D.C. Cir. 2002).

In addition, the defendants argued that with a final judgment in Hungary, international comity should respect the result. "When possible, the decisions of foreign tribunals should be given effect in domestic courts," but a special reason for declining comity exists when the foreign judgment is "contrary to the crucial public policies of the forum in which enforcement is requested." *Laker Airways Ltd. v. Sabena, Belgian World Airlines*, 731 F.2d 909, 931, 937 (D.C. Cir. 1984).

The plaintiffs opposed, and since the motion was largely denied, the court's opinion itself is also a review of the plaintiffs' arguments. The threshold elements were not complicated, the court stated:

> The Complaint clearly alleges substantial and non-frivolous claims that the Herzog Collection was taken without just compensation and for discriminatory purposes. Specifically, it alleges that despite efforts by the Herzog family to prevent the confiscation of their artwork by hiding the bulk of it in the cellar of one of the family's factories in Budafok, the Hungarian government, in collaboration with the Nazis, discovered the hiding place and confiscated its contents as part of a larger campaign of asset seizure and genocide against Hungarian Jews.

De Csepel v. Republic of Hungary, 808 F. Supp. 2d 113, 128–129 (D.D.C. 2011). As to the specifics, the court acknowledged the general presumption that a sovereign's taking of property from its own citizen does not violate international law, but agreed with the plaintiffs that the allegations as set out made the case that Hungary did not consider Jews to be Hungarian citizens by the time of the takings at issue during the war, and with respect to the unfairness and extortion thereafter, the Herzogs and de Csepels were no longer Hungarian by any measure thanks to the treatment that they had received. Critically, the court looked past the precise technicalities of citizenship in 1944 when Hungarian Jews were literally being rounded up by the hundreds of thousands for summary execution:

> [I]t is clear that under these extraordinary facts, the government of Hungary thought otherwise and had *de facto* stripped her, Ms. Weiss *de Csepel*, and all Hungarian Jews of their citizenship rights. Consequently, the alleged Hungarian "citizenship" of plaintiffs' predecessors does not preclude the application of the expropriation exception in this case.

Id. at 130, *citing Cassirer, 461 F. Supp. 2d 1157, 1165–66.* In addition, the court held, even if only abstractly, the Hungarian government's actions might raise issues as to the international aspects of the property takings, here it cannot ignore that the entire action was taking place in coordination with, if not at the express direction of, the German army. No domestic taking rule would shield the actions of the SS or the Wehrmacht against Hungarian Jews. *De Csepel*, 808 F. Supp. at 130. Furthermore, *Cassirer* was persuasive, the court stated, such that the FSIA contained no requirement that the sovereign defendant be the one who was fully responsible for the taking; if Germany were viewed as the actor in the taking of the Herzog collection, then Hungary's disputed possession of it today made it subject to suit under the FSIA. *Id.* As in the case against the Spanish museum, the court viewed the essential question as the status of the defendant in possession of the property, not the identity of the sovereign wrongdoer at the time of the taking.

The court also addressed the defendants' arguments about the impact of the 1973 treaty and Hungary's 1991 and 1992 laws regarding the plaintiffs' claims. However, the 1973 agreement with the United States applied only to takings from persons who were U.S. citizens at the time of the takings, not from Hungarians. This is because the 1973 treaty was grounded in the principle of espousal, which is the process by which a state acts on behalf of its *own* citizens to settle claims against another state. The United States could not have espoused claims for Hungarians in 1944. *Id.* at 133. Although the 1992 Hungarian law did allow for compensation for wartime takings, the court did not agree with Hungary's interpretation of the treaty that it meant to settle all such claims, but rather to provide one possible avenue of redress. Thus, "plaintiffs' claim that the Herzog Collection was taken in violation of international law is substantial and non-frivolous, and therefore, it adequately satisfies the second requirement of the FSIA's expropriation exception." *Id.* at 131. Moreover, by this point the question of exhaustion of remedies abroad moved from a central point of the analysis to a footnote because by the time *Cassirer* was decided, the D.C. circuit had held that a plaintiff invoking the expropriation exception is not required to exhaust local remedies before litigating in the United States. *Id.* at 131, n.3, *citing Agudas Chasidei Chabad v. Russian Fed'n*, 528 F.3d 934, 948–49 (D.C. Cir. 2008).

Chabad is a case that casts a long shadow over FSIA Holocaust restitution claims. Agudas Chabad is a constituent institution in Brooklyn, New York, of the worldwide Chabad-Lubavitch movement, an Orthodox Jewish community focused on the teachings of a lineage of successive charismatic leaders known in each respective generation as the Rebbe. In 2005, Agudas Chabad sued the Russian Federation, the Russian Ministry of Culture and Mass Communication, the Russian State Library, and the Russian State Military Archive, seeking the return of the collection from the leader of the worldwide Chabad-Lubavitch movement, the Rebbe. By the early twentieth century, the accumulated library included thousands of religious books, manuscripts, and other documents. One portion of the library was seized in 1917 by the emerging Bolshevik government from a warehouse in which the fifth Rebbe had placed it for safekeeping in the face of the advancing German army during the First World War as the Tsarist regime collapsed. The Russian State Library (where those objects ended up after the dust settled) rejected the fifth and then the sixth Rebbe's pleas for their return in the 1920s. Over the next twenty years, the sixth Rebbe moved from Soviet territory to Latvia to Poland, from which he fled upon the German invasion in 1939. The remaining portions of the library still in his possession were left behind, collected by the German army, and ultimately captured by the Soviet Union at the end of the war. That portion is currently held by the Russian State Military Archive. The sixth Rebbe survived the war and settled in the United States, where he and his followers have been attempting to retrieve the library ever since. They and the then-seventh Rebbe (who died in 1994 without an official successor) achieved initial success in 1991–1992 as the Soviet Union collapsed, but political forces in the nascent Russian Federation apparently thwarted their early judicial victories by having the results set aside.

After the suit was filed in the United States, the defendants collectively moved to dismiss the Complaint, arguing that they were entitled to sovereign immunity. The plaintiffs countered with the expropriation exception of the FSIA. The U.S. District Court of the District of Columbia denied the motion to dismiss, and the U.S. Court of Appeals for the District of Columbia Circuit affirmed the order. In affirming the lower ruling, the D.C. Circuit analyzed carefully whose property rights were at issue, *i.e.,* a specific Russian's or Soviet's (the Rebbe's) property, as opposed to the worldwide organizations. Russia claimed sovereign immunity for that part of the library that was seized by the Bolsheviks and then appropriated by the Russian Federation after the collapse of the Soviet Union on the argument that it was not these plaintiffs' (the movement writ large) property, but rather that the library at best could be claimed by the fifth or sixth Rebbe—both long deceased and not parties to the case. The D.C. Circuit found that the initial victory in the Russian court in 1991, overruled by executive action, however, established sufficiently the movement's ownership rights to constitute a retaking in 1991–1992 (as opposed to 1917–1925) of that part of the library, potentially in violation of international norms such that the FSIA stripped the defendants' immunity. The D.C. Circuit affirmed the District Court's rejection of the Russian defendants' other arguments about exhaustion of remedies as they related to the remainder of the library, as well as *forum non conveniens.*

In view of all this, the *de Csepel* court found *Chabad* instructive on the commercial nexus analysis as *de Csepel*, citing *Weltover* as well.

See Weltover, 504 U.S. at 614 ("[W]hen a foreign government acts...in a manner of a private player within [a market], the foreign sovereign's acts are 'commercial' within the meaning of the FSIA."). The court rejected Hungary's request to import the language of § 1603(e), just as the Ninth Circuit had done in *Cassirer* and, more important, to the court in D.C., the D.C. circuit had in *Chabad* stated:

> Congress took the trouble to use different verbs in the separate prongs, and to define the phrase in the first prong. Russia wants us to turn that upside down and obliterate the distinction Congress drew. Moreover, we see no anomaly in applying the "commercial activity definition set forth in § 1603(d).... The substantiality requirement of § 1603(e) is thus inapplicable.

Id. at 132, *citing Chabad*, 528 F.3d at 947. As to the specifics, the *de Csepel* court was satisfied that the allegations of the Complaint met them:

> [T]he Museums and University have loaned art to museums located in the United States and received reciprocal benefits in exchange; encouraged United States tourism and allowed United States visitors to purchase admission tickets over the internet; published guidebooks in English featuring paintings from the Herzog Collection which are sold to visitors from the United States at the museum gift shop, which accepts U.S. credit cards; authored and promoted books and other publications about the paintings, and sold these books online through Amazon; accepted orders for printed reproductions of the paintings directly from U.S. residents and shipped those prints directly to the U.S.; engaged in tourist advertising in the U.S. (including promotional brochures that promote works comprising a portion of the Herzog collection); and with respect to the University, participated in student exchange programs and the United States Fulbright Program. (Compl. ¶¶ 32-33.) These examples are more than sufficient to amount to "commercial activity" for jurisdictional purposes under the FSIA.

De Csepel, 808 F. Supp. at 132.

As noted above, the court rejected Hungary's contention that the 1973 treaty settled claims with respect to persons who were Hungarians (or more to the point, not Americans) at the time of the wartime taking. *Id.* at 133. Both Hungary and the United States apparently made this point explicitly during negotiations, over and above the fact that the court did not consider the treaty language capable of any other interpretation. The plaintiffs produced a 1973 letter from the State Department that is a "universally accepted principle of international law that a state does not have the right to ask another state to pay compensation to it for losses sustained by persons who were not its citizens at the time of loss." *Id.* More recently, the State Department's Office of the Legal Adviser had confirmed that the treaty "did not settle or discharge claims of U.S. nationals who became U.S. nationals after their claims arose." *Id.* Even if the United States had the power to settle claims for noncitizens, it was clear to the court that it had not intended to do so in 1973.

Lastly, the court rejected the argument that a 1954 decree concerning art in the possession of the museums was an alleged taking that might fall within the treaty. The 1954 museum decree applied to art that was in the custody of a Hungarian museum and whose owner was either unknown or had left the country without permission, which the Complaint disputed. *Id.* at 134. In addition, even though partial compensation may have been paid, that fact did not preclude seeking full compensation because the payment was not a settlement. *Id.*

With jurisdiction established, the court addressed whether the plaintiffs had stated a claim that could proceed and whether that claim should be litigated in the United States. As to the former, the court was satisfied that the allegations of an agreement for safekeeping after the war was sufficient to state the bailment claim that was central to plaintiffs' claim:

> [P]laintiffs have pled that defendants, while recognizing the ownership rights of the Herzog Heirs, exercised possession and control over the Herzog Collection in such a manner as to imply a bailment relationship. (See Compl. ¶¶ 36, 70-73, 99). In addition, plaintiffs charge that Hungary made public representations concerning Holocaust-looted property in the 1947 Peace Treaty that

> are consistent with plaintiffs bailment theory. (Compl. ¶ 69). ("The 1947 Peace Treaty among Hungary and the Allies confirmed that Hungary was to act solely as a custodian or trustee of looted or heirless property [and that] under no circumstances could Hungary itself possess any right, title or interest in the property.").

Id.

Turning to the forum, the court noted the burden on defendants to satisfy the initial requirement that the alternative forum proposed was adequate. *Id.* at 138. The court would not acknowledge that Hungary had met even this generally low burden because the Hungarian courts had not taken a consistent position with regard to all Holocaust-era artwork. However, the court noted that plaintiffs' belief that they would receive a less favorable outcome is not generally enough to establish that the alternative forum is inadequate. It assumed the adequacy of Hungary in considering the public and private factors. *Id.*

The court recognized the fallacy of the language and translation argument. "Relevant depositions and documents would require translation regardless of where this matter is heard." *Id., citing Chabad*, 466 F. Supp. 2d at 29 (rejecting cost of translating documents as a significant factor where documents would require translation regardless of forum). Interestingly, the court found it significant that it had the power to attach Hungary's property in the United States in aid of execution on a judgment, further weighing in plaintiffs' favor. The court was entirely dismissive of Hungary's equally dismissive treatment of the traditional presumption against disturbing plaintiffs' choice of forum. *Id.* at 139. The forum is even more appropriate because the District of Columbia is actually designated within the FSIA itself as a proper one, weighing in favor of the plaintiffs as a central forum with enhanced efficiency (the ultimate basis for the *forum non conveniens* argument).

As to whether the plaintiffs had stated a timely claim, the court noted that the conversion-based claims accrued when the plaintiffs demand the property and the defendant refused, or when the defendant "takes some action that a reasonable person would understand to be either an act of conversion or inconsistent with a bailment." *Malewicz*, 517 F. Supp. 2d. at 335, citing *In re McCagg*, 450 A.2d 414, 416 (D.C. 1982). The court found plaintiffs' arguments persuasive that the statute should be tolled during the Communist era, after which the plaintiffs promptly commenced negotiations. Further, the plaintiffs had alleged that Hungary actively misled them for years and, most important:

> [P]laintiffs' bailment action could not have arisen during the period in which they were engaged in good-faith negotiations with the Hungarian government, as defendants had not yet "absolutely and unconditionally" refused plaintiffs' demand for return of the Collection.

Id. at 141. Finally, given how strenuously Hungary had argued that plaintiffs were required first to go to Hungary, the court held that the Nierenberg litigation tolled any applicable statute while that action was pending. *Id.* at 142.

That left the defendants' Act of State and political question arguments. Although the analysis here was brief, it is important for subsequent cases because rather than engage in a step-by-step consideration of the elements of that doctrine, the court made a broader statement:

> [T]he sovereigns involved are Nazi Germany and their allies in the World War II-era Hungarian government. Confronted by similar facts, courts have consistently held that the act of state doctrine does not apply to the Nazi taking of Jewish property during the Holocaust. *See Chabad*, 466 F. Supp. 2d at 26 (declaring such takings "manifestly illegal"); *Bodner v. Banque Paribas*, 114 F. Supp. 2d 117, 130 (E.D.N.Y. 2000) ("The wholesale rejection of the Vichy government at the close of World War II render[s] the Act of State doctrine wholly inapplicable to this case."). There is no reason to apply a different standard to the actions taken by Hungary toward its Jewish population during World War II.

Id. at 143. With regard to political questions, the defendants had argued (for the first time in their reply brief) that the case would disrupt the executive branch's determination that Hungarian claims should be settled through the Foreign Claims Settlement Commission. The court rejected this argument, because "Plaintiffs do not challenge the 'sufficiency' of the

1973 Agreement or the awards by the Commission, they claim that such measures do not apply to them at all." *Id.* at 144.

That left only the impact of the Nierenberg litigation. Unlike domestic judgments, foreign judgments are not automatically entitled to recognition or preclusive effect in U.S. courts. *Hilton v. Guyot*, 159 U.S. 113, 16 S. Ct. 139, 40 L. Ed. 95 (1895). These foreign judgments instead rely on the principle of comity. *In re Arbitration Between Int'l Bechtel Co. & Dep't of Civ. Aviation of the Gov't of Dubai*, 300 F. Supp. 2d 112, 117 (D.D.C. 2004). In other words:

> [T]here has been opportunity for a full and fair trial abroad before a court of competent jurisdiction, conducting the trial upon regular proceedings, after due citation or voluntary appearance of the defendant, and under a system of jurisprudence likely to secure an impartial administration of justice between the citizens of its own country and those of other countries, and there is nothing to show either prejudice in the court, or in the system of laws under which it was sitting, or fraud in procuring the judgment, or any other special reason why the comity of this nation should not allow it full effect....

Hilton, 159 U.S. at 202. In view of this standard, the court held that Nierenberg had had an adequate opportunity, and that Hungary should not have to relitigate title to the eleven works that had been covered there. In that respect, the court granted the motion to dismiss over those eleven works.

As the FSIA allows, the defendants immediately appealed. The plaintiffs cross-appealed the dismissal of the claims to the eleven paintings that were the subject of the Nierenberg litigation. The D.C. circuit made some interesting observations. In response to Hungary's attack on the District Court's holding that the World War II era takings from Jews was a violation of international law regardless of the identity of the sovereign or the nationality of the victims, the Court of Appeals stated:

> Of course, we have no quarrel with the historical underpinnings of the district court's analysis. During World War II, the Hungarian government did indeed enact a series of anti-Semitic laws "designed

> to exclude Jews from meaningful roles in Hungarian society." Compl. ¶ 44. This exclusion was both symbolic, through the requirement that Jews "wear distinctive signs identifying themselves as Jewish." *De Csepel*, 808 F. Supp. 2d at 129, and physical, through expulsion "to territories under German control where they were mistreated and massacred."

Yet the Court of Appeals viewed the thrust of this Complaint somewhat differently. The plaintiffs were not seeking redress as Jews persecuted by the Nazis or their Hungarian agents, the court found that but "for the subsequent breaches of bailment agreements they say they entered into with Hungary." *De Csepel v. Republic of Hungary*, 714 F.3d 591, 598 (D.C. Cir. 2012). Given the plaintiffs' various responses to the forum non conveniens and Act of State doctrine arguments, the Court of Appeals concluded: "[I]t is incumbent upon us to address Hungary's jurisdictional challenge in light of the bailment claims the family actually brings." *Id.* The court then considered only the applicability of the commercial activity exception without ruling at all on the availability of the expropriation exception. It found that Hungary was not immune from suit under the commercial activity exception. The bailment relationship alleged by the plaintiffs was an act plainly commercial in nature and certainly of the sort that private parties could perform, with nothing uniquely sovereign about it. *Id.* at 599. It rejected Hungary's argument that the bailments, such as they were, arose out of the 1947 peace treaty and were thus uniquely sovereign. The bailment theory was not premised on that, however; it was premised on direct dealings with the government about custody of the artwork. Importantly, even without addressing the expropriation exception per se, the Court of Appeals noted that the indisputably sovereign act of seizure in 1944 or thereabouts does not make Hungary's subsequent contractual agreements sovereign in nature. *Id.* at 600.

As to whether the commercial acts had a direct effect in the United States, the Court of Appeals agreed with the District Court that they did. Unlike other cases in which there was no obvious connection to the United States, the *de Csepel* plaintiffs had alleged promises by Hungary to return the artworks at times when Hungary knew some of them to be in the United States. Thus, the failure to perform such an agreement had a direct effect in the United States, i.e., the paintings never arrived. Even though the Complaint never alleged as much explicitly, it is the natural inference of the accusations of breach of the bailment agreements. *Id.* at 601.

The Court of Appeals did not agree with Hungary that the 1947 treaty abolished its amenability to suit to the extent it ever existed. Hungary had argued that the treaty's provisions established "an exclusive treaty-based mechanism for resolving all claims seeking restitution of property discriminatorily expropriated during World War II from individuals subject to Hungarian jurisdiction." *Id.* at 602. Not quite so, held the court, because its focus was on the postwar bailment claims, to which the treaty had no application. As to the 1973 treaty, the court viewed the repudiation of the bailments as no earlier than 2008 and thus also not within that treaty. *Id.* at 603.

The D.C. Circuit spent little time dismissing Hungary's statute of limitations arguments, first noting that "dismissal is appropriate only if the complaint on its face is conclusively time-barred," *citing Firestone v. Firestone*, 76 F.3d 1205, 1209, 316 U.S. App. D.C. 152 (D.C. Cir. 1996). The court would not even entertain whether the statute had begun to run, because the Complaint was silent on whether Hungary at any point refused further negotiations. *De Csepel*, 714 F.3d at 604. The critical point is that the Complaint alleged that only in 2008 had Hungary finally refused to return the works. *Id.* Because the Complaint was filed within three years of that date, there was nothing further to discuss. *Id.*

The Court of Appeals concluded by endorsing the reasoning of the District Court with respect to the inapplicability of the Act of State doctrine as well as the political question argument and rejected the idea that plaintiffs had not stated a claim for bailment. All that remained was consideration of the *forum non conveniens* argument and the cross-appeal of the dismissal of the claims to the eleven works that had been litigated to a disputed end in Hungary. The Court of Appeals reversed the District Court and reinstated the full set of claims to recover all the works at issue. The court recited the District Court's findings on the private factor analysis that the language concerns did not shift the balance in favor of Hungary. As a result, reviewing that finding only for an abuse of discretion, the Court of Appeals found none and affirmed the holding. *Id.* at 606.

The court reversed the finding that comity obliged recognition of the Hungarian proceedings, because the Complaint squarely alleged that the proceedings had in fact lacked the requisite due process required under *Hilton*. Hungary had argued that the Herzog heirs had failed to be specific enough in what, exactly, they believed was so unfair, but the court put the burden on Hungary: "'[C]omity is an affirmative defense' for which the party seeking recognition of the judgment bears the burden of proof." *Id.* at 607, *citing Taveras v. Taveraz*, 477 F.3d 767, 783 (6th Cir. 2007). A Complaint need not anticipate and plead facts to rebut an affirmative defense. Dismissal at the Rule 12(b)(6) stage is therefore inappropriate.

On the heels of the setback for the *Cassirer* plaintiffs just a few months earlier in the Ninth Circuit, the D.C. circuit's opinion was a dramatic shift. Now, reviewing the case law in the courts of appeals, the tide had at least stalled, if not swung back to a more expansive view of the jurisdiction of U.S. courts over restitution claims. As before, however, Hungary did not take the development lightly. It has since filed multiple motions to dismiss, continuing to challenge the applicability of the FSIA to the Herzog heirs' claims, but the court deferred further rulings until discovery concluded. *See de Csepel v. Republic of Hung.*, 75 F. Supp. 3d 380 (D.D.C. 2014). After substantial jurisdictional and fact discovery, the District Court again upheld nearly all of the claims' viability under the expropriation exception in 2016 (save for two of the paintings) while concluding that the commercial activity exception did not apply. That latter point may seem odd, but the 2013 Court of Appeals' opinion addressed only the allegations of the Complaint. By contrast, the 2016 District Court opinion deals with the facts now in the record as exchanged and uncovered by the parties.

As with the Court of Appeals' decision, a significant intervening precedent in a partially unrelated case drove the result. There have been a number of cases in the last few years against Hungary for Holocaust-related claims. Cases have been filed in the same court in Washington, D.C., as well as in the U.S. District Court for the Northern District of Illinois, seeking damages from the Hungarian railroads for their complicity in the deportation of Hungarian Jews to Auschwitz. The case in Washington was dismissed in 2014 as lacking applicability under the expropriation exception and as barred by the same 1947 treaty discussed in *de Csepel.*

See Simon v. Republic of Hungary, 37 F. Supp. 3d 381, 408–24 (D.D.C. 2014); *cf Abelesz v. Magyar Nemzeti Bank*, 692 F.3d 661 (2012). On appeal, the D.C. circuit reversed, finding that the expropriation exception applied, and that the 1947 treaty, in fact, did not bar the claims. *Simon v. Republic of Hungary*, 812 F.3d 127 (D.C. Cir. 2016). *Simon* first endorsed the espousal theory that the *de Csepel* District Court had articulated, namely, that the U.S.-Hungary treaty could not be construed to waive on behalf of the United States those claims on behalf of persons who were not U.S. citizens at the time of the claims. *Simon*, 812 F.3d at 131.

With the treaty exception resolved, the *Simon* court had to consider the FSIA exceptions. The Court of Appeals repeated the settled standard that in assessing whether "rights in property taken in violation of international law are in issue," the plaintiff need only make a "non-frivolous" showing at the jurisdictional stage. *Id., citing Helmerich & Payne Int'l Drilling Co. v. Bolivarian Republic of Venezuela*, 784 F.3d 804, 811–12 (D.C. Cir. 2015); *Chabad*, 528 F.3d at 940–41. The reason for this, the Court of Appeals observed, was that in those cases the merits of the claim mirrored the jurisdictional theory because the causes of action alleged taking of property without just compensation, which is the same standard applied to consider whether a taking violates international law:

> When the jurisdictional and merits inquiries fully overlap in that fashion, a plaintiff need not prove a winning claim on the merits merely to establish jurisdiction. Rather, the plaintiff need only show that its claim is "non-frivolous" at the jurisdictional stage, and then must definitively prove its claim in order to prevail at the merits stage.

Simon, 812 F.3d at 141. The railroad claims were slightly different, however, in the Court of Appeals' view. Here, they

> plead a "violation of international laws" only to "give rise to jurisdiction" under the FSIA's expropriation exception, Compl. ¶ 207, not to establish liability on the merits. Unlike in our prior cases, consequently, the international-law violation at issue here—genocide—bears solely on jurisdiction.

Id. In such a case, the court reasoned, the bar is somewhat higher than the "non-frivolous" (*id.*) standard; instead, a plaintiff must allege facts to satisfy the jurisdictional standard.

With this in mind, the *Simon* court considered whether the claims concerned rights in property "taken in violation of international law." 28 U.S.C. § 1605(a)(3). The "question then becomes whether the takings of property described in the complaint bear a sufficient connection to genocide that they amount to takings 'in violation of international law.'" *Id.* To answer that question, the court looked to Convention on the Prevention and Punishment of the Crime of Genocide (Genocide Convention), art. 2, Dec. 9, 1948, 78 U.N.T.S. 277. It defines genocide as follows (emphasis added):

> [A]ny of the following acts committed with intent to destroy, in whole or in part, a national, ethnical, racial or religious group, as such:
> (a) Killing members of the group;
> (b) Causing serious bodily or mental harm to members of the group; [or]
> (c) *Deliberately inflicting on the group conditions of life calculated to bring about its physical destruction in whole or in part...*

Simon, 812 F.3d at 143, *citing* the Genocide Convention. The *Simon* court noted that the clause was drafted specifically in response to the expropriations that occurred during the Holocaust. Citing *de Csepel* with approval, the Court of Appeals held that the allegations and history of depriving "Hungarian Jews of the resources needed to survive as a people sufficed because: 'The Nazis...achieved [the Final Solution] by first isolating [Jews], then expropriating the Jews' property, then ghettoizing them, then deporting them to the camps, and finally, murdering the Jews and in many instances cremating their bodies'" showed the requisite genocidal intent. *Id.* at 143–44 (*citing* Amended Complaint at ¶ 82).

Even so, Hungary had also asserted what is known as the domestic takings rule in *Simon*. The Court of Appeals rejected Hungary's domestic takings argument because "[t]he domestic takings rule has no application in the unique circumstances of this case, in which, unlike in most cases involving expropriations in violation of international law, *genocide* constitutes the pertinent international-law violation." *Id.* at 144. More specifically:

> The international-law prohibition against genocide in fact was a direct reaction to the actions of sovereigns against their own citizens. The Hungarian Holocaust is a paradigmatic example. Genocidal expropriations of the property of a sovereign's own nationals thus are "tak[ings] in violation of international law" for purposes of the FSIA's expropriation exception. 28 U.S.C. § 1605(a)(3). In short, the domestic takings rule has no applicability in the discrete circumstances of this case.

Id. at 145. Genocidal takings are therefore squarely within the expropriation exception, regardless of the nationality of the perpetrator or the victim.

With a new, controlling precedent in its own circuit, it was hardly a surprise that the District Court found that the Herzog heirs had met the expropriation exception; however, interestingly enough, the court also held that the commercial activity exception did not apply. *De Csepel v. Republic of Hungary*, 169 F. Supp. 3d 143 (D.D.C. 2016). As noted above, discovery had fleshed out some additional factual details. Of the forty-four works at issue, twenty-four are claimed by the heirs of András Herzog, twelve are claimed by the heirs of Erzsébet Herzog, and eight are claimed by the heirs of István Herzog. Two of the works came into the museums' possession much later than during the war, as it turned out. Lucas Cranach the Elder's *The Annunciation to Saint Joachim* was seized by Hungary's state security agency from an attorney, Dr. Henrik Lorant. The Cranach seems to have been placed in Lorant's house by Ferenc Kelemen, who himself claimed to have been keeping it safe for Erzsébet Herzog. In 1963, John Opie's *Portrait of a Lady* was donated to the Museum of Fine Arts by an individual named Endre Gyamarthy. The court concluded that it was undisputed that at least fifteen of the works did return, at least temporarily, to the Herzog heirs after the war. Under customs and smuggling laws prohibiting the export of cultural patrimony, however, the transfers were conditional upon the explicit agreement that the paintings remained in Hungary. *Id.* at 149. Ten more appear to have been released to the family on paper, but whether the works were physically returned was in dispute. Evidence was introduced that even for those works that were physically returned, onerous conditions were imposed to consummate the official transfer. From one example:

> At acceptance, the owners are obliged to pay a duty fee of 11 per cent of the value of the privately owned artworks returned from Germany. It is understandable that the owners of larger collections and artworks of higher value do not hurry to take out their artworks, knowing that such items are in a good place.

Id. at 149-50. Thus, to obtain the return of artwork looted during the Holocaust, owners would have had to pay the fee and obtain an export license. Yet, Hungary claims present title to:

> Most of the artworks that Hungary *did* temporarily return to the Herzog family [that] were subsequently re-seized by Hungary in 1952 as part of a criminal action. After allegedly discovering that the former wife of István Herzog (Ilona Kiss) had attempted to illegally smuggle Herzog art out of the country in 1948, the Communist regime prosecuted Kiss, resulting in forfeiture proceedings. In all, twenty artworks were seized by the state, fifteen of which are at issue in this lawsuit.

Id. at 150. There was not, however, any single formal custodial or bailment contract between any of the heirs and the Hungarian museums. Summing up, the District Court organized the paintings at issue into four categories:

> (1) art acquired by defendants *after* the Holocaust; (2) art confiscated during the Holocaust that was never returned to plaintiffs; (3) art confiscated during the Holocaust that was returned to plaintiffs, and then subsequently seized back by criminal forfeiture; and finally, (4) art confiscated during the Holocaust that was returned

> to plaintiffs, and then subsequently deposited with the museums by the 1950 bailment agreement.

Id. at 151 (emphasis in original).

With all this in mind, the court analyzed the applicability of the commercial activity exception. It was dismissive of the plaintiffs' attempts for the first time to argue that the first two prongs of the commercial activity exception applied (a commercial activity carried on in the United States by a foreign state, or an act performed in the United States in connection with the commercial activity of the sovereign). The causes of action arising out of the alleged bailment contracts are not based on the present-day Hungarian commercial activity today but rather the postwar conduct of Hungary that plaintiffs argued was inconsistent with those agreements. *ÖBB Personenverkehr AG v. Sachs*, 136 S. Ct. 390, 392 (2015) (holding that the commercial acts must form the "gravamen of the complaint").

As to the third prong, a commercial act abroad causing a direct effect in the United States, the court concluded that the facts now in the record did not support this theory. Where the D.C. circuit had endorsed the allegations as sufficient because specific performance of the bailment agreements would have required delivery in the United States, the factual record was not enough to reach that conclusion. *De Csepel*, 169 F. Supp. 3d at 158. There is a distinction, however, the court noted, between contracts that necessarily implicate performance in the United States as the place of performance and those that do not implicate such a performance. The question to be answered is whether the agreements between the heirs and Hungary did that. The court agreed that the evidence supported a bailment theory for at least some of the artworks. While the form and scope of those agreements varied, and the seizure and custody of the artworks did not have a unified history, the court held that for all such agreements, the evidence was undisputed that Hungary's expectation would have been to be required to return the works in Budapest, not anywhere else, in no small part because of the strict criminal export prohibitions. *Id.* at 160-61. Indeed, the later partial performance of the bailment agreements took place in Budapest when the Museum of Fine Arts told Erzsébet that she or her agent could pick up the paintings in Budapest, but that due to the customs regulations and preservation order attached to such artifacts, they could not leave the country. *Id.* at 161. This convinced the court that nothing about the bailments meant that performance would necessarily be in the United States, and thus it lacked the direct effect required by the commercial activity exception: "There is no evidence that the bailment agreements placed any restriction on the mode of Hungary's performance at the time of execution; nor any indication that the contractual relationship vested plaintiffs with any future power to do so." *Id.* at 162.

Having dispensed with the availability of the commercial activity exception, the District Court upheld the availability of the expropriation exception on the factual record. Here, the recent opinion in *Simon* was paramount. Critically, the court stated, "[A] court is not limited to solely those jurisdictional grounds under the FSIA that overlap with a plaintiff's substantive claim." *Id.* at 163. It noted that even though the Court of Appeals had previously focused on the bailment agreements under the commercial activity exception now held to be inapplicable, *Simon* had found the expropriation exception available even for claims not primarily based on takings because of their association with the Holocaust: "Such takings, the *Simon* Court held, 'did more than effectuate genocide or serve as a means of carrying out genocide. Rather, we see the expropriations *as themselves genocide*.'" *Id.* The Hungarian defendants did not dispute that forty-two of the forty-four works at issue in the lawsuit were seized in furtherance of the Nazis' genocidal campaign, or, as their attorney was apparently pressed to concede at oral argument, "where property is taken 'in connection with a genocidal act' like the 'treatment of the Jewish people during World War II, the taking may qualify as a taking in violation of international law.'" *Id.* at 164. *Simon* also resolved the 1947 treaty's effect, flatly rejecting the same argument made by Hungarian defendants in *De Csepel*. *Simon*, 812 F.3d at 150. The *de Csepel* District Court therefore concluded that the two paintings not taken during the Holocaust, the Cranach and the Opie portrait, were not subject to the expropriation exception either.

As a fallback, Hungary contended that those paintings temporarily returned should fall outside the expropriation exception because it undermined the argument that there had been no prompt, adequate, and effective compensation required by international law. The court disagreed, noting that the seizure of paintings during the Hungarian Holocaust, resolved only when Hungary lost the war, failed any reasonable definition of prompt. As the court noted, "It is puzzling to suggest that artwork confiscated during the Holocaust as part of a campaign of genocide loses its status as property 'taken in violation of international law' because it is eventually released to its owner after years of deprivation." *De Csepel,* 169 F. Supp. 3d at 166-67.

Now, with the benefit of the *Chabad, de Csepel,* and *Simon* decisions from the Court of Appeals, the District Court had no choice but to reject Hungary's exhaustion argument. It is simply settled law now in the D.C. circuit that exhaustion is not required to invoke the expropriation exception. *See Simon*, 812 F.3d at 148; *Chabad*, 528 F.3d at 948–49; *accord Abelesz*, 692 F.3d at 678. The District Court noted in *de Csepel* the plausibility of the observation in Justice Breyer's concurrence in *Altmann* that if a claim involves a "basic expropriation claim asserting that a sovereign has taken an individual's property without just compensation," it might not qualify. *Altmann*, 541 U.S. at 714. That construct simply does not apply to the taking of Jewish property during the Holocaust; there is nothing basic or ordinary about it, and Justice Breyer's concurrence does not suggest otherwise. In addition, as was noted in *Simon*, "[W]hen the international law violation at issue is genocide, a failure to seek compensation from the foreign state is irrelevant to the jurisdictional analysis." *De Csepel*, 169 F. Supp. 3d at 168.

Lastly, the court declined to adopt a prudential exhaustion rule, that is, one where "[e]ven if plaintiffs' claims fit comfortably within the expropriation exception, defendants might suggest that the Court decline to exercise jurisdiction as a matter of international comity until plaintiffs either exhaust their domestic remedies, or demonstrate that any such attempt would be futile." *Id.* at 169. Even if adopted, however that rule applies only to provide deference by a state (here the United States) for claims for harm to its own citizens, i.e., U.S. citizens, and for claims brought by the state itself. The Herzogs were not U.S. citizens when they were harmed, and the rule would not apply even if adopted. *Id.*

None of this is happening in a vacuum in Hungary. At the time the lawsuit was filed, the right-wing government of Viktor Orbán had just been elected. While it may be wishful thinking given the similar recalcitrance of a more progressive Germany, it is difficult not to wonder how a different government might have handled the case. The case is more than six years old. There is absolutely no question that these artworks were taken from the Herzogs during the Holocaust in Hungary. There is really no remaining argument that Hungary's treaties provided any compensation either to the Herzogs or to situations in which they could apply. So why is Hungary resisting in this fashion? Why, as the Norton Simon Museum or the Thyssen-Bornemisza Museum did, is Hungary so intent on keeping what in any meaningful sense are ill-gotten gains? Such answers are always couched in why one can keep the artwork, but not whether one should keep it.

Chapter 18

Commercial Activity or Sovereign Act?

Ironically, most of the FSIA-related cases have involved foreign sovereigns other than Germany: Austria, Spain, the Netherlands, and Russia. Until 2015, the only two that did involve the country actually responsible for the war were brought under the commercial activity exception, not the expropriation exception. Both fell short, one in the U.S. District Court for the District of Tennessee and the U.S. Court of Appeals for the Sixth Circuit, and one in the U.S. District Court for the Southern District of New York and then the U.S. Court of Appeals for the Second Circuit. Both underscored that, to date, courts have not been willing to take a particularly expansive view of commercial acts in the context where Nazi-looting allegations are in play.

The New York case again involved the Mendelssohn-Bartholdy heirs. They filed suit in 2013 against the Free State of Bavaria and its Staatsgemäldesammlungen, the Bavarian State Paintings Collection, over title to *Madame Soler* by Pablo Picasso. The case invoked jurisdiction not based on the original sequence of events that befell Mendelssohn-Bartholdy, however, but on the circumstances of Bavaria's later acquisition of the painting in 1964 from Justin Thannhauser. Schoeps and his co-plaintiffs alleged that Bavaria had sent its agent to New York to buy the painting there, a factual circumstance that Bavaria denied, arguing to the contrary that the place of performance of the sale was in France.

The Complaint invoked all three clauses of the commercial activity exception, 28 U.S.C. §§ 1605(a)(2)(i)–(iii). The Complaint traces the history of the Mendelssohn-Bartholdy family and its experience in Germany under the Nazis just as the same heirs' case against the Guggenheim and MoMA had. It augmented those allegations with more specific historical analysis about the banking family itself, noting publications that targeted them specifically starting in 1933 with such menacing statements as "We are still not finished with the Mendelssohns and still have to say something about the history of this 'honorable' banking house."[171] Mendelssohn-Bartholdy was divested of his position on the Berlin stock exchange by the Statute on the Preparation of the Organic Constitution of the German Economy[172] and the Central Union of German Banking and Bankers[173] in early 1934. While these policies were effectively destroying Mendelssohn-Bartholdy's economic participation, other threats began to come his way. After the 1934 purge known as the Night of the Long Knives, in which Nazi officials, particularly from the conservative party and those that had led the Sturmabteilung (SA), were murdered by the Schutzstaffel (SS), a lead article in a publication by Nazi Party ideologist Alfred Rosenberg, *Der Weltkampf* (*World Struggle*), attempted to legitimize the murder of former Reich Chancellor von Schleicher based upon his association with the Mendelssohn family.

With so few options for economic survival available to him, the plaintiffs alleged, Mendelssohn-Bartholdy began to organize his collection for consignment. The Complaint characterized the Certificate of Inheritance as a cover, a fictive cover, to shield the collection from scrutiny as putatively in the hands of a non-Jew (his wife Elsa). The allegations of the Complaint flatly denied that there had been any wedding gift at all in 1927:

> In fact, there was no "wedding gift" in 1927. Mendelssohn-Bartholdy as well as every dealer with whom he dealt referred exclusively to Mendelssohn-Bartholdy as the owner of the artworks up until the time of his death in May 1935. Indeed, Justin Thannhauser relates specifically in his internal files that he acquired

> *Madame Soler* and the other Picasso artworks from "the Collection of Paul von Mendelssohn-Bartholdy."[174]

Mendelssohn-Bartholdy consigned *Madame Soler* to Thannhauser in 1934, as discussed above. Thereafter, the plaintiffs alleged:

> Thannhauser bought the paintings from Mendelssohn-Bartholdy in a prototypical "forced sale." Circumstantial evidence confirms, however that Thannhauser paid Mendelssohn-Bartholdy little. In the alternative, Plaintiffs allege that–after the forced consignments caused by Nazi persecution–Thannhauser stole the Painting after Mendelssohn-Bartholdy's death, when he realized that no one but Mendelssohn-Bartholdy was aware of the consignment of *Madame Soler* and the other Picasso paintings.[175]

This is admittedly unusual. Almost every complaint makes a set of factual allegations and makes alternative legal claims. This one set forth alternative factual scenarios. That raises obvious problems with the ability to carry a burden of proof; if it could be one or the other, it is difficult as a matter of logic later to say that either one is more likely than not. The Complaint alleged that none of the Mendelssohn-Bartholdy heirs knew until 2005 that he had disposed of the painting in Germany in 1935. More seriously, they accused Bavarian authorities of affirmatively concealing the Mendelssohn-Bartholdy provenance when they later acquired the paintings in the 1960s when the authors of a *catalogue raisonné* inquired. From there, the plaintiffs alleged, the inertia of ignorance of potential claims undermined any possible ability to learn the truth or pursue claims. They referred to testimony by Stuart Eizenstat on July 27, 2006, describing a pervasive silence about the issue. Lastly, they argued for the same presumption of confiscation that they had alleged in the New York museum case.

With regard to the acquisition by Bavaria of the painting, the plaintiffs accused Bavaria's agent, Halldor Soehner, of being an ex-Nazi. Soehner travelled to New York in the spring of 1964 to discuss buying *Madame Soler* from Thannhauser. They met in Thannhauser's apartment and agreed upon a price, according to the plaintiffs, of DM 1.6 million. Plaintiffs alleged that Soehner could not have done this in good faith, ignorant of the painting's history:

> As an ex-Nazi, Soehner would have known that Mendelssohn-Bartholdy and his family (the most famous German Jewish family in history) were viciously persecuted by the Nazis, e.g., Mendelssohn & Co. was "Aryanized"; one of Mendelssohn-Bartholdy's sisters had been sent to a concentration camp; and statues of Felix Mendelssohn were torn down.[176]

Against this, they alleged that Soehner had never asked from whom Thannhauser acquired the painting. Worse yet, they alleged that Soehner's financing for the purchase came from a secret plan to liquidate 113 other works in the Staatsgemäldesammlungen that had Nazi-tainted provenances; these paintings were owned by Goering, Martin Bormann, and Heinrich Hoffmann, among others.

According to the plaintiffs, the Bavarian defendants had given incorrect or inadequate responses to the heirs' queries about the painting. The plaintiffs claimed that the Bavarians had conceded that Mendelssohn-Bartholdy—and not his wife—was the one who conveyed the painting to Thannhauser, that Mendelssohn-Bartholdy was properly considered a victim of persecution, and that Soehner had travelled to New York. The response ignored the more specific details of the banker's persecution, however, according to the heirs. Bavaria rejected the prelitigation demand for the return of *Madame Soler* by stating, "[T]he sales of the pictures were not motivated by situations of financial need," and thus "that there is no connection between the sale of the artwork and the persecution of Paul von Mendelssohn-Bartholdy by the National Socialist regime."[177] After multiple meetings involving German and American counsel, Bavaria refused to discuss the matter further or submit the question to the German Advisory Commission (see Chapter 20) for a recommendation about whether the museum ought to restitute it.

The Complaint sought title to the painting and its physical return. The plaintiffs accused Bavaria not just of acquiring a painting without good title, but also of affirmatively defrauding them and other potential claimants. Interestingly, the plaintiffs also asserted a separate claim for "taking in violation of international law" within the meaning of the FSIA, but did not assert jurisdiction under the expropriation exception of § 1605(a)(3).

Bavaria moved to dismiss in its first response. The threshold argument that it made was that the commercial activity exception could not apply because the claims were not based on the commercial activity of which Bavaria was accused (buying the painting in New York), but rather were based on the allegations of Nazi persecution in the 1930s. As such, Bavaria argued, the court did not even need to enter into analysis of the direct effect test of the commercial activity exception because the statute did not apply in the first place. As Bavaria's brief framed the question:

> Here, the acts giving rise to the cause of action are Mendelssohn-Bartholdy's alleged sale of the Painting under duress in 1934/35 and Bavaria's denial of Plaintiffs' claim for possession of the Painting in 2010. In contrast, the acts needed to establish jurisdiction are Bavaria's alleged purchase of *Madame Soler* in 1964/65 in the United States. The requisite degree of closeness between the two is plainly lacking.[178]

Without conceding that point, Bavaria argued further that there was, in fact, no direct effect in the United States as the statute requires, requiring dismissal.

Bavaria pointed out that "a claim is not 'based upon' a foreign state's commercial activity in the United States unless that commercial activity constitutes the actionable conduct that allegedly harmed the plaintiff." *See Saudi Arabia v. Nelson*, 507 U.S. 349, 355 (1993). Bavaria's point, illustrated by a hypothetical, was that had Thannhauser lived in Switzerland at the time of the transaction, the result would be the same because the foundation of plaintiff's theory was still based on a German series of events, namely, the persecution of Mendelssohn-Bartholdy.

Regardless, Bavaria argued, the Complaint failed the direct effect test of the third prong of the commercial activity exception. Under Second Circuit case law, "the mere fact that a foreign state's commercial activity outside of the United States caused physical or financial injury to a United States citizen is not itself sufficient to constitute a direct effect in the United States." *Guirlando v. T.C. Ziraat Bankasi A.S.*, 602 F.3d 69, 74

(2d Cir. 2010). Instead, the effect caused by the foreign sovereign's conduct must be "legally significant."[179] In the case of a contract, the place of performance is paramount; in the case of a tort, the locus of the injury or deprivation is what matters. In the *Schoeps* case, Bavaria argued that any such deprivation was incurred in Germany and not the United States where the painting is located. Although that is not really the case (as it would absolve any sovereign defendant of an obligation to return property to someone in the United States on the theory that the property was located elsewhere), Bavaria could just as easily argued that the place of deprivation was Germany because that is where the plaintiffs were but for one of them.

Bavaria also took the unusual step of making a factual argument in its motion to dismiss that it had not, as a matter of fact, engaged in commercial activity in the United States, such that the first prong of the commercial activity exception could not be applied either and offered it thusly:

> Soehner's (and thus Bavaria's) activities in the United States in connection with the acquisition of *Madame Soler* were confined to a preliminary meeting with Thannhauser in New York. The subsequent transaction itself—including execution of the Letter Agreement in France, [the] shipment of the Painting to Munich from neighboring Switzerland, and remittance of the purchase price via the Bavarian State Bank to EBA in Liechtenstein—all took place entirely within Europe.

In this respect, the first prong becomes analogous to a question of specific jurisdiction. Under contract claims, the place of performance is what matters. The heirs' claims were not entirely contractually based; of course, they had alleged affirmatively a case of fraud. Bavaria framed the question as whether or not the contract was formed in New York or was merely a preliminary meeting that may or may not have led to a contract. If it should be the latter, then there was no commercial activity as contemplated by the statute.

The heirs understandably leaned on the allegations of their Complaint to rebut the factual theory of what had happened between Soehner and Thannhauser. Not only had they alleged the fact of the meeting (a November 11, 1964, letter to the Bavarian State Ministry of Education and Culture [the Ministry] from Soehner recounted the particulars of his meeting with Thannhauser), but also claimed that they had reached agreement on all material terms of the contract. The plaintiffs took strong issue with Bavaria's assertion that Thannhauser had not sold the painting on his own behalf in New York but had rather done so in France as an agent for the real seller, a Liechtenstein entity named L'Establissement Les Beaux Arts (EBA). Against that, they cited a contemporary report in the *Sueddeutsche Zeitung* that Soehner was in America to "scour"[180] the continent for Picassos. The insertion of EBA, they suggested, was a contrivance to avoid U.S. and New York taxes, and that even if EBA, it was wholly controlled by Thannhauser.

All this, they argued, made Bavaria a private player in the art market, not a sovereign actor. Here, Soehner's scouring of the American art market for Picassos was just that, they submitted. Further, they argued that the formation of the substance of a contract on U.S. territory was enough. *See Gibbons v. Udaras na Gaeltachta*, 549 F. Supp. 1094, 1113 (S.D.N.Y. 1982) ("[w]here, as here, the commercial activity in question centers on the formation of a contract, the United States will be found to have had a substantial contact with that activity if substantial contractual negotiations occurred here ... or if substantial aspects of the contract were to be performed here ... ").

As is so often the case, the longer the motion practice went on, the more extreme the positions became. Bavaria's reply to plaintiffs' opposition went over similar territory about the commercial activity in question. Most surprisingly, Bavaria took issue not so much at Petropoulos's opinion, but with his very competence. The reply brief stated, "Plaintiffs rely almost exclusively on a 38-page declaration by their purported expert, Jonathan Petropoulos. Petropoulos's unsupported speculation and conjecture masquerading as an 'expert' opinion is blatantly inadmissible."[181] An attack on his conclusions is to be expected. Putting quotes around his name as an expert, however, is simply preposterous. He is one of the best-known and widely respected historians on Nazi-looted art.

The court (presided over by the same judge who had expressed such concern about the confidentiality of the parties' settlement terms in the case against the Guggenheim and MoMA) held a hearing on Bavaria's motion on December 23, 2013. It observed:[182]

> [I]t appears to me . . . that the critical issue is whether the sale of the painting, in material part, was consummated in New York, or whether it was consummated abroad. If it was consummated in New York, then it might well be that sovereign immunity would not attach, because a commercial activity was carried on in the United States, thus implicating 28 U.S.C. Section 1605(a)(2)(i).

To answer this question, the court determined that it needed to hold an evidentiary hearing and not limit itself to the papers submitted. It held hearings in the late winter of 2014.

In the end, the court did not believe as an evidentiary matter that the transaction had been consummated in New York. *Schoeps v. Bayern*, 27 F. Supp. 3d 540, 546 (2014). It found as a matter of fact that Soehner had indeed come to America as the heir-apparent to the then-director of the Bavarian state museums, Kurt Martin. Soehner signed the guestbook at Thannhauser's residence between March and May of 1964. Once he returned to Munich, he wrote to Thannhauser on August 1, 1964, and requested the opportunity to meet again. This second meeting, the court found, was to be in Europe, however, not New York. He thereafter received approval from the Bavarian State Ministry to travel to Saint-Jean-Cap-Ferrat, France, "to conduct negotiations with the art trade there in the first week of the month of August 1964." *Id.* at 543. Thannhauser was there as well, because he dictated:

> [O]n "Hotel Intercontinental Genève" letterhead, "I hereby confirm the purchase of the oil painting 'Madame Soler' by Pablo Picasso by the Bavarian State Paintings Collections, Munich, from myself as commission agent. The Purchase price is 1,775,000.00 Swiss Francs . . . the full amount should be paid by August 31, 1965." Def. Ex. 32. The Letter Agreement adds the caveat that "[t]his acquisition is subject to the proviso of consent of the Bavarian State Ministry of Education and Cultural Affairs and the consent of the Purchase Commission for Modern Art with the Bavarian State Paintings Collections in Munich."

Id. By this point, the court noted, the plaintiffs had conceded that the sale had not been consummated in New York; the court made a factual finding that the parties had not reached agreement in New York. Even so, the court inferred that the motivation for this was the one offered by the plaintiffs: to avoid U.S. taxes. *Id.* at 544.

Based on all these factual conclusions, the court held as a matter of law that none of the prongs of the commercial activity exception applied. As to the first, the court found that against the requirement that the claim be based on commercial activity with substantial contact with the United States:

> In no real sense is this suit even "based upon" Bavaria's acquisition of Madame Soler in 1964-65, let alone activity in the United States. Rather, as the "Nature of Action" section of the Amended Complaint makes clear, the gravamen of this action is that title to *Madame Soler* never rightfully passed to Thannhauser in Germany because "Mendelssohn-Bartholdy consigned the Painting (to Thannhauser) in 1934 only after nearly two years of intensifying Nazi persecution."

Id. Similarly, the court rejected the idea that the claims met the substantial contact requirement:

> As has already been made clear, the evidence establishes that the only activity conducted by Bavaria in the United States in connection with its acquisition of *Madame Soler* consisted of Soehner's preliminary meeting with Thannhauser in the spring of 1964, a meeting of no legal consequence, which took place months before the occurrence of all the pertinent events—the drafting a letter agreement in France, the shipment of the painting from Vaduz to Munich, the approval of the acquisition in Munich, and the payment for the painting to EBA in Liechtenstein—all of which occurred in Europe. And even if, contrary to the evidence, a bargain for *Madame Soler* had been vetted at the initial New York meeting, an individual preliminary meeting cannot and does not by itself constitute commercial activity "having substantial conduct with the United States" under FSIA §§ 1605(a) (2) and 1603(e).

Id. at 545.

The heirs' argument under the second prong of § 1605(a)(2) did no better in the court's eyes. "Where, as here, the plaintiff 'has not argued that any non-commercial acts performed by [Bavaria] in the United States allegedly formed the basis of its complaint,' the second prong is simply 'inapplicable.'" Lastly, the court found that nothing outside the United States had caused a sufficient effect in the United States to abolish sovereign immunity under the third prong. The court had harsh words for this notion:

> In a vain attempt to satisfy this requirement, plaintiffs posit that Bavaria's purchase of *Madame Soler* even if occurring (as this Court has found) entirely outside the United States, had a supposed series of allegedly "direct effects" on the United States, ranging from "the disastrous effect of Bavaria's commercial misconduct on the policy-sensitive NY art market," to the furtherance of an alleged criminal conspiracy to evade United States taxes. See Plaintiffs' post-hearing briefing at 9. This is balderdash. While the Second Circuit has held that "[t]here is no requirement that the [direct] effect be substantial," *Servaas, Inc. v. Republic of Iraq*, 2011 WL 454501 at *2 (2d Cir. 2011), neither the alleged impact on the art market nor the alleged tax evasion are direct effects at all.

Id. at 546. With that, the case was dismissed and judgment entered on all counts for Bavaria.

The heirs appealed to the Second Circuit. The Court of Appeals deferred to the District Court's factual findings and affirmed its legal reasoning in all respects in a summary order. *Schoeps v. Bayern*, 611 F. App'x 32, 33 (2d Cir. 2015). The most notable aspect of the brief opinion came in its treatment of the District Court's findings about the thrust of the Complaint—that is, was the case really based on the 1964 transaction and not something else?

> We have a different view of the gravamen of Plaintiffs' action than that which was adopted by the District Court. But we need not decide this question, and neither did the District Court, for

> we agree with the District Court that Bavaria did not engage in relevant commercial activity having "substantial contact" with the United States.... We also agree that Plaintiffs' action is not based upon an act outside the United States in connection with a commercial activity of Bavaria that caused a "direct effect" in the United States.

Id. at 34. This is a remarkably cryptic statement. However, with the benefit of the cases considered here, it is clear that the Court of Appeals was referring to the expropriation exception. After all, the bulk of the allegations and much of the proffered testimony was about the historical persecution of the Mendelssohn-Bartholdys. This theory, as far as the papers and oral arguments reflect, was never even mentioned by the heirs' attorneys. Had they done so, in light of the rapid developments in the law at the same time, it is difficult not to wonder if the outcome might have been different, certainly as to jurisdiction. The Complaint gave an exhaustive and eloquent detail the facts of persecution and the circumstances of duress. Perhaps it would have encountered a domestic-takings argument like the ones in *Simon* and *De Csepel*, but it is unknowable now whether the District Court would have agreed. On March 21, 2016, the Supreme Court denied the heirs' petition for writ of certiorari.

The difference between commercial and sovereign acts was also central to a Tennessee case against the Federal Republic of Germany that was filed by the heirs of Walter Westfeld pursuant to the commercial activity exception of the FSIA. Fred Westfield, as administrator of the estate of Walter Westfeld, and others as representatives of relevant heirs, filed suit in the Chancery Court in Davidson County, Tennessee (Nashville). While the FSIA is a federal statute, its jurisdiction is not necessarily exclusively limited to the federal courts; when applied, it merely means that a foreign sovereign is not immune from suit. The Complaint addressed the history of Walter Westfeld, a Jewish art dealer in Wuppertal, Germany. According to the Complaint, as repression increased in 1933, Westfeld made efforts to depart from Germany and transfer his art collection and assets to the United States to support his emigration. The Complaint alleged that he was able to transfer $40,000 to his brother Robert, who at that time lived in Nashville and had changed his name to Westfield. Despite his efforts, he had still not managed to secure passage out of Germany when his passport expired in 1938. He was able to transmit one painting, *Portrait of a Man and Woman in an Interior* by Eglon van der Neer, which was eventually acquired by the Museum of Fine Arts, Boston.

In the wake of the November pogroms and Kristallnacht, Westfeld was arrested on November 15, 1938. The pretext was a currency violation, but his heirs alleged that the real purpose was to obtain leverage to acquire his art collection. The state attorney in Düsseldorf put up a portion of Westfeld's property for a forced auction at Lempertz Auction House on December 12-13, 1939. The proceeds went to the German government, not to Westfeld. He had been sentenced to three and one-half years' imprisonment and fined RM 300,000. That fine was paid by using the proceeds of the Lempertz auction, a rank confiscation by another name. The Nazis were not done with Westfeld yet, however. While imprisoned, he was brutally interrogated about an El Greco that the Gestapo sought for the Führermuseum project in Linz. This, too, was put up for sale at Lempertz.

Westfeld died in late 1942 or early 1943 in Auschwitz. As was often the case, when a murdered Jew's actual date of death was unknown, the Amtsgericht (court) in Düsseldorf, by order dated August 1, 1948, fixed his official date of death as May 8, 1945—the day of the German surrender and the end of the war in Europe.

As the Complaint described it, Westfeld's heirs were alerted to the Nazi looting of Walter Westfeld's collection when they came across a description on the Museum of Fine Arts Boston's website concerning the painting there. In that post, Victoria Reed (the same curator for provenance whose scholarship played a central role in the Seger-Thomschitz case) had written an article indicating that some of Westfeld's art may have been confiscated. The Complaint alleged that she was not initially able to identify which items were sold at the 1939 Lempertz sale, but subsequently she advised him that she had located a catalogue. This gave the full picture of the scope of the remarkable collection that had been stripped away and sold.

The Westfeld heirs sued Germany for conversion and other equitable claims. Oddly enough, despite referencing the Lempertz catalogue, the Complaint does not mention any specific works of art. Instead, it sought a constructive trust and a compulsory accounting of the paintings identified in a general sense. The jurisdictional averments of the Complaint specifically named § 1605(a)(2)—the commercial activity—as the basis for jurisdiction.

Germany removed the action to federal court pursuant to 28 U.S.C. § 1441, which allows a defendant to remove any civil action over which the federal courts would have had jurisdiction had it been filed originally in a District Court. Because a case invoking the FSIA, a federal statute, can be filed in federal court under 28 U.S.C. § 1331 ("The district court shall have original jurisdiction of all civil actions arising under the Constitution, laws, or treaties of the United States."), the removal statute gave the German defendants that right in *Westfield*.

Germany moved to dismiss. Stressing the absence of any contact with the United States by Walter Westfield, Germany contested that the commercial activity exception expired. It also augmented the factual allegations of the Complaint that it had removed with allegations contained in an earlier probate court proceeding that the plaintiffs had apparently brought to clarify their role as Westfeld's lawful heirs of who could bring the case. In that probate petition, Walter Westfeld was survived by three brothers at the time of his death: Dietrich Westfield, Robert Westfield, and Max Westfield (who had by then Anglicized their name to "Westfield"). Dietrich Westfield and Max Westfield left Germany and joined Robert Westfield in Nashville in 1940. Dietrich Westfield died in Nashville in 1967. Max Westfield was a well-known artist. Max Westfield died in Nashville in 1971.

On November 10, 1949, an estate proceeding concerning Walter Westfeld's will was opened in a German court in Düsseldorf; Dietrich Westfield was appointed as executor. After the brothers backed away from further participation out of an aversion to returning to Germany and without the resources to do so, the German court appointed Emilie Scheulen, Walter Westfeld's wife, a certificate of heirship. In 1958, Scheulen brought a case in Tennessee to recover the balance of a sum she claimed was owed by Robert Westfield to Walter Westfeld's estate.

Turning to the FSIA, the motion rightly pointed out that the Complaint was scarce, to say the least, on allegations concerning commercial activity by Germany (whether in the United States or elsewhere causing effect in the United States). Although the Complaint only referenced

§ 1605(a)(2), the motion also argued why § 1605(a)(3), even if raised, should not apply. As to the first, the motion challenged as insufficient the allegations of the conversion of Westfeld's property and the later sale for a profit. This kind of seizure, Germany argued, was a quintessentially sovereign act, regardless of what it did with the proceeds:

> The seizure of private property by the German police, and the subsequent forced sale in 1939, is clearly not an activity in which a private person can or customarily could engage. The intentional conduct alleged by Plaintiff does not qualify as "commercial activity." The activities carried out by a sovereign's law enforcement agencies, by their nature, are not activities or actions which a private party is permitted to engage.[183]

Somewhat helpfully, in contrast to positions that Germany would take in 2015–2016, Germany was candid about the true nature of the use of its sovereign authority during the Nazi period as it relates to questions posed by the FSIA.

Even if the Lempertz auction that followed the seizure could somehow be characterized as a commercial act, Germany argued, it had no direct effect in the United States as required. It challenged as too speculative the argument that the effect in the United States was to deprive the U.S. heirs of something they otherwise would have received. This, Germany argued, was not the "immediate consequence"[184] required by *Weltover*, but rather had intervening elements that break the chain of causation. Germany cited unsuccessful cases involving personal injuries abroad that held that the effects felt when the person returned home are not enough. *Texas Trading & Milling Corp. v. Fed. Rep. of Nigeria*, 647 F.2d 300, 312 n.5 (2d Cir. 1981); *Zedan v. Kingdom of Saudi Arabia*, 849 F.2d. 1511, 1514 (D.C. Cir. 1988); Martin, 836 F.2d at 95; *Zernick v. Brown & Root, Inc.*, 826 F.2d. 415, 418–419 (5th Cir. 1987); *Reers v. Deutsche Bahn AG*, 320 F. Supp. 2d 140, 149 (S.D.N.Y. 2004).

With respect to the availability of the expropriation exception, Germany took the position that the expropriation of its property of one of its own nationals failed to qualify as the predicate taking in violation of international law "confiscations by a state of the property of its own nationals, no matter how flagrant and regardless of whether compensation has been provided, do not constitute violations of international law," Germany argued, quoting *F. Palicio y Compania, S.A. v. Brush*, 256 F. Supp. 481, 487 (S.D.N.Y. 1966) and *United States v. Belmont*, 301 U.S. 324, 332 (1937). The most telling aspect of those cases is their age, which was decades before a more sophisticated consideration of the facts of art looting by the Nazis. Perhaps most absurdly, however, Germany argued that because Germany's highest court later ruled that "the laws which caused the loss of citizenship for German Jews were void *ab initio* [from the very start], because these laws constituted such a flagrant violation of the fundamental principles of justice that they must be considered void *ab initio*, and finding otherwise would validate the former German government's actions and its discrimination of Jewish German citizens," *that they were not takings at all. See* German Federal Constitutional Court (Bundesverfassungsgericht) BverfGE 23, 98, 106 - 2 BvR 557/62 - (Feb. 14, 1968). Lastly, Germany noted the absence of any allegations pleading commercial activity that would satisfy § 1605(a)(3), which was hardly surprising, as the Westfields did not plead that exception to sovereign immunity.

Germany also argued that the statute of limitations barred the claims in issue, suggesting:

> There is no allegation contained in the Federal Complaint (or the Plaintiff's Tennessee probate pleadings) which suggest that these now deceased siblings of Walter Westfield were (1) unaware of the taking of the Walter Westfield's art collection by the former German government in the late 1930s or (2) that they were unaware that the property had been sold by the former German government during the time period of 1939-1943.[185]

Germany cited the correspondence between Walter's brothers and Scheulen in Germany for the proposition that they were aware of the expropriation of property then. Ironically, given the sequence in *Seger-Thomschitz v. Museum of Fine Arts Boston*, Germany pointed out that more than the three-year statute of limitations had passed since the plaintiffs had learned of the painting at the Museum of Fine Arts, Boston—the discovery that plaintiffs alleged had spurred their present claim.

The plaintiffs countered by relying on the third prong of the commercial activity exception: an act outside the United States causing a direct effect in the United States. Plaintiffs identified "the conversion of Walter Westfeld's specific works of art and tapestries through seizure and sale, first in the 1938-1939 time period and second in the 1943-44 time period"[186] as the requisite acts. They argued that an act under the commercial activity exception need not be one in which a private person can engage, *citing Siderman de Blake v. Republic of Argentina*, 965 F.2d 699, 709 n.10 (9th Cir. 1992) for the proposition that "the FSIA does not require that every act by the foreign state be commercial for the third clause of the commercial activity exception to apply." Further, the acts in *Weltover* had a sovereign aspect (a presidential decree that had altered the maturity date of sovereign bonds): "But the issuance of the bonds was, and the decree was an act made 'in connection with' that activity. The third clause of the commercial activity exception applied." *Adler v. Federal Republic of Nigeria*, 107 F.3d 720 (9th Cir. 1997).

In addition, the plaintiffs cleverly turned on its head the argument that Germany had made defending the expropriation exception: If Nazi Germany's seizures had been declared a nullity, then they could not have been sovereign acts—as far as the law was concerned, they were not acts of the government at all. Less persuasively, the plaintiffs argued that dispossession is not necessarily sovereign because commercial seizures can and do happen by creditors.

The Westfeld heirs took on Germany's expropriation exception by arguing that the acts of Nazi Germany were not the acts of a sovereign at all, citing the Ninth Circuit holding (never revisited) in *Altmann*. They analogized the seizure of Maria Altmann's property by Erich Führer to the seizure of Westfeld's collection before the Lempertz auctions. The plaintiffs argued for the illegitimacy of a sovereign immunity defense by citing *Altmann*, *Vineberg v. Bissonnette*, *Weiss v. Lustig*, 58 N.Y.S. 2d 547, 549 (N.Y. Sup. Ct. 1945); *Menzel v. List*, and *Bernstein v. N.V. Nederlandsche-Amerikaansche Stoomvaart-Maatschappij*, as well as the legacy of the Tate Letter. The commercial component of the expropriation exception was satisfied, the plaintiffs argued, by the allegations that "the 'commercial activity' was 'the sale of the converted works by the German government on the private art market through private auction houses.'"[187] Strangely enough, after making these points, the plaintiffs disavowed any reliance on the expropriation exception: "Plaintiffs, in fact, do not allege anywhere in their Complaint that they are basing subject matter jurisdiction in this lawsuit on the expropriation exception of 28 U.S.C. §1605(a)(3)."[188]

Turning to the statute of limitations, plaintiffs argued that Tennessee law did not permit them even to bring the action until they had been duly appointed as administrators, which had happened only recently, citing several cases that were upheld as timely even though they were brought decades after the relevant events. In their case, the administrator was not appointed until February 12, 2008, less than eight months before the Chancery Court Complaint was filed. They also advanced an equitable tolling argument:

> The Defendant, the Federal Republic of Germany, which "regards itself as identical to the [Third] Reich and claims its property," *Kunstsammlungen zu Weimar v. Elicofen*, 536 F. Supp. 829, 852 n. 22 (E.D.N.Y. 1981), actively took steps that prevented Walter Westfeld and, then, his estate, from bringing suit in a timely manner. It imprisoned Walter Westfeld, who, as owner of the property, was the one person who could most reliably identify which of his assets had been seized and auctioned. Defendant also compelled through threat of force Walter Westfeld's relatives to flee the country without any resources, thereby inhibiting their ability, physically and financially, to obtain information as to the identity of the works of art and tapestries owned by him, and to determine those works of art and tapestries that actually had been converted by Defendant. (Comp., ¶¶2, 3, 12) After vicious interrogations, torture, and humiliation, Defendant sent Walter Westfeld away to Theresienstadt and then to Auschwitz, where he was exterminated, thereby eliminating once and for all the only reliable source for identifying all of the property that the Defendant had converted.

Based on this, plaintiffs argued, "Defendant should not now be permitted to plead the statute of limitations as an affirmative defense, when the very conduct of Defendant vastly complicated Plaintiffs' efforts to commence a lawsuit in a timely manner."[189]

This eloquent attack on the audacity of Germany's assertion of a timeliness defense, notwithstanding the Washington Principles, was never decided, because the District Court granted Germany's motion to dismiss pursuant to the FSIA. *Westfield v. Fed. Republic of Germany*, No. 3:09-0204, 2009 U.S. Dist. LEXIS 65133, at *2 (M.D. Tenn. July 28, 2009). Looking at a recent U.S. Court of Appeals for the Sixth Circuit case that dismissed U.S. sex abuse claims against the Vatican because "all the claims stemmed from the alleged promulgation of a policy of secrecy for clergy sexual abuse issues, and the gravamen of plaintiff's claims was the tortious conduct of priests which was allegedly facilitated by the tortious conduct of Holy See employees," the District Court concluded that the same rationale applied. *Id., citing O'Bryan v. Holy See*, 556 F.3d 361, 377 (6th Cir. 2009). Likewise, in *Garb v. Republic of Poland*, 440 F.3d 579, 582 (2nd Cir. 2006), plaintiffs who brought suit against the Republic of Poland and the Ministry of the Treasury of the Republic of Poland for the expropriation of real property from Jews in postwar Poland ran aground for the same reason. Summing it all up, the District Court held that:

> Although the treatment of Walter Westfeld by the Nazi government as alleged in the Complaint was ineffably horrendous, the Court concludes that the actions upon which Plaintiffs' Complaint is based were not taken in connection with a commercial activity of the Defendant.

Westfield, 2009 U.S. Dist. LEXIS 65133, at *16. Further:

> If the seizure is deemed to be an expropriation of property, as explained in the cases cited above, it is an action that can only be taken by a sovereign. If the seizure is deemed to have been effected for the satisfaction of a criminal fine or penalty, akin to forfeiture, it is an action that can only be taken by a sovereign through its police powers and judicial functions. In either case, the actions complained of were those unique to a sovereign power rather than a private person. The subsequent disposition of the art collection on the private art market through privately-owned auction houses does not render the initial act of seizure a commercial activity.

Id. at 17.

Judgment entered for Germany, and the plaintiffs appealed. The result was the same. *Westfield v. Fed. Republic of Germany*, 633 F.3d 409 (6th Cir. 2011). It bears noting, however, that the heirs found a receptive audience in the Court of Appeals for their argument that the acts at issue were commercial enough to be considered as such for the purposes of § 1605(a)(2), but ultimately this was insufficient because the Sixth Circuit held that there was no cognizable "direct effect." *Id.* at 414 ("[T]he Heirs quite persuasively navigate the morass of reported decisions and make a convincing argument that, based on Germany's sale of the collection at auction to raise capital, the seizure of Westfeld's artwork was sufficiently in connection with commercial activity to fall within this exception.").

Ultimately, the Sixth Circuit held that it was constrained by *Weltover* to find a direct effect only if Germany had been obliged to do something within the United States, which the Complaint did not allege. This contrasted with the bond-related cases where foreign sovereigns had promised to pay funds *in the United States*. *Id.* at 416. It held thusly:

> Seizing Westfeld's art collection caused a direct effect in Germany. Allegations that Westfeld intended to send his art collection to the United States do not broaden the scope of the direct effects. Although the action that prevented the transfer was in this case an illegal seizure and not a failure to pay, that does not distinguish the cases cited above, which recognize that a foreign country's actions do not cause direct effects in the United States merely because the entity to which it owed money planned to move the funds to the United States. While we do not question that Westfeld genuinely wished to transfer his artwork to Nashville, finding a direct effect based on plans to send property to the United States would largely eliminate the protections of sovereign immunity.

Id. It is the foreign sovereign's acts and not the plaintiffs' acts that are scrutinized. Even accepting the full weight of Germany's repression of Westfeld, unless the plaintiffs alleged that the seizure was itself to prevent the transfer to America (with that specific result in mind, rather than what happened later), there was no direct effect within the meaning of the law.

The court did make a point of rejecting the plaintiffs' argument that the nullity of Nazi Germany's anti-Semitic laws and measures somehow made Germany's actions during that era nonsovereign: "[E]ven though we agree that this Court should not recognize Westfeld's fine and imprisonment, it should still respect that they were acts of a sovereign." *Id.* at 418. Expressing the usual sympathy for the fate of Westfeld, the Court of Appeals nonetheless affirmed the dismissal.

Interestingly, as a coda to the litigation, the chain of events that brought the possible claim to the Westfields' attention came to a happier conclusion in the same year the Sixth Circuit upheld the dismissal. At the same time it was successfully defending Seger-Thomschitz's claims, the Museum of Fine Arts, Boston, did ultimately agree to reach a settlement with the Westfields over the *Portrait of a Man and Woman in an Interior* by Eglon van der Neer. In its resource website disclosing its provenance research,[190] the Museum of Fine Arts, Boston, stressed the ambiguity:

> It is not known for certain how the MFA's Portrait of a Man and Woman in an Interior left Westfeld's possession and made its way to the United States. Without further documentation, its exact provenance may never be known. However, it is difficult to imagine a scenario by which he sold the painting voluntarily in Nazi Germany, receiving proceeds over which he had free disposal.

Nonetheless, the museum reached a financial settlement with the heirs, under which the painting remains in Boston. From the museum's press release:[191]

> When the MFA purchased the Portrait of a Man and Woman in an Interior from E. and A. Silberman Galleries in 1941, the dealer told MFA curator W. G. Constable that it was "brought to this country by a refugee some time ago, and I wish I were able to supply you with more information." Silberman appears to have purchased the painting in the spring of 1941, but it has not been ascertained from whom. The gallery is no longer in existence and its records, which cannot be located, are believed to have been destroyed.

As far as the Westfields go, Fred Westfield told *The Boston Globe*, "We feel very good and very thankful for how the museum dealt with us. We had a lot of help from some of the people at the museum over the years, once we started to claim that the painting really did belong to us." "MFA Makes Amends in Probably Looting," *The Boston Globe* (Edgers, 2011).

Relatively few cases to date have squarely addressed the awkward role that Switzerland has sometimes played in the provenance of art once owned by persecuted Jews. While history has shown that it was frequently a place where after the war dealers like Kornfeld and Bernoulli acquired, if not outright laundered, titles to paintings that had previously been stolen, only one case to date has been brought to address a wartime acquisition from a person in duress that also involved Swiss territory. That case, *Orkin v. Swiss Confederation*—also brought by the heirs of Margarethe Mauthner—never really proceeded, however. The holding—that a purchase by Oskar Reinhart could not meet the requirements of the § 1605(a)(3) expropriation exception—like so many disputes, involves a cast of characters that still overshadow the issue today.

Mauthner purchased a Van Gogh pen and ink drawing, *Les Saintes Maries de la Mer*, in 1906. In 1933, she sold the drawing to Reinhart "to help fund her family's escape from the Nazis' persecution of German Jews,"[192] as the District Court later put it. Reinhart famously created his eponymous foundation in 1945 and donated some of his collection to it (but not the Van Gogh). When he died in 1965, the remainder of his collection (including the Van Gogh) went to Switzerland, which has since owned and managed the Sammlung (Collection) Oskar Reinhart in Winterthur, Switzerland.

Mauthner's great grandson Andrew Orkin filed suit in 2009 in the U.S. District Court for the Southern District of New York. He invoked the expropriation exception to seek jurisdiction over Switzerland and the Collection as its agent or instrumentality. Creatively, he also alleged that the Alien Tort Statute, 28 U.S.C. § 1350 (ATS) applied. The District Court disagreed on both counts in a brief opinion. *Orkin v. Swiss Confederation*, 770 F. Supp. 2d 612, 617 (S.D.N.Y. 2011). The central theory of Orkin's claims, the District Court inferred from the Complaint, was that Reinhart took advantage of Mauthner's "plight and desperation as a Jew in Nazi Germany to purchase the drawing at an artificially low price and, years later, donated or bequeathed the drawing to one of the defendants. As Reinhart's purchase was invalid, the theory goes, so too was receipt and retention of the drawing." *Id.* at 614.

Given that the FSIA would be the sole method to obtain jurisdiction over the Swiss Confederation, the court considered whether there had been a taking to meet the standards of § 1605(a)(3). The court saw little to dwell upon:

> In consequence, "takings" jurisdiction exists only where the property at issue passed in the first instance from the plaintiff—or, as here, the plaintiff's predecessor—to a sovereign or to some person or entity acting on a sovereign's behalf. Here, however, the drawing passed from Mauthner to Reinhart. Plaintiff does not allege that Reinhart acted in any capacity other than as a private individual.

Id. at 616.

Although the District Court did not mention the then-recent *Cassirer* case by name, it dismissed Orkin's responsive argument that the statute required only a sovereign, present-day defendant and not a sovereign taking. *Id.* at 616–17. The Alien Tort Claims Act was of no more use because that is a substantive statute creating a cause of action for "(1) tort actions, (2) brought by aliens (only), (3) for violations of the law of nations (also called 'customary international law')." *Id.* at 617. Even if Orkin had such a claim against the Oskar Reinhart Foundation as a private entity (putting aside the court's conclusion that there was no evidence that the Oskar Reinhart Foundation, rather than the Swiss Confederation, ever had the painting), it would not create jurisdiction to hear the claims.

Although the opinion was understandable from a distance, it is somewhat more puzzling on closer inspection. The logic of *Cassirer*, which flows from the language of the statute itself, does not peg the underlying "taken in violation of international law" (28 U.S.C. § 1605(a)(3)) to a sovereign act. Indeed, these many cases show why that should not be the standard. Take the case against the Museum of Fine Arts, Boston, for example. Assume that the circumstances between Reichel and Kallir were somewhat different and that there were no disputes about the price having been facially inadequate and thus a result of the chaotic and repressive circumstances faced by Vienna's Jews in 1938. If the victorious Allies rightly imposed a suspicion of duress on such transactions and the possessor could not meet the presumption—precisely because it cannot consist of the just and fair compensation required—how would that instance not be a taking in violation of international law? In addition, if it were a violation, then Switzerland would be in no different a position than Spain: a sovereign defendant in possession of a piece of property with those title issues. Further, both Lily Cassirer and Maria Altmann were victimized directly by opportunists, not the Nazi state, but they were victims of the conditions created by the Nazi regime that made it possible and that gave rise to the justifiable presumption against the validity of such transfers.

Clearly, the District Court disagreed, and the Court of Appeals for the Second Circuit did not devote much energy to the question. *Orkin v. Swiss Confederation*, 444 F. App'x 469, 470 (2011). In a summary order just a few months after the initial dismissal, the Second Circuit agreed that "[t]he term 'taken' [in § 1605(a)(3)] clearly refers to acts of a sovereign, not a private enterprise, that deprive a plaintiff of property without adequate compensation." *Zappia Middle E. Constr. Co. v. Emirate of Abu Dhabi*, 215 F.3d 247, 251 (2d Cir. 2000). It rejected Orkin's effort to distinguish this and other similar cases by relying on *Chabad* and *Cassirer* because of the sovereign character of the alleged taker in those cases. The Court of Appeals endorsed the ATS holding of the District Court as well.

PART FIVE

The Worst System in the World but All the Rest

Chapter 19

Progress or Broken Promises? Restitution Claims Procedures Among the Signatories to the Washington Conference Principles

As these many disputes show, there is essentially no public component to the ownership of potentially looted art in the United States. The one common denominator among all these cases is that none involve property over which the United States or one of the fifty states has possession or control. As a result, while the Washington Principles have rightfully, if belatedly, begun to assume greater prominence as part of the rules of decision in individual cases, the extent of the national government's ability to influence the issue is constrained by this reality. The United States has no ability to tell private citizens what to do with the property in their hands as a matter of ownership unless it runs into an unrelated principle such as customs or transportation in interstate commerce. In the execution, those have turned out to be relatively infrequent occurrences. However, at the end of the day, the extent of the federal government's unilateral options is limited by the Fifth Amendment and the Fourteenth Amendment.

That is not the case in Europe. Some of the cases that have ended up in U.S. courts intersect with the procedures and commissions that European nations have set up largely in response to the Washington Conference. Following the war, the Allied focus was on national-level restitution. The Monuments, Fine Arts, and Archives Section (MFAA) should best be remembered for its meticulous, if imperfect, research after the war. That decision to handle restitutions at the national level meant, necessarily, that the final decisions were left to the countries themselves, many of which had been Axis belligerents, and even more of whom showed a disregard for the need to track down survivors and heirs.

In response to the renewed attention of the last two decades and to the Washington Conference specifically, some European countries have set up dedicated commissions and boards to address claims for art in national collections that the claimants allege was the subject of Nazi looting. This was in implicit—and even sometimes explicit—recognition that the mechanisms available to survivors in the immediate aftermath of the war were inadequate, if not outright hostile, to the interests of righting the wrongs of the war. As a result, by the 1990s, there were large, heirless collections in many of the nations of Europe. It is therefore instructive to review at least in summary the output of those national commissions that have been created. Doing so provides context for the situations in which survivors and heirs will feel that they have no choice but to litigate, and happier instances in which national commissions provide leadership about what presumptions and conclusions ought to follow in difficult cases that often lack overwhelming proof or disproof of anything. The quality, efficiency, and effectiveness of these commissions have much to say about whether those disputes end up in U.S. courts.

When efforts at national restitution commissions gained steam again in the late 1990s, the Austrian approach was synonymous with a lack of transparency and predetermined outcomes, as the farcical outcome in the panel that addressed Maria Altmann's claim in the first instance makes clear. However, for the most part the Austrian Art Restitution Advisory Board (*Kunstrückgabebeirat*) enjoys a reputation now for thoroughness, even if some higher profile cases like the Klimt's *Beethoven Frieze* raise hard questions. By contrast, most expected a scrupulous and meticulous output from the German Advisory Commission—the full name is *Beratende Kommission im Zusammenhang mit der Rückgabe NS-verfolgungsbedingt entzogener Kulturgüter, insbesondere aus jüdischem Besitz* (the advisory commission on the return of cultural property seized as a result of Nazi persecution, especially Jewish property). The commission is better known as the Limbach Commission, named after its presiding member and former Constitutional Court Judge Jutta Limbach. Yet, the German Advisory Commission has handled only thirteen cases in as many years, and its recent output is an embarrassing mixture of historical revisionism and procedural incompetence. The United Kingdom and the Netherlands can point to a steadier path, but for the most part, the aspirational statements of the Washington Principles have gone unheeded in Europe. A brief review of that history is instructive, however, in considering why claimants turn to U.S. courts, even with respect to the restitution of objects and against defendants on the other side of the Atlantic.

Austria

As its own ten-year history's publication blurb notes, the Austrian *Kunstrückgabebeirat* (*or Beirat*) was organized in direct response to the seizure of *Portrait of Wally* and *Dead City III*. From the Austrian perspective, this was a truly shocking development in a country that still struggled with its own myth of Austria as the first victim of Nazi Germany, rather than as a nation that watched—and helped—its substantial and integrated Jewish community be destroyed. Less than two years before its government lurched to the far right under the government formed after the substantial electoral victories of Nazi apologist Jörg Haider and his Austrian Freedom Party (Freiheitliche Partei Österreichs), the Commission was formed in 1998 as part of the country's new restitution law: Bundesgesetz über die Rückgabe von Kunstgegenständen aus den Österreichischen Bundesmuseen und Sammlungen (BGBl. I Nr. 181/1998). This had been preceded by the creation of the Kommission für Provenienzforschung (Commission for Provenance Research) in February 1998, just as the *Wally* case was getting under way.

The *Kunstrückgabegesetz* of 1998 authorized the federal minister of art and culture, public service and constitution to convey works in national possession to heirs. This is not just optics. Most state collectors in Europe are forbidden from deaccessioning *any* works at all. Section one created three categories of eligible objects: (1) those originally restituted after the war that become state property in the course of proceedings related to the export ban without compensation having been paid, (2) objects subject to Austria's 1946 Nullification Act (*Nichtigkeitsgesetz*) related to invalid seizures and subsequent sales, and (3) objects otherwise not returned and which became national property as so-called heirless property. If a determination is made that the property falls within these categories but a specific heir cannot be identified, then it can be transferred to the National Foundation of the Republic of Austria for the Victims of National Socialism (Nationalfonds der Republik Österreich für Opfer des Nationalsozialismus). Any heir who receives such property does so free of lien or other restriction.

The *Kunstrückgabebeirat*, formally speaking, advises the ministry. The minister appoints the chair and other members, ostensibly seeking to balance lawyers, historians, and art historians. In 2009, the *Kunstrückgabegesetz* was amended again to address more explicitly the impact of the postwar export prohibition, the *Ausfuhrverbot*. In addition, whereas the 1998 law was limited to *Kunstgegenstände*, or works of art, the 2009 amendment broadened the applicability to include works of art and other moveable cultural property *(Kunstgegenstände und sonstiges bewegliches Kulturgut)*. Further, the territorial and temporal scope of the law expanded. Whereas the 1998 law concerned only objects affected after the *Anschluss*, and in Austria, now any object that is presently in national ownership but affected by any Nazi-era dispossession (defined as any time after January 30, 1933) is subject to review.

As noted above, its session and decision with respect to the first set of claims lodged by the Bloch-Bauer heirs was disastrous, resulting in the June 28, 1999, decision that led first to a brief court filing in Austria, followed by the landmark FSIA litigation in the United States. The commission has heard roughly 300 cases in its existence, with many restitutions and many recommendations against return. A few examples are instructive.

In 2014, Vienna's Natural History Museum (Naturhistorisches Museum) restituted 177 botanical drawings and prints to the heirs of Dr. Ernst Moritz Kronfeld. The restitution followed a 2011 recommendation by the *Kunstrückgabebeirat*. Austria returned the drawings because of the clear problems with trying to portray any 1941 conveyance by a Viennese Jew as a transaction conducted at arms' length, even without direct evidence of coercion. Just as important, it brushed away the defense that the drawings had been acquired in good faith, a dramatic change from the perspective usually taken in civil law countries such as Austria.

The *Beirat*'s opinion portrays Kronfeld as another classically—if tragically—fin de siècle, Austrian Jewish figure. He was born in the city of Lemberg in the Austrian region of Galicia in 1865, which was then part of the Austro-Hungarian empire. Lemberg was the German name for what is now known as Lvov, Ukraine, and the capital of the increasingly autonomous region (or kingdom) of Galicia. It was host to a thriving Jewish community by the time of Kronfeld's childhood in the late Austro-Hungarian empire. In adulthood, Kronfeld was editor of several magazines in Vienna, a garden historian, and botanist, best known for his collections and knowledge of the palace at the Habsburg summer palace of Schönbrunn.

The drawings and prints reflected the work of botanist Nikolaus Joseph von Jacquin and gardener Ryk van der Schot (who was later the court director of gardens and menagerie). Von Jacquin and van der Schot had participated in an Austrian expedition to the West Indies between 1754 and 1759, and the illustrations reflected their representations of the flora that they saw there. The expedition had been commissioned by Franz Stefan von Lothringen, the Holy Roman emperor and husband of Austria's iconic Empress Maria Theresia.

By 1938, the *Beirat* noted, Kronfeld was one of Austria's largest collectors of books, pictures, documents, and plans of the park at Schönbrunn. After the *Anschluss* in March of 1938, Kronfeld was required to submit the infamous standard inventory of all of his property, which as was the case for many other Viennese Jews, simply provided a handy list of prized objects for Nazis to seek out. Kronfeld offered his collection to the National Library (Nationalbibliothek) in 1940, via the antique dealer Dr. Rudolf Engel. The only surviving record of this seems to be a letter from Engel to the National Library dated January 2, 1941, which rejected the offered price of 100 Reichsmarks (a paltry sum), and asking that the materials be returned to Kronfeld.

Kronfeld died in his apartment in Vienna on March 16, 1942. According to the documentation accompanying his death, he had property worth less than RM 300 and a few clothes in his possession. Barely two months later, fourteen pictures once in the Kronfeld collection were received by the Vienna municipal collections; the pictures were transmitted by Baldur von Schirach, longtime head of the Hitler Youth and later the Gauleiter (District Leader) of Vienna. Schirach was convicted of war crimes at Nuremberg and sentenced to twenty years in prison; he died in 1974. Those fourteen pictures were restituted in an earlier proceeding. Kronfeld's wife, his sole heir, was deported to Theresienstadt in August 1942, and murdered at Treblinka in September 1942.

In November 1942, Engel offered a renewed portion of the Kronfeld collection (described as such) to the National Library. The fate of the balance of the collection during and after the war is unclear. The 177 objects resurfaced in 1988, offered again to the National Library by an antiques dealer known as "W.K." That dealer's archives indicate that the objects arrived there in 1980, of unknown provenance.

The *Kunstrückgabebeirat* acknowledged that it could not determine exactly what happened to the collection between 1942 and 1988 but concluded nonetheless (author's translation):

> These questions can be left open, because the sale by either Dr. Kronfeld or his widow would have been sales by persons in a persecuted group, and would also be void as an appropriation in connection with the deportation of Rosalia Kronfeld within the meaning of § 1 of the Annulment Acts (the determination of Rosalia Kronfeld as the sole heir and legal successor of her husband need not be analyzed further in this determination of restitution).
>
> The Advisory Council determines, therefore, that the collection of Ernst Kronfeld eventually of his widow Rosalia Kronfeld, was seized.

The works were thus restituted to surviving heir Mario Lanzer, as well as the Jewish Community of Vienna (Israelitische Kultusgemeinde), as the designated representative for any other heirs.

This decision was important for the manner of its analysis. First, it acknowledged that it cannot be determined with certainty who took Kronfeld's collection, whether by sale or outright seizure. Most commendably, however, it refused to hide behind that fact and engaged instead in inferential analysis that should be obvious to anyone: There is simply no possible way that Kronfeld could legitimately have disposed of his collection given his circumstances. The Austrian panel was not looking for a way to avoid the only real conclusion: Kronfeld was persecuted to the point of either selling the collection out of necessity, or it was stolen from him. Most refreshingly, the *Beirat* implicitly acknowledges that it does not matter which event occurred in order to conclude that the works must be returned. The decision nonetheless had the courage simply to say what was so clearly the case: that there was no scenario in which Kronfeld could have voluntarily conveyed his property. Circumstantial evidence can indeed be very convincing, especially when the collection of a recently deceased Viennese Jewish man turns up on the art market in 1942 (also after his wife died and his sole heir was murdered).

Equally welcome is the decision not to punish Kronfeld's heirs for the Natural History Museum's later good-faith acquisition. This is more typically in line with the Anglo-American property concept that a thief cannot convey good title and the concepts articulated in the London Declaration.

Another case involving the Bloch-Bauer claims also caused some controversy, but this time they were of a more nuanced but still controversial balance of competing claims, not an out-of-hand dismissal of heirs' claims. This matter involved an agreement to bypass the *Beirat* and submit the dispute to an arbitration panel, whose decision was eventually reviewed and affirmed by the local court.[193]

Klimt's *Portrait of Amalie Zuckerkandl* appears on the very same property inventory of Ferdinand Bloch-Bauer as the *Portrait of Adele Bloch-Bauer*. Altmann herself made application to the *Beirat*. However, Altmann, as heir to Bloch-Bauer, was not the only claimant in those proceedings. The Müller-Hofmann family, heirs of the subject herself, Amalie Zuckerkandl, also made claim to the paintings. They claimed that the Müller-Hofmanns were the ones who sold it to Rita Künstler, but did so only under duress (they too are Jewish).

The biggest remaining dispute was over how the painting had gone from the collection of Ferdinand Bloch-Bauer to the collection of Hermine Müller-Hofmann (Zuckerkandl's daughter). The painting was apparently commissioned by the Zuckerkandls, who then divorced, whereupon Amalie became a friend of Bloch-Bauer's.

After Bloch-Bauer fled the country, his property was seized and registered with the Nazi government. Dr. Erich Führer was designated as Ferdinand Bloch-Bauer's representative, but interestingly enough Bloch-Bauer remained in contact with Führer, who was able to arrange an export license for a Kokoschka portrait of Bloch-Bauer himself. However, the Klimts (*Amalie Zuckerkandl* and the *Portrait of Adele Bloch-Bauer*) remained in Austria. Altmann's representatives argued that the painting could not have come to Müller-Hofmann via Führer without duress; Ferdinand Bloch-Bauer had fled for his life and, they argued, none of his sales could have been free from undue influence.

Critically for this discussion, the arbitration panel rejected that argument. It found, as a matter of fact and after weighing the evidence and credibility of the witnesses, that it was just as likely that Bloch-Bauer had *asked* Führer to sell or give the painting to Müller-Hofmann. Without much supporting evidence or discussion, it rejected the idea that the RM 1,600 sales price was presumptively low for that time, which likewise doomed the claims by the Müller-Hofmanns in the same proceeding.

The panel concluded, noting the considerable documents and witnesses, that (author's translation):

> The most plausible possibility is that the painting may have been given by Dr. Führer to Ms. Müller-Hofmann at the inducement of Ferdinand Bloch-Bauer without exchange or consideration, with whom Führer was in regular contact.[194]

The panel also noted that Bloch-Bauer had bought the painting *twice* from Amalie Zuckerkandl to support her financially, as evidence supported the idea that he later had it given to her family. That is to say, he had assisted her financially before, and the panel thought it plausible that he would have done so again (particularly given the risk as a Jew still living in Austria). The panel then rejected both groups' claim to the painting.

The foregoing is a far murkier trail than the one that the *Portrait of Adele Bloch-Bauer I* and *II* followed. It is tragic, and the panel may well have been wrong. Also important, as noted above, is that in many continental legal systems a later possessor can have good title, even if her predecessor did not. Again, whether Künstler took the painting in good faith is a difficult question.

More recently, the *Beirat* recommended against restitution of the iconic *Beethoven Frieze* by Klimt at Vienna's Secession museum, a claim brought by the Lederer family. The *Frieze* was formally restituted after the war but without an export license. According to the family, Austria would only grant an export license for the family's other art if they agreed to sell the *Frieze* to Austria at a bargain rate. Eventually, a sale was consummated in 1973 for $750,000, which the family asserts was a fraction of its value.

The *Beirat* focused at length on the correspondence between the Lederer family and Austrian officials. Ultimately, the committee was unpersuaded that the Austrian government had actually forbidden (as opposed to discouraged) the export of the painting. Therefore, even though Austria revised its laws in 2009 to recognize that the export prohibition could justify restitution, the committee would not deem it sufficiently coercive to recommend restitution.

The claimants wasted little time in challenging the decision, declaring it wrongly decided. In a press release, they questioned whether they had received all relevant documents and further stated (author's translation):

> We question whether something secretive may have happened. The Republic of Austria has delivered its verdict without giving those concerned a chance to review the files and give an opinion. The rules of the proceeding and the current execution of the Art Restitution Law violated several aspects of fundamental rights. We plan to ask the European Court of Human Rights in Strasbourg to review these severe legal defects. Moreover, we want to explore opportunities that are offered by U.S. jurisdiction.[195]

Austria's case can best be described, in the best and worst sense, as complicated. It started as a pariah, stubbornly defending postwar behavior while refusing to acknowledge the complicity in the Nazi period. Yet its evolution is meaningful and real. In that sense, it deserves plaudits for administering a system that at least gives confidence that a particular claim will be heard seriously.

Germany

The same can no longer be said for Germany, at least at the national level. The progress in Germany, which is otherwise so admirably out in front of issues of historic accuracy and responsibility for the Holocaust, has been surprisingly regressive. As West Germany emerged from occupation by the Allies—remembering, of course, there was no undivided nation again until 1990—West Germany passed a law taking effect in 1957 to address restitution, the Bundesrückerstattungsgesetz—the Federal Restitution Law, or BRüG. This law had a self-contained limitations period, however, expiring in the 1980s. The now reunited Federal Republic of Germany endorsed the Washington Principles, and in 1999 adopted the so-called joint declaration in the form of an agreement between the national government and the sixteen individual federal states, or Lander: the *Gemeinsame Erklärung der Bundesregierung, der Länder, und der kommunale Spitzenverbände zur Auffindung und zur Rückgabe NS-verfolgungsbedingt entzogenen Kulturgutes, insbesondere aus jüdischem Besitz.*[196] The *Gemeinsame Erklärung* pledges the public museums of the national and state governments to use their best efforts to identify affected items. In turn, a 100-page manual, or *Handreichung*, was published to flesh out the principles.

Thereafter, the advisory commission was founded. Since its founding, the *Beratende Kommission im Zusammenhang mit der Rückgabe NS-verfolgungsbedingt entzogener Kulturgüter, insbesondere aus jüdischem Besitz* has been colloquially known as the Limbach Commission, named after its longtime presiding member Jutta Limbach, a former constitutional court (Bundesverfassungsgericht) judge. It met for the first time on July 14, 2003. Yet, unlike the substantial output of the Austrian Kunstrückgabebeirat, in thirteen years the Limbach Commission has managed only to hear one case per year, more or less. It is only available when the museum in possession agrees to appear, to which some (like the Bavarian State Paintings Collection) have been notoriously resistant.

Until recently its membership has been static, with no requirement of inclusion of any particular profession or life experience. It has been, in a word, calcified, devoted more to defending its supposed independence than to demonstrating any actual legal or historical competence.

Initially, the Limbach Commission's decisions evinced sophisticated analysis. In one of its first decisions, Limbach considered a claim for restitution from the collection of Julius and Clara Freund, German Jews who were persecuted as such. After Julius died in his British exile in 1941, Clara sold their collection in desperation in Switzerland. Both the owner and the artwork were outside of Nazi Germany (United Kingdom and Switzerland), and they were paid a near-market price. Yet, the larger picture was clear, and the Limbach Commission recommended restitution for a collection that was clearly sold under duress. In 2008, it recommended that the German *Land* of Hessen pay Karl Ernst Baumann compensation amounting to 10,000 euros for *Portrait der Familie von Ditfurth* by Johann J. August von der Embde. In 2009, the commission recommended that the German federal government return *Peasant Girl without a Hat and with a White Headcloth* (1897) by Wilhelm Leibl to the heirs of Dr. Alexander Lewin. On the other hand, in 2007 the commission recommended against returning the poster collection of Hans Sachs that his heirs later won in court, language from the latter of which has been cited there and in the United States for the enunciation of German law on sales by Jewish collectors under duress.

By 2014, however, the committee's baseline views had shifted. In 2013, the descendants and heirs of the consortium that owned the famed Welfenschatz (Guelph Treasure) submitted their case to the commission. From a 1931 exhibition catalogue at the Fogg Museum at Harvard, the collection consisted of:

> [R]eliquaries, crosses, portable altars, and other ecclesiastical objects. The earliest object in the collection was a cloisonné medallion, dating probably from the eighth century. The most significant of the objects date from the eleventh and twelfth centuries, a period of great artistic brilliance.[197]

The Stiftung Preussischer Kulturbesitz (SPK), the foundation that administers the major Berlin museums, including the Kunstgewerbemuseum where the Welfenschatz is located, rejected the claim, arguing in the first instance that the consortium had foreign shareholders who were co-owners of what was sold (presumably to contest the standing of these claimants). More centrally, the SPK pointed out that the sale was the intended outcome for the collection at the time of its acquisition in 1929, before the political pressure came to bear. Moreover, the SPK asserted, by 1934–35 there was no interest from others buyers, a reasonable explanation for which was the worldwide financial crisis, not political persecution. That supposed lack of interest was simply incorrect, however, as a specific museum in Herrenhausen bei Hannover was specifically warned off further interest by Prussian state Nazi officials.

Ultimately, the commission was persuaded by the idea that the Great Depression, not duress, was the reason for the depressed price, and recommended that the Guelph Treasure stay where it was. As the report noted (author's translation):

> Although the Commission is aware of the severe fate of art dealers and their persecution in the Nazi era, there are no indications that suggest that the art dealers and their business partners in the case to be assessed by the Commission were under duress—even from Goering; in addition, one had to deal with the effects of the global economic crisis in 1934/1935.[198]

The commission also stressed the availability of the sale proceeds at the time to the dealer as evidence that the sale was a commercial transaction, not a forced sale (author's translation).

> As a result of these findings, the Advisory Commission of the belief that the sale of the Guelph Treasure was not a persecution-induced forced sale. It therefore cannot recommend a return of the Guelph Treasure to the heirs of the four art dealers and any other former co-owners.[199]

This was flatly contradicted, however, by expert opinion that the sale price was barely a third of the real value, as well as the uncomfortable fact that some of the proceeds were paid into the usual blocked accounts. The dispute is presently in litigation in the United States in Washington, D.C., with arguments pending about the FSIA jurisdictional application of *Altmann, de Csepel,* and *Cassirer,* among other cases discussed here.[200]

As if in defensive reaction, the commission has become even more conservative. Later the same year it ruled against the heirs of Clara Levy for Lovis Corinth's *Three Graces.* Clara Levy was a textile manufacturer who was persecuted by the Nazis. The painting was in the collection of Ludwig Levy, Clara's husband, who bequeathed it to her on his death in 1921. Clara lived in Berlin and emigrated to Schleifmühle, Luxembourg, in 1939, where her son Fritz managed a factory. The Corinth painting went with her. Clara died there in 1940.

According to a declaration given by Paula Levy (Fritz Levy's former girlfriend and later wife and heir), a part of Clara's household effects was shipped to New York. It is on the circumstances of this shipment that the case turns. A bill of lading produced by Paula supposedly states "Lovis Corinth, The Three Graces."[201] The bill of lading is also stamped "New York, Dec. 5/41 19 . . . the property entered by this Bill of Lading manifested on Steamer San Francisco arrived at New York June 3/40 Compagnie Generale Transatlantique Hol Lesquette."[202] The remainder of Clara's effects remained in Luxembourg until the invasion by German troops in May of 1940 and thereafter were seized by the German Reich.

Sometime between 1940 and 1941, the Corinth painting was located in the Buchholz Gallery in New York City operated by Curt Valentin. Valentin and Karl Buchholz were a primary destination for much of the "degenerate" art that was seized by the Nazis and sold for hard currency abroad. Art dealer Siegfried Rosengart in Lucerne later wrote in a 1951 letter that he had heard reports from New York that Valentin "had acquired [the painting] about ten years ago at a Public Auction Sale."[203] Rosengart sold the painting in 1949 on commission for the Buchholz Gallery to Prof. Dr. Max Huggler, director of the Kunstmuseum Bern and brought it to Bern. The Bavarian State Paintings Collection (Bayerische Staatsgemäldesammlungen) acquired the painting from Huggler in 1950.

In 1959, Paula Levy, represented by attorney Henry Zacharias, brought a restitution claim for money damages against the Federal Republic of

Germany as Fritz Levy's widow and heir. The claim listed the belongings allegedly seized by the German authorities, including seventeen unspecified pictures: eight out of the office, and nine out of the hall. The commission found that the Corinth could not have been among the eight in the office because it was not shown in the factory; and it could not have been in the hall because Rita Hubbard, one of Clara's granddaughters, later recalled that it had hung in the dining room. The 1959 claim was apparently denied on the finding that no transfer of property from abroad to the German Reich could be detected, a dubious result to be sure.

In 2002, Clara Levy's heirs made an application for the return of the Corinth painting, arguing that it was confiscated from Clara's effects before the 1940 shipment left Luxembourg and that the painting never reached the family members in New York who were its intended recipients. The authenticity of the signature of Clara's daughter Else Bergmann on the supposed receipt was also challenged.

The Bavarian State Paintings Collection rejected the claim on the theory that it could perceive neither an outright misappropriation, nor a sale under duress. From the transfer to Clara's daughter Else Bergmann, Bavaria inferred a free-willed transfer, confirmed (in Bavaria's view) by Else's signature and the receipt stamp by Valentin's gallery. Bavaria placed great reliance on the letter from Rosengart that (supposedly) describes the public auction of the painting in the United States. In the words of the Limbach Commission (presumably paraphrasing Bavaria's initial rejection of the claim; author's translation):

> There are no known instances of Valentin using works seized from the persecuted in Germany or areas occupied by German troops. There would be no clue that Valentin had received the painting from German troops in the second half of 1941.[204]

In going on to reject the request that the Bavarian museums restitute the painting now, the Limbach Commission starts from the premise that the undisputed fact that Clara Levy and her heirs were persecuted as Jews, and/or had to flee and conceal themselves, does not necessarily lead to the conclusion that the Corinth painting is itself the object of Nazi looting. That is a relatively facile assertion, however; *no* claimant can or should win restitution merely by alleging status or persecution. This is the definition of a straw man contention: once the flimsy contention is raised, it is easy ostensibly to knock it down.

The commission relied principally on two offers of proof, one potentially persuasive and one almost useless. The appearance of the painting's name on the bill of lading is clearly a problem for the claimants. A reasonable person could conclude (assuming it looks as the commission describes) that the painting did indeed arrive in New York, shipped by Clara Levy to her daughter, who from there sold the work at auction. The commission concluded, not unreasonably, that the fact that Paula Levy later came to have the bill of lading likely means that the shipment did indeed arrive at the family's location.

However, the commission's citation to Paula Levy's description in the (seemingly speciously denied) 1959 claim reveals the weakness in the recommendation. Why would it matter what Paula said about where the paintings were? She would not necessarily have had knowledge of where Clara had hung the painting at a time when Paula's relationship to Fritz is not explained.

Reviewing all this, the commission concluded that it was "extremely unlikely"[205] that the painting would have been sent to New York by the Nazis after they seized it, simply because it was not of the style labeled "degenerate" (implying that stylistically favored paintings would have been retained).

This too, does not withstand logical scrutiny. Most directly, it gets the dates wrong, finding it implausible that the Nazis would have shipped art to New York in late 1941 with the war under way. If the painting arrived in New York as the commission believes, however, it was *in early 1940*, not late 1941. In addition, the United States and Germany were not at war in either 1940 or 1941 (at least until December). While conditions were obviously tense, nonintervention was a major political movement in the United States, and paintings labeled "degenerate" and removed from German museums were absolutely flowing to America—and Valentin's gallery—throughout that interval. The conclusion that the resale back to Europe in 1949 or 1950 proves good title as of 1941 is nonsensical.

The commission's reliance on Valentin's own Jewish background as insulation from suspicion regarding the painting's title also falls flat. First, whether or not one believes it was justified under the circumstances, there is no question that art seized in Germany (particularly museums) flowed through Valentin to the American market. Many believe that Germany's own conduct justifies that, but it certainly happened. Second, for anyone to contend in 2014 that the mere fact of Jewish ancestry lays to rest any further inquiry simply hasn't paid attention to the Gurlitt saga.

None of this answers another unanswered but important question, however: the significance of why the painting was shipped to America, even if the sequence was exactly as the commission says. To put this in perspective, consider the circumstances of Clara Levy and her family in 1940. They had fled their own country and had found refuge and economic stability in a neutral country that, like Switzerland (but not Belgium), had been spared the brunt of the German army's mischief in the First World War. Then, in 1940, the German army swept west, absolutely unstoppable. Did Clara Levy have a choice about what to do with her property? What was not sent, sure enough, was promptly seized. To perceive free will in any part of that chain of events is to not understand the situation at all.

The Levy claim opinion waives this lack of free choice away without actually addressing it, stating that there can be "no doubt"[206] that if there were an auction in New York, the heirs then received a fair market price for the painting at the time. However, why is that so clear? For a panel that increasingly exploits the existence (as there is in all these cases) of minimal doubt, to make a bold declaration that there is "no doubt" of something as speculative as that strains credulity.

Limbach's slide into moral relativity was just beginning. In 2015, after being sued in the United States over the Welfenschatz, the advisory commission recommended against restitution to the heirs of George Behrens, a Jewish banker. The claim concerned the heirs of George Eduard Behrens, a Hamburg banker and owner of *Pariser Wochentag* (*Paris Weekday*) by Adolph von Menzel. As his heirs pointed out, they had suffered almost immediate persecution in 1933 after the Nazi ascension to power. According to the advisory commission opinion, Behrens sold the painting at some point in 1935. The exact date was not known, but it was after September 15, 1935, when the Nuremberg Laws were enacted. According to the City of Düsseldorf (where the painting now is), the painting was sold first to a dealer and then to the city. Behrens was arrested by the Hamburg police after Kristallnacht in 1938 and then deported to the Sachsenhausen concentration camp in 1939. The bank, L. Behrens & Söhne, ceased operations on May 31, 1928, and was liquidated as of December 31, 1938. After paying the confiscatory flight taxes, Behrens managed to escape to Cuba through Belgium and France.

Despite all this, the advisory commission concluded that the 1935 sale was *not* the result of persecution. First, citing the Düsseldorf position (effectively endorsed by the result), it states (author's translation):

> Jewish private banks were hardly affected in the early years of the Nazi regime in their business.

Now speaking not for Düsseldorf, but for itself and its reasoning, the advisory commission concludes (author's translation):

> The Commission of course does not fail to recognize that George E. Behrens belonged to those persons collectively persecuted for racist reasons as "Non-Aryan" after the adoption of the "Reich Citizenship" Law of September 15, 1935, that he was in concentration camp custody from November 1938 until March 1939, that he had to liquidate his bank, and to emigrate accompanied by great property losses. The Commission considers the situation at the time of the sale of the Menzel painting, however, for the bank and for the family, to be quite another.[207]

This implies that life was somehow not that bad for Jewish bankers in Germany before 1935. If that were somehow unclear, it goes on to say:

> Undoubtedly there had been a massive anti-Semitic agitation in Germany since the beginning of 1933, as well as anti-Jewish excesses and a changing legal situation with the introduction of the "Aryan clause" for employment in the civil service. It is, however, undisputed in the historical record that Jewish private banks in the early years of the Third Reich were not directly affected.[208]

Lastly (author's translation):

> The Ministry of Economic Affairs, until the end of the Schacht era was interested in trouble-free operation of the Jewish banks and fought successfully against anti-Semitic advances in this area for several years. With the decline of the economic crisis, the Jewish banks experienced an economic boom, which passed on to the banking house of L. Behrens & Söhne as well.[209]

The "Schacht era," referring to Minister of Economics Hjalmar Schacht, was hardly the halcyon days for German Jews. Schacht spoke out on occasion and later broke with the regime, but it hardly follows that Jewish bankers were free from interference. Particularly on the heels of the Welfenschatz decision that was so focused on price and the market, the two decisions together imply that the Great Depression was over in 1935 for some (when it suits), but not for others (when it doesn't).

Matters came to a head in 2016. In a move that is symbolic of the tattered legitimacy of the German advisory commission concerning Nazi-looted art in state museums, the heirs Alfred Flechtheim suspended the Limbach process concerning *Violon et encrier* (*Violin and Inkwell;* 1913) by Juan Gris in the Stiftung Kunstsammlung Nordrhein-Westfalen (Art Collections Foundation of Northern Rhineland/Westphalia) in Düsseldorf. Dr. Michael Hulton of San Francisco, California, Flechtheim's great-nephew and heir, instructed his attorneys to put on hold the process after disputes about the fairness of the proceedings. In a letter to the Commissioner for Culture and the Media, Monika Grütters, accompanying their press release, Dr. Hulton's attorneys issued a scathing criticism of the proceedings and asked the advisory commission not to make any recommendation about the painting in Düsseldorf until a further investigation into the procedural missteps could be completed.

As discussed above, Flechtheim represented many of the stars of the Expressionist movement, like George Grosz and Max Beckmann. After January 1933, however, Flechtheim simply could not stay in Germany. Less than two months after Hitler became chancellor, members of the Kampfbund forcibly stopped an auction held by Flechtheim in Düsseldorf. He fled and left his galleries in the hands of his long-time employees. This trust was soon betrayed. His gallery space in Düsseldorf was appropriated by his assistant Alex Vömel (a Nazi Party member) in 1933, who cheerfully advertised his new gallery explicitly in the prior location of the Galerie Flechtheim. Curt Valentin was a Flechtheim employee before he established the Galerie Buchholz in New York.

Flechtheim's niece, Rosi Hulisch, made efforts to sell some of his inventory while she herself was subject to racial persecution. The Juan Gris painting was sold in 1934 in London, which Flechtheim's heirs have argued was the result of his persecution. The museum bought the work on the international market in 1964.

In 2014, Dr. Hulton and the Düsseldorf museum agreed to submit the matter to the advisory commission. The commission had previously considered Flechtheim's fate in evaluating a request for recommendation in April 2013. That claim concerned a painting by Oskar Kokoschka (*Portrait of Tilla Durieux*) that Vömel had sold in 1934 to a collector whose foundation was later absorbed by the Wallraf-Richartz Museum, which later conveyed it to the Museum Ludwig in Köln (Cologne). The Köln government refused to return the painting, arguing that the 1934 price was consistent with a fair market value. The advisory commission concluded as follows in that case:

> In the absence of evidence to the contrary, it is to be assumed that Alfred Flechtheim abandoned the disputed painting because of his situation of persecution. The Nazi-persecuted loss of the painting is therefore affirmed.[210]

Quite unlike the regrettable direction the advisory commission has taken of late, this put the burden on the German possessor to prove the legitimacy of its possession and not on the heirs of the persecuted.

On the Gris matter, a hearing of sorts was conducted, though these are more a matter of sequential presentations than anything like an evidentiary hearing. Only half the panel attended. It was after the hearing that things went awry. Dr. Hulton's attorneys advised the advisory commission that they would follow up by letter for the entire panel regarding evidentiary matters discussed at the hearing and did so three days later. Yet, when they followed up, they were told that the February 15, 2016, follow-up had not been circulated to the panel, and the advisory commission was already deliberating its recommendation. Combined with other irregularities in the procedure, Dr. Hulton concluded that the process was unfair. Dr. Hulton said in a press release:

> I am thankful for the recognition of the terrible fate of my uncle and his family that the Commission gave in the case of the return of the Oskar Kokoschka paintings three years ago. Distinct from that time, however, I am alarmed in this case at the degree of information that was exchanged and the lack of transparency in the process that I experienced before and during the hearing, and that I had no opportunity to present my concerns to the entire Commission. This gives no respect to the families of Nazi victims and is not what I expect from Germany.

However, just two weeks later, the advisory commission issued a decision anyway, giving now-standard dismissive treatment to complaints about its fairness.

The *New York Times* reported in March 2016 that Germany would pay for "at least"[211] one more year of the Gurlitt/Schwabinger task force, which had recently concluded its initial term of appointment amidst criticism of the German government's handling of the case. Most shockingly, however, was that while apparently attending Oscar parties in California, Monika Grütters categorically rejected recent suggestions (including those from members of her own organization) that the advisory commission that issues recommendations about claims for looted art in German museums should include a member of the Jewish community. In perhaps the most tone-deaf statement of many to date, she said, "We did not do this, and for good reason," because such member "would be the only voice who would be prejudiced."[212]

In one stroke, the minister of culture of the Federal Republic of Germany rejects out of hand that a Jewish member of the advisory commission could be objective. All the other German members were apparently above reproach, but not a Jewish participant. The statement is even more ironic because the suggestion that the advisory commission add a member of the Jewish community was suggested by none other than

Hermann Parzinger, president of the SPK. Catrin Lorch noted (author's translation) that:

> But isn't this also true for Germans? They advise only in disputes about the return of art in German museums. In the Advisory Commission founded by the former Constitutional Judge Jutta Limbach, was comprised of up to eight "voluntary, high-ranking individuals appointed from the scientific community and public life." Among them in the past were only Germans.[213]

After a drumbeat of criticism, Germany caved to pressure to include Jewish members of the commission. The German government announced the addition of three new members in November 2016: Raphael Gross, director of the Simon Dubnow Institute for Jewish History in Leipzig, Gary Smith, the former director of the American Academy in Berlin, and Marion Eckart-Höfer, former president of the Federal Administrative Court. Gross has been the director of the Dubnow Institute since 2015, and is a historian of Jewish history and culture. Smith has taught the philosophy of art and culture in Germany and the United States. Eckart-Höfer is a respected jurist who has been retired since 2014, who interestingly enough comes from a well-established artistic family. Each and all of them are qualified and serious people, and one hopes that they will bring some fresh air and analytical vigor to the panel. Since their appointment, there have been two recommendations either for compromise or restitution. The advisory commission will also now be available for disputes between private parties. Only recently, it announced some basic rules of procedure, long a sore spot among participants as well.

As journalist Stefan Koldehoff wrote in the *Frankfurter Allgemeine Zeitung*, however, the "cardinal birth defect"[214] of the advisory commission is that the German museums have no obligation to participate. German representative of the Jewish Claims Conference Rüdiger Mahlo rightly told the *Süddeutsche Zeitung* that "[t]he one-sided right of appeal for victims should be the core of the reform in order to make the advisory commission an effective organization for the restitution of Nazi looted art."[215]

How did it come to this in the country that has, on other issues of historical understanding, performed so admirably—and by members of a generation who have no direct responsibility? Is it just guilt fatigue? The ongoing fiasco of the Gurlitt affair may offer some explanation. On the first Sunday in November 2013, the German weekly magazine *Focus* published a bombshell revelation: hundreds of paintings worth upwards of a billion dollars[216] had reportedly been found in the apartment of an elderly Munich man, Cornelius Gurlitt, that were, could have been, or might be, Nazi looted art. The more details that emerged, the stranger the story became. While the dramatic claims of the value of the art turned out to be premature and overstated, it quickly became clear that this was a real story. Gurlitt's trove, which was first reported as an improbable assembly of works, was in fact the legacy of his father, Hildebrand Gurlitt. Hildebrand had been a well-known dealer and academic from Dresden. Most important, Hildebrand was appointed one of the four dealers permitted to trade in degenerate art after 1937. Late in the war, he fled from Dresden after the firebombing of February 13–14, 1945, and settled in Aschbach. He was interrogated after the war by the MFAA's S. Lane Faison for whom he spun a convincing but purely fictional account of having lost his entire collection in the bombing. He was permitted to return to public life and was eventually elected president of the Kunstverein in Düsseldorf. Hildebrand died in a car accident in 1956, followed a few years later by the passing of his wife (Cornelius's mother), leaving Cornelius in possession of the hidden collection.

In early 2012, Cornelius was traveling from Switzerland to Munich on a train. While customs and border enforcement are ordinarily a nonevent in Schengen-zone Europe, a German official noticed him returning late on the same day he had left Germany, which piqued the official's attention. Any cash greater than 10,000 euros must be declared. It was not unusual for travelers to retrieve cash from Swiss banks without declaring it, so the officials questioned Gurlitt. It turned out that he had just under the monetary limit, but in the course of the conversation, the details of which are still not well known, Gurlitt apparently revealed that he had been visiting Galerie Kornfeld in Bern. The details are still secret, but the upshot was a more formal investigation and the raid on Gurlitt's apartment in early 2012. Once the officials realized the potential link to Nazi-looted art, they engaged an art historian but mostly did nothing until the *Focus* article forced their hand.

The response was part of what has become a pattern. The Bavarian minister of culture hastily proposed an amendment to federal law to extend the statute of limitations on claims. A task force of art historians was announced to investigate the provenance further, and the German minister of culture said all the usual things about fairness, making reference to the Washington Principles. As the new year started, confusion was the only consistent development. Gurlitt gave a rambling interview with *Der Spiegel* in which he talked about speaking with his pictures and defiantly refusing to return anything:

> Yes, I just won't do that. I will give nothing back willingly. Under no circumstances will I do that. But you can . . . I obviously can't do anything. When they seize it and take it away, what can I do then? I can do nothing. I have to just wait. Just that. Then I let it the first time.[217]

It was revealed that he had sold Max Beckmann's *The Lion Tamer* recently at Lempertz Auction House in Cologne; the auction house, because of the infamy in the provenance, had reached out to Flechtheim's heirs (to whom the painting had once belonged) to reach a settlement before it was auctioned. Gurlitt's attorneys created a bizarre "Gurlitt Info" website with a stock photograph of an elderly man with no relation to the case, in which they asserted that only a handful of the works of art were suspected of having been looted. Going on the offensive, Gurlitt filed a claim against the Bavarian prosecutor to get his paintings back. A "Task Force Schwabinger Kunstfund" was organized by the Bavarian government under the leadership of Ingeborg Berggreen-Merkel, but with an unknown mandate or deadline. As would become apparent, the diligent and professional work of the art historians on the panel would repeatedly be undermined by the political posturing of Grütters and other politicians.

Then, suddenly, Gurlitt struck a deal of sorts, agreeing to permit the task force to examine the collection and to return any works found to have been looted. With the ink barely dry, however, it was time for the next unexpected development: Gurlitt died. What truly surprised the world is that he had composed a recent will. Gurlitt did not merely leave his collection of paintings with their dubious provenance questions to a museum outside Germany, but he named the Kunstmuseum Bern itself as his sole heir. Gurlitt's cousin, Uta Werner, filed a challenge to the will, arguing that Gurlitt lacked testamentary capacity to make a will. The Kunstmuseum is the oldest museum in Switzerland, with more than 50,000 objects that include works by Vincent van Gogh, Franz Marc, and Henri Matisse. The museum responded by releasing a statement:[218]

> Despite speculation in the media that Mr. Gurlitt had bequeathed his collection to an art institution outside Germany, the news came like a bolt from the blue, since at no time has Mr. Gurlitt had any connection with Kunstmuseum Bern. The Board of Trustees and Directors of Kunstmuseum Bern are surprised and delighted, but at the same time do not wish to conceal the fact that this magnificent bequest brings with it a considerable burden of responsibility and a wealth of questions of the most difficult and sensitive kind, and questions in particular of a legal and ethical nature. They will not be in a position to issue a more detailed statement before first consulting the relevant files and making contact with the appropriate authorities.

In February 2014, the task force made its first recommendation about Henri Matisse's *Seated Woman*, claimed by the heirs of renowned Paris art dealer Paul Rosenberg. Chair Ingeborg Berggreen-Merkel issued a statement that (author's translation):

> Even if it could not be documented with certainty under what circumstances Hildebrand Gurlitt came into the possession of the work, the task force comes to the conclusion that it is Nazi-looted art from the rightful property of the collection of Paul Rosenberg. This result also takes into account that after 70 years, not all questions can be answered definitively, but it is nonetheless the object of the Washington Principles that fair and just solutions should be found.
>
> Our expert opinion will be made available to the probate court for use in determining if the work should be restituted to the heirs of Paul Rosenberg, as a result of the still-undecided legal issues.

> This ultimate decision rests in the hands of the heirs/legal successors of Cornelius Gurlitt, who declared himself ready shortly before his death to restitute according to the Washington Principles. This duty is binding on his heirs.[219]

That was not accompanied by any details about when or how the painting would be returned, however.

Less than a month later, the claimants' patience started to wear thin. David Toren, a 91-year-old New York lawyer, sued Germany in the United States District Court for the District of Columbia. The lawsuit sought the return of *Two Riders on the Beach* (*Zwei Ritter am Meer*) by Max Liebermann, one of the iconic images that became associated with the Gurlitt affair immediately after its disclosure in *Focus*. Toren, a resident of New York, left Germany at age fourteen in 1939. His great uncle, David Friedmann, lived in Breslau, the capital of Silesia (now part of Poland, known as Wrocław). As the Complaint explained, the Nazis catalogued and seized Friedmann's art collection in 1939–40, and the Liebermann painting appears on those records. A letter dated December 5, 1939, was attached to the Complaint, which addressed as-yet unseized Jewish collections in Breslau, including Friedmann's, as well as that of well-known collector Hans Sachs, interestingly. Thereafter, the Complaint attached a letter to Hildebrand Gurlitt dated August 28, 1942, which described the Liebermann as available. The author's name is not legible on the letter.

The Complaint sought recovery under several theories, but they fell into two groups: the first was bailment and the other was wrongful possession. As to the latter, Toren alleged that he was the true owner and that Germany was wrongfully in possession of the work. Under common law, he could recover the painting, its value, or some combination thereof.

The bailment argument clearly drew on the recent success of the *de Csepel* plaintiffs in the Court of Appeals. The distinction, however, was that whereas *de Csepel* alleged that the heirs of Baron Herzog (the collector's) came to an agreement with Hungary after the war to hold his art in its museums although they did not demand its return until recently (thus avoiding the statute of limitations), Toren alleged that Germany's unilateral decision to hold the seized art from 2012 to present in pursuit of finding its owners constitutes a bailment agreement with those then-unnamed and unknown owners.

Jurisdictionally, the case did not follow the *Altmann* approach using the expropriation exception. Instead, the Complaint relied on the commercial activity exception, arguing that the commercial effect that Bavaria's seizure of the paintings caused was a breach of the constructive bailment agreement. Because Toren was in the United States, he argued, the effects of the breach—again, caused by the seizure in Munich—happened in New York and satisfied the statute. Gurlitt was not named as a defendant. Germany eventually moved to dismiss, but the case was dismissed by agreement because the Liebermann is one of a small handful of works to have actually been returned to claimants.

Slightly less than a year after the initial discovery, the German federal cabinet announced the official formation of the German Center for Cultural Property Losses (*Deutsches Zentrum Kulturgutverluste*). Citing its "awareness of the special responsibility for the reworking of Nazi art theft,"[220] the ruling Christian Democratic Union (CDU) party coalition issued this statement (author's translation):

> The Foundation for the German Center for Cultural Property Losses will raise the [level] of provenance research into Nazi-looted art to a new level. Its goal is to coordinate, strengthen, and expand the countless activities and facilities of provenance research. In this way, it will be ensured that wrong will be punished through the strengthened state support.[221]

The announcement stated that the Federal Republic of Germany will contribute 4 million euros per year, while the sixteen German federal states (Bundesländer) will collectively add about 600,000 more. This initially seemed liked a positive development. However, 5 million euros is not as much as it sounds. Read closer, the intention was to build out the existing Lost Art Coordination Center in Magdeburg. True to form, this announcement served more as a triumphal, mission-accomplished moment to burnish Grütters's reputation more than a genuine change in commitment. At its core, the center remains an auxiliary tool for German museums that are faced with a claim, not a comprehensive examination of museum collections. Little has changed since other than ups and downs in the contested will filed by Gurlitt's cousin and the ill-conceived plan to hold an exhibition of the disputed works in Germany that no one seems to have thought about before announcing.

It must be said that the simplest explanation for all this is that the political will is lacking to find real answers as opposed to the optics of a contrived solution. Is there any further evidence for this contention? Regrettably, yes. In June 2016, journalists Catrin Lorch and Jörg Häntzschel published an explosive revelation in *Süddeutsche Zeitung* titled "The Munich Looted Art Bazaar," which reported on the work of the Commission for Looted Art in Europe (CLAE). The article reported that the government of Bavaria sold artworks returned to it by the famed Monuments Men after World War II that were supposed to be restituted to the victims of Nazi looting. Not only was the art given back to the German state on the explicit condition that it be restituted to the victims of Nazi art plunder, in some cases it was literally returned to the families of Nazi officials, such as Emmy Goering (Hermann's daughter) and Henriette von Schirach rather than to the victims themselves. Less than a month after the Federal Republic of Germany's toxic and revisionist reply brief in the Welfenschatz case (which argued, among other things, that individual claimants cannot sue because the U.S. policy was national-level restitution), the ramifications are far reaching for Germany's self-professed adherence to the Washington Conference Principles on Nazi-Confiscated Art of 1998. While the specific artwork in question may be less significant than most of the works found in Cornelius Gurlitt's apartment in 2012, the revelation is in many ways much, much worse. The underlying CLAE scholarship cannot be praised enough.

Some initial context is important. While the recent *Monuments Men* movie, for example, focused on the race to save noteworthy artifacts while hostilities were still ongoing, the far greater proportion of the MFAA's work was the task of dealing with the vast quantities of art in Nazi hands when the war ended. As is now well known, the United States and other allies opted for an approach of national-level restitution. That is to say, rather than search Europe for individual victims, the Allies returned the objects to the government of the country from which they were taken. The Allies returned some 10,600 objects to Bavaria with explicit instructions "that the investigation into the ownership of the pictures be continued."[222]

As the Washington Conference and subsequent studies have shown, this massive and laudable work often allowed the government in question simply to ignore the problem thereafter. Worse, in the modern era of restitution, recalcitrant European sovereign defendants have argued to U.S. courts that individual heirs have no standing to file claims because lawsuits conflict with the policy that the United States adopted after the war. Germany took this position in the Welfenschatz litigation as recently as June 2016.

As the revelation confirmed, the response in Bavaria was a complete sham. The investigation centered on a painting hanging in the Xanten cathedral, *Dutch Plaza*, by an unknown Dutch painter after a painting by Jan van der Heyden. It was stolen from a Jewish family in Vienna in 1938, the Krauses. Yet this and many other works were not returned to the families that survived or to their heirs but to Nazis like Baldur von Schirach (one-time minister of education and later Gauleiter of Vienna) or Heinrich Hoffmann.

Gottlieb Kraus was born in Bohemia in 1867, then very much part of the Austrian Empire. He and his wife Mathilde were quintessential members of Vienna society. The Krauses collected drawings by Rudolf von Alt and romantic landscapes by Georg Waldmüller. After the *Anschluss*, they were required, like all Austrian Jews, to register their property and to identify themselves as "Isaac" and "Sara" rather than their real names. They left Vienna, heading toward Prague (a common and tragic choice by Vienna's Jews and other targets of the Nazi regime). Their possessions and house in the leafy, hill neighborhood of Grinzing (near where the Reichels lived) were auctioned off and the proceeds going to the Nazi government.

The research also skillfully paints a parallel narrative of Henriette von Schirach, Baldur's wife. While her husband was properly punished as a war criminal, not the least of which because of his role in the deportation of 185,000 Austrian Jews, she quietly retired to Munich. She lived, incredibly, in the same neighborhood that Cornelius Gurlitt did, under her maiden name, Hoffmann. Yet, while the Krauses obtained no relief from the Bavarian government, Henriette Hoffmann von Schirach did. Hermann Goering's widow also made a successful personal appeal to the general director of the Bavarian State Paintings Collection.

The most important point is this: The scandal cements Bavaria's role as the worst outlier among the German federal states (so much so that several dozen U.S. representatives sent a disapproving letter to the Bavarian government recently). It also underscores why Germany's plaintive claims to be leading the way in restitution are wrong. This scandal also shatters one of the most dangerous ideas often whispered around the edges of restitution cases: Claimants only care about the most valuable works.

Far more so than the Gurlitt case, in which it could at least be said that the privacy rights of an individual citizen at least ostensibly explained the secrecy, this is a far-reaching scandal. Rather than the resignations that should immediately have been in order, various promises were made to examine what happened.[223] Another generation is passing away, which only adds to the urgency, and therefore, the likelihood of further litigation.

United Kingdom

The German and Austrian commissions underscore the highs and lows that have occurred when the various stakeholders have attempted to fulfill the Washington Principles. For obvious reasons, they are in many ways the most important such commissions because of the roles of those respective countries' participation in plundering art belonging to European Jews. England, France, and the Netherlands have also made efforts to create a resolution mechanism of sorts. Unique among them, in England, the issue is not about art taken from its one-time residents but rather art that entered the marketplace and eventually ended up in the United Kingdom. Like other Western countries, sensitivity to the issue grew in the 1990s. In June 1998, leading up to the United Kingdom's participation in the Washington Conference, the National Museum Directors' Conference convened a Spoliation Working Group. It created a "Statement of Principles and Proposed Actions" that proposed a "UK wide survey of objects which institutions currently believe might have been wrongfully taken during the Holocaust and World War II period."[224] Building on databases that were created in response to the Spoliation Working Group, the UK established in February 2000 the Spoliation Advisory Panel (SAP). The SAP's mandate is to review claims concerning cultural objects currently in the possession of a national museum.

One of the initial obstacles to the SAP's work was that national museums were often independently barred by law from removing objects from their collections. This was addressed by a 2009 law, the Holocaust (Return of Cultural Objects) Act of 2009, which stated that it was an "Act to confer power to return certain cultural objects on grounds relating to events occurring during the Nazi era,"[225] defined as the period between January 30, 1933, and December 31, 1945. Where the SAP has recommended return, and the Secretary of State has approved the recommendation, the museums affected may return the property in question. These recommendations are not mandatory, however, and may be declined by the museum in question.

As a legal proposition, the SAP relies heavily on two bases, the London Declaration of 1943 and British Military Law No. 59 (BML; a modification of the American Military Government Law No. 59). BML No. 59 stated:

> . . . it shall be presumed in favour of a claimant that a transaction entered into between January 1933 and May 1945 which involves any transfer or relinquishment of property during a period of persecution by any person who was directly exposed to persecutory measures on racial grounds shall be presumed to constitute an act of confiscation.

As noted earlier, that presumption can be rebutted by proving that a fair purchase price was paid to which the seller had free right of disposal. The SAP charter lists a series of factors to be considered.

Once it reviews the case, the SAP can recommend restitution of the object(s), payment of some kind of compensation, a display of the object's history and provenance that highlights the Nazi persecution involved, or advising direct negotiations.

As of August 2014, the SAP had considered fourteen claims.

The Netherlands

Quite unlike the United Kingdom, the Netherlands was invaded, occupied, and subjected to massive looting by its citizens. Goering in particular was ruthless in seeking out Dutch collections, as noted above, working hand in glove with Alois Miedl targeting collectors like Goudstikker, but Goering and Miedl were also together in grim competition with the occupation administration and the Dienstelle Mühlmann, the administrative office overseeing occupied Holland (named after Kajetahn Mühlmann). Hildebrand Gurlitt was one of the German buyers given access to this illicit market.

After the war and the restoration of the Dutch government, the Netherlands established the Council for Restoration of Rights (Raad voor het Rechtsherstel). In 1945, it also set up the Netherlands Art Property Foundation (Stichting Nederlands Kunstbezit, or SNK). The SNK first focused on the significant collections that had been targeted and worked to restitute such collections to their former owners. In 1949 and 1950, the SNK conducted three exhibitions to publicize the art for which the owners were sought. These restitution-related tasks were eventually transferred to the Bureau for Restoration Payments and the Restoration of Property (Bureau Herstelbetalings- en Recuperatiegoederen), which continued its work until being closed in the 1950s when a prescribed limitations period expired. Everything that remained in state custody is held by the Netherlands Art Property Collection, or Art Property Collection (Nederlands Kunstbezitcollectie), administered by the Ministry of Education, Culture and Science. It was held with the understanding that not everyone might have seen the art, and it would be kept until further claims could be made.

Against this unresolved backdrop, movement began in the late 1990s. The Netherlands Museums Association undertook a two-step investigation into the provenance of national collection objects entitled "Museum Acquisitions 1940–48,"[226] conducted between 1998 and 1999, and the "Museum Acquisitions from 1933 onwards," from 2009 to 2013.[227] At the same time, the Origins Unknown Committee (Commissie Herkomst Gezocht) was getting under way, and the Origins Unknown Agency (Bureau Herkomst Gezocht) was tasked with investigating all items in the Art Property Collection. The Origins Unknown Committee, also called the Ekkart Committee after its chairman, Rudi Ekkart, published reports in 2001, 2003, and 2004. The committee called for a more generous restitution policy, urging a reversal of the burden of proof to assume that any Jewish property transfer was involuntary, and a relaxation of the burdens of proof. The committee proposed an interesting corollary to these views, however, for art dealers. Namely, it argued, "[T]he art trade's objective is to sell its trading stock so that the majority of the transactions, even at the Jewish art dealers, were principally carried out in the usual way."[228]

This momentum surrounded the establishment of the Restitutions Committee in 2001, an independent advisory panel intended to fulfill in part the commitments of the Washington Principles. Formally named the Advisory Committee on the Assessment of Restitution Applications for Items of Cultural Value and the Second World War, the Restitutions Committee was created by a decree on November 16, 2001. The seven-member panel must include a chair and vice chair with master's degrees in law, a historical expert on the Second World War, an art history expert, and a musicology expert (notably different from the Limbach Commission's membership). The Restitutions Committee has two primary tasks: (1) to advise the Minister for Education, Culture and Science on objects taken involuntarily directly related to the Nazi regime that are currently in Dutch national custody; and (2) to issue opinions on disputes concerning ownership of such objects between the original owner or heirs on the one hand, and non-State possessors on the other hand.

Most decisions since the establishment of the Restitutions Committee have concerned objects in the Art Property Collection. The second category effectively constitutes a binding arbitration and is unique among the various national restitution commissions. Article 3 of its document states the principles on which it makes such recommendations, citing the Washington Principles, the circumstances under which the art was lost, and, interestingly, the significance of the work to the claimant and the collection in possession.

France

Like the Netherlands, France was overrun and ruthlessly plundered by the occupying German army and private art market actors who were given access to the spoils of this activity, most notoriously by the ERR. France also adopted the London Declaration in exile and legislation on April 21,

1945. This legislation made a distinction between transactions that had taken place against the will of the original owner versus actions by an official empowered by the German authorities and a general deprivation of rights. The first type moved even further past the rebuttable presumption of duress and declared the transaction as null ab initio—without any effect from the moment it occurred. In the latter, however, the original owner (not the possessor) had the burden of proof to establish that the transaction had been illegitimate.

An agency was created to oversee restitution of spoliated works, the Office for Private Property and Interests (Office des Biens et Intérêts Privés; OBIP). This OBIP established an Artwork Recuperation Committee (Commission de Récupération Artistique, or CRA). The CRA put together a list of cultural property that had been removed from France, known as the *Répertoire des Biens Spoliés en France Durant la Guerre de 1939-1945,* which was distributed widely to museums, galleries, and art dealers in France, Germany, and Austria. The CRA ended its work in 1949. All works that had been returned to France but not claimed were sold by the government, with the exception of roughly 2,000 works deemed to be of notable significance. That remainder was named the Musées Nationaux Récupération (MNR).

In many ways, France was at the very center of renewed attention in the 1990s. This was for a few reasons. First, Americans' and international buyers' interest in French art were at an all-time high. Impressionist exhibitions, catalogues, and merchandise reached the point of cliché. Second, *The Rape of Europa*, easily the single most influential book and scholarship on the topic of looted art, focused on the activities of the ERR and looted French art in particular. This brought uncomfortable attention to things like the very existence of the MNR, still in state hands. A study was commissioned to study the looting of art from French Jews between 1940 and 1944, known as the Mission Mattéoli (once again taking on the name of its chair). In reviewing the MNR, 200 pieces were determined definitively to have been looted, with the remainder having been moved through the French art market of the time. Building on the Mission Mattéoli's conclusions and analysis, an independent commission for France was proposed: the Commission for the Compensation of Victims of Spoliation Resulting from the Anti-Semitic Legislation in Force during the Second World War

(Commission pour l'indemnisation des victimes de spoliations intervenues du fait des législations antisémites en vigueur pendant l'Occupation or the CIVS). The CIVS is comprised of two judges of the Court of Cassation, two members of the Court of Auditors, two university professors, and two other members deemed qualified and usually connected to the French Jewish community. In keeping with French procedure, the process is more inquisitorial than adversarial: the claimant submits a request, and the CIVS investigates. It may conduct interviews, seek and review documents, but the presentation is not made by the claimant to the decision maker.

These investigations result in recommendations that, as in most of the national panels, are nonbinding. The volume is impressive; by April 2014, the CIVS had handled more than 28,000 cases and produced an even greater number of recommendations, frequently for compensation. Like all the commissions except the Netherlands's commissions, the CIVS's work is limited to objects in national possession and does not extend to works in private hands.

Limited Progress Elsewhere

Of the dozens of countries in Europe that signed the Washington Principles, France, England, Austria, and Germany are the only major players even to address the cursory and usually badly inadequate laws enacted in the 1940s and 1950s, which quickly expired in that era. Other European efforts have ranged from token, to ineffective, to downright hostile.

As part of the International Council of Museums (ICOM) Museum and Politics Conference in St. Petersburg in 2014, Dr. Wesley A. Fisher and Dr. Ruth Weinberger, on behalf of the World Jewish Restitution Organization (WJRO) and the Conference on Jewish Material Claims Against Germany (Claims Conference), gave an overview of recent history and addressed each country one by one. The report takes a high-level view at what progress has been made.

How one views the report from there really is a matter of outlook. At first blush, this quote is terribly depressing:

> Of the 50 countries for which summaries are appended to this report, only 4 may be said to have made major progress towards

> implementing the Washington Conference principles and the Terezin Declaration, while an additional 11 have made substantial progress in this regard.[229]

The report was complimentary of the information made available in Germany but noted that most research is still conducted by the museums themselves, making any progress necessarily slow. Belgium, Luxembourg, Norway, Slovakia, and France were designated as having made substantial progress. France failing to make the top category should be regarded as a disappointment, however, because of its importance.

That is as good as it gets, unfortunately. From there, the only question in the report is just how bad the offenders are. Progress in nearly all of Eastern Europe is regarded as nonexistent (in addition to those discussed specifically later: Belarus, Bosnia, Bulgaria, Estonia, Latvia, Macedonia, Poland, Romania, Serbia, Slovenia, and Ukraine).

Italy is singled out for particular criticism. Italy has pursued antiquities, museums, even curators, to the ends of the earth (even objects found in international waters), so one might expect a comparable effort with regard to Nazi-looted art closer to home (Italy's established Jewish community fared well by comparison until late in the war and Mussolini's collapse, after which the Nazis took over the persecution in earnest). Not so, regrettably. The report states succinctly:

> It does not appear that provenance research is taking place in Italy, nor is there a legislative background that would allow for the restitution of cultural and religious property.[230]

Hungary is also worked over in the report:

> About 90-92% of the artworks taken out of the country were returned between 1945 and 1948, with approximately 20% remaining in Hungary's cultural institutions – including artworks looted from Hungarian Jews. The National Gallery and the Museum of Fine Arts are known to hold looted art. Despite numerous legal attempts, the heirs to the Herzog collection, the Hungarian banker Baron Mor Lipot Herzog, who had collected

> between 1,500 and 2,500 artworks, have been denied any restitution. In 2010, the heirs to the Herzog collection filed a lawsuit in the United States against Hungary. The Herzog collection is not the only collection of Jewish artworks kept by Hungarian cultural institutions. According to experts in the field, Hungarian museums still store several hundred works of art obtained under questionable circumstances.
>
> Hungary has never set up a historical commission to investigate Hungary's role and participation in the financial and physical annihilation of its Jews, and it has not initiated any provenance research by its cultural institutions. While a few restitutions have taken place, important works of art have consistently been kept from being restituted to their rightful owners.[231]

Many other countries are criticized for giving lip service to the Washington Principles but doing little else. In the end, there is no question that the state of affairs now relative to 1997 is night and day. However, there is clearly more to be done.

Chapter 20

A Tragic Fate: Conclusions and Possibilities

The last twenty-five years have seen an explosion in the awareness of an interest in the subject of art looted by the Nazis and their allies between 1933 and 1945. With it has come a parallel expansion of efforts to seek the restitution of those artworks. Of those efforts, actual litigation is a minor subset, and of that litigation, cases in America a smaller proportion still. So what do these cases show us, if they show us anything? The answer reflects both on the effectiveness of neutral legal principles and American forums to address old grievances generally, and of the passions and motivations of those involved. In addition, if recent events offer any guidance, it may well be that a wavering commitment to the Washington Principles means that litigation in America will increase.

Another consideration is the cultural effect that the litigations have had. Complaints about lawyers, particularly American lawyers, are hardly news. Yet, just as reductive diatribes about tort claims obscure the real effect that consumer law, for example, has had on issues such as product safety, all the denigration in the world does not change the fact that U.S. litigation has moved the course of the restitution of Nazi-looted objects as much as any other development in the modern era.

In terms of the legal issues, the broad trends remain that the passage of time, cumulatively, presents the biggest challenge to claims. With some irony, the greater the awareness of the issue increases, the harder it is for plaintiffs to establish that they could not have known of the claim and thus avoid the statute of limitations. It is not as simple as that, particularly as archives overseas remain inaccessible. However, a considerable challenge remains convincing judges that the larger issue justifies giving a plaintiff a chance to prove his or her case in court despite decades having passed since the event occurred. Judges—rightly—are not in the position to make exceptions as a matter of course. As a result, skillful advocacy plays a key part in the course of any dispute that lands in court.

2016 brought an unexpected and significant change to the law of time limitation defenses. An unusual coalition of Democrats and Republicans (including, for example, Charles Schumer of New York and Ted Cruz of Texas, two politicians seldom on the same side of any issue, let along during the most divisive presidential campaign in memory, in which Cruz was still a candidate at the time) introduced the Holocaust Expropriated Art Recovery Act (S. 2763, the HEAR Act) that drew welcome attention to the ongoing challenges to the restitution of Nazi-looted art. The sponsors submitted the bill in April 2016 to standardize, at the federal level, the statute of limitations for claims for alleged Nazi-looted art; the Act proposed a universal six-year limitation period for claims in U.S. state and federal courts. This would eliminate any confusion of the sort that followed from California's attempted revisions of its statute of limitations; the problem with the California law was that the Ninth Circuit concluded that it intruded on the prerogatives of the federal government. There is no dispute that Congress and the president could thus enact such a law because the Ninth Circuit's ruling that it was for Congress, not individual states, to regulate such issues.

In the summer of the same year, the Senate Judiciary Committee convened a hearing. Senator Chuck Grassley's expediting of the hearing was also a sign that a vote might follow. This is important because recent bills to amend the FSIA as it pertains to looted-art claims, for example, have never even had a hearing in the Judiciary Committee, let alone gotten a vote (they did pass the House first).

At the time the bill was introduced, it seemed perhaps to be a presidential primary stunt by Senator Ted Cruz on the eve of the New York primary, but a hearing on the bill left the strong impression that the bill stood a real chance to progress. Given the current political climate, the hearing was almost shockingly bipartisan. It is important to remember, however, that despite a healthy dose of self-congratulation by the senators in attendance, the bill did not ensure any particular restitution and will still leave available defenses that several of the participants decried as inconsistent with U.S. policy.

Most accounts of the hearing focused on the star power of the witnesses, which is understandable but not terribly relevant. Actress Helen Mirren, who played Maria Altmann in the movie depiction of that restitution saga, spoke eloquently about the tragedy of loss suffered by the victims and survivors of Nazi looting. More concretely, Simon Goodman, author of *The Orpheus Clock* and member of the Gutmann-Goodman family that brought the Edgar Degas *Landscape with Smokestacks* case, spoke from personal experience about what Mirren had depicted onscreen. Likewise, Ronald Lauder decried the assertion of statutes of limitations as an avoidance of substance, which is true. Lauder said:

> When the United States endorsed the Washington Principles in 1998 and the Terezin Declaration in 2009, the U.S. committed itself to the recovery of art that was confiscated by the Nazis during the Holocaust. Our adherence to this commitment requires that resolution of such cases be based on the merits of each case and not on procedural technicalities or the capacity of one party to outspend, or outwait, the other. There are museums here in the United States that have been waiting out the clock to pass the Statute of Limitations. This also forces claimants to spend enormous amounts of money on legal fees – another strategy to make them give up.
>
> This is not justice. Stalling claims is an abuse of the system. Sadly, there are museums that feel no need to uphold the Washington Principles. Many other institutions do the very least that is required and not much more.[232]

Quite right, but as the bill was originally worded when he said this, it would still have allowed possessors to wait out claims; they would just have to wait a little longer.

Far more helpful were the comments of Monica Dugot of Christie's and Agnes Peresztegi, president of the Commission for Art Recovery. Dugot—an articulate advocate for many years for transparency and provenance research—responded to questions from Senator Al Franken and others about the challenges that face claimants, the overwhelming and decentralized information that is available, and the need for expertise. Peresztegi skillfully answered queries from Senator Orrin Hatch about the power of Congress to override state law statutes of limitations, rightly pointing out the interstate nature of the art market, and the failure of California's efforts to revise its statute of limitations, which was struck down as interference with federal law as discussed above. Put another way, if states cannot regulate something because of preemption, then Congress certainly can.

Peresztegi also made important reference to the fact that it has been U.S. policy to support restitution since 1943—a reference to the so-called London Declaration of that year—undercutting frequent arguments seen in litigation that only national-level restitution, not individual claims, is the policy of the United States. This point should be beyond dispute, yet von Saher and others have had to litigate the issue multiple times.

After the text of the bill was revised, it was approved out of the Judiciary Committee with a recommendation for passage. Chief among the drafting changes was a clarification that would preserve any claims that would be timely in New York, though without mentioning that state specifically. Absent the HEAR Act, any claimant in New York would not trigger the statute of limitations until he or she made a demand, as litigated in the *Grosz* case, for example. The original draft of the HEAR Act would have, however, set a six-year statute of limitations from discovery of the claim, which may already have passed. The revised bill sent to the full Senate in September 2016 (and introduced verbatim in the House of Representatives) addressed this unintended consequence on New York claims by stating that any claim that is currently not barred by the statute of limitations (which would include any claim in New York in which no demand has yet been made) will be deemed to have been discovered on the effective date of the legislation, giving the claimant six years from that legislative date to bring the case. The law's six-year statute of limitations and discovery rule is an improvement insofar as it would create some uniformity and put to bed forever the disputes that drove the *Von Saher* case in particular.

New York's demand and refusal rule would have been better. However, it is critical to remember that even with the passage of this law, all of the technicalities rightly decried by the witnesses will be still be available to defendants who wanted, in Lauder's words, to wait out claimants. If that was the problem, then the HEAR Act is not a complete solution.

On December 16, 2016, President Obama signed the HEAR Act into law. *See* Pub L. No. 114-308. The HEAR Act expressly preempts all state statutes of limitations with respect to claims for Nazi-looted art like those in this case. The HEAR Act provides:

> SEC. 5. Statute of limitations.
>
> a) In general.—Notwithstanding any other provision of Federal or State law or any defense at law relating to the passage of time, and except as otherwise provided in this section, a civil claim or cause of action against a defendant to recover any artwork or other property that was lost during the covered period because of Nazi persecution may be commenced not later than 6 years after the actual discovery by the claimant or the agent of the claimant of—
>
> (1) the identity and location of the artwork or other property; and
>
> (2) a possessory interest of the claimant in the artwork or other property.

Id. For preexisting claims, the statute deems this "date of discovery" to be the effective date of the statute, *i.e.*, no sooner than December 16, 2016. Specifically:

> (c) Preexisting claims.—Except as provided in subsection (e), a civil claim or cause of action described in subsection (a) shall be deemed to have been actually discovered on the date of enactment of this Act if—
>
> (1) before the date of enactment of this Act—
>
> (A) a claimant had knowledge of the elements set forth in subsection (a); and
>
> (B) the civil claim or cause of action was barred by a Federal or State statute of limitations; or

> (2) (A) before the date of enactment of this Act, a claimant had knowledge of the elements set forth in subsection (a); and
>
> (B) on the date of enactment of this Act, the civil claim or cause of action was not barred by a Federal or State statute of limitations.

Id. Further, the HEAR Act states:

> (d) Applicability.—Subsection (a) shall apply to any civil claim or cause of action that is—(1) pending in any court on the date of enactment of this Act, including any civil claim or cause of action that is pending on appeal or for which the time to file an appeal has not expired.

Of similar importance, although less widely reported, was the HEAR Act's affirmation of U.S. restitution policy. Recall that the defendants in cases from *Von Saher*, to *de Csepel*, to *Cassirer* argued that individual civil actions for the restitution of Nazi-looted art intruded on the foreign affairs prerogative of the Executive Branch. While those courts rightly overruled that argument (see, for example, *Von Saher v. Norton Simon Museum of Art at Pasadena*, 754 F.3d 712, 723 (9th Cir. 2014)[233]), it continued to be made. The HEAR Act puts that to rest unequivocally. The HEAR Act states:

> SEC. 2. Findings.
>
> [ ]
>
> (8) While litigation may be used to resolve claims to recover Nazi-confiscated art, it is the sense of Congress that the private resolution of claims by parties involved, on the merits and through the use of alternative dispute resolution . . .

The law thus does two things: it encourages alternative dispute resolution, and it confirms that litigation is an option available to claimants. To encourage a preference for one options necessarily means that the other option is, indeed, an option. Turning again to the history of the law's bipartisan proposal and passage noted above only underscores this point. The right to have a day in court is explicitly the justification given by most of its sponsors and proponents. Indeed, as Senator Charles Grassley, chairman of the Senate Judiciary Committee, noted:[234]

> The HEAR Act thus serves two purposes: first, to ensure that laws governing claims to Nazi-confiscated art and other property further United States policy as set forth in the Washington Conference Principles on Nazi-Confiscated Art, the Holocaust Victims Redress Act, and the Terezin Declaration; and second, to ensure that claims to artwork and other property stolen or misappropriated by the Nazis are not unfairly barred by statutes of limitations but are resolved in a just and fair manner.

The HEAR Act is like all compromises: It gives everyone a bit of what they want but does not completely satisfy anyone. It eliminates battles over which statute of limitations should apply and when it should begin, providing a uniformity and certainty that anyone involved should value—particularly current possessors who may feel they have been unfairly targeted. It revives some claims that would have been barred—it might have saved one or more of Dr. Seger-Thomschitz's claims from dismissal, for example, at least at the threshold stage—no doubt to the unhappiness of current possessors, but it starts the clock with fewer exceptions, which puts pressure on heirs to determine whether there is a case to bring. That remains a challenge in cases in which the current possessor's records lack transparency, which is a detriment to claimants. However, the law at least makes sense because it sets the terms of the debate and would avoid arguments that have delayed specific cases (like *Von Saher*) for years.

Defendants, of course—and with equal skill—hearken back as much as they can to the traditional reasons for limitations periods: the difficulties of proof without witnesses and the possibility of intervening good-faith purchasers; these are all valid points in the right circumstances. As to the latter, the flashpoint remains the historical question of that good faith. Were Bernoulli, Kornfeld, and other Swiss art dealers in the 1950s good-faith purchasers? It seems hard to believe now. Yet, despite how hard it is to validate the good faith of anyone buying a painting with provenance from someone in an occupied area, those transactions, under the local law of the time, often serve to extinguish any later claim. It is reasonably likely that had the University of Oklahoma pressed the point, it would have prevailed by relying on the applicable Swiss judgment. Similarly, the theme that claimants could were not aware of their claims is undercut by incredible stories such as the Gurlitt saga or the Kraus/Bavaria fiasco.

Clearly, the most pitched battles concern the question of forced sales, though they are hardly exclusive. Indeed, the Meyer, Goodman, and Altmann cases presented no real dispute about whether the works in question were stolen, but the nastiest invective from current possessors such as Bavaria, the SPK, or MoMA has been to subtly or otherwise suggest that plaintiffs' ancestors got what they paid for. It is a worrying, and increasing, trend.

In the end, the only question that really matters is whether there is an alternative. It is not possible to paint American museums with a broad brush. Some, like the MFA, have devoted real time and resources to discovering the truth, whereas others have not. Some countries like the United Kingdom and the Netherlands have made an effort to learn the scope of problem works. Some have contemptuously refused even to try. Germany, under the culture ministry of Monika Grütters, remains committed above all to optics over substance. At the time of the Washington Conference, Austria had its head in the sand about *Portrait of Wally*, but has evolved admirably, if not universally, in its treatment of the proper presumptions and perspectives on Jewish collections at the time of the Nazi takeover.

No sweeping conclusions do justice to these stories and cases. Indeed, the stories only engender stereotypes about institutions and heirs that continue to entrench positions and create hard feelings. Unfortunately, however, as long as the art is in one location and the heirs are in another, the disputes will no doubt continue.

Acknowledgments

Remarkable teachers never leave you. This book has its roots in many places but chief among them were the study of art history and German many years ago at Williams College. Elizabeth McGowan, the first art history professor I ever had, opened my eyes to the visual expression around me and taught me innumerable lessons in brevity and expression. Thomas Kohut, professor of history, inspired and challenged me to confront and analyze primary sources in their native language. Bruce Kieffer, Gail Newman, and Helga Druxes, in addition to their classroom instruction, offered the chance to live and work in Germany in 1996, opening a lifelong engagement with its language, culture, and history. Thank you to Michael Conforti for taking a flyer on a recent graduate who was coaching rowing part time and was willing to do whatever tasks a growing museum program needed, and to Brian Allen, a true professional mentor. This book would never have happened but for those experiences.

I offer my gratitude to my partners and colleagues at Sullivan & Worcester LLP, who have supported the creation and expansion of our art law practice. Thank you in particular to Rhonda Sady for her many and patient edits to the manuscript.

Patricia Moed offered essential guidance on my book proposal. Megan Noh gave a critical review of the manuscript. Her sharp eye and analysis were indispensable. My editor, Jonathan Malysiak, is owed my special thanks for being at my side throughout this project and for his constant wise counsel.

To my parents, Agnes O'Donnell and Vince O'Donnell, who encouraged me to follow my interests for their own sake and not for what impression they made on others for as long as I can remember. For never asking me, "An art history degree? What are you going to do with that?" Thank you. To Diane and Chester Black, your love and support mean the world to me.

To Erica, Megan, Bridget, and Zachary: You inspire me to do my best and always do what's right. Our world will be well taken care of in your kind and capable hands.

Finally and most importantly, to my wife, Amy, who challenges me with her intelligence, humbles me with her patience, and graces me with her partnership: I couldn't do it without you.

Appendix of and Credits for Selected Works at Issue

Max Beckmann
Löwenbändiger (*The Lion Tamer*)
Gouache and pastel on wove paper, 90 × 59.3 cm
Private collection

Lucas Cranach the Elder, German, 1472–1553
Adam, c. 1530
Oil on panel (one of a pair), 75 × 27 ½ in. (190.5 × 69.9 cm)
Norton Simon Art Foundation

Lucas Cranach the Elder, German, 1472–1553
Eve, c. 1530
Oil on panel (one of a pair), 75 × 27 ½ in. (190.5 × 69.9 cm)
Norton Simon Art Foundation

Edgar Degas
French, 1834–1917
Landscape with Smokestacks, c. 1890
Pastel, over monotype, on textured cream wove paper, edge-mounted on board

317 × 416 mm
Purchased from the collection of Friedrich and Louise Gutmann and gift of Daniel C. Searle
1998.915
The Art Institute of Chicago

Paul Gauguin (French, 1848–1903)
Street in Tahiti, 1891, oil on canvas
45 ½ × 34 ⅞ in. (115.5 × 88.5 cm)
Toledo Museum of Art, purchased with funds from the Libbey Endowment, gift of Edward Drummond Libbey
1939.82

George Grosz
Portrait of the Poet Max Hermann-Neisse (1927/1928)
Oil on canvas, 59.4 × 74 cm
Museum of Modern Art, New York, © USA Leemage/Bridgeman Images
Art © Estate of George Grosz licensed by VAGA, New York, NY

George Grosz
Republican Automatons (1920)
Watercolor and pencil on paper, 60 × 47.3 cm
Museum of Modern Art, New York, USA Bridgeman Images
Art © estate of George Grosz/Licensed by VAGA, New York, NY

George Grosz
Self Portrait with Model (1928/1929)
Oil on canvas, 115.6 × 75.6 cm
Museum of Modern Art, New York

Gustav Klimt
Portrait of Adele Block-Bauer I (1907)
Oil, silver, and gold on canvas, 138 × 138 cm
Neue Galerie, New York
© De Agostini Picture Library, E. Lessing/Bridgeman Images

Oskar Kokoschka, Austrian, 1886–1980
Two Nudes (*Lovers*), 1913
Oil on canvas
163.2 × 97.5 cm (64 ¼ × 38 ⅜ in.)
Museum of Fine Arts, Boston
Bequest of Sarah Reed Platt, 1973.196
Photograph © 2017 Museum of Fine Arts Boston

Max Liebermann
Two Riders on the Beach (*Zwei Ritter am Meer*; 1901)
Oil on canvas, 71 × 91 cm, private collection
© Stephen Chung/Alamy Live News

Pablo Picasso
Boy Leading a Horse (1906)
Oil on canvas, 220.6 × 131.2 cm
Museum of Modern Art, New York/Bridgeman Images
© 2016 Estate of Pablo Picasso/Artists Rights Society (ARS), New York

Pablo Picasso
Le Moulin de la Galette (c. 1900)
Oil on canvas, 88.2 × 115.5 cm
Solomon R. Guggenheim Museum, New York/Bridgeman Images
© 2016 Estate of Pablo Picasso/Artists Rights Society (ARS), New York

Pablo Picasso
Madame Soler (1903)
Oil on canvas, 100 × 73 cm
Pinakothek der Moderne, Munich/Bridgeman Images
© 2016 Estate of Pablo Picasso/Artists Rights Society (ARS), New York

Camille Pissarro
La bergère rentrent des moutons (1886)
Oil on canvas, 17 × 14 ½ in.
Fred Jones Jr. Museum of Art, Norman, Oklahoma

Camille Pissarro
Rue Saint-Honoré, après-midi, effet de pluie (*Rue St. Honoré, Afternoon, Rain Effect*; 1892)
Oil on canvas, 81 × 65 cm
Thyssen-Bornemisza Museum, Madrid
De Agostini Picture Library/G. Nimatallah/Bridgeman Images

Egon Schiele
Portrait of Wally (1912)
Oil on panel, 32 × 39.8 cm
Leopold Museum, Vienna, Austria
© De Agostini Picture Library/G. Nimatallah/Bridgeman Images

Egon Schiele
Seated Woman with Bent Left Leg (Torso) (1917)
Gouache and black crayon on paper, 43.2 × 29.9 cm
Private collection

Eglon van der Neer, Dutch, 1634–1703
Portrait of a Man and Woman in an Interior
1665–1667
Oil on panel
73.9 × 67.6 cm (29 ⅛ × 26 ⅝ in.)
Museum of Fine Arts, Boston

Seth K. Sweetser Fund, 41.935
Photograph © 2017 Museum of Fine Arts Boston

Vincent van Gogh
Vue de L'Asile et de la Chapelle de Saint-Rémy (1889)
Oil on canvas, 45.1 × 60.4 cm

Vincent van Gogh
The Diggers (1889)
Oil on paper, 65.1 × 50.2 cm
Detroit Institute of Arts
Bequest of Robert H. Tannahill/Bridgeman Images

Vincent van Gogh
Les Saintes-Maries de la Mer (1906)
Drawing
Sammlung Oskar Reinhart, Winterthur, Switzerland

Francis Xavier Winterhalter
Mädchen aus den Sabiner Bergen (*Girl from the Sabine Mountains*; undated)
Oil on canvas, 74.5 × 63 cm

Iris and Max Stern Foundation, Montreal, Canada
Image of *Rue St. Honoré* in Lily Cassirer's home
Rue Saint-Honoré, après-midi, effet de pluie (*Rue St. Honoré, Afternoon, Rain Effect*) as seen in the home of Lily Cassirer in the early 1920s
Image courtesy of the Cassirer family

Endnotes

[1] *See* Ronald S. Lauder, *Plenary Session on Nazi-Confiscated Art Issues,* NAZI-CONFISCATED ART ISSUES, Washington Conference on Holocaust-Era Assets, available at the Florida Center for Instructional Technology, College of Education, University of South Florida, https://fcit.usf.edu/holocaust/resource/assets/heac4.pdf.

[2] *Id.*

[3] *See Croatia: Delegation Statement,* DELEGATION STATEMENTS, Washington Conference on Holocaust-Era Assets, available at the Florida Center for Instructional Technology, College of Education, University of South Florida, https://fcit.usf.edu/holocaust/resource/assets/heac3.pdf.

[4] *See* Ambassador Louis Amigues, Director, Archives and Records, Ministry of Foreign Affairs, *Intervention during the Plenary Session: Overview of Nazi Confiscated Art Issues* (translated from the original French by the U.S. Department of State Office of Language Services, Translating Division), DELEGATION STATEMENTS, Washington Conference on Holocaust-Era Assets, available at the Florida Center for Instructional Technology, College of Education, University of South Florida, https://fcit.usf.edu/holocaust/resource/assets/heac3.pdf.

[5] *See Hungary: Delegation Statement,* DELEGATION STATEMENTS, Washington Conference on Holocaust-Era Assets, available at the Florida Center for Instructional Technology, College of Education, University of South Florida, https://fcit.usf.edu/holocaust/resource/assets/heac3.pdf.

[6] *See Israel: Delegation Statement,* DELEGATION STATEMENTS, Washington Conference on Holocaust-Era Assets, available at the Florida Center for

Instructional Technology, College of Education, University of South Florida, https://fcit.usf.edu/holocaust/resource/assets/heac3.pdf.

[7] *Id.*

[8] *See Latvia: Delegation Statement,* DELEGATION STATEMENTS, Washington Conference on Holocaust-Era Assets, available at the Florida Center for Instructional Technology, College of Education, University of South Florida, https://fcit.usf.edu/holocaust/resource/assets/heac3.pdf.

[9] *Id.*

[10] *See Luxembourg: Delegation Statement,* "German Measures Taken Against Jews and Emigrants," DELEGATION STATEMENTS, Washington Conference on Holocaust-Era Assets, available at the Florida Center for Instructional Technology, College of Education, University of South Florida, https://fcit.usf.edu/holocaust/resource/assets/heac3.pdf.

[11] *See Poland: Delegation Statement,* DELEGATION STATEMENTS, Washington Conference on Holocaust-Era Assets, available at the Florida Center for Instructional Technology, College of Education, University of South Florida, https://fcit.usf.edu/holocaust/resource/assets/heac3.pdf.

[12] *See* Valentin Kopteltsev, ambassador and head of the Russian delegation, *Russia: The General Goals of the Conference and the Looted Art Problem,* DELEGATION STATEMENTS, Washington Conference on Holocaust-Era Assets, available at the Florida Center for Instructional Technology, College of Education, University of South Florida, https://fcit.usf.edu/holocaust/resource/assets/heac3.pdf.

[13] *Id.*

[14] *See Slovak Republic: Delegation Statement,* DELEGATION STATEMENTS, Washington Conference on Holocaust-Era Assets, available at the Florida Center for Instructional Technology, College of Education, University of South Florida, https://fcit.usf.edu/holocaust/resource/assets/heac3.pdf.

[15] *See Spanish Delegation Statement: Activities of the Spanish Commission on Holocaust-Era Assets,* DELEGATION STATEMENTS, Washington Conference on Holocaust-Era Assets, available at the Florida Center for Instructional Technology, College of Education, University of South Florida, https://fcit.usf.edu/holocaust/resource/assets/heac3.pdf.

[16] *Id.*

[17] *See* Salomo Berlinger, Special Adviser to the Commission on Jewish Assets in Sweden at the Time of the Second World War and Member of the Swedish Delegation, *Sweden: Delegation Statement,* DELEGATION STATEMENTS, Washington Conference on Holocaust-Era Assets, available at the Florida Center for Instructional Technology, College of Education, University of South Florida, https://fcit.usf.edu/holocaust/resource/assets/heac3.pdf.

[18] Stephanie Barron, DEGENERATE ART: THE FATE OF THE AVANT-GARDE IN NAZI GERMANY, Harry N. Abrams (April 15, 1991).

[19] *See* Thomas G. Borer, Ambassador and Head of Delegation, *Switzerland: Introductory Declaration,* DELEGATION STATEMENTS, Washington Conference on Holocaust-Era Assets, available at the Florida Center for Instructional Technology, College of Education, University of South Florida, https://fcit.usf.edu/holocaust/resource/assets/heac3.pdf.

[20] *Id.*

[21] *See Turkey: Delegation Statement on Holocaust-Era Assets,* DELEGATION STATEMENTS, Washington Conference on Holocaust-Era Assets, available at the Florida Center for Instructional Technology, College of Education, University of South Florida, https://fcit.usf.edu/holocaust/resource/assets/heac3.pdf.

[22] *See* Stuart E. Eizenstat, *Overview of the Washington Conference Principles on Nazi-Confiscated Art,* DELEGATION STATEMENTS, Washington Conference on Holocaust-Era Assets, available at the Florida Center for Instructional Technology, College of Education, University of South Florida, https://fcit.usf.edu/holocaust/resource/assets/heac3.pdf.

[23] *Id.*

[24] *Id.*

[25] *See* World Jewish Restitution Organization, *Report of the W.J.R.O.: Jerusalem, November 1, 1998,* submitted by Ambassador Naphtali Lavie, Vice Chairman of the Executive, DELEGATION STATEMENTS, Washington Conference on Holocaust-Era Assets, available at the Florida Center for Instructional Technology, College of Education, University of South Florida, https://fcit.usf.edu/holocaust/resource/assets/heac3.pdf.

[26] *See* Prof. Dr. Carla Schulz-Hoffmann, Deputy General Director, Bavarian State Paintings Collections, Germany, *Break-out Session on Nazi-Confiscated Art Issues: Principles to Address Nazi-Confiscated Art,* NAZI-CONFISCATED ART ISSUES, Washington Conference on Holocaust-Era Assets, available at the Florida Center for Instructional Technology, College of Education, University of South Florida, https://fcit.usf.edu/holocaust/resource/assets/heac4.pdf.

[27] Association of Art Museum Directors, *Report of the AAMD Task Force on the Spoliation of Art during the Nazi/World War II Era (1933–1945),* available at https://aamd.org/document/report-of-the-aamd-task-force-on-the-spoliation-of-art-during-the-nazi/world-war-ii-era.

[28] *Id.*

[29] *Id.*

[30] American Alliance of Museums, *Recommended Procedures for Providing Information to the Public about Objects Transferred in Europe during the Nazi Era,*

available at http://www.aam-us.org/docs/default-source/professional-resources/nepip-recommended-procedures.

31 *Id.*

32 Association of Art Museum Directors, *Art Museums and the Identification and Restitution of Works Stolen by the Nazis* (May 2007), available at https://aamd.org/sites/default/files/document/Nazi-looted%20art_clean_06_2007.pdf.

33 *Id.*

34 Portrait of Wally (Gravitas Ventures 2012).

35 *Id.*, interview with Rudolph Leopold.

36 "Wally's Journey," Lecture by Jane Kallir, Museum of Jewish Heritage, August 18, 2010. Available at http://www.gseart.com/Articles/Wallys-Journey-37.php.

37 Portrait of Wally (Gravitas Ventures 2012).

38 *Id.*

39 Glenn Lowry, Testimony to the U.S. House of Representatives Banking Committee, February 12, 1998.

40 Portrait of Wally (Gravitas Ventures 2012).

41 Tim Rutton, "In NPR actions, were all things considered?" *Los Angeles Times*, March 19, 2005

42 Portrait of Wally (Gravitas Ventures 2012).

43 Howard Reich, *$6.5 million will end Picasso fight,* Chicago Tribune, August 10, 2005.

44 *Id.*

46 *See* In der Schiedssache Majken Hofmann usw., 7 Mai 2006 (In the Arbitration of Majken Hofmann, et al., May 7, 2006).

47 *See Vineberg v. Bissonnette*, Case No. 1:06-cv-00211-ML-IDA (D. R.I.), Memorandum of Law in Support of Plaintiff's Motion for Preliminary Injunction and Expedited Review, Docket No. 41, at 2 (May 10, 2007), *citing* Bissonnette's Aff. in Supp. of 12(b) Mot. to Dismiss and/or for Stay filed with the Court and dated Dec. 28, 2006, Docket No. 23, ¶ 7(i) (advising U.S. Court of value asserted in German proceedings as approximately €60,000 or $80,000).

48 *See Vineberg v. Bissonnette*, Case No. 1:06-cv-00211-ML-IDA (D. R.I.), Defendant, Maria Louise Bissonnette's Memorandum of Law in Opposition to Plaintiff's Motion for Summary Judgment, Docket No. 71, at 5 (July 31, 2007).

49 *See Bakalar v. Vávra,* Case No. 1:05-cv-03037-WHP (S.D.N.Y.), Letter to Court from William L. Charron, May 6, 2008, Docket No. 185 (May 6, 2008).

50 *See Bakalar v. Vávra*, Case No. 1:05-cv-03037-WHP (S.D.N.Y.), Opinion and Order dated September 2, 2008, Docket No. 220, at 14 (September 2, 2008).

[51] *Id.* at 16.

[52] *See Von Saher v. Norton Simon Museum*, No. 091254 (Supreme Court), Brief of Amicus Curiae of the United States of America, May 27, 2011.

[53] Statements at oral argument from recording of *Marei Von Saher v. Norton Simon Museum of Art, et al.*, No. 12-55733, available at http://www.ca9.uscourts.gov/media/view.php?pk_id=0000011212.

[54] *See Museum of Fine Arts Boston v. Seger-Thomschitz*, Case No. 1:08-cv-10097-RWZ, Affidavit of Jonathan Petropoulos in Opposition to Motion of the Museum of Fine Arts, Boston's Motion for Summary Judgment on the Statute of Limitations, Docket No. 43, at ¶ 15 (October 21, 2008).

[55] *See Museum of Fine Arts Boston v. Seger-Thomschitz*, Case No. 1:08-cv-10097-RWZ, Declaration of Victoria Reed in Support of Museum of Fine Arts, Boston's Motion for Summary Judgment Based on Statute of Limitations, Docket No. 28, (the "Reed Declaration") at ¶ 40 (September 19, 2008).

[56] *Id.* at ¶ 44.

[57] *Id.*

[58] *Id.* at ¶ 54.

[59] *Id.* at ¶ 55.

[60] *See Museum of Fine Arts Boston v. Seger-Thomschitz*, Case No. 1:08-cv-10097-RWZ, Dr. Claudia Seger-Thomschitz's First Amended Answer and Counterclaim, Docket No. 19, at ¶ 56 (July 21, 2008).

[61] Reed Declaration at ¶ 57.

[62] *Id.* at ¶ 57, Exhibit 65.

[63] *Id.*

[64] *See Museum of Fine Arts Boston v. Seger-Thomschitz*, Case No. 1:08-cv-10097-RWZ, Memorandum of Points and Authorities in Support of Museum of Fine Arts, Boston's Motion for Summary Judgment Based on Statute of Limitations, Docket No. 35, at 6–7 (September 19, 2008).

[65] *Id.*

[66] *See Dunbar v. Seger-Thomschitz*, Case No. 08-711, Complaint, Docket No. 1, at ¶ 8 (January 22, 2008).

[67] *Id.*

[68] *See Dunbar v. Seger-Thomschitz*, Case No. 08-711, Sarah Blodgett Dunbar's Memorandum in Support of Motion for Partial Summary Judgment on Her First Amended Complaint and Motion for Summary Judgment on Defendant's Counterclaims, Docket No. 16-1, at 7 (October 6, 2008).

[69] *See Dunbar v. Seger-Thomschitz*, Case No. 08-711, Affidavit of Sarah Blodgett Dunbar, at ¶ 9 (dated October 3, 2008; filed October 6, 2008).

[70] *See Dunbar v. Seger-Thomschitz*, Case No. 08-711, Sarah Blodgett Dunbar's Memorandum in Support of Motion for Partial Summary Judgment on Her

First Amended Complaint and Motion for Summary Judgment on Defendant's Counterclaims, Docket No. 16-1, at 6 (October 6, 2008).

[71] *See Dunbar v. Seger-Thomschitz,* Case No. 08-711, Answer and Counterclaim, Docket No. 10, at ¶ 6 (June 27, 2008).

[72] *Id.* at ¶ 72.

[73] *See Dunbar v. Seger-Thomschitz,* Case No. 08-711, Sarah Blodgett Dunbar's Memorandum in Support of Motion for Partial Summary Judgment on Her First Amended Complaint and Motion for Summary Judgment on Defendant's Counterclaims, Docket No. 16-1, at 6 (October 6, 2008).

[74] *See Dunbar v. Seger-Thomschitz,* Case No. 08-711, Opposition of Dr. Claudia Seger-Thomschitz to Plaintiff's Motion for Summary Judgment, Docket No. 35, at 16 (December 15, 2008).

[75] *See Dunbar v. Seger-Thomschitz,* Case No. 08-711, Declaration of Jonathan Petropoulos in Opposition to Motion for Summary Judgment of Plaintiff and Counterclaim-Defendant, Docket No. 35-3, at ¶ 6-13 (December 15, 2008).

[76] *Id.* at ¶ 10.

[77] *Dunbar,* 638 F. Supp. 2d at ¶ 665.

[78] *See Detroit Institute of Arts v. Ullin, et al.,* Case No. 2:06-CV-10333 (E.D. Mich.), Defendants' Answer to Complaint, Affirmative Defenses, and Counterclaims, Docket No. 24, at ¶ 123 (April 27, 2006).

[79] *Id.* at ¶ 145.

[80] *Id.* at ¶ 152.

[81] *Id.* at ¶ 165.

[82] *See Detroit Institute of Arts v. Ullin, et al.,* Case No. 2:06-CV-10333 (E.D. Mich.),Brief in Support of Plaintiff and Counter-Defendant the Detroit Institute of Arts' Motion to Dismiss Counterclaims, Docket No. 27-2, at 18 (June 19, 2006).

[83] *See Detroit Institute of Arts v. Ullin, et al.,* Case No. 2:06-CV-10333 (E.D. Mich.), Defendants' Brief in Opposition to Plaintiff's Motion to Dismiss, Docket No. 31, at 3 (August 7, 2006).

[84] *Id.* at 7, fn. 6.

[85] *Id.* at 8.

[86] *Id.* at 14.

[87] *See Grosz et al. v. Museum of Modern Art,* Case No. 1:09-cv-03706-CM-THK, Verified Complaint, Docket No. 1, at ¶ 63 (April 10, 2009).

[88] *Id.* at ¶ 141.

[89] *See Grosz et al. v. Museum of Modern Art,* Case No. 1:09-cv-03706-CM-THK, Plaintiffs' Memorandum of Law in Opposition to Defendant's Motion to Dismiss the Amended Complaint, Docket No. 23, at 4 (June 25, 2009).

[90] *Id.* at p. 8.

[91] *Id.* at p. 14.

[92] *See Grosz et al., v. Museum of Modern Art,* Case No. 1:09-cv-03706-CM-THK, Order on Letter Motion, Docket No. 43 (August 31, 2009).

[93] *See Grosz et al., v. Museum of Modern Art,* Case No. 1:09-cv-03706-CM-THK, Endorsed Letter, Docket No. 82 (October 2011).

[94] *See Grosz et al., v. Museum of Modern Art,* Case No. 1:09-cv-03706-CM-THK, Motion for Stay, Docket No. 85 (December 2, 2011).

[95] *See Grosz et al., v. Museum of Modern Art,* Case No. 1:09-cv-03706-CM-THK, Order, Docket No. 86 (December 6, 2011).

[96] *See Schoeps v. The Museum of Modern Art et al.*, Case No. 1:07-cv-11074-JSR, Complaint, Docket No. 1, at ¶ 8 (December 7, 2007). The case was originally captioned with the museums as plaintiffs, but the District Court restyled the caption to reflect Schoeps's status as the claimant.

[97] *Id.* at ¶ 14.

[98] *Id.* at ¶ 16.

[99] *Id.* at ¶ 24.

[100] *Id.*

[101] *Id.* at ¶ 28.

[102] *Id.* at ¶ 31.

[103] *Id.* at ¶ 36.

[104] *Id,* at ¶ 39.

[105] *Id.* at ¶ 60.

[106] *Id.* at ¶ 63.

[107] *See Schoeps v. The Museum of Modern Art et al.*, Case No. 1:07-cv-11074-JSR, Order, Docket No. 31 (March 26, 2008).

[108] *See Schoeps v. The Museum of Modern Art et al.*, Case No. 1:07-cv-11074-JSR, Letter Opinion of Dr. Wolfgang Ernst, Docket No. 32-2, at 3 (April 1, 2008).

[109] *See Schoeps v. The Museum of Modern Art et al.*, Case No. 1:07-cv-11074-JSR, Opinion and Order, Docket No. 38, at 8 (April 14, 2008).

[110] *Id.* at p. 10.

[111] *See Schoeps v. The Museum of Modern Art et al.*, Case No. 1:07-cv-11074-JSR, Declaration of Evan A. Davis in Support of Plaintiffs' Motion for Summary Judgment, Docket No. 59, Exhibit 31A (author's translation) (October 20, 2008).

[112] *Id.*

[113] *See Schoeps v. The Museum of Modern Art et al.*, Case No. 1:07-cv-11074-JSR, Memorandum of Law In Support of the Museum of Modern Art and the Solomon R. Guggenheim Foundation's Motion for Summary Judgment, Docket No. 55, at 7 (October 20, 2008).

[114] *Id.* at p. 26.

[115] *See Schoeps v. The Museum of Modern Art et al.*, Case No. 1:07-cv-11074-JSR, Order, Docket No. 84, at 2 (December 31, 2008).

[116] *See Schoeps v. The Museum of Modern Art et al.*, Case No. 1:07-cv-11074-JSR, Order, Docket No. 89 (January 8, 2009).

[117] *See Schoeps v. The Museum of Modern Art et al.*, Case No. 1:07-cv-11074-JSR, Memorandum Order, Docket No. 134, at 1 (March 24, 2009).

[118] *Id.* at 3.

[119] *Id.* at p. 4, contrasting *Metropolitan Museum Historic Dist. Coalition v. De Montebello*, 20 A.D.3d 28, 37-38, 796 N.Y.S.2d 64 (1st Dep't 2005).

[120] *Id.* at 4.

[121] *Id.* at 6.

[122] *See Meyer v. Board of Regents of the University of Oklahoma*, Case No. 1:13-cv-03128-CM, Amended Complaint, Docket No. 34, at ¶ 51.

[123] *Id.* at ¶ 62.

[124] *See Meyer v. Board of Regents of the University of Oklahoma*, Case No. 1:13-cv-03128-CM, Memorandum Decision and Order Dismissing Action as Against the Oklahoma Defendants for Lack of Personal Jurisdiction, Docket No. 55, at 2 (May 14, 2014).

[125] *Id.* at 3.

[126] *Id.* at 4–5.

[127] *Id.* at 8.

[128] *See Meyer v. Board of Regents of the University of Oklahoma*, Case No. 1:13-cv-03128-CM, Order Transferring Case to the Western District of Oklahoma, Docket No. 65, at 2 (April 7, 2015).

[129] *Id.* at 3.

[130] *See* Opening Statement by Mike Reynolds, Testimony before the Oklahoma House Conference Committee on Government Modernization and Accountability, May 13, 2014, available at http://returnthepissarro.blogspot.com/.

[131] Lorne Fultonberg, *Students protest OU painting with football flyover,* News Channel 4, first posted September 5, 2015, available at http://kfor.com/2015/09/05/students-protest-ou-painting-with-football-flyover/.

[132] *Id.*

[133] *Id.*

[134] Graham Bowley, *University Negotiates to Return Pissarro to Jewish Family,* New York Times, December 4, 2015.

[135] *Id.*

[136] *See Malewicz et al. v. City of Amsterdam*, Case No. 1:04-cv-00024-RMC, Amended Complaint, Docket No. 4, at ¶ 9 (January 9, 2004).

[137] *Id.* at ¶ 11.

[138] *Id.* at ¶ 18.

[139] *Id.* at ¶ 23.

[140] *See Malewicz et al. v. City of Amsterdam*, Case No. 1:04-cv-00024-RMC, The City of Amsterdam's Motion to Dismiss the Amended Complaint in its Entirety, Docket No. 17, at 4 (April 30, 2004).

[141] *Id.* at 5.

[142] *Id.* at 12.

[143] *Id.* at 15.

[144] *See Malewicz et al. v. City of Amsterdam*, Case No. 1:04-cv-00024-RMC, Memorandum of Points and Authorities in Opposition to Defendant's Motion to Dismiss Plaintiffs' Amended Complaint, Docket No. 19, at 3 (September 3, 2004).

[145] *Id.* at 8.

[146] *Id.* at 17.

[147] *Id.* at 29.

[148] *Id.* at 36.

[149] *Id.* at 40.

[150] *See Malewicz et al. v. City of Amsterdam*, Case No. 1:04-cv-00024-RMC, Statement of Interest of the United States, Docket No. 26, at 4 (December 22, 2004).

[151] *Id.* at 7.

[152] *Cassirer v. Kingdom of Spain*, 616 F.3d 1019, 1023–24 (9th Cir. 2010).

[153] *Id.* at 1032.

[154] *See Cassirer et al. v. Kingdom of Spain et al.*, Case No. 2:05-cv-03459-JFW-E (C.D. Cal.), Memorandum and Order Regarding Defendant's Motion to Dismiss, Docket No. 159, at 3 (May 24, 2012).

[155] *Id.* at 14–15.

[156] *Id.* at 31.

[157] *Id.* at 33.

[158] *See* 2010 Cal. Stat. ch. 691, § 1.

[159] *See Hungary: Delegation Statement,* DELEGATION STATEMENTS, Washington Conference on Holocaust-Era Assets, available at the Florida Center for Instructional Technology, College of Education, University of South Florida, https://fcit.usf.edu/holocaust/resource/assets/heac3.

[160] *Id.*

[161] *See de Csepel v. Republic of Hungary*, Case No. 1:10-cv-01261-ESH (D.D.C.), Motion to Dismiss by The Republic of Hungary, the Hungarian National Gallery, the Museum Of Fine Arts, the Museum of Applied Arts, and the Budapest University of Technology and Economics, Docket No. 15, at 15 (February 15, 2011).

[162] *Id.* at 16.

[163] *Id.* at 32.
[164] *Id.* at 38.
[165] *Id.*
[166] *Id.*
[167] *Id.* at 42.
[168] *Id.* at 43.
[169] *Id.* at 52.
[170] *Id.*
[171] *See Schoeps et al., v. Freistaat Bayern*, Case No. 1:13-cv-02048-JSR (S.D.N.Y.), Complaint, Docket No. 1, at ¶ 89 (March 27, 2013).
[172] *Id.* at ¶ 101.
[173] *Id.*
[174] *Id.* at ¶ 133.
[175] *Id.* at ¶ 146.
[176] *Id.* at ¶ 177(a).
[177] *Id.* at ¶ 207.
[178] *See Schoeps et al., v. Freistaat Bayern*, Case No. 1:13-cv-02048-JSR, Free State of Bavaria's Memorandum of Law in Support of its Motion to Dismiss the Second Amended Complaint for Lack of Subject Matter Jurisdiction Under the FSIA, Docket No. 18, at 14 (November 26, 2013).
[179] *Id.* at p. 17.
[180] *See Schoeps et al., v. Freistaat Bayern*, Case No. 1:13-cv-02048-JSR, Opposition of the Plaintiff Mendelssohn-Bartholdy Heirs to Motion of Bavaria to Dismiss the Second Amended Complaint for Lack of Subject Matter Jurisdiction, Docket No. 22, at 5 (December 10, 2013).
[181] *See Schoeps et al., v. Freistaat Bayern*, Case No. 1:13-cv-02048-JSR, Free State of Bavaria's Reply in Further Support of its Motion to Dismiss the Second Amended Complaint for Lack of Subject Matter Jurisdiction Under the FSIA, Docket No. 25, at 9 (December 17, 2013).
[182] *See Schoeps et al., v. Freistaat Bayern*, Case No. 1:13-cv-02048-JSR, Transcript of Hearing Held December 23, 2013, Docket No. 32, at 2 (January 8, 2014).
[183] *See Westfield et al., v. Federal Republic of Germany*, Case No. 3:09-cv-00204 (M.D. Tenn.), Defendant's Memorandum of Law Supporting Motion to Dismiss Complaint Pursuant to Rule 12, Docket No. 10, at 18 (April 6, 2009).
[184] *Id.* at 20.
[185] *Id.* at 26.
[186] *See Westfield et al., v. Federal Republic of Germany*, Case No. 3:09-cv-00204 (M.D. Tenn.), Plaintiffs' Response in Opposition to Defendant's Motion to Dismiss, Docket No. 20, at 14 (May 22, 2009).
[187] *Id.* at 25–26.

[188] *Id.* at 30.

[189] *Id.* at 43.

[190] *See Nazi-Era Provenance Research,* MFA.org, available at http://www.mfa.org/collections/provenance/nazi-era-provenance-research.

[191] *See Provenance Outreach Conducted by Museum of Fine Arts, Boston, Results in Agreement to Retain Ownership of Eglon Van Der Neer's Portrait of a Man and Woman in an Interior,* press release, Museum of Fine Arts Boston (June 26, 2011), available at http://mfas3.s3.amazonaws.com/MFA_Van%20der%20Neer%20press%20release.pdf.

[192] Orkin v. Swiss Confederation, 770 F. Supp. 2d 612, 614 (S.D.N.Y. 2011).

[193] Oberster Gerichtshof [OGH] [Supreme Court] April 1, 2008 Docket No. 5 Ob 272/07x, Beschluss Des Obersten Gerichthofs (Austria).

[194] *See* In der Schiedssache Majken Hofmann usw., 7 Mai 2006 (In the Arbitration of Majken Hofmann et al.), May 7, 2006.

[195] Press release: "Representative Weber regarding the Beethoven Frieze: Decision not legally tenable" ("Erbenvertreter Weber zu Beethovenfries: Entscheidung rechtlich nicht haltbar - Fall für internationale Gerichte"), http://www.ots.at/presseaussendung/OTS_20150306_OTS0152/erbenvertreter-weber-zu-beethovenfries-entscheidung-rechtlich-nicht-haltbar-fall-fuer-internationale-gerichte.

[196] Full text available at https://www.kulturgutverluste.de/Content/08_Downloads/DE/Gemeinsame-Erklaerung.pdf?__blob=publicationFile&v=11.

[197] *See The Guelph Treasure, Notes* (Fogg Art Museum), Vol. 2, No. 6 (Jun., 1931), at 333–337.

[198] *See* Recommendation of the Advisory Commission for the Return of Nazi-persecuted cultural property in the "Guelph Treaure" case (Empfehlung der Beratenden Kommission für die Rückgabe NS-verfolgungsbedingt entzogener Kulturgüter zum Fall „Welfenschatz"), https://www.kulturgutverluste.de/Content/06_Kommission/DE/Empfehlungen/14-03-20-Empfehlung-der-Beratenden-Kommission-im-Fall-Welfenschatz.pdf?__blob=publicationFile&v=7.

[199] *Id.*

[200] On March 31, 2017, the U.S. District Court for the District of Columbia denied the motion to dismiss made by the SPK and Germany. The District Court found FSIA jurisdiction and agreed with the plaintiffs that the allegations of a sale made under duress fit within the expropriation exception because, as in *de Csepel*, the deprivation of the economic means to survive is an element of genocide, which is a quintessential violation of international law. Germany's arguments that it was immune from review over takings from its own citizens was rejected. *Philipp et al. v. Federal Republic of Germany et al.*,

Civil Action No. 15-cv-266 (CKK), 2017 U.S. Dist. LEXIS 48460 (D.D.C. Mar. 31, 2017).

201 *See* Recommendation of the Advisory Commission for the Return of Nazi-persecuted cultural property concerning the picture "Three Graces" by Lovis Corinth (Empfehlung der Beratenden Kommission für die Rückgabe NS-verfolgungsbedingt entzogener Kulturgüter zum Bild „Drei Grazien" von Lovis Corinth), https://www.kulturgutverluste.de/Content/06_Kommission/DE/Empfehlungen/14-08-21-Empfehlung-der-Beratenden-Kommission-im-Fall-Levy-BSTGS.pdf?__blob=publicationFile&v=5.

202 *Id.*

203 *Id.*

204 *Id.*

205 *Id.* (author's translation).

206 *Id.* (author's translation).

207 *See* Recommendation of the Advisory Commission for the Return of Nazi-persecuted cultural property, in partcular from Jewish ownership, in the matter "Behrens" Düsseldorf (Beratende Kommission für die Rückgabe NS-verfolgungsbedingt entzogener Kulturgüter, insbesondere aus jüdischem Besitz, Empfehlung der Beratenden Kommission in der Sache „Behrens ./. Düsseldorf"), available at https://www.kulturgutverluste.de/Content/06_Kommission/DE/Empfehlungen/15-02-03-Empfehlung-der-Beratenden-Kommission-im-Fall-Behrens-Duesseldorf.pdf?__blob=publicationFile&v=7.

208 *Id.*

209 *Id.*

210 *See* Recommendation of the Advisory Commission for the Return of Nazi-persecuted cultural property, in partcular from Jewish ownershipm, under the chair of Prof. Dr. Limbach in the matter of Flechtheim ./. Cologne (Beratende Kommission für die Rückgabe NS-verfolgungsbedingt entzogener Kulturgüter, insbesondere Besitz, hat unter Vorsitz von Frau Prof. Dr. Limbach zum Fall Flechtheim ./. Köln Stellung genommen), https://www.kulturgutverluste.de/Content/06_Kommission/DE/Empfehlungen/13-04-09-Empfehlung-der-Beratenden-Kommission-im-Fall-Flechtheim-Koeln.pdf?__blob=publicationFile&v=6.

211 Alison Smale, *Germany to Continue Funding to Establish Provenance of Looted Art,* New York Times, March 3, 2016.

212 *Id.*

213 Catrin Lorch, *Grütters' Lapsus,* Sueddeutsche Zeitung, March 9, 2016.

214 Stefan Koldehoff, *Beschwerde nicht vorgesehen,* Frankfurter Allgemeine Zeitung, November 14,2016.

[215] Catrin Lorch, *Vermittler oder Entscheider?*, SUEDDEUTSCHE ZEITUNG, November 9, 2016.

[216] *See* Alex Shoumatoff, *The Devil and the Art Dealer,* VANITY FAIR, March 19, 2014.

[217] Özlem Gezer, *Gespräch mit einem Phantom,* DER SPIEGEL, November 11, 2013.

[218] *See* Museum of Fine Arts Bern Press Release (May 7, 2014).

[219] *See TASKFORCE-Gutachten bestätigt NS-Raubkunstverdacht des Gemäldes von Henri Matisse „Sitzende Frau" (1921),* Lost Art Internet Database (lostart.de), available at http://www.lostart.de/Content/02_Aktuelles/2014/14-06-11%20PM%20Taskforce%20Matisse1.html;jsessionid=03206226FEC04120FDE65A92875F7523.m1?nn=6044.

[220] *Deutsches Zentrum Kulturgutverluste ist ein Meilenstein,* CDU/CSU press release, October 8, 2014, available at https://www.cducsu.de/presse/pressemitteilungen/deutsches-zentrum-kulturgutverluste-ist-ein-meilenstein.

[221] *Id.*

[222] Catrin Lorch and Jörg Häntzschel, *Münchner Raubkunst Bazaar,* SUEDDEUTSCHE ZEITUNG, June 25-26, 2016.

[223] *See* Press Release (Munich) "The Doors of the State Paintings Collections Are Open for Claimants and Scientists—Intensive Provenence Research at the Pinakothek („*Die Türen der Staatsgemäldesammlungen stehen für Geschädigte und Wissenschaftler offen—Intensive Provenienzrecherche der Pinakothen*") July 1, 2016.

[224] *Fair and Just Solutions? Alternatives to Litigation in Nazi-looted Disputes: Status Quo and New Developments*, Evelien Campfens, (ed.), Eleven International Publishing, at 63 (2015).

[225] *Id.* at 66.

[226] *Id.* at 74, citing *Museum Acquisitions After 1933, an Overview Survey* (*Museale Verwervingen vanaf 1933, 'Over het Onderzoek'*), available at www.musealeverwervingen.nl/36/0ver-het-onderzoek.

[227] *Id.*

[228] *Id.* at 75, citing Ekkart Committee, "Recommendations for the restitution of artworks of art dealers" (28 January 2013).

[229] Wesley A. Fisher and Ruth Weinberger, *Holocaust-Era Looted Art: A Current World-Wide Overview,* the Conference on Jewish Material Claims Against Germany, ICON Museum & Politics Conference, World Jewish Restitution Organization, September 10, 2014, available at http://art.claimscon.org/wp-content/uploads/2014/11/Worldwide-Overview.pdf.

[230] *Id.*

[231] *Id.*

[232] *See* testimony of Roland Lauder to the Senate Judiciary Committee, Subcommittee on the Constitution, Subcommittee on Oversight, Agency Action, Federal Rights and Federal Courts, June 7, 2016, available at https://www.judiciary.senate.gov/meetings/s-2763-the-holocaust-expropriated-art-recovery-act_reuniting-victims-with-their-lost-heritage.

[233] "Von Saher is just the sort of heir that the Washington Principles and Terezin Declaration encouraged to come forward to make claims, again, because the Cranachs were never subject to internal restitution proceedings . . . . Perhaps most importantly, this litigation may provide Von Saher an opportunity to achieve a just and fair outcome to rectify the consequences of the forced transaction with Goering during the war, even if such a result is no longer capable of being expeditiously obtained." *Von Saher v. Norton Simon Museum of Art at Pasadena*, 754 F.3d 712, 723.

[234] *See* Holocaust Expropriated Art Recovery Act of 2016, Report to Accompany S. 2763, Calendar No. 654, Report 114-394.

Glossary of Names, Terms, and Concepts

Act of State doctrine—a prudential doctrine suggesting that courts should abstain from hearing cases in which they otherwise have jurisdiction if the claim concerns an act by a government against one of its own citizens. The Act of State doctrine is why most claims of confiscation in the Soviet Union have not been heard in U.S. courts.

Adverse possession—property doctrine under which a trespasser can become the owner of a piece of property. Pursuant to a statutory period, typically twenty years, the adverse possessor must use the property continuously, exclusively, and in a fashion that would put the true owner on notice with the opportunity to eject the trespasser.

Marilyn Alsdorf—a collector in Chicago who purchased *Femme en Blanc* by Pablo Picasso, later the subject of litigation with Thomas Bennigson.

Maria Altmann—born Maria Victoria Bloch in Vienna in 1916. She was a member of the Bloch family, a successful Austrian Jewish family, the daughter of Gustav Bloch and Marie Therese Bauer. Her uncle, Ferdinand Bloch-Bauer, was a sugar magnate and patron of the arts.

American Alliance of Museums (AAM)—the largest industry association of American museums, including art museums.

Anschluss—the annexation of Austria by Germany in 1938, strongly advocated in advance by Austrian National Socialists, led by Arthur Seyss-Inquart. After months of uncertainty about a possible union with Nazi Germany, Hitler invited Austrian chancellor Kurt von Schuschnigg to Germany in February 1938. Schuschnigg initially agreed to hold a plebiscite vote on the union, but then changed course. Schuschnigg then resigned, ordering the Austrian army not to resist the Germans. Ostensibly on an invitation for "aid," the German army entered Austria on March 13, 1938. Chaotic scenes followed in Vienna in particular, with Jews dispossessed of their homes and possessions by mobs. Jews of all ages were forced to scrub the sidewalks with small brushes while leering crowds mocked them, in what became known as "Reibpartie," or "scrubbing parties."

Art Loss Register (ALR)—created in London in 1990, the ALR built off the work of the International Foundation for Art Research (IFAR) in creating a database of artworks on which claims (including but not limited to claims of Nazi looting) had been placed. As awareness of looted art increased, the ALR became one of the earliest searchable databases.

Aryanization—the term used by Nazi officials to describe the transfer of business and property from Jewish owners to approved, Aryan ones.

Association of Art Museum Directors (AAMD)—an association of the directors of the most prominent fine art museums in the United States.

Bailment—the legal relationship that pertains to temporarily holding property for another. Bailment can be express, according to a contract, or implied (under specific circumstances, such as when you temporarily give your property to a valet).

David Bakalar—owner of *Seated Woman with Bent Left Leg (Torso)* by Egon Schiele; he brought suit for declaratory judgment in New York against the heirs of Fritz Grünbaum.

Bayerische Staatsgemäldesammlungen (Bavarian State Paintings Collection; BSGS)—an agency of the State of Bavaria, the BSGS oversees the collections of the major museums in Munich. Current possessor of and defendant in case regarding *Madame Soler* by Pablo Picasso.

Thomas Bennigson—Carlotta Landsberg's grandson and heir, litigant against Marilyn Alsdorf over title to *Femme en Blanc* by Pablo Picasso.

Else Bergmann—Clara Levy's daughter. Bergmann's role in the import of *Three Graces* by Lovis Corinth was a key part of the dispute over ownership of the painting. *Three Graces* was imported to New York, and whether Levy had shipped it to her daughter was a key point of contention.

Christoph Bernoulli—Swiss art dealer now notorious for purchases of looted art in Switzerland in the 1950s supposedly without knowledge of their prior circumstances; one-time owner of *La bergère rentrent des moutons* by Camille Pissarro.

Maria-Louise Bissonnette—stepdaughter of Karl Wilharm, defendant in litigation over *Mädchen aus den Sabiner Bergen* (*Girl from the Sabine Mountains*) by Francis Xavier Winterhalter.

Adele Bloch-Bauer—Maria Altmann's aunt and subject of Gustav Klimt's *Portrait of Adele Bloch-Bauer I* and *Portrait of Adele Bloch-Bauer II,* both of which were the subject of the litigation with Austria. The terms of her 1925 will expressing a desire that the painting be left to Austria were the subject of much dispute.

Ferdinand Bloch-Bauer—Adele Bloch-Bauer's husband and Maria Altmann's uncle, who fled to Switzerland after the *Anschluss.*

Sarah Reed Blodgett—a Portland, Oregon, collector who bequeathed *Two Nudes (Lovers)* by Oskar Kokoschka to the Museum of Fine Arts Boston and the mother of Sarah Blodgett Dunbar.

Lea Bondi—Viennese art dealer and owner of the Würthle & Sohn (Würthle and Son) gallery there. Bondi's gallery was Aryanized by Friedrich Welz, who acquired property from Bondi and other Jews in this fashion. Bondi won restitution of the gallery after the war, but Welz claimed that *Portrait of Wally* had been confiscated as part of the collection of Heinrich Rieger, another persecuted Austrian Jew.

Bundesdenkmalamt (BDA)—the Austrian Federal Office for the Preservation of Historical Monuments. The existing commission for the preservation of cultural heritage established under Emperor Franz Joseph, it fell to the BDA to oversee the restitution of some 8,000 Nazi-looted objects returned to Austria by the MFAA after the war.

Burden of proof—in any civil case, one party bears the burden to prove that the result it seeks is more likely to have occurred than not.

California Code of Civil Procedure Section 354.3—California's 2002 attempt to extend the statute of limitations to December 31, 2010, for actions regarding the recovery for works of fine art alleged to have been stolen during the Holocaust era (defined as 1929 to 1945). The law was eventually struck down by the U.S. Court of Appeals for the Ninth Circuit because the Ninth Circuit concluded that the law was preempted by the foreign affairs power of the executive branch of the U.S. government.

Lilly Cassirer—owner of *Rue Saint-Honoré, après-midi, effet de pluie* (*Rue St. Honoré, Afternoon, Rain Effect*) by Camille Pissarro; subject of litigation with the Thyssen-Bornemisza Museum in Madrid; grandmother of Klaus (Claude) Cassirer. Lilly survived the war and died in Cleveland, Ohio, in 1962.

Claude (né Klaus) Cassirer—grandson of Lilly Cassirer; original plaintiff in litigation against Spain and the Thyssen-Bornemisza Museum. He died while the litigation was pending.

Collective Declaration of 1999 (*Gemeinsame Erklärung der Bunderegierung, der Länder, und der kommunale Spitzenverbände zur Auffindung und zur Rückgabe NS-verfolgungsbedingt entzogenen Kulturgutes, insbesondere aus jüdischem Besitz*)—the declaration among the German federal government and its sixteen federal states to implement the Washington Principles.

Comity—the principle that courts of one nation ought to respect the judgments and acts of another, as distinguished from the Full Faith and Credit Clause of the Constitution that requires U.S. states to honor each other's judgments.

Commissie Rechtsverkeer in Oorlogstijd (CORVO)—a Dutch postwar commission that was empowered to accept or reject suspect transactions.

Commission de Récupération Artistique (CRA)—the French government entity charged with researching artworks and collections that had been looted during the Vichy regime.

Conference on Jewish Material Claims Against Germany (Claims Conference)—founded in 1951, the Claims Conference was created to negotiate with Germany on behalf of victims of Nazi persecution.

Conversion—a common law claim for the unlawful dominion and control over property. This claim is often brought in parallel to a replevin claim because if the property is no longer available, its value may be a substitute remedy.

Council for Restoration of Rights (Raad voor het Rechtsherstel)—commission set up after the war in the Netherlands to begin to sort out the return of looted art.

David de Csepel, Angela Maria Herzog, and Julia Alice Herzog—heirs of Baron Herzog and plaintiffs in litigation against Hungarian museums.

Declaratory judgment—a procedural claim that asks a court to make a declaration regarding the state of the parties' rights. On its own, it will not typically include any mandatory relief like the return of property.

Degenerate Art Action—1937 program in which disapproved modern art deemed degenerate was taken out of German museums and exhibited separately with corresponding derogatory commentary and labels. Less ideologically pure, the Nazis also sold these works, then among the most valuable in the world, for hard currency abroad (most notoriously at the Galerie Fischer auction in Lucerne). A select group of four art dealers (Hildebrand Gurlitt, Karl Buchholz, Ferdinand Möller, and Bernhard Böhmer) were given a monopoly over this trade.

Detroit Institute of Arts (DIA)—owner of *The Diggers* by Vincent van Gogh; the DIA brought a declaratory judgment action after receiving demands from the heirs of Martha Nathan.

Devisenschutzkommando (DSK)—the German Financial Exchange protection Commando, which often worked hand in hand with the Einsatzstab Reichsleiter Rosenberg (ERR).

Diversity jurisdiction—pursuant to 28 U.S.C. § 1332, if the parties have diverse citizenship (meaning from different states or countries) and the matter in dispute exceeds $75,000, a case can be brought in federal court.

Sarah Blodgett Dunbar—a plaintiff in a declaratory judgment action pertaining to *Portrait of a Youth* (1910) by Oskar Kokoschka.

Einsatzstab Reichsleiter Rosenberg (ERR)—the special Nazi unit organized under and named after Nazi ideologue Alfred Rosenberg, author of *The Myth of the Twentieth Century* (*Der Mythos des 20. Jahrhunderts*), a notoriously racist screed written in the late 1920s. The

ERR was principally involved in the organized theft of French and Dutch collections.

Equitable defenses—a remnant of the Court of Chancery in England; equitable defenses are exception to the legal result on some ground of fairness. The defendant asserting an equitable defense ordinarily bears the burden of proof.

Leon Fischer and Milos Vavra—heirs of Fritz Grünbaum and claimants for *Seated Woman with Bent Left Leg (Torso)* by Egon Schiele.

Alfred Flechtheim—a renowned dealer in Berlin and Düsseldorf and pioneer of modernist art patronage, who was targeted swiftly such that he had to flee Germany immediately after the 1933 takeover by the Nazis.

Reichfluchtsteuer (Reich flight tax)—the final insult to those Jews who were able to escape Germany alive; they were subjected to this additional tax at confiscatory levels on their remaining money for the privilege of being allowed to leave.

Foreign Cultural Exchange Jurisdictional Clarification Act, Public Law 114-319—a law proposed multiple times in the U.S. Congress to exclude loans of artwork that enjoy protection under the Immunity From Seizure Act (IFSA) from the definition of commercial activity necessary to satisfy the expropriation exception of the Foreign Sovereign Immunities Act. It passed Congress and was signed into law in December 2016.

Foreign Sovereign Immunities Act (FSIA), 28 U.S.C. § 1605 *et seq.*—the U.S. federal statute that provides the exclusive set of circumstances in which a foreign nation, its political subdivisions, or its instrumentalities may be sued. Sovereign entities are entitled to a presumption of immunity from suit absent consent or a statutory exception, and the FSIA provides a number of bases on which that sovereign immunity can be abrogated in federal court.

Forum non conveniens—like the Act of State doctrine, a prudential abstention doctrine that dismisses a case when a more appropriate forum exists elsewhere but to which the court lacks the power to transfer.

Fred Jones Jr. Museum of Art—an art museum at the University of Oklahoma; a defendant in the lawsuit over Camille Pissarro's *La bergère rentrent des moutons.*

Erich Führer—a Viennese attorney who was appointed head of the Bloch-Bauer estate for the purpose of its liquidation.

Fund for (Hilfsfonds) Assistance to Political Persecutees—a postwar Austrian fund to compensate Austrian Jews for property losses.

Dr. Karl Garzarolli—postwar director of the Austrian National Gallery. Garzarolli was involved in the acquisition of *Portrait of Wally*, before exchanging it with Dr. Rudolph Leopold for other paintings, after Lea Bondi had sought Leopold's assistance in retrieving *Portrait of Wally*. Dr. Garzarolli was also instrumental in acquiring *Portrait of Adele Bloch-Bauer I* and the other paintings that had belonged to Ferdinand Bloch-Bauer. Dr. Garzarolli claimed that Adele had bequeathed the paintings to the museum, but concealed from Bloch-Bauer's heirs the will that made clear she had left them to her husband, expressing only an unenforceable preference that he leave them to the National Gallery (which, after being chased out of his home by the Nazis, would have been out of the question).

Galerie Gutekunst & Klipstein—a Swiss gallery; predecessor in title to the Galerie St. Etienne of *Seated Woman with Bent Left Leg (Torso)* by Egon Schiele.

Galerie St. Etienne—New York gallery opened by Otto Kallir after he left Austria, seller of *Seated Woman with Bent Left Leg (Torso)* by Egon Schiele to David Bakalar in 1963.

***Gesetz zur Wiederherstellung des Berufsbeamtentums* (Law for the Restoration of the Civil Service)**—one of the first national enactments intended to purge Jews and other political enemies from the important civil service; the law subjected existing employees to strict racial criteria for employment. It took effect April 7, 1933, and was used, among other things, to bolster the administration of state museums with Nazi Party loyalists.

Gleichschaltung—the idea that the Nazis could impose a single worldview on German society.

Good-faith purchaser—someone who acquires property without any knowledge that it may have been stolen. In the United States, a good-faith purchaser will typically lose to the true owner, whereas in many European countries the good-faith purchaser acquires title and extinguishes the claims of the original owner.

Desirée (Desi) von Halban-Kurz Goudstikker—the widow of Jacques Goudstikker; Desi survived the war and made efforts to recover his lost collection from the Dutch government.

Jacques Goudstikker—probably the most successful interwar art dealer in the Netherlands. Targeted specifically by Hermann Goering, he signed over his gallery under duress and fled the country before dying aboard the SS *Bodegraven*, one of the last ships to leave the occupied Netherlands.

Lilian and Martin Grosz—heirs of the painter George Grosz, they brought a claim against the Museum of Modern Art in New York for Grosz's *Portrait of the Poet Max Hermann-Neisse* (1928); *Self Portrait with Model* (1929); and *Republican Automatons* (1920). The court disagreed with their position about when MoMA had refused to return the paintings, and ruled that the claims were barred by the statute of limitations.

Fritz Grünbaum—an Austrian Jewish collector and stage actor, interned and murdered in Dachau.

Elisabeth Grünbaum—wife of Fritz Grünbaum, sister of Mathilde Lukacs.

Hildebrand Gurlitt—an art dealer and authorized seller of "degenerate" art; he successfully convinced the Monuments Men that his collection had been lost in the firebombing of Dresden. The collection was not destroyed and was found some seventy years later in his son's apartment in Munich.

Cornelius Gurlitt—son of Hildebrand Gurlitt. The discovery of some 1,200 works of art in his apartment, suspected of having connections to Nazi-looted art, set off an international scandal. It was revealed in 2013 that they had been seized in 2012 as part of a tax investigation after Cornelius aroused the suspicion of a customs agent on a train home from Switzerland.

Friedrich Bernhard Gutmann—the grandson of Bernhard Gutmann, heir to the family banking business at the Dresdner Bank, and owner of *Landscape with Smokestacks* by Edgar Degas.

Théophile Hansen—Viennese architect who designed many of the monumental buildings that encircle the *Ringstrasse* around the city center. The public buildings in particular conform to stylistic types as to their function: the Parliament building is Neoclassical, the city hall is Neogothic, the museums are Neorenaissance, and so on. Hansen also designed many of the palaces, or "Palais," large private residences that were owned in many instances by successful Viennese Jews, such that the Ringstrasse was pejoratively referred to as "Zionstrasse," or "Zion Street," by anti-Semitic factions. Hansen's buildings define the visual character of central Vienna.

Angela Maria Herzog and Julia Alice Herzog along with David de Csepel—heirs of Baron Herzog and plaintiffs in litigation against Hungarian museums.

Baron Mór Lipot Herzog—a Jewish art collector in Budapest, Hungary, during the first half of the twentieth century. Over his lifetime, he assembled a fabled art collection that spanned Old Masters and more modern paintings, including those of the Impressionists.

Holocaust Claims Processing Office (HCPO)—a division of the New York State Department of Financial Services, the HCPO advocates on behalf of Holocaust victims and their heirs by seeking the just and orderly return of assets to their original owners.

Holocaust Expropriated Art Recovery (HEAR) Act, Pub L. No. 114-308—law that standardized at the federal level a six-year statute of limitations for claims to Nazi-looted art.

Holocaust Victims Redress Act (HVRA) of 1998—a 1998 law that endorsed the concept of returning looted art to its former owners. Courts have held, however, that the HVRA did not provide a private cause of action for claimants to sue, making the effect of the law somewhat tentative.

Otto Kallir—formerly Otto Nierenstein; a Viennese dealer who purchased *Two Nudes (Lovers)* by Oskar Kokoschka from Oskar Reichel.

Franz Kieslinger—a Nazi art appraiser who assessed the considerable collection of Fritz Grünbaum pursuant to the *Verzeichnis* he was required to complete and file.

Immunity From Seizure Act (IFSA; 22 U.S.C. § 2459)—a 1965 law that immunizes any cultural object from judicial seizure while it is in the United States. Only objects whose owners (or borrowers) have applied for and been given immunity before entering the United States enjoy this immunity. Immunity from seizure relates only to the property's actual seizure, however. It does not mean that the owner cannot be sued in the United States. Put another way, a defendant who is not immune from suit under the Foreign Sovereign Immunities Act can be sued on a claim related to an object that is immune from seizure, subject to the restrictions of the Foreign Cultural Exchange Jurisdictional Clarification Act of 2016.

Interlocutory appeal—an exception to the usual rule that only a final judgment may be appealed, interlocutory appeals are most relevant in FSIA cases in which a sovereign defendant who loses a motion to dismiss may immediately appeal that ruling.

Kommission für Provenienzforschung (Commission for Provenance Research)—an Austrian commission created in February 1998, succeeded by passage of Restitution Law and the *Kunstrückgabebeirat.*

***Kunstrückgabebeirat* (Austrian Art Restitution Advisory Board)**—a federal panel that advises state-owned museums in Austria on claims for allegedly Nazi-looted art. It was formed pursuant to the 1998 restitution law, the *Bundesgesetz über die Rückgabe von Kunstgegenständen aus Österreichischen Bundesmuseen und Sammlungen* (BGBl. I Nr. 181/1998). Initially the subject of fierce criticism after the board declined to recommend the restitution of Gustav Klimt's *Portrait of Adele Bloch-Bauer I* and other works to Maria Altmann, its output and sensitivity has improved dramatically in recent years.

Kunstrückgabegesetz—the Austrian Art Restitution Law of 1998. This law authorized the Austrian Federal Minister of Art and Culture, Public Service and Constitution to convey works in national possession to heirs. This was an important grant of authority because works may not otherwise be removed from public collections for any reason. The law created three categories of eligible objects: (1) those originally restituted after the war that become state property in the course of proceedings related to the export ban without compensation having been paid; (2) objects subject to Austria's 1946 Nullification Act (*Nichtigkeitsgesetz*) related to invalid seizures and subsequent sales; and (3) objects otherwise not returned and which became national property as so-called heirless property. If a determination is made that the property falls within these categories but a specific heir cannot be identified, then it can be transferred to the National Foundation of the Republic of Austria for the Victims of National Socialism (*Nationalfonds der Republik Österreich für Opfer des Nationalsozialismus*).

Laches—an equitable defense, laches will defeat a claim that otherwise is timely under the statute of limitations where the possessor's reasonable reliance on the plaintiff's inaction prejudiced the possessor in some important way.

Carlotta Landsberg—a German Jewish woman and owner of *Femme en Blanc* by Pablo Picasso; later the subject of litigation between Thomas Bennigson and Marilyn Alsdorf.

Ronald Lauder—the former U.S. ambassador to Austria, president of the World Jewish Congress, and former honorary chair of the board of trustees of the Museum of Modern Art in New York. Founder of the Neue Galerie museum in New York.

Erich Lederer—a family member of owners of the *Beethoven Frieze* by Gustav Klimt that was restituted to him but subjected to Austria's export ban; his heirs unsuccessfully petitioned the *Kunstrückgabebeirat* to return the work in 2015.

Lempertz Auction House—a prominent action house in Cologne, Germany. The collection of Walter Westfeld was sold there around December 12 or 13, 1939. *The Lion Tamer* by Max Beckmann, formerly of the Alfred Flechtheim Galerie and later in the possession of Hildebrand and Cornelius Gurlitt, was sold there as well shortly before the collection in Cornelius's possession was found in 2012, as was *Mädchen aus den Sabiner Bergen* (*Girl from the Sabine Mountains*) from the forcible sale of the Max Stern collection.

Rudolph Leopold—an important collector and expert on Schiele; also the namesake and director for life of the Leopold Museum.

Clara Levy—owner of *Three Graces* by Lovis Corinth. Levy was a textile manufacturer who was persecuted by the Nazis. *Three Graces* had been in the collection of Ludwig Levy, Clara's husband, who bequeathed it to her on his death in 1921. Clara lived in Berlin and emigrated to Schleifmühle, Luxembourg, in 1939, where her son, Fritz, managed a factory. The Corinth painting went with her. Clara died there in 1940.

Limbach Commission (Beratende Kommission im Zusammenhang mit der Rückgabe NS-verfolgungsbedingt entzogener Kulturgüter, insbesondere aus jüdischem Besitz)—also known as the Advisory Commission; named for the late presiding member Jutta Limbach, a former constitutional court judge. The Limbach Commission issues recommendations to German museums about whether to restitute works alleged to have been taken by the Nazis. The Advisory Commission's recommendations are nonbinding.

London Declaration—the Inter-Allied Declaration against Acts of Dispossession committed in Territories under Enemy Occupation and Control. The 1943 London Declaration was the beginning of the Allies' legal framework to deal with looted property and art.

Mathilde Lukacs—sister of Elisabeth Grünbaum, found to be the prior owner of *Seated Woman with Bent Left Leg (Torso)* by Egon Schiele before it was with the Galerie Gutekunst.

Margarethe Mauthner—a German Jew; Mauthner owned *Vue de l'Asile et de la Chapelle de Saint-Rémy*, a painting by Vincent van Gogh.

Paul von Mendelssohn-Bartholdy—a Jewish banker in Berlin. He was member of the illustrious Mendelssohn extended family. His ancestors and relatives included the family patriarch and philosopher Moses Mendelssohn, the renowned composer Felix Mendelssohn (who was von Mendelssohn-Bartholdy's great uncle, born Jakob Ludwig Felix Mendelssohn Bartholdy), Felix's sister Fanny, and his banker grandfather (also named Paul Mendelssohn-Bartholdy).

Léone Meyer—the daughter of Raoul Meyer and Yvonne Bader Meyer. Yvonne was the daughter of Théophile Bader, the founder of the Groupe Galeries Lafayette. Raoul and Yvonne owned a painting by Camille Pissarro, *La bergère rentrent des moutons,* that was the subject of litigation with the Fred Jones Jr. Museum of Art at the University of Oklahoma.

Alois Miedl—a Munich-born banker who had lived in the Netherlands for some time. Hermann Goering and Miedl devised a complicated scheme to target the collections of Dutch Jews after the country was occupied.

Military Government Law No. 59—one of a series of Allied decrees after the war, compelling the return of stolen property to its true owner regardless of good-faith acquisition in the interim.

Möbelaktion—the "furniture action" undertaken by the occupying Germans in France in which vast collections of French Jews' furnishings and decorative arts were seized.

Monuments, Fine Arts, and Archives Section (MFAA)—the renowned unit responsible for the security of works of art while the war was still waging and for the collection and return of cultural property after the war ended; now known to history as the Monuments Men.

Museum of Fine Arts Boston—a defendant in the case brought by Claudia Seger-Thomschitz over Oskar Kokoschka's *Two Nudes (Lovers)*.

Martha Nathan—a German Jewish woman who owned *The Diggers* by Vincent van Gogh.

Nationalfonds der Republik Österreich für Opfer des Nationalsozialismus (National Foundation of the Republic of Austria for the Victims of National Socialism)—established in 1995. It renders payments to victims of National Socialism (Nazism)—in particular, those who had previously received little or no compensation, those in need of special assistance, or those whose personal circumstances warrant relief.

Wally Neuzil—subject of *Portrait of Wally* by Egon Schiele.

N.Y. Arts and Cultural Affairs Law § 12.03—New York state law that provides a number of rules concerning fine arts sales and commissions. The final paragraph contains a provision against the seizure of any work of art "enroute to or from, or while on exhibition or deposited by a nonresident exhibitor at any exhibition held under the auspices or supervision of any museum, college, university or other nonprofit art gallery, institution or organization within any city or county of this state for any cultural, educational, charitable or other purpose not conducted for profit to the exhibitor." The law was successfully invoked by the Museum of Modern Art and the Leopold Museum when seeking to quash the grand jury subpoena seizing *Portrait of Wally*. That was only the beginning, however, because immediately after the Court of Appeals decision quashing the New York grand jury subpoena, the painting was seized pursuant to a federal subpoena, which kept the work in New York for another decade while the case was litigated.

Netherlands Art Property Collection or Art Property Collection (Nederlands Kunstbezitcollectie)—administered by the Ministry of Education, Culture and Science, the Collection holds everything that was returned to the Netherlands for possible restitution that was not returned to individuals.

Netherlands Art Property Foundation (Stichting Nederlands Kunstbezit, or SNK)—the SNK first focused on the significant collections that had been targeted and worked to restitute such collections to their former owners. In 1949 and 1950, the SNK conducted three exhibitions to publicize the art for which the owners were sought.

Lynn Nicholas—author of *The Rape of Europa*. The publication of this book shortly after the end of the Cold War was seminal in reviving interest in and understanding of the extent of Nazi art looting.

***Nichtigkeitsgesetz* (Nullification Act)**—Austria's 1946 law related to invalid seizures and subsequent sales.

Night of the Long Knives (*Nacht der langen Messer*)—1934 purge in which Nazi officials, particularly those from the conservative party and those who had led the SA, were murdered by the SS. The event was the beginning of the SS's ascendance within the Nazi hierarchy.

Norton Simon Museum—current possessor of *Adam* and *Eve* by Lucas Cranach; litigant against Marei von Saher over title to the paintings.

Office des biens et intérêts privés (OBIP)—created in 1944 in France to gather works recovered from Germany but whose owners were unknown.

Ordinance for the Registration of Jewish Property—the April 26, 1938, law that affirmatively required Jews in Germany and Austria to list and register their personal and real property with the *Vermögensverkehrstelle* (property registration office). These lists, the *Verzeichnis über das Vermögen von Juden* (Inventory of the Property of Jews), were often then used by Nazi officials as guides for property to seek out and keep for themselves. Whether a work of art was on a particular *Verzeichnis* has been a hotly contested issue in litigation.

Origins Unknown Agency (Bureau Herkomst Gezocht or Ekkart Committee)—named after its chairman, Rudi Ekkart; also subsequent to the Washington Conference, this Dutch agency was tasked with investigating the origins of any work in the Art Property Collection.

Origins Unknown Committee (Commissie Herkomst Gezocht)—a post-Washington Conference committee to assess the collections in the Nederlands Kunstbezit-Collectie for possible return.

Andrew Orkin—the great-grandson and heir of Margarethe Mauthner who brought suit against Elizabeth Taylor and the Swiss Confederation for the Van Gogh's *Vue de L'Asile et de la Chapelle de Saint-Rémy* and *Les Saintes-Maries de la Mer*, respectively.

Personal jurisdiction—the concept of whether one can be sued in a particular jurisdiction. Personal jurisdiction is either general (an overall pattern of conduct or business that renders a party present in a particular jurisdiction) or specific (the party has committed an act or participated in a transaction in that place that is the subject of the case). States have long-arm statutes that set the circumstances under which a party is subject to jurisdiction, but that analysis is also subject to an overall due-process evaluation, that is, whether fundamental fairness would permit the party to be forced to defend itself in that location.

Jonathan Petropoulos—leading historian of the history of Nazi-looted art and frequent expert witness in litigation in U.S. courts.

Sarah Reed Platt—collector who bequeathed *Two Nudes* (*Lovers*) by Oskar Kokoschka to the Museum of Fine Arts, Boston. Platt also owned another Kokoschka, *Portrait of a Youth* (1910). Both had once belonged to Oskar Reichel, and both were the subject of claims by Dr. Claudia Seger-Thomschitz. Platt's daughter, Sarah Blodgett Dunbar, brought a declaratory action against Seger-Thomschitz in Louisiana to resolve the dispute.

Preemption—Under Article VI of the United States Constitution, federal laws will preempt or displace state laws when either the laws conflict (conflict preemption) or the federal law occupies a particular field entirely (field preemption).

Prescription—another word for *adverse possession;* the prescription allows the current possessor to eventually become the true owner if he or she exercises control in a manner that would put the true owner on notice for more than a prescribed period (usually twenty years). A long-standing, common-law principle related to land, only Louisiana allows the practice for personal property in the United States.

Provenance—the ownership history of a work of art; the chain of title.

Oskar Reichel—a Viennese Jewish doctor and art collector in Vienna. He was the prior owner of paintings at the center of litigations involving the Museum of Fine Arts, Boston, and Sarah Blodgett Dunbar.

***Reichskammer der bildenden Künste* (Reich Chamber of the Visual Arts; RBK)**—a subdivision of the Reichskulturkammer, the RBK had power over all cultural trade, and the power to exclude Jews from it.

***Reichskommissar für die besetzten niederländischen Gebiete* (Reich Commissioner for the Occupied Dutch Territories)**—the German civilian administration of the occupied Netherlands, headed by Arthur

Seyss-Inquart, who had been the chancellor of Austria when it acceded to the annexation (the *Anschluss*) by Germany.

Reichskulturkammer—the Reich Culture Chamber, the umbrella organization under Joseph Goebbels intended to imprint on German society the Nazis' view of culture.

***Reichsministerium für Volksaufklärung und Propaganda* (Reich Ministry for Public Enlightenment and Propaganda or RVP)**—the cabinet-level administration overseen by Joseph Goebbels to control the dissemination of all news and propaganda to influence the German public.

Replevin—a common-law claim for the return of a piece of property. A replevin action asks the court to compel the property's possessor to return it to the claimant.

Heinrich Rieger—a persecuted and ultimately murdered Viennese Jew whose collection was confused with Leo Bondi's after works belonging to both ended up at the Belvedere in Vienna.

Sammlung Oskar Reinhart (Oskar Reinhart Collection)—this Swiss museum was the defendant in the case brought by Andrew Orkin for Van Gogh's *Les Saintes Maries de la Mer*.

Jakob Scheidwimmer—an official of the *Reichskammer der bildenden Künste*, he obtained a warrant to search Lilly Cassirer's home and later supposedly purchased *Rue Saint-Honoré, après-midi, effet de pluie* (*Rue St. Honoré, Afternoon, Rain Effect*) by Camille Pissarro from her for 900 Reichsmarks.

***Schutzstaffel* (SS)**—the principal paramilitary organization of the Nazi regime once in power. Led by Heinrich Himmler and his chief deputy Reinhard Heydrich, the SS conspired to displace the SA as the primary instrument of force. Himmler eventually reorganized all police forces in Germany under the SS, in particular the Gestapo (*Geheime Staatspolizei*, or Secret State Police). The SS had many other military units and is synonymous with the worst atrocities of the Holocaust.

Daniel Searle—a collector who purchased *Landscape with Smokestacks* by Edgar Degas and donated it to the Art Institute of Chicago.

Claudia Seger-Thomschitz—an heir of Oskar Reichel and claimant in cases against the Museum of Fine Arts, Boston, and Sarah Blodgett Dunbar.

Halldor Soehner—an agent for Bavaria who traveled to New York in 1964 to discuss purchasing Pablo Picasso's *Madame Soler* from Justin Thannhauser.

Sovereign immunity—in most court systems, a sovereign cannot be sued without its consent or some law or rule that abrogates that immunity.

Spoliation Advisory Panel (SAP)—in the United Kingdom, the SAP's mandate is to review claims concerning cultural objects currently in the possession of a national museum.

Statute of limitations—the time within which a claim must be filed or be deemed waived. Ordinarily set by statute, most states provide that property claims must be brought within three years of the loss or discovery by the plaintiff of the circumstances leading to the claim. New York takes a different approach; the statute for conversion claims does not begin to run on a claim against a good-faith purchaser until the plaintiff makes a demand and the defendant refuses to return the property. (There is no demand and refusal rule against the thief or someone who acquires it in bad faith.)

Stedelijk Museum in Amsterdam—the defendant in the claims brought by the heirs of Kazimir Malewicz after the works in question were loaned to the Menil Collection in Houston while immune from seizure under the Immunity from Seizure Act.

***Stiftung Preussischer Kulturbesitz* (SPK, Prussian Cultural Heritage Foundation)**—the SPK was created after World War II and the dissolution of the Prussian state by the Allies. The SPK succeeded to the art and cultural property previously owned by Prussia. It now oversees the State Museums of Berlin (*Staatliche Museen zu Berlin*).

Max Stern—the son of Julius Stern and the proprietor of Galerie Julius Stern, which specialized in Dutch and Flemish Old Masters, as well as German paintings.

George Stroganoff—Stroganoff claimed that *Adam* and *Eve* by Lucas Cranach the Elder (later owned by Jacques Goudstikker and claimed by Goudstikker's heirs) had been taken from him by the Soviet Union. The Soviet Union conducted several high-profile fire sales of expropriated "bourgeois" art at Berlin galleries just before the Nazis' rise to power in an effort to raise foreign currency that the Soviet command economy could not provide. Stroganoff eventually sold the Cranachs in 1971 to the Norton Simon Art Foundation, and they went from there to the well-known museum of the same name. They remain there today.

Sturmabteilung **(SA)**—literally "storm detachment," often called "storm troopers," the SA was the paramilitary component of the Nazis' rise to power. The SA fomented political and electoral violence, disrupting meetings of Socialists, trade unionists, and Communists and threatening people at the polls. The SA was led by Ernst Röhm, who was murdered in the aftermath of the Night of the Long Knives.

Summary judgment—the procedure by which a court determines that there are no material facts still to be sorted out such that a purely legal question is ready for resolution by the court. If any facts that are necessary to the legal analysis are in dispute, then summary judgment is not appropriate.

Robert H. Tannahill—a collector in Detroit who purchased *The Diggers* by Van Gogh from Georges Wildenstein, Alex Ball, and Justin Thannhauser.

Tate Letter—the 1949 letter by State Department official Jack Tate that expressed that the foreign policy of the United States was to relieve any constraints on jurisdiction over claims for looted property.

Terezin Declaration—a declaration after the conference of the same name (on June 30, 2009) largely reaffirming the Washington Conference Principles.

Justin Thannhauser—an art dealer involved in one way or another in the provenance of *Madame Soler, The Diggers, Head of a Woman, The Absinthe Drinker, Moulin de la Galette*, and *Boy Leading a Horse*.

Thyssen-Bornemisza Museum—the defendant in litigation over *Rue Saint-Honoré, après-midi, effet de pluie* (*Rue Saint Honoré, Afternoon, Rain Effect*) by Camille Pissarro.

Title—the ownership of a piece of property.

Toledo Museum of Art—the defendant in the litigation over by *Street Scene, Tahiti* by Paul Gauguin.

Tolling—whether by statute or in equity, tolling suspends the calculation of a deadline, typically a statute of limitations. Tolling is often argued where certain facts are unknown or unknowable.

Unjust enrichment—an equitable claim in the absence of an enforceable contract, unjust enrichment allows a plaintiff to seek recovery when allowing the defendant to retain some property or economic benefit would be unfair.

Milos Vavra—see entry for Leon Fischer.

Curt Valentin—art dealer and one-time employee of Alfred Flechtheim. Valentin is a controversial figure for his role in selling modern art at his Galerie Buchholz in New York that had been removed from German museums as degenerate by the Nazis.

***Verordnung zur Ausschaltung der Juden aus dem deutschen Wirtschaftsleben* (Order Regarding the Elimination of Jews from the German Economy)**—as part of the escalating institutional repression of German and Austrian Jews after Kristallnacht, the November 12, 1938, law forbade Jews from a wide range of economic activity.

***Verzeichnis über das Vermögen von Juden* (Inventory of the Property of Jews)**—pursuant to the Ordinance for the Registration of Jewish Property of April 26, 1938, Jews were required to file lists of all their property. Such declarations of fine art in particular were often used as wish lists for unscrupulous officials to target.

Robert Vineberg—a trustee of the Max Stern estate and plaintiff in the case against Maria-Louise Bissonnette over *Mädchen aus den Sabiner Bergen* (*Girl from the Sabine Mountains*) by Francis Xavier Winterhalter.

Völkisch—the movement in parallel with Nazism that placed heavy emphasis on the so-called folk aspects of Germanity. Often used as a contrast to Jewish traits, Nazi and *völkisch* propaganda tried to argue in favor of the superiority of supposedly innate ethnic German (or Aryan) traits.

Marei von Saher-Langenbein—the Goudstikkers' daughter-in-law (wife of their son, Edouard) and claimant in the litigation over *Adam* and *Eve* by Lucas Cranach against the Norton Simon Museum.

Washington Conference—the 1998 conference organized by the United States Department of State to address the legacy of property displaced and looted by German governments and armed forces. One of the products of the Washington Conference was the Washington Conference Principles on Nazi-Confiscated Art.

Washington Conference Principles on Nazi-Confiscated Art—a series of principles agreed to at the Washington Conference about the handling of claims to looted art. Pledged to by nations, not individuals or museums, the Washington Principles are best known for their encouragement of "fair and just solutions," a phrase that has proved both useful and problematic.

Friedrich Welz—a Nazi functionary who Aryanized the Würthle & Sohn (Würthle and sons) Gallery owned by Lea Bondi.

Walter Westfeld—a Jewish art dealer in Wuppertal, Germany. Westfeld made efforts to depart from Germany and transfer his art collection and assets to the United States to support his immigration.

Dr. Karl Wilharm—buyer of *Mädchen aus den Sabiner Bergen* (*Girl from the Sabine Mountains*) by Francis Xavier Winterhalter at Lempertz Auction house subsequent to its seizure from Max Stern.

World Jewish Restitution Organization (WJRO)—established after the fall of the Iron Curtain, the WJRO addresses restitution of Jewish property in Europe, excepting Germany and Austria.

Bibliography

Alfred Flechtheim: Raubkunst und Restitution (Andrea Bambi and Axel Drecoll, eds., Schriftenreihe der Vierteljahrshefte für Zeitgeschichte, Band 110).

William Sheridan Allen, The Nazi Seizure of Power: The Experience of a Single German Town, 1922–1945 (Franklin Watts, rev. ed. March 1, 1984).

Stephanie Barron, Degenerate Art: The Fate of the Avant-Garde in Nazi Germany (Harry N. Abrams, April 15, 1991).

Monica Bohm-Duchen, Art and the Second World War (Princeton University Press, January 19, 2014).

Robert Edsel, The Monuments Men: Allied Heroes, Nazi Thieves, and the Greatest Treasure Hunt in History (Center Street, September 3, 2009).

Ersessene Kunst: Der Fall Gurlitt (Johannes Heil and Annette Webter, eds., Metropol, 2015).

Fair and Just Solutions?: Alternatives to Litigation in Nazi-Looted Art Disputes: Status Quo and New Developments (Evelien Campfens, ed., Eleven International Publishing, January 15, 2015).

Hector Feliciano, The Lost Museum: the Nazi Conspiracy to Steal the World's Greatest Works of Art (Basic Books, 1st ed. May 12, 1997)

Klaus Fischer, Nazi Germany: A New History (Bloomsbury Academic, September 1, 1996).

Stephen Green, Reluctant Meister: How Germany's Past is Shaping Its European Future (Haus Publishing, expanded ed. November 15, 2014).

Catherine Hickley, The Munich Art Hoard: Hitler's Dealer and His Secret Legacy (Thames & Hudson Ltd., September 21, 2015).

Meike Hoffmann and Nicola Kuhn, HITLERS KUNSTHÄNDLER: HILDEBRAND GURLITT 1895–1956 (C.H. Beck, 1st ed. March 9, 2016).

HOLOCAUST RESTITUTION: PERSPECTIVES ON THE LITIGATION AND ITS LEGACY (Michael J. Bazyler and Roger P. Alford, eds., NYU Press, December 25, 2005).

Victor Klemperer, I WILL BEAR WITNESS: A DIARY OF THE NAZI YEARS, 1933–1941 (Modern Library, new edition, November 15, 1999).

Victor Klemperer, I WILL BEAR WITNESS: A DIARY OF THE NAZI YEARS, 1942–1945 (Modern Library, April 3, 2001).

Stefan Koldehoff, DIE BILDER SIND UNTER UNS: DAS GESCHÄFT MIT DER NS-RAUBKUNST UND DER FALL GURLITT (Galiani-Berlin, March 8, 2014).

Jennifer A. Kreder, *State Law Holocaust-Era Art Claims and Federal Executive Power*, 105 NW. U. L. REV. COLLOQUY 315 (2011).

Jennifer A. Kreder, *Fighting Corruption of the Historical Record: Nazi-Looted Art Litigation*, 61 U. KAN. L. REV. 75 (2012).

Jennifer A. Kreder, *The New Battleground of Museum Ethics and Holocaust Era Claims: Technicalities Trumping Justice or Responsible Stewardship for the Public Trust?*, 88 OR. L. REV. 37 (2009).

Jennifer A. Kreder, *The Holocaust, Museum Ethics and Legalism*, 18 S. CAL. REV. L. & SOC. JUST. 1 (2008).

Erik Larson, IN THE GARDEN OF BEASTS: LOVE, TERROR, AND AN AMERICAN FAMILY IN HITLER'S BERLIN (Broadway Books, 1st ed. May 10, 2011).

Sophie Lillie, WAS EINMAL WAR. DIE ENTEIGNETEN KUNSTSAMMLUNGEN WIENS (Czernin Verlag, 1st ed. November 10, 2003).

Melissa Müller and Monika Tatzkow, LOST LIVES, LOST ART: JEWISH COLLECTORS, NAZI ART THEFT, AND THE QUEST FOR JUSTICE (Vendome Press, 1st ed. November 1, 2010).

Lynn Nicholas, THE RAPE OF EUROPA: THE FATE OF EUROPE'S TREASURES IN THE THIRD REICH AND THE SECOND WORLD WAR (Vintage, December 22, 2009).

Anne-Marie O'Connor, THE LADY IN GOLD: THE EXTRAORDINARY TALE OF GUSTAV KLIMT'S MASTERPIECE, PORTRAIT OF ADELE BLOCH-BAUER (Knopf, February 7, 2012).

Olaf Peters, DEGENERATE ART: THE ATTACK ON MODERN ART IN GERMANY 1937 (Prestel, April 21, 2014).

Jonathan Petropoulos, THE FAUSTIAN BARGAIN: THE ART WORLD IN NAZI GERMANY (Oxford University Press, 1st ed. March 30, 2000).

Jonathan Petropoulos, ART AND POLITICS IN THE THIRD REICH (The University of North Carolina Press, February 1, 1996).

Judith Prowda, VISUAL ARTS AND THE LAW: A HANDBOOK FOR PROFESSIONALS (Lund Humphries, 2013).

Susan Ronald, HITLER'S ART THIEF: HILDEBRAND GURLITT, THE NAZIS, AND THE LOOTING OF EUROPE'S TREASURES (St. Martin's Press, 1st ed. September 22, 2015).

Anders Rydell, HITLERS BILDER: KUNSTRAUB DER NAZIS - RAUBKUNST IN DER GEGENWART (Campus Verlag, 1st ed. October 2, 2014).

Birgit Schwartz, AUF BEFEHL DES FÜHRERS: HITLER UND DER NS-KUNSTRAUB (Theiss, Konrad, 1st ed. August 1, 2014).

William L. Shirer, THE RISE AND FALL OF THE THIRD REICH: A HISTORY OF NAZI GERMANY (Rosetta Books, reissue ed. October 23, 2011).

Timothy Snyder, BLOODLANDS: EUROPE BETWEEN HITLER AND STALIN (Basic Books, First Trade Paper Edition. October 2, 2012).

Timothy Snyder, BLACK EARTH: THE HOLOCAUST AS HISTORY AND WARNING (Tim Duggan Books, September 8, 2015).

Frederic Spotts, HITLER AND THE POWER OF AESTHETICS (Overlook Books, April 2004).

Nicholas Stargardt, THE GERMAN WAR: A NATION UNDER ARMS (Basic Books, October 13, 2015).

Bayard Taylor, THE HOLY ROMAN EMPIRE (Kindle edition, July 2, 2013).

Frederick Taylor, EXORCISING HITLER: THE OCCUPATION AND DENAZIFICATION OF GERMANY (Bloomsbury Press, 1st ed. May 10, 2011).

Anja Tiedemann, DIE "ENTARTETE" MODERNE UND IHR AMERIKANISCHER MARKT: KARL BUCHHOLZ UND CURT VALENTIN ALS HÄNDLER VERFEMTER KUNST (SCHRIFTEN DER FORSCHUNGSSTELLE "ENTARTETE KUNST", BAND 8) (De Gruyter, November 15, 2013).

Ana Filipa Vrdoljak, INTERNATIONAL LAW, MUSEUMS AND THE RETURN OF CULTURAL OBJECTS (Cambridge University Press, 1st ed. September 1, 2008).

Edmund de Waal, THE HARE WITH AMBER EYES: A FAMILY'S CENTURY OF ART AND LOSS (Farrar, Straus and Giroux, August 31, 2010).

Tina Walzer and Stephan Templ, UNSER WIEN. »ARISIERUNG« AUF ÖSTERREICHISCH (Aufbau-Verlag, 2001).

Steve Wick, THE LONG NIGHT: WILLIAM L. SHIRER AND THE RISE AND FALL OF THE THIRD REICH (St. Martin's Press, reprint ed. August 2, 2011).

U.S. Committee on Financial Services, United States House of Representatives, *Review of the repatriation of Holocaust art assets in the United States*, Serial No. 109-113, July 27, 2006.

Index

B

C

G

N

Y

Z